# OXFORD MODERN LANGUAGES AND LITERATURE MONOGRAPHS

# Javier Marías's Debt to Translation

*Sterne, Browne, Nabokov*

GARETH J. WOOD

OXFORD
UNIVERSITY PRESS

# OXFORD

UNIVERSITY PRESS

Great Clarendon Street, Oxford OX2 6DP,
United Kingdom

Oxford University Press is a department of the University of Oxford.
It furthers the University's objective of excellence in research, scholarship,
and education by publishing worldwide. Oxford is a registered trade mark of
Oxford University Press in the UK and in certain other countries

British Library Cataloguing in Publication Data
Data available

Library of Congress Cataloging in Publication Data
Data available

ISBN 978–0–19–965133–7

Printed in Great Britain
on acid-free paper by
MPG Books Group, Bodmin and King's Lynn

# *Acknowledgements*

To begin, my warmest thanks go to two people: Eric Southworth, who supervised the doctoral thesis on which this book is based, has been and continues to be the finest friend and mentor I could wish for; my partner, Mary Ann Lund, has offered support and affection in equal measure and at just the right times.

Elide Pittarello and Xon de Ros were kind enough to act as my D.Phil. examiners at the University of Oxford and I would also like to thank Stephen Roberts and John Rutherford who read the manuscript for OUP and whose comments I found immensely supportive and helpful.

I owe my gratitude to the AHRC and Exeter College, Oxford for their financial support and to the *Bulletin of Hispanic Studies* and *Bulletin of Spanish Studies* for permission to reproduce material. Helen Buchanan, Javier Marías, Montse Vega, and Jon Wynne-Tyson offered patient assistance with my enquiries and helped my researches no end. I would like to thank the production team at OUP for their diligent preparation of this book and Dominic Moran for the decade of friendship that has underpinned its writing.

This book is dedicated to my parents, Richard and Ann.

# Contents

*Acknowledgements*                                                          v

*List of Abbreviated Titles of Marías's Works*                             ix

Introduction                                                                1

1. An Overview of a Career in Translation                                  18

2. The Why? And the How?                                                   41

3. Sterne Challenges                                                       70

4. Following the Precedent: Marías's Shandean Novel                        97

5. Competing with Illustrious Forerunners: Browne,
   Borges, and Bioy Casares                                               139

6. Browne, *El siglo*, and the Depiction of Tyranny                       168

7. The Continuing Presence of Browne                                      196

8. Nabokov                                                                226

9. The Culmination of his Art: *Tu rostro mañana*                         258

Conclusion                                                                321

*Bibliography*                                                            327

*Index*                                                                   347

# List of Abbreviated Titles of Marías's Works

The following abbreviations will be employed in the text and footnotes. The author's name has been abbreviated to **JM** in footnotes where he is the sole author of a work.

| | |
|---|---|
| *AVC* | *A veces un caballero* (Madrid: Alfaguara, 2001) |
| *BS* | *Baile y sueño* (Madrid: Alfaguara, 2004) |
| *CFM* | *Cuando fui mortal* (Madrid: Alfaguara, 1996) |
| *CTB* | *Corazón tan blanco* (Madrid: Alfaguara, 1999 [1992]) |
| *DNA* | *Demasiada nieve alrededor* (Madrid: Alfaguara, 2007) |
| *EHS* | *El hombre sentimental* (Madrid: Alfaguara, 1999 [1986]) |
| *EMT* | *El monarca del tiempo* (Barcelona: Reino de Redonda, 2003 [1978]) |
| *EOOL* | *El oficio de oír llover* (Madrid: Alfaguara, 2005) |
| *ES* | *El siglo* (Madrid: Alfaguara, 2000 [1983]) |
| *FL* | *Fiebre y lanza* (Madrid: Alfaguara, 2002) |
| *HMC* | *Harán de mí un criminal* (Madrid: Alfaguara, 2003) |
| *LDL* | *Los dominios del lobo* (Madrid: Alfaguara, 1999) |
| *LF* | *Literatura y fantasma: edición ampliada* (Madrid: Alfaguara, 2001 [1993]) |
| *MBPM* | *Mañana en la batalla piensa en mí* (Madrid: Alfaguara, 2000 [1994]) |
| *MED* | *Mientras ellas duermen* (Madrid: Alfaguara, 2000 [1990]) |
| *MS* | *Mano de sombra* (Madrid: Alfaguara, 1997) |
| *NET* | *Negra espalda del tiempo* (Madrid: Alfaguara, 1998) |
| *PP* | *Pasiones pasadas* (Madrid: Alfaguara, 1999 [1991]) |
| *SACF* | *Seré amado cuando falte* (Madrid: Alfaguara, 1999) |
| *TLA* | *Todas las almas* (Madrid: Alfaguara, 2000 [1989]) |
| *TRM* | *Tu rostro mañana.* Also abbreviated as the novel's three separate volumes: *FL*, *BS*, and *VSA* |
| *VF* | *Vida del fantasma: cinco años más tenue* (Madrid: Alfaguara, 2001 [1995]) |
| *VSA* | *Veneno y sombra y adiós* (Madrid: Alfaguara, 2007) |

# Introduction

This is a book about translation and literary influence. It takes as its subject the most important contemporary Spanish novelist, Javier Marías (1951), who worked as a literary translator for a significant portion of his early career. Since then, he has maintained that the years he spent rendering in Spanish works of literature in English were the perfect writer's apprenticeship. This study has, therefore, two main aims. Firstly, it examines his claims to the influence of three of those he translated, Laurence Sterne, Sir Thomas Browne, and Vladimir Nabokov. It does so by submitting those translations to close textual analysis and then standing them alongside the author's fiction to see how they have shaped and informed it. Secondly, to ensure that the discussion of literary influence is embedded in an understanding of Marías's fiction, it analyzes those novels and short stories on their own terms, at the same time as seeing how they have been wrought by the author's translation practice.

Marías is the author of eleven novels, two volumes of short stories, a dozen book-length translations, thirteen collections of literary and journalistic articles, as well as a fourteenth on football (he has written a weekly column in Spain's national press since 1994). His most recent fiction, in particular *Corazón tan blanco* (*A Heart So White*, hence *CTB*, 1992), *Mañana en la batalla piensa en mí* (*Tomorrow in the Battle Think on Me*, hence *MBPM*, 1994), and *Tu rostro mañana* (*Your Face Tomorrow*, hence *TRM*, 2002–2007), has seen his star rise to the extent that he is considered a serious candidate for the Nobel Prize for Literature.[1] A life-long resident of Madrid, in the years before his earnings from writing alone were sufficient to maintain him financially, he spent periods living and working in the United Kingdom, Italy, and the United States. He carries the title Xavier I, fourth King of Redonda, although, as we shall see in Chapter 1 of this study, it is not as wanton an eccentricity as might at first appear. Since 2000 he has also become an editor and publisher of translated works, both commissioning new ones and recouping the rights to the translations he wrote himself, reissuing them under his own imprint,

---

[1] See, for example, Sarah Emily Miano, 'Betrayal of a Blood Brother', *The Observer*, Books section, 8 May 2005, p. 16.

the Reino de Redonda press. His pre-eminent position among Spain's writers has seen him win a host of national and international awards, including the Premio de la Crítica (1993), Premio Rómulo Gallegos (1994–1995), Prix Femina (1996), IMPAC Prize (1997), Premio Salambó (2003), Premio Miguel Delibes (2004), European Literary Award (2011), as well as the Premio Nacional de Traducción (1979) for his version of Sterne's *The Life and Opinions of Tristram Shandy, Gentleman* (1759–1767). Reception of his works in the United Kingdom and the United States has been helped in no small measure by his having found in Margaret Jull Costa a translator of truly exceptional talents. We ought to consider the IMPAC Prize a joint award for her efforts in rendering *A Heart So White*, the winning novel, in English.[2] In April 2008, Marías took up his seat in the Real Academia Española, an entrance that, although somewhat belated, given that his nomination had been mooted as far back as mid 1994, nevertheless confirmed his place among his nation's cultural élite.[3] Despite being an unashamedly literary author—his novels often hinge on intertextual references to Shakespeare and are written in 'endlessly unspooling, self-revising sentences'—he has been translated into more than thirty languages and sold in excess of five million copies worldwide.[4] Running alongside this popular success has been the praise of illustrious contemporaries, among them John Ashbery, Roberto Bolaño, J. M. Coetzee, Margaret Drabble, Orhan Pamuk, and W. G. Sebald. In 2006, the editors of *The Paris Review* paid Marías the compliment of asking him for an interview in the long-running 'Art of Fiction' series. According to *El País*, Spain's largest-selling newspaper, such an accolade was to 'entrar a formar parte del parnaso' ('to join the pantheon of greats') alongside writers who had for many years been the object of his admiration and, in the cases of Isak Dinesen, William Faulkner, and Nabokov, his efforts as a translator.[5]

[2] On Marías's popularity in Britain, see Alexis Grohmann, 'Pérfida Albión: La (escasa) presencia de la narrativa española reciente en el Reino Unido', *Quimera*, 273 (2006), 36–40.

[3] Marías was voted into the Real Academia de la Lengua on 29 June 2006 and gave the address that marks the official entrance into the institution on 27 April 2008. As early as 1995, he revealed that, a year and a half before, a group of academics had wanted to put his name forward for nomination but that he had rejected the idea on the grounds that his father, Julián, was already a member: 'con un Marías en la Academia hay bastante' ('one Marías in the Academia is quite enough'). See Interview with Jaime López at the following URL: http://www.javiermarias.es/PAGINASDEENTREVISTAS/TribunaSept95.html (accessed 23 February 2008). With the death of his father in late 2005, he no longer had reason to feel the same reluctance and accepted the nomination.

[4] John Ashbery, 'Books of the Year', *Times Literary Supplement*, 1 December 2006, p. 7.

[5] Enrique Murillo, '"La vida es un mal novelista": "The Paris Review" abre las puertas a Javier Marías en el gran círculo literario anglosajón', *El País*, 15 January 2007, p. 48. For Marías's *Paris Review* interview, see 'Javier Marías: The Art of Fiction No. 190', *The Paris Review*, 179 (2006), 10–42.

That he should have received such a tribute in the English-speaking world could hardly seem more appropriate, given his labours as a translator to increase the availability and understanding in Spain of literature in that language. A fact often mentioned, but seldom elaborated upon, by critics of his work is that, for more than twenty years from the early 1970s onwards, he devoted considerable energy to translating into Spanish works of literature in English. Despite an already considerable bibliography of studies and articles dealing with diverse aspects of his output—as literary essayist, newspaper columnist, novelist, short story writer—those that offer any appraisal of his translation career can be counted on the fingers of one hand. As Maarten Steenmeijer has put it, 'Las traducciones de Marías siguen siendo...un importante campo abierto a la investigación' ('Marías's translations remain...an important field open to research').[6] This book casts the first stone into that neglected well and offers close textual analysis of Marías's translations of Sterne, Browne, and Nabokov as well as showing how their influence has shaped his subsequent writings.

It is axiomatic to the point of cliché that translation acts as a crucial bridge between literary traditions across linguistic, national, and even temporal boundaries. In Spain itself, the blossoming of the Realist and Naturalist novel in the 1880s would have taken a very different form had it not been for the translations of Émile Zola that arrived in the country at the start of that decade. Without the rediscovery of so many ancient Greek texts, not least Aristotle's *Poetics*, the European Renaissance would have been a very different enterprise from the one we know today. Translation offers renewal through contact with a crucially, sometimes dangerously, different culture. And yet, as George Steiner has observed, 'the translator...is often a ghostly presence' and, particularly in the Hispanic field, translation has received precious little academic attention.[7] It is rarely mentioned by critics of Benito Pérez Galdós, for example, that one of his first efforts at creative writing was a translation of Dickens's *The Pickwick Papers*.[8] In 1891, his one-time lover, Emilia Pardo Bazán, set herself to a translation of *Les*

[6] Maarten Steenmeijer, 'Javier Marías, columnista: el otro, el mismo', in *Cuadernos de narrativa: Javier Marías*, ed. by Irene Andres-Suárez and Ana Casas (Madrid: Universidad de Neuchâtel/Arco, 2005), pp. 255–73 (p. 257).

[7] George Steiner, *After Babel: Aspects of Language and Translation*, 3rd edn (Oxford: Oxford University Press, 1998), p. 284.

[8] Galdós describes Dickens in his memoirs as 'mi maestro más amado' ('my most beloved master') and recalls the translation he had written in 1868 for 'un periódico de Madrid' ('a Madrid newspaper'). Benito Pérez Galdós, *Obras inéditas*, ed. by Alberto Ghiraldo, 12 vols (Madrid: Renacimiento, 1923–1930), X: *Memorias* (1930), p. 213. His translation was originally published in serial form as Charles Dickens, 'Las aventuras de Pickwick', *La Nación* (Madrid), 9 March–8 July 1868. Galdós's version is available in book form: Charles Dickens, *Aventuras de Pickwick*, trans. by Benito Pérez Galdós, ed. by Arturo Ramoneda, 2 vols (Madrid: Ediciones Júcar, 1989).

*frères Zemganno* by Edmond de Goncourt, in the midst of one of her most
fertile creative periods.[9] A year later her increasing engagement with femi-
nism was focused in no small way through John Stuart Mill's *The Subjection
of Women* (1869), which she translated and published in her 'Biblioteca de
la Mujer' series as *La esclavitud femenina*. Galdós's friend and Pardo Bazán's
enemy, Leopoldo Alas, devoted the final months of his life to completing a
version of Zola's novel *Travail* (1901), a labour that marks a fitting endpoint
to more than two decades spent reflecting on the Frenchman's novelistic
achievements.[10] Although their work in this field has attracted sporadic
commentary from critics, no systematic study of the importance of translation in nineteenth-century Spain has been attempted. And this despite the
fact that, for each of these writers, time away from their own autonomous
projects was a huge investment of effort and energy. At the turn of the
twentieth century, Miguel de Unamuno put his unschooled English to use
translating Thomas Carlyle and Herbert Spencer into Spanish, though
again this seems to have attracted little notice.[11] Perhaps the most startling
case is that of Carmen Martín Gaite, who had met the ageing Unamuno
when she was a young girl. She went on to become not only the most gifted
female novelist of her generation but also one of its most prolific translators.
The range and eclecticism of her efforts in the field of translation are little
short of astonishing. Across more than thirty years and from English,
French, Galician, German, Italian, and Portuguese, Martín Gaite translated
works by, among others, Charlotte and Emily Brontë, José Maria Eça de
Queirós, Gustave Flaubert, Natalia Ginzburg, Primo Levi, C. S. Lewis,
George MacDonald, Fernando Pessoa, Rainer Maria Rilke, Italo Svevo,
Oscar Wilde, William Carlos Williams, and Virginia Woolf.[12] Such versatil-
ity has merited not one study, in spite of the large amount of critical

[9] Edmond de Goncourt, *Los hermanos Zemganno*, trans. by Emilia Pardo Bazán
(Madrid: Saenz de Jubera, 1891).
[10] Émile Zola, *Trabajo*, trans. by Leopoldo Alas, 2 vols (Barcelona: Maucci, 1901). Alas's
translation is also available in the following scholarly edition: Émile Zola, *Trabajo*, trans. by
Leopoldo Alas, ed. by Francisco Caudet (Madrid: Ediciones de la Torre, 1991). Comment
on Alas's attitudes and achievements as a translator can be found in John Rutherford,
'"Esos pobres truchimanes": Leopoldo Alas y la traducción literaria', in *Leopoldo Alas. Un
clásico contemporáneo, 12–16 Noviembre de 2001*, ed. by Araceli Iravedra Valea et al., 2 vols
(Oviedo: Universidad de Oviedo, 2002), I, 289–302.
[11] Thomas Carlyle, *La revolución francesa*, trans. by Miguel de Unamuno, 2 vols (Madrid:
Avrial, [n.d.]); Herbert Spencer, *La Beneficencia*, trans. by Miguel de Unamuno (Madrid:
La España Moderna, [1893]); Herbert Spencer, *De las leyes en general* (Madrid: [Tordesil-
las], [1909]); Herbert Spencer, *Exceso de legislación* (Madrid: [Tordesillas], [1910]).
[12] The following is, as far as I can ascertain, a complete list of Martín Gaite's translations.
In each case, I have given the earliest edition of the works I have been able to identify.
Unless otherwise stated they were translated solely by her: *Ocho siglos de poesía gallega:
antología bilingüe*, ed. and trans. by Carmen Martín Gaite and Andrés Ruiz Tarazona
(Madrid: Alianza [1972]); Felipe Alfau, *Cuentos españoles de antaño* (Madrid: Siruela,

attention devoted to her work as a diarist, essayist, feminist, novelist, and short story writer. The authors of the most recent book-length survey of her writings underestimate the range of her talents, giving her credit for translations from only four of the six languages from which she worked, and devote no more than half a page to discussion of this aspect of her career.[13] This book argues for the centrality of translation to Spanish literature in the modern period by offering a case study of Marías, the sheer breadth of whose literary tastes is comparable to those of Martín Gaite. In addition to the authors already mentioned, he chose to translate among others Joseph Conrad, Thomas Hardy, Wallace Stevens, Robert Louis Stevenson, and W. B. Yeats; the genres of individual works by each of them range, moreover, from the prose tract (Browne, Yeats) to autobiography (Conrad), poetry (Faulkner, Nabokov, Stevens, Stevenson), the novel (Sterne), the novella (Dinesen), and the short story (Hardy). I show in this study how Marías's prose style and imaginative vocabulary were formed in dialogue with Sterne, Browne, and Nabokov as he rewrote their works in his own language. His example offers proof of Steiner's claim that the translator 'enriches his tongue by allowing the source language to penetrate and modify it', since much that Marías learnt from those he translated is still traceable and observable in his writing today.[14] Most obviously this occurs

---

1991); Emily Brontë, *Cumbres borrascosas* (Barcelona: Bruguera, 1984); Charlotte Brontë, *Jane Eyre* (Barcelona: Alba, 1999); Gabriel Joseph de Lavergne, *Cartas de amor de la monja portuguesa Mariana Alcoforado* (Barcelona: Círculo de lectores, [2000]); José Maria Eça de Queirós and José Duarte Ramalho Ortigão, *El misterio de la carretera de Sintra* (Madrid: [Nostromo], [1974]); Eva Figes, *Actitudes patriarcales: las mujeres en la sociedad*, 2nd edn (Madrid: Alianza, 1980); Gustave Flaubert, *Madame Bovary* (Barcelona: Bruguera, 1982); Natalia Ginzburg, *Querido Miguel* (Barcelona: Lumen, 1989); Natalia Ginzburg, *Nuestros ayeres* (Madrid: Debate, 1996); Primo Levi, *Historias naturales* (Madrid: Alianza, 1988); Primo Levi, *El sistema periódico* (Madrid: Alianza, 1987); C. S. Lewis, *Una pena observada* (Madrid: Trieste, 1988); C. S. Lewis, *Una pena en observación* (Barcelona: Anagrama, 1994); George MacDonald, *La princesa y los trasgos* (Madrid: Siruela, 1995); Fernando Pessoa, *El marinero* (Alcalá de Henares: Fundación Colegio del Rey, 1990); Charles Perrault, *Bruno Bettelheim presenta los Cuentos de Perrault* (Barcelona: Crítica, 1980); Rainer Maria Rilke, *Cartas francesas a Merline, 1919–1922* (Madrid: Alianza, 1987); John Ruskin et al., *Cuentos de hadas victorianos*, trans. by Carmen Martín Gaite et al. (Madrid: Siruela, 1993); Ignazio Silone, *Vino y pan* (Madrid: Alianza, [1968]); Italo Svevo, *Senectud* (Barcelona: Bruguera, 1982); Italo Svevo, *Corto viaje sentimental* (Madrid: Alianza, 2008); Oscar Wilde, *El retrato de Dorian Grey* ([Madrid]: Salvat, [1970]); William Carlos Williams, *Viaje hacia el amor y otros poemas* (Madrid: Trieste, 1981); Virginia Woolf, *Al faro* (Barcelona: Edhasa, 1978).

[13] Catherine O'Leary and Alison Ribeiro de Menezes, *A Companion to Carmen Martín Gaite* (Woodbridge: Tamesis, 2008), p. 202. In fact, their omission is doubly frustrating because the authors remark elsewhere on the influence of several of these writers—Ginzburg, Levi, Svevo, Woolf—on Martín Gaite's work. See pp. 38, 57, 60, 74, 192–3, 198. Why they do not make the connection between influence and translation is something of a mystery.

[14] Steiner, p. 67.

when a particular passage from a work he translated has become a habit of thought, the best encapsulation of an idea, an imaginative touchstone. An example can be found in an article he published in late 2005. There he describes his reasons for lining the bookshelves of his Madrid home with toy soldiers, a habit apparently intended to remind him of the humility of the writer's profession. Those soldiers were the protagonists of the first tentative narratives he developed while playing as a child:

> Y si bien se mira, esos juegos en los que uno decidía, siguiendo ciertas reglas o convenciones y buscando siempre la verosimilitud de toda emulación, los destinos y peripecias de sus soldaditos o de sus muñecos, son probablemente el primer paso en firme para escribir ficción.[15]

> (And if you look at it closely, those games, in which, following certain rules or conventions and always seeking the verisimilitude that is essential to mimesis, you decided the fates and vicissitudes of your toy soldiers or dolls, are probably the first firm steps towards writing fiction.)

Not only do the soldiers help to keep his feet on the ground by reminding him of the 'orígenes tan modestos' ('such modest origins') out of which his career grew, they also remind him of one of his favourite poems, 'Say Not of Me' by Stevenson. The Scottish author suffered throughout his life from a weak constitution, one that prevented him from following his forebears into the family firm, building lighthouses on the remotest outcrops of the Scottish coast. In 'Say Not of Me', translated by Marías in 1980, he pleads that posterity should not look with scorn on his choice of a literary vocation over a manual one. Rather than believe him to have 'declined/The labours of my sires.../To play at home with paper like a child':

> Decid más bien: *En la primatarde del tiempo/una esforzada familia se sacudió de las manos/la arena del granito, y, mirando en la distancia/cómo a lo largo de la resonante costa sus pirámides/y altas memorias atrapaban al agonizante sol,/sonrió con contento, y a esta pueril tarea/dedicó en torno al fuego las horas de su anochecer.*[16]

> (Say rather that: *In the afternoon of time/A strenuous family dusted from its hands/The sand of granite, and beholding far/Along the sounding coast its pyramids/And tall memorials catch the dying sun,/Smiled well content, and to this childish task/Around the fire addressed its evening hours.*)

---

[15] Javier Marías, 'Esta pueril tarea', in *Demasiada nieve alrededor* (Madrid: Alfaguara, 2007), pp. 141–3. This article collection hence referred to as *DNA*.

[16] Robert Louis Stevenson, *De vuelta del mar: Poemas*, trans. with notes by Javier Marías, 2nd edn (Madrid: Hiperión, 1998), pp. 52–3. Marías quotes the poem in full in the article cited above, adding comment between the first four lines and the seven-line section here quoted.

Stevenson's pregnant phrase—'this puerile task', 'esta pueril tarea'—serves Marías synecdochically as a reminder that writers should think twice before attributing great weight to an activity that can easily inspire self-importance in its practitioners.[17]

The confessional article on his fear of flying, 'Aviones Marineros', is another text where we find Marías quoting from his translations. When discussing the impersonal relationship modern-day passengers have with aircraft, he contrasts their indifference with the deeply affectionate terms in which Conrad talks about the vessels he skippered during his years at sea. Marías quotes two substantial passages from his Spanish version of *The Mirror of the Sea*, Conrad's memoir of that period, in which the latter evokes the fondness and respect that often hardened old sea dogs would lavish on their boats:

> Y aún más adelante relató Conrad las conmovidas palabras, casi una oración fúnebre, del capitán de un bergantín que se había hundido: 'Ningún otro barco podía haberse portado tan bien...Era pequeño, pero era un buen barco. No me causaba inquietud. Era fuerte. En el último viaje vinieron a bordo mi mujer y mis dos hijos. Ningún otro barco habría aguantado tanto el espantoso tiempo que durante días y días tuvo que atravesar antes de quedar desarbolado hace dos semanas. Estaba completamente agotado, eso es todo. Podéis creerme. Resistió días y días bajo nuestros pies, pero no podía resistir eternamente. Ya fue bastante. Me alegro de que todo haya terminado.'[18]

> (And later still Conrad related the heartfelt words, almost a funeral oration, uttered by the captain of a brigantine that had sunk: 'No ship could have done so well...She was small, but she was good. I had no anxiety. She was strong. Last voyage I had my wife and two children in her. No other ship could have stood for so long the weather she had to live through for days and days before we got dismasted a fortnight ago. She was fairly worn out, and that's all. You may believe me. She lasted under us for days, but she could not last for ever. It was long enough. I am glad it is over.')

Were we to analyse this passage in greater depth, we would want to examine the parallels between his sensibility and that of his Spanish translator: while Conrad laments in *The Mirror of the Sea* the passing of the sailing ship, which was faced with obsolescence following the advent of the paddle-steamer, Marías juxtaposes the love and respect men of a bygone era bestowed on their boats with the blasé attitude of modern air passengers. We might seek

---

[17] This favourite quotation also appears in Marías's 'Retrato imaginario del artista en casa', in his *Pasiones pasadas* (Madrid: Alfaguara, 1999), pp. 85–9 (p. 87) and 'Javier Marías: The Art of Fiction No. 190', p. 18.

[18] Javier Marías, 'Aviones marineros', *Granta en español*, 1 (2004), 23–30 (p. 28).

to determine the extent to which the echoing of Conrad in 'Aviones marineros' artistically complements the aim of Marías's piece, which I take to be an encouragement to the reader to perceive the romance of these ships of the sky: he ends the article with the hope that in future pilots will narrate the stories of their planes, much as Conrad might have done with a ship: what Marías calls 'un poco de literatura, o, lo que es lo mismo, un poco de unicidad; un poco de historia, pasado y vida' ('a bit of literature, or, what amounts to the same thing, a bit of uniqueness; a bit of history, past, and life').[19] As translation, we would further examine what Conrad's words lose and gain in their passage from one language to another. In the original, the deeply moved sea-captain refers to his ship as 'her' and 'she'—'She was strong. Last voyage I had my wife and two children in her'—heightening the sense of closeness and a deeply felt loyalty.[20] Although Marías explains earlier in 'Aviones marineros' that boats are among the only words in English to receive a gender, grammatical accuracy in Spanish dictates that the subject of the verbs in these sentences be the masculine singular 'barco'. What is lost in this instance, he makes up for when translating the captain's first statement—'No ship could have done so well'.[21] In applying to the boat the verb 'portarse', which is suggestive of human behaviour and not frequently used of inanimate objects, Marías helps to restore something of its personification in English.

What these two examples demonstrate is that Marías's translations of Stevenson and Conrad have become part of his literary vocabulary. But by placing the quotations in new contexts, their implications are subtly changed, as Marías is well aware:

> He traducido mucho, y también por eso no tengo el ansia de la originalidad. Al contrario, tengo bien clara la posibilidad de las repeticiones; ya que las repeticiones nunca son las mismas, no pueden serlo jamás y pueden aportar significados nuevos.[22]

> (I have translated a lot, and also for that reason I don't feel the anxiety of originality. On the contrary, I'm well aware of the potential for repetitions; since repetitions are never the same, they never can be and they can always bring new meanings to bear.)

Ilse Logie too points out that:

> Es innegable que Marías considera al escritor un 'inter-pres', en el sentido etimológico de 'el que habla en el medio', que pone textos a la disposición

[19] 'Aviones marineros', p. 30.
[20] Joseph Conrad, *The Mirror of the Sea* and *A Personal Record* (London: Dent, 1946), p. 146.
[21] *The Mirror of the Sea*, p. 146.
[22] Caterina Visani interview. http://www.javiermarias.es/main.html (accessed 4 June 2008).

*does he translate well?*
*does he translate humbly?*
*has he learnt from his translations?*

de sus lectores, replanteando así el principio de autoría, ya que en nuestra época, ser autor de un escrito consiste—como tan bien lo supo Borges—más en descubrirlo y adueñarse de él que en inventarlo.[23]

(There is no doubt that Marías considers the writer as an 'inter-pres', in the etymological sense of 'he who speaks in the middle', who puts texts at his readers' disposal, and in doing so invites us to reconsider the idea of authorship, since in our time, being the author of a piece of writing—as Borges was so well aware—consists more of discovering it and taking possession of it than of inventing it.)

If, as seems to be the case, both Marías and his critics are conscious that he is deliberately weaving allusive webs by echoing the works he has translated, the task of those critics should be to explore those webs. What do they mean? How do they contribute to his writing? What do they show us about the possibilities for linguistic cross-fertilization through translation? These are the questions I seek to answer in this book by relying on close textual analysis of individual instances of these allusive practices.

There are several reasons why Marías scholars might be interested in his translations. Perhaps the most obvious is the question of quality: does he translate well? Fernando Valls bemoans the tendency among Spanish literary journalists to 'alabar una traducción siempre que esté hecha por un escritor. Por un escritor de ficción, se entiende…a mayor nombre mejor traducción' ('praise a translation as long as it's by a recognized author. An author of fiction, that is… the bigger the name the better the translation').[24] Has Marías benefited from such tacitly endorsed but critically unsubstantiated approval? I argue that he has not. Does he translate humbly? Nabokov warned that, when a talented writer turns his hand to translation, there is an inherent danger that 'he will drown the foreign masterpiece under the sparkling ripples of his own personal style'. Such a translator, rather than 'dressing up like the real author,…dresses up the author as himself'.[25] Again, I argue that Marías does not try to upstage the illustrious forerunners whose work he is translating. However, by far the most tantalizing reason for studying Marías's translations are the author's repeated claims to have learnt much from the task of writing them: 'traducir es, naturalmente, un grandísimo ejercicio literario, un ejercicio

---

[23] Ilse Logie, 'La traducción, emblema de la obra de Javier Marías', in *El pensamiento literario de Javier Marías*, ed. by Maarten Steenmeijer, Foro Hispánico, 20 (Amsterdam: Rodopi, 2001), pp. 67–76 (p. 68).

[24] Fernando Valls, *La realidad inventada: Análisis crítico de la novela española actual* (Barcelona: Crítica, 2003), p. 37.

[25] Vladimir Nabokov, 'The Art of Translation', in *Lectures on Russian Literature*, ed. by Fredson Bowers (London: Weidenfeld & Nicolson, 1982), pp. 315–21 (p. 319).

magnífico'[26] ('translating is, naturally, a great literary exercise, a magnificent exercise'); 'A aquel que quiera escribir...yo le recomendaría que tradujera...yo he notado en mi propia prosa flexibilidad y soltura después de traducir' ('I would recommend to any aspiring writer that they do some translation...I've noticed flexibility and fluency in my own prose after translating'); 'Si a mí me preguntaran en una escuela de letras qué es lo que se debe enseñar, yo podría decir: traducir. Me parece el mejor ejercicio para un escritor'[27] ('If they were to ask me what should be taught in a writing school, I would say: translation. I think it's the best exercise for a writer'); 'ya había traducido a Conrad y a Sterne, entre otros, y...noté mi "instrumento" más afinado que antes, gracias al extraordinario ejercicio literario que supone la traducción'[28] ('I had already translated Conrad and Sterne, among others, and...I noticed that my "instrument" was more finely tuned than before, thanks to the extraordinary literary exercise that translation demands'). From this representative sample of the assertions made in interviews conducted between 1988 and 2001, it is clear that Marías believes translation to have honed his skills as a writer, shaping his prose for the better to the point where he actively encourages others to follow his example. This book will show that, far from being an empty boast, his awareness of how translation has shaped his own writings bespeaks a lively sensitivity to the literary debts he has accrued. He has explored the latter in essays, interviews, lectures, prologues, and translator's notes demonstrating a perspicacious ability to act as critic of his own work. Running alongside this authorial commentary on his own praxis will be close comparison of his translations and his own writings. Central to the argument lies the belief that, at its best, translation can be as profound an engagement with another writer's work as it is possible to achieve. Another celebrated practitioner of the art, Edith Grossman, puts the point well:

> In the process of translating, we endeavor to hear the first version of the work as profoundly and completely as possible, struggling to discover the linguistic charge, the structural rhythms, the subtle implications, the complexities of meaning and suggestion in vocabulary and phrasing, and the ambient cultural inferences and conclusions these tonalities allow us to

---

[26] Interview with Javier Marías conducted by Caterina Visani. Text available at the following URL: http://www.javiermarias.es/PAGINASDEENTREVISTAS/entrevista-CaterinaVisani.html (accessed 6 June 2008).

[27] Sol Alameda, 'Javier Marías: el éxito europeo de un indeciso', *El País Semanal*, 10 November 1996, pp. 58–64 (p. 62).

[28] Juan Gabriel Vásquez, '"Tengo a veces la sensación de no estar ya vivo"', *Lateral*, 82 (2001), 13–15 (p. 13–14).

extrapolate. This is a kind of reading as deep as any encounter with a literary text can be.[29]

Marías's case both exemplifies and expands on Grossman's insight since translation has shaped his literary imagination and prose in readily discernible ways.

Isabel Cuñado boldly (and bizarrely) claims that the task I have pursued is old news:

> Es de sobra conocida la influencia que autores como Thomas Browne, Laurence Sterne, Henry James y Joseph Conrad han tenido sobre el escritor madrileño (a los que yo añadiría E. T. A. Hoffmann, Isak Dinesen, Jorge Luis Borges y Juan Rulfo).[30]

> (The influence that authors like Thomas Browne, Laurence Sterne, Henry James, and Joseph Conrad have had on the Madrid author is well known [to whom I would add E. T. A. Hoffmann, Isak Dinesen, Jorge Luis Borges, and Juan Rulfo].)

If this body of knowledge is as commonly held as she asserts, why does she cite no studies, articles, or critical material to substantiate her claim? Moreover, does her act of adding four further names to the list spontaneously create even more shared knowledge? Although Cuñado does not mention them, to date three researchers have offered appraisals of aspects of Marías's translation career: Luis Pegenaute has briefly examined Marías's version of *Tristram Shandy*; Ilse Logie has looked at how translation underpins Marías's hermeneutic vision but acknowledges that she is hampered by not having had access to any of the texts he translated; most importantly, Alexis Grohmann has discussed how translating Browne and Conrad shaped Marías's 1983 novel *El siglo* (hence *ES*) and gone some way towards assessing the influence of *Tristram Shandy* on his later *Negra espalda del tiempo* (*Dark Back of Time*, hence *NET*, 1998).[31] In *Coming Into One's Own: the Novelistic Development of Javier Marías*, Grohmann's approach to the translation of Browne and Conrad forms part of a wider enquiry into the development of the author's prose style. It has been a

[29] Edith Grossman, *Why Translation Matters* (New Haven and London: Yale University Press, 2010), p. 9.

[30] Isabel Cuñado, *El espectro de la herencia: la narrativa de Javier Marías*, Portada Hispánica, 17 (Amsterdam: Rodopi, 2004), p. 12.

[31] Luis Pegenaute, 'The Unfortunate Journey of Laurence Sterne Through Spain: The Translation of his Works into Spanish', *The Shandean*, 6 (1994), 24–53; Logie, 'La traducción, emblema de la obra de Javier Marías'; Alexis Grohmann, *Coming Into One's Own: the Novelistic Development of Javier Marías* (Amsterdam: Rodopi, 2002); Alexis Grohmann, 'Literatura y errabundia', in *Antes y después del "Quijote"*, ed. by Robert Archer et al. (Valencia: Biblioteca Valenciana/Association of Hispanists of Great Britain and Northern Ireland, 2005), pp. 373–81.

great help to establish a dialogue with his conclusions in my own work, as will become clear in chapters that follow on Sterne and Browne.

A striking aspect of Marías's career is that his advocacy of reading and translating literature in English has not been without consequences for his standing in Spain's literary world. In the words of his friend and fellow novelist Eduardo Mendoza, recognition in his home country has come 'con cuentagotas y como a desgana' ('like blood from a stone and as if reluctantly').[32] While his early novels were dismissed as themselves sounding like translations from English, the emphasis placed by interviewers on his success outside Spain hints at a view of him as having left his literary roots behind and lost interest in his home country. This tired parochialism has also affected another of Spain's most successful cultural exports, the film director Pedro Almodóvar, whose worldwide acclaim appears to have made him more enemies than friends back home. The Spanish cinematic establishment studiously ignores his works when, each year, the nominations are announced for the national film awards, the Goyas, seemingly on the basis that Almodóvar is no longer theirs to reward. In Marías's case, when his 'suspicious' success outside Spain is coupled with his strident criticism of his fellow citizens' social habits or voting tendencies in his weekly newspaper column, it is not difficult to see why he should be a divisive figure. Perhaps the best illustration of his uncompromising, but highly principled stance as a public intellectual is offered by his decision in December 2002 to sever all ties with the magazine *El Semanal*, where he had published a weekly column for the previous eight years.[33] *El Semanal*, a Sunday supplement syndicated to many of Spain's regional newspapers, boasted in the years Marías was writing for it a readership of up to four million people, though with only limited circulation in Madrid and Barcelona.[34] His acrimonious departure was caused by the editors' suppression of an article he had written in solidarity with his fellow columnist Arturo Pérez-Reverte and in their joint condemnation of Spain's Catholic Church. Pérez-Reverte had attracted public criticism for a forthright attack on the Church and its then leader, Pope John Paul II, prompting Marías to leap to his colleague's defence the following week. He used his column to deliver a second broadside against that most tarnished of institutions. But it was at this point that trouble flared. Doubtless fearful of the reaction of readers and sponsors after Pérez-Reverte's article had already caused a considerable stir, the editors at first deferred

---

[32] Eduardo Mendoza, '"Laudatio" de la puntuación', *El País*, 30 June 2006, p. 50.

[33] Marías's association with *El Semanal* began in December 1994.

[34] Marías explains the nature of *El Semanal*'s editorial arrangements in the following interview: Javier Marías and Michel Braudeau, 'À propos d'un certain Javier Marías', *La Nouvelle Revue Française*, 584 (2008), 1–20 (pp. 14–15).

publication of Marías's coruscating piece, then refused outright to print it, at which point he resigned from the magazine.[35] In his view, Spain had endured press censorship for quite long enough during his lifetime and he had no intention of working for a publication that would not uphold freedom of speech. The wider reasons for Marías's antipathy towards the Catholic Church are not far to find in his articles and include the scorn it demonstrated towards Spain's secular institutions in justifying the religious wedding of Letizia Ortiz to Felipe de Borbón, the heir to the Spanish throne, in 2004: apparently the fact that she was a divorcée was no obstacle to her marrying because her previously contracted civil marriage had no real validity in the eyes of the Church anyway.[36] Further irritants for Marías come in the form of the millions of euros the Church continues to receive courtesy of the Spanish taxpayer in spite of the fact that the country is allegedly a secular state.[37] For him as for many of his compatriots, the close collaboration between the Church and General Francisco Franco's dictatorial regime remains a lingering stain on the former's moral and spiritual authority.[38]

Where some might see deliberate controversialism in Marías's stance, others would perceive a particular understanding of the role of the public intellectual. His articles challenge his fellow citizens to be more engaged, more civilized, and more reflective members of a democratic society. He has stated several times that, when choosing subjects for his columns, he tries to discuss topics where his views might shake the easy consensus of politically correct thought or knee-jerk response. In seeking such a role, he is setting himself up as a polemical figure but a nevertheless essential cog in the wheel of a healthy democracy. He has used his platform to act as a coherent critic of political correctness, the pact of silence around Franco's dictatorship, the frivolousness of contemporary society, and successive governments of different political persuasions both at home and abroad. The better to retain his ideological independence, he has consistently refused to participate in literary competitions or cultural events that

[35] The article, entitled 'Creed en nosotros a cambio', was eventually published in Javier Marías, *Harán de mí un criminal* (Madrid: Alfaguara, 2003), pp. 317–19. This article collection hence referred to as *HMC*.
[36] Javier Marías, 'Hacia el Día Mundial del Orgullo Cardenalicio', in *El oficio de oír llover* (Madrid: Alfaguara, 2005), pp. 143–5. This article collection hence referred to as *EOOL*.
[37] Javier Marías, 'El encapuchado abuso', in *EOOL*, pp. 50–2.
[38] Javier Marías, '"Botellón" de encapuchados', in *DNA*, pp. 192–4. See also Vincente Molina-Foix, *New Cinema in Spain* (London: BFI, 1977), p. 4. According to Helen Graham, the precise role played by the Church during the Civil War and its aftermath remains to be explored by researchers, who find their way to ecclesiastical archives barred by institutional prevarication. See her *The Spanish Civil War: A Very Short Introduction* (Oxford: Oxford University Press, 2005), p. 145.

are sponsored by the Spanish state, setting himself apart from a great majority of his contemporaries. He has also ensured that his weekly articles do not just become wrappers for the following day's fast food by publishing them in collected volumes: *Mano de sombra* (1997), *Seré amado cuando falte* (1999), *A veces un caballero* (2001), *Harán de mí un criminal* (2003), *El oficio de oír llover* (2005), *Demasiada nieve alrededor* (2007), and *Lo que no vengo a decir* (2009).[39]

We shall see in the first chapter of this study that Marías grew up in a Spain still ruled by Franco and in a family environment where the dictator's shadow loomed especially large. He has been quick to remind his readers that well within living memory—his own memory—Spain did not enjoy free elections, uncensored newspapers, or an independent judiciary. With that in mind, he believes in the need for an engaged and informed dialogue with the society one inhabits, lest in neglecting it one should wake up to discover that its easy privileges have been lost through lack of vigilance. Those years spent in enforced close proximity to the inane rhetoric of a right-wing dictatorship left a deep mark on the young author. So nauseated was he by the relentless recourse to unquestioning national pride that was the hallmark of official discourse under Franco that he, along with many of his artistic contemporaries, rejected their homeland outright as either a subject or setting for their work. Cuñado has argued in her monograph, *El espectro de la herencia: la narrativa de Javier Marías*, that the novelist's works throughout the 1980s and 1990s showed traces of the repressed desire to address recent national history and the traumas of a collective past: a desire repressed because of this early antipathy towards all that smelt strongly of Spain. The roots of his decision to become a translator can also be traced, in part at least, to that same antipathy. But, as I have already indicated, any suggestion that Marías stands aloof from his homeland today is simply wrong. His novels and articles represent a deep and thoughtful engagement with Spain's twentieth-century history and contemporary society. His long-standing interest in betrayal, the knowability of others, the nature of war, and the benevolence of memory in forgetting a traumatic past all find their seeds

---

[39] On this point, Maarten Steenmeijer has written: 'Como es el caso de sus cuentos, ensayos, artículos y otros escritos publicados de forma dispersa, Marías se ha empeñado en reunir todas sus columnas en forma de libro sin que mediara en ello ninguna presión de los editores. De esta manera, el autor dio a entender que, a su juicio, sus columnas son algo más que textos publicados en periódicos de ayer que nadie quiere ya' ('As is the case with his short stories, essays, articles, and other pieces published in a dispersed fashion, Marías has insisted on collecting all of his columns together in book form without publishers pressing him to do so. In this way, the author made clear that, in his view, his columns are something more than texts published in yesterday's paper that nobody wants any longer'). See 'Javier Marías, columnista: el otro, el mismo', pp. 259–60.

in the experiences of both his family and his nation during the Civil War and its aftermath. The novels of what most critics agree is his mature period, from *El hombre sentimental* (*The Man of Feeling*, hence *EHS*, 1986) onwards, are first-person narratives written by men approaching middle age who are endeavouring to put unsettling events behind them. They share a detached, observational mode; an apparent aloofness behind which often lurks deep disquiet over how to find a place in a world which offers no obvious personal, ethical, or narrative certainties. The elucidation of how the author develops fiction of both national and universal resonance through their voices will be the subject of discussion in Chapters 4, 7, and 9 of this study. Chapter 6 examines Marías's novel *ES*, written immediately prior to *EHS*, in which he begins tentatively to address the subject of Spain's Civil War and the question of why human beings should seek underhand control over others' destinies. There, Marías builds the portrait of his central protagonist, a police informant, with substantial recourse to the writings of Sir Thomas Browne. The resonances of the Civil War, the figure of the informant, and why human beings should dishonestly seek to control one another's destinies echo through his penultimate novel, *TRM*, the subject of the concluding chapters of this study.

Such has been my way of approaching both Marías's fiction and how the translation of Sterne, Browne, and Nabokov helped to shape it. The first two chapters of this study establish a framework by answering three basic questions: What did he translate? Why did he translate? And how does he translate? Chapter 1 thus answers the first of these by giving a biographical sketch of Marías, explores in detail his activities as a translator, and elucidates the particular influences and personal tastes that guided his choices at a given juncture. Chapter 2 looks at his reasons for becoming a translator. It contextualizes his early ambivalence towards his homeland within a wider body of opinion by finding common ground between his views and those of his contemporaries. The final section of that chapter also explores his stance in relation to the theory of translation, asking where he stands on two of the most enduring issues to have shaped that discipline: whether translation is in itself a creative art and whether translators should bring the foreign text to their reader (naturalize it) or allow its otherness to remain intact. In the remainder of my work I have used the vocabulary and insights of Translation Theory sparingly as a useful critical idiom. As a matter of personal preference, I have limited the amount of theoretical discussion overall in order to free up space to discuss Marías's novelistic preoccupations and practice. He espouses the belief—one I share wholeheartedly—that novels remain among the best art forms in which to interrogate human experience in a sustained and

Translation theory?

complex way.[40] I have taken the view that it is discussion of such lasting matter that will provide both the greatest interest and insight for the reader curious to learn more about Marías, rather than the advancement of yet more theoretical approaches to the art of translation.

In the main body of this study (Chapters 3 to 7), I have divided into discrete chapters discussion of the assessment of Marías's qualities as a translator from the particular impact that activity had on his work. In doing so I have contributed to the understanding not only of his career as a translator but also of the works translation has done much to shape. As far as possible, I avoid discussing his echoing of Sterne, Browne, and Nabokov out of the context of individual works and their larger meanings. And so, for example, when examining the Brownean allusions in *ES*, I do so in the context of how and why they are used to characterize the central protagonist. The third chapter offers a literary analysis of Marías's version of *Tristram Shandy* while the fourth examines how he used the precedents offered by Shandean autobiography as a model for *NET*. Chapter 5 analyzes his version of the fifth chapter of *Hydriotaphia* while comparing it to that written by Jorge Luis Borges and Adolfo Bioy Casares, for reasons I explain there. The sixth and seventh chapters discuss the ways in which Marías has alluded to or quoted Browne in the novel *ES* and the short story 'Cuando fui mortal'. Chapter 8 then breaks this mould by offering an overview of how continued contact with Vladimir Nabokov—through reading and even the condensed translation and rewriting of the latter's novel *Lolita*—has shaped Marías's thinking and literary persona, as well as his short story 'Mientras ellas duermen' and the novel *MBPM*. The final chapter is in two parts and offers, by way of a conclusion to this study, an analysis of his penultimate and most ambitious novel, *TRM*. There I bring together all that we have learned about the author's praxis and preoccupations, and use it to interpret what seems likely to be his crowning achievement.

My insertion of an adverb of probability in that last sentence is a function of studying a living author who, as this book goes to press, has just published his latest novel, *Los enamoramientos* (2011). The potential pitfalls of such study are well documented. However, the benefits of writing about an author who has given, and continues to give, consistently illuminating press interviews, as well as attracting reviews in newspapers and magazines across the world, have been considerable. I have made extensive use of such material in my work, helped immeasurably by Montse Vega, the founder of what must be among the best websites in the world

---

[40] Javier Marías, 'Contar el misterio', in *Literatura y fantasma: edición ampliada* (Madrid: Alfaguara, 2001), pp. 117–23. This article collection hence referred to as *LF*.

devoted to a living author—www.javiermarias.es. That Marías's readers should enjoy such a facility is not without its ironies given that the author himself is a Luddite who neither owns nor uses a computer, still writes on an electric typewriter, and sends his correspondence by post and fax.[41] I have provided references to that website for some of the interviews in more difficult-to-find journals and magazines. For the benefit of readers unfamiliar with Spanish, English translations of Spanish quotations have been included. Unless otherwise stated, they are my own. A final point to mention is that in the text that follows and for the sake of stylistic variation, I have used the terms 'translation', 'rendering', and 'version' synonymously.

---

[41] Marías's worn-on-the-sleeve resistance to modern technology has earned him gentle ribbing in Spain's press. See for example Francisco Cantalapiedra, 'El misterio del móvil de Javier Marías', *El País*, 6 February 2004, p. 51.

# 1

# An Overview of a Career in Translation

To establish a context within which to discuss Marías's career as a translator we must first establish three things: what did he translate, why did he translate, and how did he translate? I devote the following two chapters to answering those questions. The first offers a biographical sketch of the author's career to date, with the emphasis placed on his early years and work as a translator. In it I endeavour to indicate the sort of family environment he grew up in, one that was shaped by early misfortune but also steeped in literary culture and an outward-looking perspective. I give a comprehensive account of his translation career, highlighting where possible what the driving forces behind his choices and decisions were, and showing how, in more recent years, Marías has devoted time to consolidating his legacy in this area. The second chapter examines what I have called the why and how: why it was that the youthful Marías turned to translation as a way of honing his skills as a writer and how he approaches translation from a theoretical perspective. It seeks, moreover, to place his decision in the context of a wider discontent with indigenous Spanish cultural heritage shared by many influential writers in the early 1970s. It then traces his reading in the field of Translation Theory and examines his two most significant theoretical essays on the art.

Javier Marías was born on 20 September 1951, the fourth son of Dolores Franco and Julián Marías, the philosopher and disciple of José Ortega y Gasset (1883–1955). Though he had a comfortable and apparently contented upbringing, his birth came at a moment when two recent misfortunes continued to make themselves felt in the family home. The first was the death of his parents' eldest child, Julianín, who had succumbed to illness on the 25 June 1949. His loss was felt acutely and they continued to mourn their dead son for years to come, such that the spectre of the dead brother he never knew loomed large on Javier's childhood horizon. The second misfortune had a more sinister tinge and not only coloured Javier's future attitudes but has also featured prominently in his novels and short stories. At the end of the Spanish Civil War, Julián Marías, who had fought and written in support of the Republican cause, fell victim to the newly formed Nationalist government's attempts to rid the country of the so-called 'anti-Spain'. In his anxiety to purge those who had opposed his rise to power, General Franco signed into law the Ley de Responsabilidades Políticas ('Law of Political Responsibility', February 1939) and with it a stringent system of retrospective justice under which Republican sympathizers could be tried for 'crimes' against the state committed during the war. A then 'friend' of Julián seized the opportunity to rid himself of an academic rival and denounced him to Francoist law-enforcers.[1] Julián was imprisoned for four months until his case came to trial and only freed after the intervention of a good Samaritan during the legal proceedings saved him from further detention or worse. This good Samaritan apparently told the court that not only was there no substance to the allegations levelled against Julián but that they were fuelled by nothing more than envy of his achievements. In spite of this happy outcome, the very fact of the allegations—substantiated or not—did lasting damage to his reputation. He was now a pariah as far as the state-run university system was concerned, a status further compounded when he refused to swear allegiance to the principles of the Movimiento Nacional ('National Movement')—Franco's blend of Falangist and Catholic doctrine. Julián was not allowed to work as a university teacher or newspaper columnist for years to come. To keep the wolf from the door, he took up an activity he had begun to cultivate before the outbreak of war and that was ideally suited to someone not permitted to publish under his own name in Spain; if he could not openly publish there, he could at least put his name to the words of others through the translations of influential thinkers that he produced. His record as a translator is in fact a formidable one: he produced eight book-length translations from French, German, and Latin in the decade after the Civil War and was later to collaborate on translations from ancient Greek.[2] Dolores Franco, Javier's mother, also published, in 1941, a translation of selected letters by

---

[1] Neither Julián nor Javier Marías has ever publicly named the traitorous friend, although as the reader will see in Chapter 9 of this study, the latter has given sufficient clues in his fiction to facilitate his identification. The Spanish literary critic José Carlos Mainer names Julián Marías's nemesis without compunction. See José Carlos Mainer, *Tramas, libros, nombres: Para entender la literatura española, 1944–2000* (Barcelona: Anagrama, 2005), p. 220.

[2] Unless otherwise stated all of the following works were translated by Julián Marías alone. Aristóteles, *Ética a Nicómaco*, trans by Julián Marías and María Araújo (Madrid: Instituto de Estudios Políticos, 1959); Aristóteles, *Política*, trans by Julián Marías and María Araújo (Madrid: Instituto de Estudios Políticos, 1951); Paul Hazard, *La crisis de la conciencia europea (1680–1715)* (Madrid: Pegaso, 1941); Gottfried Wilhelm Leibniz, *Discurso de metafísica* (Madrid: Revista de Occidente, 1942); Max Scheler, *De lo eterno en el hombre* (Madrid: Revista de Occidente, [1940]); Lucio Anno Séneca, *Sobre la felicidad* (Madrid: Revista de Occidente, [1943]).

Napoleon, entitled *De Córcega a Santa Elena*.[3] Strangely enough, Marías
seems not to have discovered until after his mother's death that she had
undertaken this piece of translation.[4] Although it is tempting to see causal
links between the future direction Marías's career would take and these
parental precedents, I do not draw such direct inferences. Rather, what
these precedents demonstrate is the kind of environment into which
Marías was born: one that was intellectually engaged, open-minded, and
multilingual.

Translators' pay being what it was, and some would say still is, Julián
Marías's translation work was never going to suffice to keep the family
afloat and so both husband and wife ran a private academy for American
students in Madrid. Julián Marías then accepted a visiting lectureship in
the United States where he was building a considerable reputation through
the philosophical works he published in Latin America. It was the first of
these sojourns in America, arranged by the exiled poet Jorge Guillén, that
saw the Marías family, including the month-old Javier, spend the rest of
1951 and half of 1952 in Wellesley (Massachusetts). Among his father's
students, Javier acquired the nickname 'el *baby* de Wellesley' ('the Wellesley baby').[5] His first memories of his father are of a man dressed like an
American academic of the 1950s and his first memories at all are of the
abundant New England snow.[6] In one of the strange symmetries that his
life offers, Marías was to return to Wellesley in 1984 to give a lecture
course on *Don Quijote*, emulating Vladimir Nabokov, one of his literary
idols.

On their return home, the family settled once more into the flat on the
Calle de Covarrubias where Javier had been born. From the evocation
he wrote in 1990 of Chamberí, the Madrid district where he grew up, one
gleans that his early childhood was spent reading Richmal Crompton's
William stories, watching films at the plentiful cinemas, and playing with
his brothers on the British-made double-decker buses that trawled up and
down the streets.[7] When he was seven years old, the family moved to the

---

[3] In the article 'Las amigas de Lolita', Javier Marías refers to the anthology she edited of
writings on Spain, *España como preocupación*, as 'el único libro que completó' ('the only
book she finished writing'). See his *A veces un caballero* (Madrid: Alfaguara, 2001), pp.
38–40 (p. 39). This article collection hence referred to as *AVC*.

[4] For confirmation of this anomaly, see 'Javier Marías: The Art of Fiction No. 190', p. 24.

[5] Julián Marías, *Una vida presente*, 3 vols (Madrid: Alianza, 1988–1989), II: *Memorias
II: 1951–1975* (1989), p. 49.

[6] JM, '"Que por mí no quede"', in *Vida del fantasma: cinco años más tenue* (Madrid: Alfaguara, 2001), pp. 444–7. (This article collection hence referred to as *VF*); Carmen Pérez-
Lanzac, 'El último caballero', *Marie Claire* (Spanish edition), January 2005, pp. 90–2 (p. 91).

[7] JM, 'En Chamberí', in *Pasiones pasadas* (Madrid: Alfaguara, 1999), pp. 64–7. This
article collection hence referred to as *PP*.

Calle Vallehermoso, a home Marías describes with great affection as so full of books that he and his brothers were obliged to negotiate the obstacle course of piled volumes in their games around the flat. Nevertheless: 'Lo cierto es que, pese a todos estos inconvenientes, aún hoy no concibo una casa acogedora y cómoda en la que las paredes no estén tapizadas de libros de alegres cantos y también de cuadros empotrados' ('What is certain is that, despite all those inconveniences, even today I cannot imagine a welcoming and comfortable home whose walls are not lined with brightly-edged books with pictures nestling between them').[8] If the photos that often accompany Marías's press interviews are anything to go by, he has taken this lesson very much to heart: his home on Madrid's Plaza de la Villa is lined from floor to ceiling with bookcases.

It was in the reading he undertook as a child that Marías acquired his literary vocation since the desire to read more of what he liked prompted him to pick up his pen and try to reproduce what had brought him so much pleasure.[9] Unlike the nineteenth-century novelist Pardo Bazán, who somewhat earnestly claimed her favourite books as a child were the Bible, the *Iliad*, and *Don Quijote*, Marías makes no secret of the humble origins of his art.[10] His attitude is mirrored by other prominent members of his generation in Spain, among them Antonio Muñoz Molina, Arturo Pérez-Reverte, and Fernando Savater, who likewise trace their love of the literary back to the comic strips and Jules Verne novels they read as children.[11] Writing in 2005 about a schoolfriend who had recently died,

---

[8] JM, 'La biblioteca invasora', in *PP*, pp. 68–72 (p. 70).

[9] Although Marías has repeated this view on numerous occasions, it is formulated with particular clarity in the following exchange with Arturo Pérez-Reverte: 'Yo empecé a escribir porque me gustaba leer. Y empecé como creo que deben empezar todos los escritores jóvenes, emulando. Existe la imitación, que puede estar bien o mal; el remedo es peor. Y existe la emulación; es uno de los motores principales de la historia y de la vida humana. Es el deseo de ser como aquel a quien uno admira y de hacer lo mismo que aquel a quien uno admira. Yo empecé a hacer unos garabatos que querían ser como *Los tres mosqueteros* o como Guillermo Brown. A mí me daban mucho goce esos libros y los quería emular' ('I began writing because I liked reading. And I started as I think all young writers must start, by emulating. There is such a thing as imitation, which can be good or bad; poor imitation is worse. And there is such a thing as emulation, which is one of the main motivating factors behind history and human life. It is the desire to be like the person that you admire and do the same thing as the person that you admire. I began writing a few scrawls that were trying to be like *The Three Musketeers* or like William Brown. Those books gave me a great deal of pleasure and I wanted to emulate them'). Juan Cruz, 'Javier Marías y Arturo Pérez-Reverte: el agua y el aceite', *La Nación*, AND Cultura section, 18 August 2007, pp. 12–17 (p. 16).

[10] Pardo Bazán made the claim in the 'Apuntes Autobiográficos' ('Autobiographical Sketch') that prefaced the first edition of her novel *Los pazos de Ulloa* (1886). See her *Obras completas*, ed. by Federico Carlos Sáinz de Robles et al., 3 vols (Madrid: Aguilar, 1963–1973), III: *Cuentos/Crítica literaria*, ed. by Harry L. Kirby (1973), p. 704.

[11] See Antonio Muñoz Molina, *Pura alegría* (Madrid: Alfaguara, 1998), p. 206; Juan Cruz, pp. 13–14; Fernando Savater, *La infancia recuperada*, 10th edn (Madrid: Taurus, 2002).

Marías recalled how much the playground games they had enjoyed years before found their imaginative centre in the comics and adventure stories they read: 'nos veo ejerciendo de romano y cartaginés, de griego y troyano, de esbirro de Richelieu y mosquetero, por supuesto de vaquero e indio' ('I can see us now playing at being Roman and Carthaginian, Greek and Trojan, Richelieu's henchman and Musketeer, [and] of course cowboy and Indian').[12] Later, he attended the Colegio Estudio, a liberal Madrid school whose ethos owed much to the Institución Libre de Enseñanza. Despite Franco's ban on co-education, the school taught boys and girls alongside one another, meaning that whenever state inspectors arrived each sex would scatter to separate class rooms to maintain the illusion of compliance.

Throughout his teenage years, the family spent summers in Soria, the Castilian town made famous by Antonio Machado's poems. During this period, he wrote the first pieces of fiction to which he thought it worth putting a name: at fourteen, the short story 'La vida y la muerte de Marcelino Iturriaga' ('The Life and Death of Marcelino Iturriaga'), and a year later, his first novel, *La víspera*, which was written in the home of the literary critic Heliodoro Carpintero.[13] The former was published in a Barcelona newspaper whereas the latter has never seen the light of day.[14] His association with Soria and the home of Carpintero continued for years to come. Speaking in May 2005, he recalled undertaking his first serious translation work—a selection of Hardy's short stories—while in Carpintero's flat. In more recent years—another symmetry—he has rented that same apartment and used it as a retreat in which to write, free from the demands and noise of Madrid.[15]

However, to return to his later teenage years, clearly he yearned to broaden his horizons. His early experiences of travel, reading foreign literature, seeing all the European and Hollywood films he devoured as a youngster could hardly fail to awaken his interest in the world beyond Spain's borders. Fortunately, his uncle, the maverick film director Jesús Franco, offered him the chance to do so. Sergio Vila-Sanjuán identifies the latter's influence as running in the opposite direction to that of Marías's upstanding, intellectual parents:

---

[12] JM, 'El amigo niño', in *EOOL*, pp. 299–301.
[13] See JM, 'Dignidad y decoro', in *Mano de sombra* (Madrid: Alfaguara, 1997), pp. 211–13. (This article collection hence referred to as *MS*); 'La dificultad de perder la juventud', in *PP*, pp. 221–37.
[14] 'La vida y la muerte…' was eventually collected into the expanded edition of *Mientras ellas duermen*. See JM, *Mientras ellas duermen*, rev. edn (Madrid: Alfaguara, 2000), pp. 13–20. This short story collection hence referred to as *MED*.
[15] Elide Pittarello, *Entrevistos: Javier Marías* (Barcelona: RqueR, 2005), pp. 12–14; JM, 'Novela y espías en Soria', in *HMC*, pp. 96–9 (p. 96).

Quizá para compensar, Javier Marías había sido expuesto también desde joven a una influencia compensatoria, la de su tío Jesús—'Jess'—Franco, el más conocido director de películas de terror a la española, con frecuentes incursiones en el género erótico, campeón en el formato de bajo presupuesto y una figura algo descabellada y no demasiado bien vista por el siempre recto y ponderado padre de Javier, don Julián Marías.[16]

(Perhaps to offset their effect, Javier Marías had been exposed from a young age to a compensatory influence, that of his uncle Jesús—'Jess'—Franco, the most renowned director of Spanish-style horror films, with frequent forays into erotica, champion of the low-budget format and a slightly ridiculous figure who was not always looked upon favourably by Javier's upstanding and measured father, Don Julián Marías.)

Jesús (or Jess) Franco's early career had included working as a second-unit director under the great Orson Welles on *Chimes at Midnight* (1965), Welles's masterful adaptation of Shakespeare's *King Henry IV* and *King Henry V*.[17] Since then his tastes have not remained quite so mainstream and he is infamous in the film industry for his low-budget, soft-porn, gore fests. He it was who lent Marías the Paris flat in which he wrote much of his first published novel, *Los dominios del lobo* (1970). Following his first year at the Complutense in Madrid, he spent six weeks in the French capital, managing to watch no fewer than eighty-five films in its unrivalled cinemas, while surviving on a diet of bread and mustard. Despite needing to busk on the Champs Elysées to supplement the meagre funds he had brought with him from Spain, by the time he left, the novel was practically complete.[18]

More importantly for our purposes, Jesús Franco was the first person to commission his nephew to translate written English. In preparation for a film eventually entitled *El conde Drácula*, Franco asked his nephews Carlos (Franco) and Javier, to translate horror film scripts for him. It would appear that the script to which Franco eventually put his name was an amalgamation of their work. Where the manuscripts of those translations are now, I have been unable to ascertain. In the unlikely event of their appearing at some time in the future, they will offer a fascinating insight

---

[16] Sergio Vila-Sanjuán, *Pasando página: autores y editores en la España democrática* (Barcelona: Destino, 2003), p. 163.

[17] Doubtless, part of Marías's affection for the film stems from this family association. It features prominently in *MBPM*.

[18] Marías's musical repertoire was impressively varied, as he revealed in conversation with Ángela López: 'En aquella época me servía de Dylan, Leonard Cohen y hasta Crosby, Still [*sic*] and Nash, más algunos espirituales que me sabía. En música sí que he sido muy extranjerizante' ('At that time I used to sing [Bob] Dylan, Leonard Cohen, and Crosby, Still[s], and Nash, plus a few spiritual numbers I knew. When it comes to music I have certainly incorporated a lot of foreign material into my tastes'). See Ángela López, '"La Academia no parece lugar muy divertido"', *La clave*, 197 (2005), 78–81 (p. 79).

into Marías's grasp of English during his early university career. Another early piece of translation work was to 'corregir y pulir la traducción argentina de aquel libro tan malo que gozó de enorme éxito, *Love Story*' ('to correct and polish the Argentine translation of that terrible book that enjoyed such success, *Love Story*'). Marías describes revising the translation of Erich Segal's tear-jerking novel in the company of a then friend, Gustavo Pérez de Ayala, calling the task 'uno de mis primeros trabajos remunerados' ('one of my first paid jobs').[19] The first Argentine translation of *Love Story*, entitled *Historia de amor*, appeared in 1970, the same year as the original English, which was released in anticipation of the better-known film version. There, the translation was credited to Eduardo Gudiño Kieffer whose work, we must assume, Marías and his colleague were called in to polish at the last minute.[20]

If Jesús Franco provided Marías with an early outlet for his linguistic talents, it was Juan Benet who helped him begin to build a reputation as a writer. By trade a civil engineer, Benet's literary vocation, though obvious in his student days according to his friend Carmen Martín Gaite, did not reach fruition until he was nearly forty.[21] His essay *La inspiración y el estilo* (1966) and the novel *Volverás a Región* (1967) became emblematic texts for the rising generation of writers (for reasons I shall examine more closely in Chapter 2). A man of formidable culture, an Anglophone, and devotee of William Faulkner, Benet became a mentor to the young Marías. Following their introduction in 1970, Benet read, enjoyed, and helped to publish *Los dominios del lobo*. In a prologue Marías wrote to that novel in 1987, he describes with nostalgia the acrobatics he used to perform on Madrid's Paseo de Recoletos for the benefit of Benet and a gathering crowd of spectators: those antics the climax of convivial nights out, one assumes.[22] The present study will seek to elucidate some of the ways in which Marías's presence among the 'tertulianos' ('members of his literary get-togethers') of Benet's circle shaped the writer he became.

During that same year (1970), Marías began specializing in Filología Inglesa ('English Philology') at university under the guidance of a language teacher—Mr White—whose retirement he would later mark with a heartfelt appreciation.[23] His second novel, *Travesía del horizonte* (*Voyage*

---

[19] JM, 'Los antiguos amigos', in *DNA*, pp. 264–6 (p. 265).

[20] Erich Segal, *Historia de amor*, trans. by Eduardo Gudiño Kieffer (Buenos Aires: Emecé, 1970).

[21] See 'Dos textos inéditos de Carmen Martín Gaite', in Juan Benet, *La inspiración y el estilo (Con dos textos inéditos de Carmen Martín Gaite)* (Madrid: Alfaguara, 1999), pp. 225–69 (pp. 227–35).

[22] JM, 'Prólogo de 1987', in *LDL*, pp. 9–16 (p. 13).

[23] JM, 'La profesión de Mr White', in *MS*, pp. 90–2.

*Along the Horizon*), was finished and published in 1972. After graduating in Filosofía y Letras ('Philosophy and Arts'), he set to work as a translator. Commissions arrived to translate short stories by first Thomas Hardy, then John Updike, the former courtesy of his soon-to-be boss, Jaime Salinas. Although Salinas had managed to persuade Benet to turn his hand to translation long enough to write a Spanish version of F. Scott Fitzgerald's *This Side of Paradise* (1920, Benet's version entitled *A este lado del paraíso*, 1968), the experience was evidently not one Benet wished to repeat since he never translated again. Marías meanwhile caught the bug.

In 1974, he moved to Barcelona to work under Salinas as an 'asesor literario' ('literary scout') for the publishing house Alfaguara. The commissioned selection of seven short stories by Thomas Hardy appeared as *El brazo marchito y otros relatos* the same year.[24] In May, a version of 'The Grave by the Handpost'—'La tumba de la encrucijada'—translated by him also appeared in the *Revista de Occidente*; a footnote on the first page announcing the imminent publication of the Alianza collection indicates that the separate appearance of a single story was intended to foment interest in the forthcoming volume.[25] As far as I have been able to ascertain, the Alianza selected edition was the second translation of Hardy short stories into Spanish. Until then, only José Donday's version of the single tale 'The Three Strangers' was available in translation to Spanish readers.[26] His first published translation was, however, the short story 'Museums and Women' ('Museos y mujeres') by John Updike, which appeared in March of that same year.[27] Again, the purpose of the story's appearance seems to have been to alert readers to the imminent publication of a larger collection in book form: in this instance 'Museos y mujeres' is the title story of an edition of selected Updike stories Noguer were to publish later that year.[28] Curiously, Noguer employed Andrés Bosch to

---

[24] The dedication to the Reino de Redonda edition of *El brazo marchito* reads: 'Este octavo volumen del Reino de Redonda está dedicado a Jaime Salinas, Embajador en Islandia o "Eddison of Ouroboros", que hace treinta años tuvo la temeridad generosa de darle a quien lo tradujo su primera oportunidad' ('This eighth volume in the Kingdom of Redonda series is dedicated to Jaime Salinas, Ambassador in Iceland or "Eddison of Ouroboros", who thirty years ago had the generous temerity to give he who translated it his first chance'). See Thomas Hardy, *El brazo marchito y otros relatos*, trans. by Javier Marías (Barcelona: Reino de Redonda, 2003), p. 5.

[25] Thomas Hardy, 'La tumba de la encrucijada', trans. by Javier Marías, *Revista de Occidente*, 134 (1974), 166–82 (p. 166).

[26] See Thomas Hardy et al., *Los tres forasteros y otras narraciones*, trans. by José Donday (Barcelona: Sociedad General Española de Librería, 1929).

[27] John Updike, 'Museos y mujeres', trans. by Javier Marías, *Revista de Occidente*, 132 (1974), 261–73.

[28] See 'Museos y mujeres', p. 273.

translate that volume and Marías's version of 'Museums and Women' was not used.[29]

Once he had taken up his job at Alfaguara, Marías soon became familiar with the task of making underexposed foreign authors available to a Spanish audience. There he formed part of a team that included Benet, Juan García Hortelano, and Luis Goytisolo whose job it was to identify and acquire the rights to foreign fiction which would prove marketable in Spanish translation.[30] It was through this role that Marías was able proudly to claim the distinction of enabling the first publication of Thomas Bernhard in Spanish. Having read *Trastorno* in 1976 in French translation, he fought hard to see a Spanish version through to publication.[31]

It is worth highlighting the importance of this job for his burgeoning career as a translator. Although he continued to accept commissions to translate works into Spanish, he also became more proactive in suggesting to publishers works he would like to translate. Working for a period of years in the publishing industry generally and in the marketing of foreign fiction more particularly must have given him both the confidence and the expertise to persuade editors to accept his offers to translate certain works. To this day he continues to promote authors he likes and make their work available in Spanish, most obviously through his Reino de Redonda press, though his work as a translator has taken a back seat in recent years. Although the point may be an obvious one, his job at Alfaguara must also have been a financial necessity since his earnings as a literary translator—often less than 1 per cent of profits from sales—would not have been sufficient to keep body and soul together.

The different challenges presented by Hardy and Updike could not be starker. Updike writes in clear, modern, American English, whereas Hardy's vocabulary is obscure and his dialogue often in dialect.[32] Hardy is also a strange choice for a translator who has repeatedly voiced his opposition to 'costumbrismo'[33] and regionalism in literature.[34] In the whole English

[29] See John Updike, *Museos y mujeres*, trans. by Andrés Bosch (Barcelona: Noguer, 1974), pp. 9–24.

[30] For further recollections on Salinas's time at Alfaguara, see Rafael Conte, 'Las paellas (republicanas) de "Tito" Jaime', *El País*, 27 November 2003, p. 14.

[31] JM, 'Mi trastorno', in *LF*, pp. 353–6.

[32] Marías mentions the 'dificultades descriptivo-campestres' ('the difficulties thrown up by descriptions of rural life') and the wish to consult with the author over the difficulties he had in rendering the obscure rural vocabulary in *NET*, pp. 194–5.

[33] There is no direct translation for 'costumbrismo' in English. In Spanish, the term refers to a genre of writing in vogue from the early nineteenth century onwards which described, celebrated, and occasionally satirized local customs. The nearest equivalent in English would be 'localism' or, perhaps too strongly, 'parochialism'.

[34] Luis H. Castellanos, p. 26.

canon, it would be difficult to think of another writer whose work is so closely bound up with a particular place and time—rural South Dorset in the second half of the nineteenth century. Perhaps we might speculate that the supernatural elements of stories like 'The Withered Arm' and 'Barbara of the House of Grebe' appealed to the Marías who had enjoyed ghost stories as a child. We might also wonder whether what seems provincial in Spanish writing, because of Marías's innate familiarity with it, when encountered in English writing, has an air of the exotic or fascinatingly new.

Whatever the challenges offered by Hardy and Updike, they can be as nothing compared to those presented by Sterne's *Tristram Shandy*, which Claudio Guillén commissioned Marías to translate after the latter had expressed desire to undertake the project. Marías's four-year silence as a translator from 1974 to 1978 is attributable to his intensive work on Sterne's masterpiece, work rewarded in 1979 with the Premio Nacional de Traducción. In the intervening period he wrote the short story 'La dimisión de Santiestéban' (1975) and the novel *El monarca del tiempo* (1978 hence *EMT*).

He lived for most of this period (1974–1977) in a Barcelona flat he shared with Mercedes de Azúa, sister of his friend and collaborator, Félix, who lived in the flat above. While Azúa beavered away upstairs translating Diderot, Marías slaved at his version of Sterne. Their collaboration alongside Vicente Molina-Foix on *Tres cuentos didácticos* (1975), a volume of three short stories intended to show solidarity among the new generation of Spanish prose writers, had a reprise in 1979.[35] A shared love of Vladimir Nabokov prompted them to issue a selection of his poems and chess problems in *Poesía* magazine, the former translated by Marías, the latter by Azúa.[36] 'Dieciocho poemas y dieciocho problemas' were taken from Nabokov's *Poems and Problems* (1970). One might well ask what prompted Marías, who has never published a line of his own poetry, to translate poems by an author also renowned for his achievements in prose. The answer, I think, lies in the desire to provide Spanish readers with access to previously untapped areas of a writer's work. In the same issue of *Poesía*, Marías published 'Fragmento', a poem by Frank O'Hara.

He repeated the exercise at the end of 1979, this time working alone on poems by William Faulkner. If in the case of Nabokov, his admiration was shared by Azúa, in the case of Faulkner, that admiration was shared by Benet. By 1997, when he published his essays on and translations of

---

[35] Marías's contribution was the aforementioned 'La dimisión de Santiestéban'.
[36] Vladimir Nabokov, 'Dieciocho poemas', *Poesía*, 4 (1979), 70–84.

Faulkner in a separate volume, Marías had become aware that trends in
literary criticism were squeezing the American out of the Western canon
because '[era] culpable de los cuatro pecados capitales de nuestros pacatos
y oportunistas tiempos...era varón, era blanco, era anglosajón y no es
difícil tildarlo...de machista' ('[he] was guilty of the four cardinal sins of
our prudish and opportunistic times...he was male, he was white, he was
Anglo, and it is not difficult to accuse him...of being a chauvinist').[37]
Firstly, how prevalent the politically correct agenda was in academic circles in the late 1970s and, secondly, how aware Marías would have been
of it, are questions that fall beyond my ability to judge. Certainly, by the
time he was assembling the anthology of material on Faulkner that would
become *Si yo amaneciera otra vez* (1997), he had recognized the need for
strong voices to shout over the chorus of disapproval that Faulkner's name
now provoked.

In December 1979 the Barcelona publisher Blume issued a Spanish
facsimile edition of Edith Holden's *Country Diary of an Edwardian Lady*.
Marías was among a group of translators commissioned to translate the
poems that punctuate the text. He and Luis Alberto de Cuenca are
acknowledged as the translators of the featured extracts from Edmund
Spenser, of which there are six. The names of two further translators are
also supplied, the first as having rendered in Spanish the extracts from
Shakespeare and the second those from Keats and Coleridge. On the face
of it, these indications ought to guide us to the poems Marías translated
for the Holden volume. They do not. Strong evidence to back this assertion is provided by the fact that the two versions of poems by Robert
Louis Stevenson that Holden includes are remarkably similar to the translations Marías published the following year in *De vuelta del mar*, his
anthology of Stevenson's verse: in one case the translations are identical
verbatim and, in the other, the slight differences are of syntax, not diction, easily accounted for by the minor changes a translator might make
between drafts.[38] For example in the first verse of 'The House Beautiful',
the Holden text reads 'Un charco estremecido ante la puerta...Así es
ahora el lugar en que habito' ('A shivering pool before the door,..., Such
is the place that I live in') whereas Marías's final text reads 'ante la puerta
un charco estremecido...así es el lugar en que ahora habito' ('Before the

[37] JM and Manuel Rodríguez Rivero, *Si yo amaneciera otra vez: William Faulkner—Un entusiasmo* (Madrid: Alfaguara, 1997), p. 13.
[38] See the versions of 'The House Beautiful' and 'The Vagabond' included in Edith Holden, *La felicidad de vivir con la naturaleza: el diario de Edith Holden*, trans. by Javier Marías et al., (Barcelona: Blume, 1979), pp. 138, 173; compare with *De vuelta del mar*, pp. 17–18, 137.

door a shivering pool,...such is the place that I live in').[39] Thus it seems likely that either Marías himself or someone working from his drafts of the Stevenson poems translated the versions as they appeared in the Holden volume. Her text contains numerous other poems by Robert Browning, Robert Burns, John Clare, and William Wordsworth. Who is to say that Marías did not also translate some of them?

When it came to issuing *De vuelta del mar* as a single volume, it appears to have been the only instance in his translation career when his work was in direct competition with that of another translator. Marías it was who suggested an edition of Stevenson's poems to Hiperión. Yet a rival had been thinking along identical lines. In an interview conducted in 1977 the poet José María Álvarez (who had been included in Castellet's influential avant-garde anthology *Nueve novísimos poetas españoles* [1970]) spoke of his anxiety to put to bed as soon as possible the translations of Stevenson's poetry on which he had been working.[40] As Álvarez also points out, Stevenson's verse remained unpublished in Spanish and a translation was long overdue. A footnote to the interview text just cited reveals that Álvarez did indeed finish the collection, the rights to which were acquired by Hiperión in 1979. The fact that Marías's *De vuelta del mar* appeared only a year later would seem to indicate that either Marías's versions were bought first or the publishers made a qualitative decision as to the respective merits of the two translators. Álvarez's edition of Stevenson's poems, called simply *Poemas*, did eventually appear in 1994 with an introduction dated 1980.[41] Even then Álvarez's translation did not supplant Marías's version: Hiperión reprinted the second edition of *De vuelta del mar* in 1998.[42]

From this story so far, two unifying elements link the works Marías translated into Spanish. The first of these is their previous unavailability in the language. While Marías claims always to have 'elegi[do] sus originales' ('chose[n] his originals') when deciding what to translate, we need to clarify exactly what he means, in the light of the fact that he was often commissioned to translate works he might not otherwise have

---

[39] Leaving aside the capitalization of the first word in each line, there are twelve differences between the two translations of 'The House Beautiful'; of these, four are changes in punctuation, two changes in word order, and two more changes in the capitalization of the words 'tierra' and 'su' when it refers to God. Another three discrepancies appear to be amendments of earlier carelessness: the misreading of the English word 'muser' as 'muses'; translation of the word 'page' by 'playa' or 'expands' by 'sueñe'.

[40] Csaba Csuday, *Al otro lado del espejo: Conversaciones con José María Álvarez* (Murcia: Universidad de Murcia, 1987), p. 252.

[41] See Robert Louis Stevenson, *Poemas*, trans. by Txatro Santos and José María Álvarez (Madrid: Hiperión, 1994).

[42] For an article praising Marías's translation see Fernando Savater, 'Stevenson: La canción del valor', in his *Amor a R. L. Stevenson* (Santander: Límite, 1998), pp. 29–34.

attempted—Hardy and Updike the two most obvious candidates in that regard.[43] What we would best conclude from his claim is that working as a translator never became a financial necessity. In short, it never became drudge work and he did not dislike the commissions he received; we can only speculate that, if he disliked them, he turned them down.

A second unifying element also emerges among some texts: interest in Nabokov he shared with Azúa, in Faulkner he shared with Benet, and in Stevenson with Álvaro Pombo. He mentions in the 'Nota sobre el texto' ('Textual note') to *De vuelta del mar* that he and Pombo discussed the poem 'Requiem', which adorns Stevenson's grave on the Samoan island of Upolu, during a late-night stroll through the streets of Madrid.[44] This sense of a community of shared enthusiasms comes through strongly in Marías's next chosen project—Conrad's *The Mirror of the Sea*. Benet had devoted an entire chapter of *La inspiración y el estilo* to 'el buque fantasma' ('the ghost ship'), where he examines the nineteenth-century vogue for, and the later decline of, narratives of the sea. The image of the ghost ship is one that eludes the realist novel's need for resolution and explanation, surviving as an enigma and appealing to all who would be, in Benet's eyes, true novelists:[45] 'Al no ser resuelto el misterio, el barco continúa, haciendo guiñadas, su insensata travesía y en la imaginación del lector la estampa se cristaliza y eterniza, el misterio prevalece y la inquietud no conoce el reposo' ('The mystery remaining unresolved, the ship continues on its winking, senseless way and in the reader's imagination the image crystallizes and becomes eternal, the mystery persists and the disquiet knows no rest').[46] The passages of *The Mirror of the Sea* in which Conrad describes drifting and battered ships are indeed among the best his memoir has to offer. And yet, according to Benet, what in other writers was the gratuitous exploitation of areas of mystery was in Conrad just the faithful record of a remarkable maritime career. Marías's translation was published, with a prologue by Benet, in 1981. The mentor praised his protégé highly for the skill and effort in rendering Conrad in Spanish:

> No creo que exista—ni será fácil que se repita—una traducción de Conrad de tal perfección. Soy testigo del inmenso trabajo que se ha tenido que tomar Javier Marías—quien está a punto de convertirse en un Erasmo de la traducción—para concluir esta labor que, me consta, ha estado en varias ocasiones en un tris de arrastrarle al abandono.[47]

---

[43] JM, 'Desde una novela no necesariamente castiza', in *LF*, pp. 51–69 (p. 55).
[44] JM, 'Nota sobre el texto', in *De vuelta del mar*, p. 7–11 (p. 11).
[45] *La inspiración*, pp. 177–92.
[46] *La inspiración*, p. 183.
[47] Juan Benet, 'Prólogo', in Joseph Conrad, *El espejo del mar: Recuerdos e impresiones*, trans. by Javier Marías, 7th edn (Madrid: Hiperión, 2003), pp. 7–12 (p. 11).

(I doubt that there is in existence—nor is it likely that there will be again—a translation of Conrad that reaches such perfection. I can bear witness to the enormous effort that Javier Marías—who is about to become an Erasmus of translation—has had to make to complete this task, one that, I know, has more than once brought him very close to quitting.)

It is in that same prologue that Benet describes his discovery of *The Mirror of the Sea*—in its French translation—during a tedious engineering trip to Sweden. He had thought he had read Conrad's complete works a few years before and his discovery of the memoir that became one of his favourite books highlighted a gap not yet covered by Spanish translators. Marías's *El espejo del mar* filled that gap. Once again it was his approach to Hiperión that prompted its publication.

1983 saw the publication of his fourth novel, *ES*, which showed how the writers he was translating were beginning to influence his own fiction: echoes of Sir Thomas Browne, whose prose he was continuing to translate as part of an ongoing project, and Conrad feature prominently in the text. Later that year and following in the footsteps of Molina-Foix and Azúa, Marías took up the post of lecturer by decree in the sub-faculty of Spanish at Oxford University, a position he occupied for the next two years. During this decisive period in his creative development, he was working on four separate projects. He had first to finalize translation and publication of Isak Dinesen's *Ehrengard* (1963, JM's version 1984), then went on to translate Yeats's *The Celtic Twilight* (1893, JM's version *El crepúsculo celta*, 1985).[48] Work was also ongoing on his versions of Sir Thomas Browne's *Religio Medici* (1643), *Hydriotaphia* (1658), and 'On Dreams' (a miscellaneous tract that remained unpublished at Browne's death in 1682). He had begun work on them in 1982 and they finally saw print in 1986. By the end of 1985 he had finished a commissioned translation of John Ashbery's 'Self-portrait in a convex mirror', which was published in *Poesía* magazine.[49]

Marías requested a term's leave from Oxford in order to spend the autumn of 1984 at Wellesley College, returning to not only the same university that had welcomed him as a child but also the same flat. Vladimir Nabokov's ghost haunted him there for two unconnected reasons: because the Russian had once occupied the flat above and because

---

[48] It is worth pointing out that Alexis Grohmann wrongly identifies Marías as the translator of the volume Isak Dinesen, *Últimos cuentos* (Madrid: Debate, 1990). In fact he only wrote a prologue to that work; the translator was Alejandro Vilafranca del Castillo. See *Coming Into One's Own*, p. 291.

[49] John Ashbery, 'Autorretrato en espejo convexo', trans. by Javier Marías, *Poesía*, 25 (1985–1986), 87–106. He subsequently published his translation, with nineteen minor revisions, in book form. See John Ashbery, *Autorretrato en espejo convexo*, trans. by Javier Marías (Madrid: Visor, 1990).

Marías was delivering a lecture series on *Don Quijote*, just as Nabokov had (in)famously done.[50]

On his return to Oxford, Marías's interest in the failed poet John Gawsworth grew after an unannounced visit from the Gawsworth enthusiast Roger Dobson. In pursuit of information on Gawsworth's career as an anthologizer of ghost stories, Marías came across several of the works he would later publish as *Cuentos únicos* (1989), a selection of interwar British short stories.[51] As we shall see shortly, he could scarcely have imagined how far the pursuit of Gawsworth's legacy would take him when he wrote about his career in 'El hombre que pudo ser rey' (1985), *Todas las almas* (*TLA*, 1989), and 'Un epigrama de lealtad' (1989). Once his Oxford contract had come to an end, he did not linger and instead went to live in Venice, where he wrote much of his fifth novel, *EHS* (1986). That same year he published a translation of Wallace Stevens's 'Notes Towards a Supreme Fiction', again in *Poesía*.[52]

The year 1987 was Marías's busiest as a translator and culminated with his acceptance of a post as a teacher of Translation Theory at his old university, Madrid's Complutense.[53] Whether or not he was consciously preparing to teach translation by gaining as much practical experience as possible, I do not know. However, it is the case that he accepted commissions from *El País* to translate Anthony Burgess's short story, 'A Meeting in Valladolid', and an article by Joseph Brodsky, on top of an already considerable schedule.[54] His valuable collaboration with *Poesía* bore fruit again when he published translations of the J. D. Salinger short story 'El corazón de una historia quebrada' and W. H. Auden's 'Dichtung und Wahrheit' in the same issue.[55] Almost simultaneously, two more translated

[50] Nabokov's lectures on *Don Quijote* are published as *Lectures on Don Quixote*, ed. by Fredson Bowers (London: Weidenfeld & Nicolson, 1982). They are infamous for their strange approach to the novel, with Nabokov insisting that it is a cruel text where the reader is asked to laugh at the knight errant's repeated torture.

[51] *Cuentos únicos*, trans. by Javier Marías and Alejandro García Reyes (Madrid: Siruela, 1989).

[52] Wallace Stevens, 'Notas para una ficción suprema', trans. by Javier Marías, *Poesía*, 26 (1986), 71–98. As in the case of Ashbery, he subsequently published it as Wallace Stevens, *Notas para una ficción suprema*, trans. by Javier Marías (Valencia: Pre-Textos, 1996).

[53] In his later article 'Lección de lengua', Marías describes himself as having taught Translation Theory 'en tres países diferentes' ('in three different countries'), those being, presumably, Spain, United Kingdom, and United States. Although Translation Theory was not part of the Oxford syllabus when Marías was lecturing there, he did teach translation. His claim tells us also that he must have done some lecturing on translation in addition to his course on *Don Quijote* while at Wellesley in 1984. See *MS*, pp. 247–9 (p. 247).

[54] Anthony Burgess, 'Encuentro en Valladolid', trans. by Javier Marías, *El País Semanal*, 26 July 1987, Libros section, pp. 1–12; Joseph Brodski, 'Catástrofes en el aire', trans. by Javier Marías, *El País*, 25 October 1987, pp. 42–3.

[55] W. H. Auden, 'Dichtung und Wahrheit (Un poema no escrito)', trans. by Javier Marías, *Poesía*, 29 (1989), 57–83. Once again, this long poem was later published in book form. See W. H. Auden, *Un poema no escrito*, trans. by Javier Marías (Valencia: Pre-Textos, 1996).

Salinger short stories appeared in *Sur Exprés*—'La larga puesta de largo de Lois Tagget' and 'Las dos partes implicadas'. The Spanish audience was lucky indeed to be able to read them since their original English versions are lost in obscurity. The reclusive and elusive Salinger had by 1987 maintained a creative silence for twenty-two years (one that remained unbroken at his death in January 2010). In Marías's words, 'hasta los más optimistas empiezan a desesperar de volver a echarse a los ojos un texto firmado por él' ('even the most optimistic are beginning to despair of seeing a text signed by him ever again').[56] Given Salinger's recalcitrance, his fans resorted to illegal practices to make available the works he had published in journals and magazines but refused to issue in a collected edition; hence the unauthorized, undated, two-volume *The Complete Uncollected Short Stories of J. D. Salinger* (issued by an enterprising but unidentified publisher) from which Marías was able to translate the three works that were unknown in Spain until then. He justified the decision on the basis that, whereas diligent American readers could track down the journals and magazines where the stories first appeared, that option was and is not open to Spanish readers.[57] This was not the first such anomaly he was inadvertently to create. By issuing Spanish translations of Richmal Crompton's novel, *The House* (1926) and short story collection, *Mist* (1927), through the Reino de Redonda press, Marías gave Spanish readers access to texts that had never received so much as a second edition in Britain.[58]

Marías taught Translation Theory at the Complutense until 1992, by which time his practical experience of the art was on the wane. Demands on his time as his profile grew both at home and abroad will have made the poorly remunerated activity even less appealing. Alongside these increasing demands we ought also to consider the dangers of artistic contagion, dangers to which George Steiner eloquently draws attention:

[56] See Marías's 'Nota Previa' in J. D. Salinger, 'Dos cuentos inéditos', trans. by Javier Marías, *Sur Exprés*, 5 (1987), 99–114 (p. 101).
[57] Today, copies of *The Complete Uncollected Short Stories of J. D. Salinger* are so scarce that their price puts them beyond the reach of all but the most deep-pocketed of book collectors. The irony of the stories being accessible to a Spanish readership while they remained out of reach of most English readers was not lost on at least one Spanish critic: Félix Romeo Pescador asked, rhetorically, in an article on Marías, '¿alguien ha leído la versión original inglesa de unos estupendos relatos de J. D. Salinger, el oculto, que tradujo Javier Marías?' ('Has anyone read the original English versions of the brilliant short stories by J. D. Salinger, the hidden man, that Javier Marías translated?'). See his 'Javier Marías por sus propios ojos', *Invitación a la lectura*, 8 (1990), 1.
[58] In fact, both works are now practically impossible to find; when they do appear for sale, their price is so inflated that only the most devoted rare-book hound would consider buying them. Marías recalled in conversation with me that in order to get a copy of *The House* from which the translator could work he was forced to apply to Crompton's literary executors for a photocopy of the original novel.

Acts of translation add to our means; we come to incarnate alternative energies and resources of feeling. But we may be mastered and made lame by what we have imported. Writers have ceased from translation, sometimes too late, because the inhaled voice of the foreign text had come to choke their own.[59]

Marías mentioned in a televised interview with Hilario Pino just this fear as one of his reasons for leaving translation to one side: 'Hace tiempo que traduzco más bien poco porque escribir y traducir son actividades, desde mi punto de vista, demasiado similares como para mantener las dos de una manera continuada' ('For a while now I have been doing very little by way of translation because writing and translating are, from my perspective, too closely related for me to maintain them both consistently').[60] In 1992 he translated no more than two poems by Keith Douglas, 'Como matar' and 'Oxford'. His decision to translate only brief texts since then can be accounted for by, on the one hand, waning interest and, on the other, the huge commercial success that greeted *CTB*, success that raised his profile to the point where the media demands on him meant he had precious-little time for his own fiction, let alone translation. Aside from the odd labour of love and one onerous task, his career as a translator could be said, if not entirely to have ceased, certainly to be on the back burner.

Since then, what time he has devoted to his translations has been to consolidate work aleady done. As the footnotes above show, he ensured that his versions of Ashbery and Stevens appeared in single volumes that are more accessible than the journals in which they first appeared. He continued that consolidation by publishing his translations of Faulkner and Nabokov as the separate volumes *Si yo amaneciera otra vez* (1997) and *Desde que te vi morir* (1999) respectively.[61] Moreover, he has regained publishing and copyright control over most of the substantial prose works he translated. Although the reasons are not immediately apparent, the event that helped him to do so was the abdication in his favour, of Jon Wynne-Tyson, the third King of Redonda.

Marías became acquainted with Wynne-Tyson when the latter, in his role as executor of the literary estates of M. P. Shiel and John Gawsworth, got wind of Marías's having published Gawsworth's short story 'How It

---

[59] Steiner, p. 315.

[60] Interview with Hilario Pino. For text see the following URL: http://www.javiermarias.es/PAGINASDEENTREVISTAS/CNN.html (accessed 2 January 2008).

[61] These volumes consist of the translations from the late 1970s along with biographical and literary-critical essays by Marías. Azúa's translation of Nabokov's chess problems also makes an appearance. Manuel Rodríguez Rivero includes in the Faulkner volume a travelogue of a journey through the American's home state.

Happened' (one of the *Cuentos únicos*) without copyright permission. The obscurity into which Gawsworth had plunged after death meant that Marías did not even know that Gawsworth had a literary estate to which he need apply. He and Wynne-Tyson came to an amicable agreement over the rights to be paid and their cordial correspondence continued as the former pursued his interest in the elusive Gawsworth. Realizing that Marías represented perhaps his best hope of divesting himself of the irksome responsibilities that went with the mythical Realm of Redonda— attacks from false pretenders to the throne, intrusive and tedious interest from journalists—Wynne-Tyson began to hint at a possible transfer of sovereignty to an initially coy Marías. Such was the indirectness of these two scrupulously polite men that Wynne-Tyson eventually wrote, 'I am sure there is some Spanish dance that could be compared with the exquisite delicacy of our recent exchange' and further wondered, '[p]erhaps I should come down on my heels more audibly'.[62] Later in 1997 the abdication was agreed and Marías was (nominally) crowned. Although the best accounts of the history of this most eccentric of literary realms are to be found in Marías's novel *NET* and Wynne-Tyson's autobiography, *Finding the Words: A Publishing Life* (2004), I will briefly summarize its history here.[63] The Kingdom of Redonda takes its name, though lays no physical claim, to a tiny, uninhabited island in the Antilles: to my knowledge only two of its four 'kings' to date have even visited the island that was first discovered and named by Columbus on his voyages to the New World. At its inception, the title of King of Redonda was a fanciful soubriquet apparently dreamt up by the father of the novelist and short story writer M. P. Shiel during the latter's childhood in the West Indies. Late in Shiel's life and by now in England, he appears to have used the title and its picturesque history as a means of attracting publicity, aided and abetted by the opportunistic poet and barfly John Gawsworth. On Shiel's death, Gawsworth inherited the title and traded relentlessly on its shallow fame, principally among the Soho publicans who wrote off his lengthening bar tabs in deference to the trade attracted by their novelty 'monarch'. Gawsworth's slow descent into alcoholism and penury is detailed with exceptional candour and compassion by Wynne-Tyson, one of his few sober and faithful friends. To him fell the task of overseeing the literary estates of Shiel and Gawsworth after years of dependency on drink had taken the latter's life. All until Wynne-Tyson was able to divest himself of the

---

[62] Letter from JW-T to JM dated 1 January 1997. Reproduced by permission of the author.
[63] Jon Wynne-Tyson, *Finding the Words: A Publishing Life* (Norwich: Michael Russell, 2004), pp. 158–95.

responsibilities and pass them on to Marías. Few real burdens weigh on the Redondan monarch other than those of administering the literary estates of the first two kings and naming a court, something each of the successive incumbents has chosen to do.

Rather than remain a passive monarch, however, Marías seized the opportunity offered by the Redondan Realm to accomplish two things. The first of these was the setting up of the first Spanish cultural prize—the Premio Reino de Redonda—open exclusively to foreigners. Candidates are nominated by the court of Redondan Dukes Marías has named since inheriting the throne. Each duke nominates three authors, artists, film-makers, or cultural commentators whose achievements merit interna-tional recognition, and the person with the highest number of nominations receives the award. In the event of a tie, Marías has the casting vote. To date the winners have been J. M. Coetzee (2001), Sir John Elliot (2002), Claudio Magris (2003), Eric Rohmer (2004), Alice Munro (2005), Ray Bradbury (2006), George Steiner (2007), Umberto Eco (2008), Marc Fumaroli (2009), Milan Kundera (2010), and Ian McEwan (2011). Although the financial gain to be had from the prize is not huge—the several thousand euros awarded come out of Marías's own pocket—the prestige of being nominated by a jury that one Spanish journalist has referred to, not unjustly, as 'el jurado más importante del mundo' ('the most important jury in the world') ought to be considerable.[64] That jury counts among its members not only the Dukes nominated by Marías but also the previous winners, who receive a dukedom in addition to their prize. Thus the Redonda prize has been or will be decided by, in addition to those listed above, Pedro Almodóvar, António Lobo Antunes, John Ashbery, Antony Beevor, William Boyd, A. S. Byatt, Guillermo Cabrera Infante, Francis Ford Coppola, Agustín Díaz Yanes, Pere Gimferrer, Edu-ardo Mendoza, Orhan Pamuk, Arturo Pérez-Reverte, Francisco Rico, Fernando Savater, W. G. Sebald, Mario Vargas Llosa, Luis Antonio de Villena, and Juan Villoro. The second opportunity offered by the Redon-dan crown was the founding of the Reino de Redonda press. Its debut was the first translation of Shiel into Spanish, *La mujer de Huguenin*. Owning his own publishing house, Marías quickly realized, gave him the chance to regain control over his translations. The fact that he should have expended so much time and energy preparing the Redonda editions of his translations indicates their centrality to his output. His conviction that translation and his own fiction do not differ substantially in the degree of creativity they demand receives corroboration in his anxiety both to keep

---

[64] Manuel Rodríguez Rivero, 'Sillón de orejas', *El País*, Babelia section, 10 April 2010, p. 16.

them in print and to retain control over how they appear. To date, he has reissued under the Reino de Redonda imprint his versions of Browne, Dinesen, Yeats, Hardy, Conrad, and an expanded *Cuentos únicos*, ensuring that they are both in print and available in editions the quality of which make them more durable and desirable than trade paperbacks.

Of these only the Conrad presented problems: due to Hiperión's retention of copyright and Marías's reluctance to pay them for the privilege of republishing his own work, he decided to undertake a new translation of *El espejo del mar*. In the process, he also offered students of his translations a potential insight into his evolving attitude to the task. In the event, this insight is as shallow as the sea is deep. A detailed examination of both texts reveals that there are 332 differences between versions. Unfortunately, the differences reveal little about evolving attitudes. Rather, Marías's 'new' version is a lesson in the artful avoidance of copyright infringement. Most of the changes could have been undertaken without reference to the original English. One-hundred and seventeen of them I would consider neutral alterations which do not change the meaning in any substantial way. They include substitution of 'aproximadamente' ('approximately') by 'más o menos' ('more or less'),[65] 'realizar' ('to carry out') by 'llevar a cabo' ('to carry out'),[66] 'obliterado' ('obliterated') by 'arrasado' ('destroyed'),[67] 'tierna' ('tender') by 'afectuosa' ('affectionate'),[68] 'se escuchaba' ('could be heard') by 'se oía' ('could be heard'),[69] and 'echarse' ('to dive') by 'lanzarse' ('to dive').[70] Another third of the amendments, 146 to be precise, are accounted for in similarly artful fashion; removal of the 'leísmo' ('tendency to use indirect object pronouns where direct object pronouns suffice') of the earlier version; the addition and suppression of commas; removal of the personal 'a' when referring to inanimate objects (usually ships); changes in the word used for boat ('buque' ['ship'] often changed to 'barco' ['boat'], 'barco' ['boat'] to 'navío' ['barque']);[71] changes to impersonal expressions ('uno puede' ['one can'] to 'se puede' ['one can'], for example);[72] accenting of capital letters and changes in capitalization; numbers expressed as words, rather than figures; and the change in dialogue from familiar to polite forms of address. While some of these changes may warrant reflection, 300 alterations in a

[65] Conrad, 2003, p. 18; Conrad, 2005, p. 34.
[66] Conrad, 2003, p. 30; Conrad 2005, p. 50.
[67] Conrad, 2003, p. 109; Conrad, 2005, p. 159.
[68] Conrad, 2003, p. 95; Conrad, 2005, p. 140.
[69] Conrad, 2003, p. 145; Conrad, 2005, p. 208.
[70] Conrad, 2003, p. 161; Conrad, 2005, p. 228.
[71] Conrad, 2003, pp. 42, 44, 51, 55, 56; Conrad, 2005, pp. 65, 68, 78, 83, 84.
[72] Conrad, 2003, p. 57; Conrad, 2005, p. 87.

text 262 pages in length is not a substantial rewriting. It is clear that instead Marías took the path of least resistance.

However, it is to events of the late 1990s that we must return to find the reasons for Marías's placing his activity as a translator lower down his list of priorities. While his profile as a writer of international standing grew on the back of the success of *CTB* and *MBPM*, the demands on his time increased exponentially to the point where trips to his bolt-hole in Soria became essential if he was to find time to write. In what must be a unique case in the recent history of Spanish publishing, it was not until *CTB*'s German translation appeared that the success began to snowball. Picked up by the small publishing house Klett-Cotta, Elke Wehr's German version, *Mein Herz so weis* received the ringing endorsement of the influential critic Marcel Reich-Ranicki on his television programme, *Das Literarische Quartett*: 'Yo creo que, de hecho, ésta es, definitivamente, una de las novelas más importantes que he leído en los últimos años. Es que no puedo recordar una calidad comparable' ('I believe that in fact this is, definitively, one of the most important novels that I have read in recent years. The fact is that I can't recall a comparable level of quality').[73] Reich-Ranicki's intervention, coupled with further favourable reviews, helped to keep the novel in the German best-seller lists for over a year. Uniquely, however, the German success helped to push *CTB* back into the Spanish best-seller lists, demonstrating how quickly information now travels across European cultural boundaries, as Ulrike Killer puts it.[74] By 2002 it had sold over a million copies in Austria, Germany, and Switzerland. Until this point, Marías was regarded as a writer with a modest public profile, a status that one critic in 1990 attributed to the fact that he had issued his early works through no fewer than five different publishers.[75] Such a lack of continuity will undoubtedly have made consolidating sales and publicity more difficult, particularly in the Spanish publishing industry which is heavily reliant on 'Novedades' and a quick turnover of titles: if a book sells slowly, it is quickly pulled from the display tables and returned to the publishers to be warehoused.

[73] The programme was broadcast on 13 June 1996. Translation of the transcript by Isabel Moya. See *10 años de* Corazón tan blanco *de Javier Marías* ([n.p.]: Alfaguara, [n.d.]), p. 105.
[74] Killer was the novel's German distributor. See Vila-Sanjuán, pp. 346–7.
[75] Félix Romeo Pescador writes that 'La obra de Javier Marías tuvo en el tiempo cortes tremendos, lapsus enormes y despistes editoriales de primera magnitud (Edhasa, La Gaya Ciencia, Seix Barral, Alfaguara fue el peregrinar de las prensas hasta llegar a Anagrama) que no favorecieron, ni mucho menos, que sus aciertos expresivos se llegaran a conocer' ('Javier Marías's output suffered tremendous cuts in time, huge blunders, and publishing slips of real gravity (from Edhasa, to La Gaya Ciencia, to Seix Barral, to Alfaguara was his round of the presses until his arrival at Anagrama) that did anything but help the diffusion of his expressive talents'). Pescador, p. 1.

When the commercial success of *CTB* at home and abroad, with its concomitant press interviews and promotional work, are coupled with his weekly newspaper column, Marías found himself with far less time for writing, let alone translation. His work in the latter field was limited to the labours of love to which I referred above. While on his way back from receiving the 1997 IMPAC prize for the English translation of *CTB*, Seamus Heaney's poem 'Postscript', displayed on a billboard in Dublin airport, caught his eye. He copied it down and translated it in his weekly column for *El Semanal* magazine. The poem is an encouragement to the addressee to take a trip out to the Flaggy Shore on Ireland's West coast, a plea to step out of the maelstrom and appreciate the natural beauty too often overlooked in our busy lives. What more vivid illustration of Marías's predicament could be offered and how much must he have appreciated the sentiment to take the trouble to reproduce it in Spanish?[76] In fact, he alluded to this incident in an interview several years later: '[el poema m]e pareció deslumbrante, lo anoté y lo hice mío. No es algo tan raro. Los jóvenes, cuando les gusta una canción de rock, la escriben y la repiten sin cesar, como si quisieran quedársela' ('I thought [the poem] was stunning, I wrote it down and made it my own. It's not such a strange thing. Young people, when they like a rock song, they write it down and repeat it non-stop, as if they wanted to keep it with them').[77] Note his use of the possessive—'lo hice mío'—his sense that translation can be as much an act of appropriation as of homage.

His last outing in recent years was the 2001 translation of Yeats' poem 'At Galway Races', undertaken as a personal favour to his good friend the philosopher Fernando Savater and included in the latter's account of the turf, *A caballo entre milenios*.[78] Given his silence since then, scholars interested in his translation career are perhaps easily haunted by the spectres of projects in which he has expressed interest but never undertaken. In 1989, he mentioned wanting one day to translate Faulkner's *The Wild Palms* (1939) and Eliot's 'The Love Song of J. Alfred Prufrock'.[79] That urge has yet to be fulfilled. We might note that, as in the cases of Browne, Stevens, and Stevenson his choices as a translator coincide with those of the great Argentine essayist and short story writer Jorge Luis Borges. The latter

---

[76] JM, 'Un poema' in *SACF*, pp. 117–19. For the original English, see Seamus Heaney, *Opened Ground: Poems 1966–1996* (London: Faber and Faber, 1998), p. 444.

[77] Andrés Rodríguez, 'El universo Marías', *Dominical*, 12 December 2004. Text available at the following URL: http://www.javiermarias.es/ByS/entrevistas2.html (accessed 3 October 2007).

[78] See W. B. Yeats, 'En las carreras de Galway', trans. by Javier Marías, in Fernando Savater, *A caballo entre milenios* (Madrid: Aguilar, 2001), p. 343.

[79] JM, 'Mi libro favorito', in *LF*, pp. 398–401 (p. 399).

translated a brief passage from *Religio Medici* and, in collaboration with Bioy Casares, the fifth chapter of *Hydriotaphia*, as we shall see in Chapter 5 of this study. Borges had also put his name to a translation of *The Wild Palms*, published in Buenos Aires in 1940, though scholars remain divided on the question of whether or nor it is his own work.[80] That Marías should express a desire to retranslate a work that has already received the benefit of a Spanish rendering by so illustrious a forerunner tells us that he regards Borges as more of a rival to be superseded than a peer to be emulated. In the introduction to *Si yo amaneciera otra vez*, Marías dispatches Borges's version of *The Wild Palms* with four dismissive words, claiming that he translated it 'bastante mal, por cierto' ('pretty badly, in fact').[81] I shall discuss this matter further in Chapter 5.

To say that Marías has ceased to translate is, of course, false in at least one important respect. As he had done in *CTB* and *MBPM*, he continues to translate passages from Shakespeare in order to incorporate them into his novels. His penultimate novel, *TRM* features translated passages from *Hamlet, King Henry IV, King Henry V, King Richard III, Macbeth,* and *Othello*. Critics have yet to give substantial treatment to his engagement with the Bard and it remains as one of the many tantalizing research projects Marías's work invites. However, my own summary of his translation career now addresses the questions of why he turned to translation and how he translates.

[80] See Douglas Day, 'Borges, Faulkner, and *The Wild Palms*', *The Virginia Quarterly*, 56 (1980), 109–18.
[81] *Si yo amaneciera otra vez*, p. 14.

# 2

# The Why? And the How?

## WHY TRANSLATE?

In 1984 Marías's mentor Juan Benet suggested a straightforward argument for the opening up of Spain's cultural borders to foreign influence:

> Y por lo mismo que no podemos vivir de nuestros propios recursos y medios y estamos obligados a importar artículos esenciales para nuestra supervivencia, no podemos depender de la cultura nacida dentro de nuestras fronteras para llevar una vida satisfactoriamente culta.[1]

> (And for the same reason that we cannot live exclusively off our own means and resources and are obliged to import the products that are essential to our survival, we cannot depend entirely on the culture born within these borders to lead a satisfactory cultural life.)

As so often in this period of Spain's intellectual history, his views succinctly articulate a wider body of opinion. In that same year, Marías delivered the lecture 'Desde una novela no necesariamente castiza' (hence 'Desde'[2]), in which he explained why he had been trying for nearly a decade to breathe new life into Spain's cultural edifice. His attempts thus far had taken the form of the translations of Updike, Hardy, Sterne, Nabokov, Faulkner, Stevenson, and Conrad he had published, as well as his work for Alfaguara recommending and seeing into print foreign authors whose work he liked. Why had he reacted so strongly against the cultural norms prevailing in Spain in the early 1970s that he felt renewal was necessary? Why did he choose translation as the specific form his reaction would take? I devote the first section of this chapter to answering these questions.

To begin, I shall examine 'Desde' in detail and alongside the stated views of Marías's artistic contemporaries. In 'Desde', he summed up the opinions that had shaped his trajectory until that point and I wish to establish the common ground that exists between the members of his

---

[1] Juan Benet, 'La cultura de la transición', in *Páginas impares* (Madrid: Alfaguara, 1996), pp. 193–202 (p. 201).
[2] JM, 'Desde una novela no necesariamente castiza', in *LF*, pp. 51–69.

generation of writers. From there a picture will emerge of Spain's cultural landscape in the late Franco and transition years that contextualizes Marías's move towards translation in a wider body of opinion. Put simply, like many of his fellow citizens who had grown up surrounded by the jingoistic rhetoric so beloved of the ideologues of Francoism, he was tired of a literary and national heritage that must have seemed ubiquitous and inescapable. Again like others, he found in that fervent but moronic espousal of the *patria* ('homeland') and *Hispanidad* ('Spanishness') grounds for considerable scepticism, tipping over eventually into straightforward antipathy for such numbingly reiterated values. The education that Franco intended would form the minds of God-fearing and patriotic Spaniards had precisely the opposite effect from that envisaged and Marías, along with many other members of his artistic generation, began to look elsewhere for their heritage because all that surrounded them at home smelt too pungently of the nationalistic ideology they had learnt to despise. So virulent, in fact, was the antipathy Marías felt for his country conceived of as the subject or even setting for a literary work that it was not until his fifth novel, *EHS*, that he allowed the action to take place in Spain. As we shall see in Chapter 5, in his fourth novel, *ES*, he was writing a version of Spain's twentieth-century history, as well as addressing questions directly related to the country's Civil War, but did so without naming his homeland once or explicitly setting the action there. In his case this antipathy towards Spain went hand in hand with a particular antipathy towards his nation's novelistic tradition. His espousal of a certain escapist, iconoclastic mentality has led some to link him with the 'Novísimos',[3] the poets named after José María Castellet's anthology, *Nueve novísimos poetas españoles* (1970) and the comparison is a useful one.

I want to show that Marías's views are best understood as forming part of wider trends in Spanish contemporary thought. Specifically, his scepticism about the ability of literature to fight political causes chimes with that of Benet and Juan Goytisolo, two leading members of the preceding generation of writers. All three believed that attempts by novelists under Franco to undermine his authority through their works had failed both politically and artistically. Moreover, several of Marías's most influential contemporaries had already reached or were reaching identical conclusions as to the long-term effects of exposure to too much nationalist propaganda: it tended to foster extreme dislike for, rather than pride in, one's country. All of these factors combined to persuade Marías to look beyond Spain's borders for his literary heritage. A childhood spent reading Dumas,

---

[3] As is clear from context, this term refers to a group of writers anthologized together in 1970. Literally, 'novísimos' might be translated as 'newest of the new'.

Crompton, et al. rendered this an easy conclusion to reach, as did a degree in English philology. From there it was a desire to learn from these foreign masters that led him to cultivate the art of translation.

As indicated, in November 1984, Marías gave the lecture 'Desde' to an audience in Austin, Texas. In it he described the gestation of his novels to date—*Los dominios del lobo, Travesía del horizonte, El monarca del tiempo,* and *ES.* Of these, the first two represent the carefree exercise of his literary gifts. *Travesía del horizonte* is a whimsical parody of turn-of-the-century stories of mystery and adventure, as Grohmann has shown.[4] When writing *Los dominios del lobo,* he took himself off to Paris in search of space and privacy—what Elide Pittarello calls 'una bohemia tan corta y suavizada' ('a bohmenian period as short as it was toned down'). He was not alone in wanting to flee Spanish shores to find the imaginative freedom to write.[5] Eduardo Mendoza describes the 'despreocupación' ('the carefree feeling') he felt the summer he wrote *El misterio de la cripta embrujada* (1978) in New York, far from Spain's troubled transition to democracy.[6] By his own account, Marías wrote *Los dominios del lobo* 'desde la irresponsabilidad más absoluta y desde la casi absoluta inocencia' ('from a position of the most total irresponsibility and almost complete innocence'): 'Lo que hacía la inocencia menos absoluta que la irresponsabilidad era, justamente, la conciencia de no desear escribir necesariamente sobre España ni necesariamente como un novelista español' ('What made the innocence less complete than the irresponsibility was, precisely, the awareness of not necessarily wanting to write about Spain or necessarily like a Spanish novelist').[7]

Central to his initial rejection of Spanish literary and cultural heritage was Francoist education policy:

> Era la nuestra la primera [generación] que en verdad no había conocido otra España que la franquista, y se nos había tratado de educar en el amor a España desde una perspectiva grotescamente triunfalista. A la hora de la rebeldía contra esa educación, la consecuencia no podía ser otra que un virulento desprecio no ya hacia esa España cotidiana y mediocre, sino hacia todo lo español, pasado, presente y casi futuro. Con la intolerancia propia de lo que éramos, aspirantes a literatos jóvenes y airados...llevamos a cabo una muy simplista operación de identificación de lo español con lo franquista. Y decidimos dar la espalda a toda nuestra herencia literaria, ignorarla casi por completo.[8]

---

[4] *Coming Into One's Own,* pp. 36–54.
[5] Elide Pittarello, 'Guardar la distancia', in JM, *El hombre que parecía no querer nada,* ed. by Elide Pittarello (Madrid: Espasa Calpe, 1996), pp. 11–31 (p.11).
[6] Eduardo Mendoza, 'Nota del autor', in *El misterio de la cripta embrujada,* 6th edn (Barcelona: Seix Barral, 2002), pp. 5–8 (pp. 6–7).
[7] 'Desde una novela no necesariamente castiza', p. 55.
[8] 'Desde una novela no necesariamente castiza', p. 57.

(Ours was the first [generation] that had really known no other Spain than Franco's, and the attempt had been made to inculcate in us a love of Spain from a grotesquely triumphalist perspective. When the time came to rebel against that inculcation, the consequence could not have been anything other than violent contempt not just for that everyday, mediocre Spain, but also for all that Spain had been, was then, and almost even would be in the future. With the intolerance that is characteristic of the people we were then—aspiring angry young writers... we carried out a very simplistic operation of associating everything Spanish with Francoism. And we decided to turn our backs on our entire literary heritage, to remain almost completely unaware of it.)

As he indicates, such a decision could appear petulant with the benefit of hindsight.[9] Nevertheless, the novelist Antonio Muñoz Molina (1956–) echoes his assessment in his lecture 'La invención de un pasado'. Just as Marías had done, Muñoz Molina described how Francoist indoctrination shaped his early view of Spain in an address delivered in the United States, this time at Harvard University in 1993:

> Los españoles, al menos los que nacimos y nos formamos después de la guerra civil, hemos vivido la paradoja de no poder o no saber vincularnos a nuestro propio pasado intelectual y político en un país regido por la preponderancia fósil del pasado. Para nosotros la palabra tradición sólo podía significar oscurantismo e ignorancia, del mismo modo que las palabras patria o patriotismo significaban exclusivamente dictadura.[10]

> (We Spaniards, at least those of us who were born and educated after the Civil War, have lived with the paradox of not being able or knowing how to link ourselves to our own intellectual and political heritage in a country governed by the fossilized preponderance of the past. For us the word tradition could only mean obscurantism and ignorance, in the same way that the words homeland or patriotism meant only dictatorship.)

The development of Francoist indoctrination through the perverse interpretation and teaching of Spain's history has been well documented by recent scholars. Carolyn Boyd and Ángel Luis Abós have examined how the ideologues of the Movimiento Nacional sought to construct a narrative

---

[9] Marías concedes that in rejecting the legacy of their immediate literary forbears, he and his contemporaries committed 'alguna que otra injusticia' ('one or two injustices'). *Quimera* magazine conducted a survey in 2002 of academics, critics, and writers to determine which had been the best novels of the twentieth century in Spain. There Marías listed Cela's *La colmena* (*The Hive*), Laforet's *Nada* (*Nada*), Ferlosio's *El Jarama* (*The River*), and *La aventura equinoccial de Lope de Aguirre* by Sender; hardly the choices of a man disenchanted with the novelistic tradition under Franco. See Fernando Valls, 'El porqué de una encuesta, de unas preguntas', *Quimera*, 214–15 (2002), 10–28 (pp. 20–1). It is also the case that while lecturing at Oxford University, Marías delivered a course on the novel under Franco.

[10] Antonio Muñoz Molina, *Pura alegría* (Madrid: Alfaguara, 1998), p. 202.

of Spanish history which would serve the interests of the totalitarian regime.[11] As Boyd puts it, 'The syllabi attributed the political and cultural achievements of the patria to the quintessential embodiments of the racial virtues like the Cid, Cardinal Cisneros, and the duke of Alba'.[12] Writers of Spain's 1898 generation, notably Maeztu, Ganivet, and Unamuno, had their work selectively represented and interpreted to encourage a desire for national unity around ideas of Hispanidad, and, in the immediate aftermath of the Civil War, the push towards Empire.[13]

At home, Marías could witness a countervailing tendency: his father Julián saw his task in this period as one of keeping alive the true legacy of Ortega y Gasset, Unamuno, and others who had done so much to drag Spanish thought into the forefront of European ideas before the outbreak of civil war.[14] In 1944, Javier's mother, Dolores Franco, had published *La preocupación de España en su literatura*, an anthology of texts by writers from the Golden Age to the then present, the unifying theme of which was their concern with the problem of Spain—her decadence, renewal, and national character.[15] She inserted a proviso in the Introduction to the effect that hers was not intended as a political volume, merely as a literary study.[16] That proviso could be seen as an answer to the increased politicization of rhetoric on the subject of nationhood in 1940s Spain. And yet, despite her efforts, the anthology was embroiled in a censorship row, the absurdity of which says much about the Francoist state. As Julián Marías explains in his autobiography, his wife's book had problems negotiating Franco's censors, who were concerned that in the original title, *España como preocupación*, 'Dolores, Franco, España y preocupación hace muy mal efecto' ('Dolores, Franco, Spain and concern together make a very bad impression').[17] Dolores was obliged to change the title to *La preocupación de España en su literatura* and it was not until 1960 that the book was republished under its original name.

Hand in hand with the official narrative of national essence went a rejection of nineteenth-century liberalism and, more importantly, of the Second Republic.[18] Although Boyd points to the diminishing importance

[11] Ángel Luis Abós, *La historia que nos enseñaron (1937–1975)* (Madrid: Foca, 2003).

[12] Carolyn Boyd, *Historia patria: politics, history, and national identity in Spain, 1875–1975* (Princeton: Princeton University Press, 1997), p. 243.

[13] Abós, p. 30. Franco had hoped that his military and logistical support for Hitler during the Second World War would be rewarded with colonial possessions in North Africa.

[14] Julián Marías, II, pp. 216–17.

[15] Julián Marías, I, p. 337.

[16] Dolores Franco, *España como preocupación* (Madrid: Alianza, 1998), p. 28.

[17] Julián Marías, I, p. 337. Dolores is obviously a woman's name in Spanish, but its literal meaning is 'pains'.

[18] Boyd, *Historia patria*, p. 244.

of history teaching as a legitimizing force for the regime after the 1950s, she also acknowledges that changes in official policy were slow to filter down to teachers:[19] they continued to use exclusively the tendentious textbooks of the early Franco years long after they were considered obsolete.[20] Given the school he attended, it seems unlikely that Marías would have been exposed to teachers who truly believed the official nonsense. It could be said that Muñoz Molina, who attended school in rural Jaén, was more likely to have come across an unleavened version of the official line. However, the fact that the two writers coincide in their views ought to remind us that it is not only in the classroom that the state's indoctrination takes place. Franco ensured that public rallies, state television, the NODO ('Noticiarios y Documentales'—official newsreels broadcast on television and more importantly in cinemas), cultural events, and political rhetoric all banged the same jingoistic drum.

While on the one hand Marías's aversion to all things Spanish was shaped by a process of official indoctrination which produced the exact opposite result to that desired, he rejected his country's novelistic tradition on more straightforward aesthetic grounds: 'la tradición novelística española es, además de escasa, pobre; además de pobre, más bien realista; y cuando no es realista, con frecuencia es costumbrista' ('Spain's novelistic tradition is, as well as meagre, poor; as well as poor, more often than not realist; and when it isn't realist, it's often provincialist').[21] For this aspiring writer, the Spanish novel had little to recommend it, with the exceptions of *La Regenta, Don Quijote,* and the works of Valle-Inclán. The frequency with which themes of national renewal and character appear in the fiction of each new Spanish generation seemed to Marías absurd when English, French, or Russian novels had so wide a breadth of subject matter to offer. That view was compounded by the generation immediately preceding his own whose attempts to combat the regime in print were, in his opinion, politically and artistically unsuccessful. He was far from alone in forming such a view.

As early as 1966, Benet described the pitfalls of writing novels whose purpose was subsumed in wider social or political goals. Benet, who became what Jo Labanyi has called 'a somewhat reluctant mentor' to the generation of writers who began publishing in the 1970s, argued that literary style was the aspect of a writer's craft to which any aspiring novelist must pay closest attention:[22] it is the acquisition of a distinctive voice through style that will give a work its longevity; causes and political situ-

[19] Boyd, pp. 283–4.      [20] Boyd, p. 280.
[21] 'Desde una novela no necesariamente castiza', p. 55.
[22] Jo Labanyi, 'Literary Experiment and Cultural Cannibalization' in *Spanish Cultural Studies: An Introduction*, ed. by Helen Graham and Jo Labanyi (Oxford: Oxford University Press, 1995), pp. 295–9 (p. 298).

ations come and go but a writer's voice will endure as long as it retains its style. Benet develops the argument that the Flaubert who wrote *L'Éducation sentimentale* (1869) was one who had tried to write a novel out of a sense of duty at odds with his artistic ambitions. The result is a failure:

> el lector cierra *L'Éducation sentimentale* con la sensación de haber sido obligado a escuchar contra su voluntad un relato que no le importa nada y lamentando al mismo tiempo que el escritor haya pasado por alto las pocas anécdotas—lo que él consideró superfluo—que podían haberlo divertido.[23]

> (The reader closes *L'Éducation sentimentale* with the feeling of having been made to listen against his will to a story which does not interest him in the slightest and lamenting at the same time that the writer has passed over the few episodes—that which he considered superfluous—that might have kept him entertained.)

Flaubert had maintained that he wished *L'Éducation sentimentale* to be the moral chronicle of his generation, and this is where, according to Benet, his error lay. So intent was Flaubert on providing us with a cogent portrait of his age that he failed to breathe into it the life that would have made it artistically successful. There can be little doubt that Marías had either absorbed these views or reached identical conclusions independently, since when Caterina Visani raised the subject of politically committed literature in an interview she undertook with him in 1988 he answered by paraphrasing Benet: 'Es muy difícil que un buen texto nazca de la necesidad o de la obligación, deberes externos al propio escritor' ('It is very unlikely that a good text will be born out of the sense of necessity or obligation, duties external to the writer himself').[24] Moreover, in a 1979 essay in which he appealed for literature to be viewed as 'algo universal y atemporal que no entiende de barreras lingüísticas ni de fronteras geográficas' ('something universal and atemporal that does not comprehend linguistic barriers or geographical borders'), he referred to Benet's characterization of the style of much Spanish writing as 'el estilo tabernario' ('the low style'):[25] the phrase is Benet's, taken from *La inspiración y el estilo*, where Marías's mentor complains that the style of much Spanish writing after the Golden Age has been dogged by an excessive popularism.[26]

---

[23] *La inspiración*, pp. 171–2.
[24] Caterina Visani interview. http://www.javiermarias.es/PAGINASDEENTREVISTAS/ entrevistaCaterinaVisani.html (accessed 4 July 2008). It is not uncommon in Marías's works to find this sort of unacknowledged paraphrasing or echoing. Marías makes no secret of Benet's status as his mentor and one can only assume that either Marías had so internalized these ideas that he no longer remembered their origin, or the two men had arrived independently at the same conclusions. The former suggestion seems the more likely of the two.
[25] JM, 'La nueva máscara de lo de siempre', in *VF*, pp. 217–21 (p. 220).
[26] See *La inspiración*, pp. 111–76.

*debate – unidos debate*

Benet argued more specifically in a later essay that the novelists of Spain's social realist school had put, to paraphrase Gide, *les bons sentiments* before *bons livres*: 'un simple paseo por los pueblos y suburbios de la España de los años 50 era mucho más sobrecogedor que la lectura de veinte novelas de la así llamada escuela realista' ('a walk through the villages and suburbs of Spain in the 1950s was far more moving than reading twenty novels of the so-called realist school').[27] Juan Goytisolo delivered a similarly damning assessment of the novelists of his generation who had sought to fight Franco from the pages of their novels. He acknowledged that he too had been writing realist literature of a particularly insipid kind and warned that, despite belonging to a literary tradition that could draw on Cervantes and Mariano José de Larra, Spanish writers had apparently lost the ability to smile.[28] This was a view shared by Marías's collaborator Félix de Azúa, for whom Spanish literary circles at this period were characterized by 'una seriedad... una severidad, escurialense, fúnebre, de tanatorio' ('a seriousness... a severity as if from the forbidding Escorial palace, funeral, morgue-like'); an atmosphere the 'Novísimos' sought to alleviate.[29]

In their anxiety to serve political ends, Goytisolo argued that, through their works, he and his contemporaries had failed to boost either their political cause or the wider interests of literature itself. The small print runs and limited sales of much protest literature of the period would corroborate such a view.[30] With prophetic accuracy, Goytisolo predicts the judgement that will fall on his generation.

> Digámoslo con claridad: las generaciones venideras nos pedirán cuentas, sin duda, de nuestra actual conducta cívica, pero no tomarán a ésta en consideración si, paralelamente a nuestra responsabilidad moral de ciudadanos, no manifestamos nuestra responsabilidad artística como escritores. No basta, en efecto, reclamar la libertad: tenemos que probarla desde ahora con la autenticidad y responsabilidad de nuestras obras.[31]

> (Let us be clear: the generations to come will doubtless ask us to justify our current civic conduct, but they will not take the latter into consideration if, at the same time as looking to our moral responsibility as citizens, we do not demonstrate our artistic responsibility as writers. Indeed it is not enough to

[27] Juan Benet, 'La novela en la España de hoy (1980)', in *La moviola de Eurípides y otros ensayos* (Madrid: Taurus, 1981), pp. 23–30 (p. 28).

[28] Juan Goytisolo, *El furgón de cola* (Madrid: Seix Barral, 1976), pp. 86–7.

[29] Félix de Azúa, 'Sobre el tiempo y las palabras. Los Novísimos', in *Lecturas compulsivas: Una invitación* (Barcelona: Anagrama, 2003), pp. 201–9 (p. 207).

[30] See Labanyi, pp. 295–6. According to her, many protest novels sold no more than two thousand copies and were probably bought by like-minded dissident intellectuals who were already in sympathy with the protest being made.

[31] Goytisolo, p. 87.

demand our freedom: we have to prove it from now on with the authenticity and responsibility of our works.)

For his part, Benet argued that we should be grateful for the fact that Cervantes, Sterne, Flaubert, Dickens, and Proust had rejected calls from their contemporaries to treat the pressing social issues of their day. Had they not resisted, the Western canon would be the poorer for it.[32]

In October 1981, we find the philosopher Fernando Savater arguing once more that the truly successful artist must avoid becoming the mouthpiece for views that do not grow naturally out of his or her creative impulse. His emergence in the late 1970s as a social commentator and columnist is highlighted by Chris Perriam as a key moment in Spain's recent intellectual past.[33] In October 1981, Savater delivered a lecture entitled 'La soledad solidaria del poeta' (subsequently published in *Quimera*), in which he argued that solitude and marginalization are essential to the writer's capacity to produce great art. Whether consciously or not, Savater reproduces a similar argument to that defended by Benet fifteen years earlier.

> ¿Hará falta decir que hay poetas que están dispuestos enseguida a prestar cualquier servicio con tal de abandonar una soledad que a ellos no les sirve para nada? Pero esos nunca tendrán mirada propia, sino que servirán de pantalla para la proyección de imágenes ajenas, quizá respetables, estimables, defendibles, pero irremediablemente ajenas y, por tanto, nunca poéticas. En cuanto el poeta con vocación de servicio pierde su soledad, renuncia a su voz y se convierte en portavoz.[34]

> (Does it need me to point out that there are poets who are ready to lend immediately any service as long as it gets them away from a solitude with which they can do nothing? But they will never possess their own vision, rather they will act as screens for the projection of others' images, perhaps respectable, laudable, defensible images but irredeemably belonging to others, and for that reason never poetic. As soon as the poet with a vocation for service loses his solitude, he renounces his voice and becomes a mouthpiece.)

In 'Desde' Marías rejects any suggestion that his generation were not politically engaged. It was simply that their fight against the regime was played out not in the pages of their works but on the streets of Madrid. In his autobiography Savater gives ample account of his student militancy and resultant imprisonment.[35] Needless to say this did

[32] 'La novela en la España de hoy (1980)', p. 28.

[33] Chris Perriam et al., *A New History of Spanish Writing: 1939 to the 1990s* (Oxford: Oxford University Press, 2000), p. 23.

[34] Fernando Savater, 'La soledad solidaria del poeta', *Quimera*, 15 (1982), 5.

[35] Fernando Savater, *Mira por dónde: Autobiografía razonada* (Madrid: Taurus, 2003), pp. 187–204. For a more general account of student militancy against Franco, see Rosa Pereda, *Contra Franco 1968–1978* (Barcelona: Planeta, 2003).

not stop an early reviewer of *Los dominios del lobo*, quoted by Marías, from lecturing him on the need to talk to Spanish readers about Spanish realities.[36] Benet's insights in *La inspiración y el estilo* prove prophetic once again: he had warned that a writer who does not pursue political goals in his fiction will face the criticism of his more 'engaged' contemporaries:

> Y lo primero que se le ocurre, ante el colega que no sangra por la misma herida y que se ha propuesto una meta algo diferente de la suya, es tildarle de escapista y estetecista, unos adjetivos que se emplean en tono despectivo por mucha gente cuyo fuerte, sin duda, no es el rigor verbal.[37]

> (And the first thing that occurs to him, faced with the colleague who is not bleeding from the same wound and who has set himself a different goal from his own, is to accuse him of being an escapist and an aesthete, terms employed with a pejorative tone by plenty of people whose forté is clearly not linguistic rigour.)

Marías continues his account of his literary beginnings:

> Pero, al declinar la herencia natural, nos sentimos libres de abrazar cualquier tradición, y es de imaginar que los escritos primerizos de los novísimos, vistos en conjunto y a cierta distancia, deben de ofrecer un aspecto delirantemente ecléctico, por no decir esquizofrénico.[38]

> (But in rejecting our natural inheritance, we felt free to embrace any tradition, and one imagines that the first literary efforts of the 'novísimos' group, viewed as a whole and from a certain distance, must offer a feverishly eclectic, not to say schizophrenic aspect.)

He goes on to describe the different forms their eclecticism took: Savater looked to Cioran, Azúa to Beaudelaire, Leopoldo María Panero to British ghost stories, Luis Antonio de Villena to W. B. Yeats and Catullus. His circle had embraced as one the notion that literary influence could come from any quarter. The opposition they experienced was considerable and the insults aimed at the 'Novísimos' coruscating; Azúa recalls that, among other things, they were accused of 'frivolidad' ('frivolity') and 'mariconería' ('poofery').[39] Marías's delight in Anglophone literary forbears led to him being described as 'angloaburrido' ('Anglodull') by the writer Francisco Umbral. (An international cultural climate in which English-speaking and particularly US products have become so ubiquitous that they are in danger of swallowing up other linguistic traditions is perhaps

---

[36] 'Desde una novela no necesariamente castiza', p. 55.
[37] *La inspiración*, p. 222.
[38] 'Desde una novela no necesariamente castiza', p. 58.
[39] 'Sobre el tiempo y las palabras', p. 204.

the best explanation for this kind of antipathy.)[40] Needless to say, Umbral's intemperate way of putting the point across does not lend weight to his argument.

The echoes here of a long-standing debate in which the avant-garde must justify its reliance on foreign literary models are not far to find. T. S. Eliot and Borges both contributed to such debates when the necessity arose in their home countries. In his essay, 'Tradition and the Individual Talent' (1919) Eliot first concedes that, '[e]very nation, every race, has not only its own critical turn of mind; and is even more oblivious of the shortcomings and limitations of its critical habits than of those of its creative genius'.[41] He then goes on to argue the need for a globalizing approach to the canon:

> Yet if the only form of tradition, of handing down, consisted in following the ways of the immediate generation before us in a blind or timid adherence to its successes, 'tradition' should positively be discouraged. We have seen many such simple currents soon lost in the sand; and novelty is better than repetition.[42]

When Borges came to write 'El escritor argentino y la tradición' (1951), his own manifesto advocating the acceptance of foreign literary models by Argentine letters, he is rejecting the perception that literature can only depict a particular national and historical moment; he is also rebutting critics who accused him of insufficient literary nationalism. As he points out, those who criticize him and others 'simulan venerar las capacidades de la mente argentina pero quieren limitar el ejercicio de esa mente a unos cuantos temas locales, como si los argentinos sólo pudiéramos hablar de orillas y estancias y no del universo' ('[nationalist critics] pretend to revere the capacity for invention of the Argentine mind but want to limit its exercise to a handful of local themes, as if we Argentines could only talk about rough neighbourhoods and ranches and not of the universe').[43] Part of Borges's technique in refuting such criticisms is to use a typically Argentine novel—*Don Segundo Sombra* (1926)—as a way of showing how the reshaping of foreign models by home-grown authors could be viewed as

[40] This fear is the subject of Steiner's final reflections in *After Babel*. There he warns of 'imported English, with its necessarily synthetic, "pre-packaged" semantic field, is eroding the autonomy of the native language-culture. Intentionally or not, American-English and English, by virtue of their global diffusion, are a principal agent in the destruction of natural linguistic diversity. This destruction is, perhaps, the least reparable of the ecological ravages which distinguish our age' (p. 494).

[41] T. S. Eliot, *Selected Essays* (London: Faber and Faber, 1953), p. 13.

[42] Eliot, p. 14.

[43] Jorge Luis Borges, *Obras completas*, ed. by María Kodama, 15th edn, 4 vols (Barcelona: Emecé, 2004), I: *1923–1949*, 271.

equally creative: '[E]s decir, Kipling, y Mark Twain, y las metáforas de los poetas franceses fueron necesarios para este libro argentino, para este libro que no es menos argentino por haber aceptado esas influencias' ('[T]hat's to say that Kipling and Mark Twain, and the metaphors employed by French poets were necessary for this Argentine book, for this book which is no less Argentine for having accepted those influences').[44] He endorses the idea that Argentine writers should above all strive for artistic achievement: '[t]odo lo que hagamos con felicidad los escritores argentinos pertenecerá a la tradición argentina' '[e]verything that we Argentine writers do felicitously will belong to Argentine tradition'.[45] His phrase 'con felicidad' implies perhaps both good writing and a sense of fun. Benet too anticipates a utopia where writers will concentrate all their energies on writing well, though his will have more sombre aims at its core:

> Poco a poco la novela en España, como en cualquier otro país, irá a ocupar su específico lugar para cumplir su específica misión: dar testimonio de la poca fortuna y mucha desgracia que el hombre puede esperar lo mismo en 1980 que en 1680; y que esa pequeña dosis de ventura y esa montaña de infortunio es obra exclusiva de él, de su ambigua naturaleza, de su torpe sociedad y de su insuficiente ciencia.[46]

> (Little by little the Spanish novel, as in any other country, will come to occupy its specific place and to fulfil its specific mission: testify to the scant good fortune and much adversity that man can expect, the same in 1980 as in 1680; and to the fact that his small dose of happiness and mountain of misfortune are his work alone, the product of his ambiguous nature, his lumbering society, and his insufficient knowledge.)

Marías had also taken the view that his path lay in absorbing the influence of the foreign writers he most admired. And yet, whereas he, Benet, Azúa, Savater, and a host of others looked to literature beyond Spain's borders for their inspiration, Muñoz Molina recalls that '[l]a cultura de la resistencia española se movía en un mezquino sistema de antagonismos': 'En la universidad, en los tiempos tristes del dogmatismo antifranquista, cualquier militante de izquierda podía reprocharle violentamente a uno su afición a los Beatles y a los Doors, que al parecer pertenecían a la cultura del imperialismo' ('the culture of Spain's political resistance operated in a small-minded system of antagonisms: at university, in the dark days of anti-Francoist dogmatism, any left-wing militant could violently reproach you your liking of The Beatles or The Doors, bands that apparently belonged to the culture of imperialism').[47] The fact that Marías was

---

[44] Borges, *Obras completas*, I, 271.      [45] Borges, *Obras completas*, I, 273.
[46] 'La novela en la España de hoy (1980)', pp. 29–30.
[47] *Pura alegría*, p. 207.

untroubled by such dogmatic attitudes can probably be put down to the circles in which he moved: his father was an erudite and cosmopolitan academic who had shown his children the United States at a young age; Benet was a man of immense culture and a devotee of William Faulkner; Molina Foix and Azúa were well-travelled young writers and translators.

What Marías goes on to describe in 'Desde' is his realization that there needed to be a change in the precise terms in which foreign influence manifested itself in his work. The parody of other literary and cinematic genres that underpinned *Los dominios del lobo* and *Travesía del horizonte* did not offer a tempting model for the future. He realized that his 'actitud "extranjerizante a ultranza" no podía durar eternamente' ('attitude of "embracing the foreign come what may" could not last for ever'). However, the path back was not as easy as it might have seemed:

> me había alejado tanto de mi propia carne, como aquel insigne crítico había venido a llamar mi realidad, que no podía salvar las distancias de un salto. Por lo demás debo confesar (y no me duelen prendas) que a mis veintitrés años, aún en pleno periodo de formación, no tenía especial urgencia por decir ni contar nada en particular.[48]

> (I had moved so far away from my own flesh, as that famous critic had ended up calling my reality, that I could not recover the distance travelled in one leap. Besides which I should confess [and I don't have any qualms about admitting] that at the age of twenty-three, still in the throes of growing up, I didn't feel any special urgency to say or tell anything in particular.)

To remain active as a writer while he sought greater maturity and subject matter he could call his own, he turned to translation. To avoid becoming a 'falso cosmopolita' ('fake cosmopolitan')—a literary curiosity whose wanton embrace of all things foreign made him a stranger to his own readers—he translated works of literature in English into Spanish. Though we might detect an incongruity here, Marías does not. By translating works in English by American, British, Danish, and Irish writers, he believed that he was enriching the versatility of his Spanish: 'traducir es naturalmente un grandísimo ejercicio literario, un ejercicio magnífico. Es un poco como un actor... que debe renunciar a su estilo para adoptar otro' ('translating is, naturally, a great literary exercise, a magnificent exercise. It is rather like an actor...who must renounce his style in order to adopt another').[49] And the experiment bore fruit. By 1978 and the publication of *El monarca del tiempo*, he felt that: 'había cruzado por fin la línea de sombra y alcanzado la madurez y la osadía necesarias para ser intérprete

---

[48] 'Desde una novela no necesariamente castiza', p. 62.
[49] Caterina Visani interview. http://www.javiermarias.es/PAGINASDEENTREVIS-TAS/entrevistaCaterinaVisani.html (accessed 24 February 2008).

de mí mismo' ('I had finally crossed the shadow line and reached the maturity and daring necessary to become an interpreter of myself').[50] He borrows Conrad's phrase 'the shadow line' to express the acquisition of artistic maturity at his 'veintisiete años' (twenty-seven years), whereas Eliot had maintained that the acquisition of 'the historical sense'—'a perception, not only of the pastness of the past, but of its presence' was essential to any writer who wished to 'continue to be a poet beyond their twenty-fifth year':

> The historical sense, which is a sense of the timeless as well as of the temporal and of the timeless and of the temporal together, is what makes a writer traditional. And it is at the same time what makes a writer most acutely conscious of his place in time, of his own contemporaneity.[51]

The crucial point for the great essayist and Marías is the moment at which one's eyes are opened to the possibilities beyond specific temporal, linguistic, or national boundaries. Translation was for Marías the means of gaining that awareness.

Thus we can see that his decision to take up translation was based on three interdependent reasons. Firstly, he wanted to broaden his cultural horizons beyond the stultifyingly politicized vistas that were on offer at home. Secondly, his upbringing, early reading, travel, and friendships all showed him that his natural literary inheritance was not limited to Spain but could encompass much further afield than the narrow confines of his national tradition. Thirdly, he saw that translation would allow him to hone the versatility of his style while he sought a voice of his own. Given these ideologically charged motivations, the questions surrounding how Marías chooses to translate assume a greater weight and become loaded with significance. As Lawrence Venuti suggests:

> Because translating traffics in the foreign, in the introduction of linguistic and cultural differences, it is equally capable of crossing or reinforcing the boundaries between domestic audiences and the hierarchies in which they are positioned. If the domestic inscription includes part of the social or historical context in which the foreign text first emerged, then a translation can also create a community that includes foreign intelligibilities and interests, an understanding in common with another culture, another tradition.[52]

The translator can bring a text to the reader or leave its cultural otherness intact. The translator can either facilitate contact with that alien quality

---

[50] 'Desde una novela no necesariamente castiza', p. 65.
[51] Eliot, p. 14.
[52] Lawrence Venuti, 'Translation, Community, Utopia', in *A Translation Studies Reader*, ed. by Lawrence Venuti, 2nd edn (London: Routledge, 2004), pp. 482–502 (p. 489).

(by guiding the reader's hand through footnotes or a domesticated rendering of what seems least familiar) or alternatively can leave the otherness of the original intact and let the reader sink or swim. Such matters come down to tactics and temperament. How might the translator best attract his community of readers? With the carrot of conciliation or the stick of confrontation? I devote the following section of this chapter to examining how Marías addresses these theoretical issues.

## MARÍAS AND THE THEORY OF TRANSLATION

Marías wrote his two most detailed and significant statements on the theory of translation in 1980 and 1982 during an intense period of practical experience. We saw in the preceding chapter that at this time his version of *Tristram Shandy* was still warm off the press, as were his renderings of poems by Faulkner, Nabokov, O'Hara, and Stevenson; work must also have begun on his versions of Browne. Perhaps not surprisingly it was to the translation of poetry that Marías turned in the first of these essays 'Ausencia y memoria en la traducción poética'. What becomes clear is that he had been gaining practical experience in tandem with theoretical knowledge. Equally clear is the fact that much of the latter was at the time cutting-edge. He quotes or name-checks Nabokov's foreword to his version of *The Song of Igor's Campaign* (1960), Octavio Paz's *Traducción: literatura y literalidad* (1971), Steiner's *After Babel* (1975), as well as more canonical work by Walter Benjamin—'Die Aufgabe des Übersetzers' (1923)—and Ortega y Gasset—'Miseria y esplendor de la traducción' (1937).[53] The last of these appears to have exercised a particularly strong influence, although that ought not to surprise us, perhaps, given that Marías's father was among the world's leading experts on Ortega's thought: the latter would be a natural reference point for Javier.

What Marías sets out to achieve in 'Ausencia y memoria en la traducción poética' is the rehabilitation of poetry translation as a creative act. He begins by setting out what he sees as the generally held view on translation that it differs from creativity, conceding that, when the translated text is nothing more than a chemistry textbook, there is little that one can put up against the argument.[54] He continues that Paz, Benjamin, and Steiner are probably those who have come closest to acknowledging the creativity inherent in translation. Paz's assertion that translation and creativity are 'operaciones gemelas' ('twin operations'), meets with a smile of

[53] JM, 'Ausencia y memoria en la traducción poética', in *LF*, pp. 371–82 (p. 371).
[54] 'Ausencia y memoria en la traducción poética', p. 371.

approval that gradually fades in the realization that for the Mexican writer they remain distinct entities. Steiner too is met with initial approval as Marías seizes on the suggestion in *After Babel* that all interpretative acts have translation at their core. According to Steiner's theory, every act of reading a text involves a process of decipherment and interpretation that is multiply subtle and extraordinarily difficult to describe:

> The complete penetrative grasp of a text, the complete discovery and recreative apprehension of its life-forms (*prise de conscience*), is an act whose realization can be precisely felt but is nearly impossible to paraphrase or systematize.[55]

Nor is the complete apprehension of a text a trifling task. Rather, Steiner sees it as the product of much gruelling scholarly labour. He lists the daunting array of familiarities a complete reader must gain: with the history of the language, matters of immediate historical and cultural context, the author's complete works including juvenilia and posthumous writings. In much the same way, Nabokov listed the competencies he saw as the prerequisite for any translator who was to undertake successfully Pushkin's *Eugene Onegin*:

> Anyone who wishes to attempt a translation of *Onegin* should acquire exact information in regard to a number of relevant subjects, such as the fables of Krilov, Byron's works, French poets of the eighteenth century, Rousseau's *La Nouvelle Heloïse*, Pushkin's biography, banking games, Russian songs related to divination, Russian military ranks of the time as compared to Western European and American ones, the difference between cranberry and lingenberry, the rules of the English pistol duel as used in Russia, and the Russian language.[56]

This almost psychotic inventory, hovering as it does on the edges of self-parody, gives ample idea of its author's idiosyncratic understanding of translation, which he saw as unethical whenever it did not display the most slavish literalism.

However, Steiner's theory that interpretation underpins all linguistic exchange corroborates the idea that to rewrite a foreign text in one's own language is itself a re-creative act: one involving the interpretation of multiple inflections of meaning embedded in social convention, historical usage, and the private discourse of the original author's style. Or it would corroborate such an idea, were it not for the fact that his theory places translation at the heart of all interpretative acts and therefore makes

---

[55] Steiner, p. 26.
[56] Vladimir Nabokov, 'Problems of Translation: "Onegin" in English', *Partisan Review*, 22 (1955), 496–512 (p. 506).

translation no different from reading a contemporary author in one's own language. For Marías, that leaves the place of translation unaltered within a wider system, the nature of which is now recognized as translational.[57] Steiner concedes that there is true creativity in his interpretative vision only at the highest reaches of acquired understanding:

> Where the most thorough possible interpretation occurs, where our sensibility appropriates its object while, in this appropriation, guarding, quickening that object's autonomous life, the process is one of 'original repetition'. We re-enact, in the bounds of our own secondary but momentarily heightened, educated consciousness, the creation by the artist. We retrace, both in the image of a man drawing and of one following an uncertain path, the coming into form of the poem.[58]

Having examined this selection of recent theories on the degree of creativity inherent in translation, Marías proceeds to outline arguments that undermine the idea that translation is not creative. For example, he refutes the notion that the work under translation is not the translator's autonomous creation by citing the example of Nabokov and Beckett. They not only wrote in two languages but translated their own works from one to the other, blurring our conception of the original moment of inspiration as dependent on particular linguistic identity. Not all authors fulfil this criteria, however, and Marías admits that their special cases cannot be considered emblematic or universal. He then makes a second concession by admitting that

> El factor mencionado sería muy discutible, pero aceptable en primera instancia, en la novela o el ensayo, por ejemplo. En ambos suele haber un argumento (al menos lo había en la novela tradicional), una línea de imaginación o de pensamiento que impone una determinada sucesión narrativa o conceptual en el texto traducido. Pero en la poesía esta imposición es cuando menos, mucho menor—y quizá de distinta índole—, y es en su cenagoso terreno donde vamos a plantearnos la existencia de esa supuesta originalidad.[59]

> (The factor just mentioned would be very debatable but acceptable, in the first instance, in the case of the novel or the essay, for example. In both there is usually a plot or argument [at least there was in the traditional novel], an imaginative thread or thought pattern which imposes a particular narrative or conceptual sequence on the translated text. But in the case of poetry this imposition is, at least, far smaller—and perhaps of a different sort—and it is in its murky territory where we are going to consider the existence of that alleged originality.)

---

[57] 'Ausencia y memoria en la traducción poética', p. 372.
[58] Steiner, p. 27.
[59] 'Ausencia y memoria en la traducción poética', p. 375.

He is arguing that poetry tugs at the boundaries of linguistic convention and so the proscription of meaning is diminished, whereas a novel or essay contains more definite indications as to sequences of events and hence meanings. The translation of poetry 'es un acto de creación que toma como motivo, inspiración, fuente, causa, impulso o recuerdo una experiencia literaria que hace reconocible' ('it is an act of creation that takes as its reason, inspiration, source, cause, impulse or memory a literary experience that it makes recognizable').[60] He cites the examples of Eliot's 'The Waste Land' and 'Prufrock', noting that no one has called either work a plagiarized version of Baudelaire or Dante, despite the fact that both poems contain their translated lines. Here Marías is not arguing like for like. There is a difference between placing others' poetry within a new artistic context and translating in its entirety an already existing poem and calling it one's own. Whilst there may be creativity in rendering in one's own tongue a poem one has read in a second language, it remains distinct from placing translated meanings in contexts alien to the original poem.

In the most persuasive section of his essay, Marías echoes Steiner's model of how literary translation takes place, what the latter calls the 'hermeneutic motion'. According to that model, the first movement towards translation is one of trust that there is something in the foreign text which can be apprehended and adequately rendered in one's own tongue.[61] The second is that of aggression, the translator 'invades, extracts, and brings home':

> Every schoolchild, but also the eminent translator will note the shift in substantive presence which follows on a protracted or difficult exercise in translation: the text in the other language has become almost materially thinner, the light seems to pass unhindered through its loosened fibres.[62]

The third stage is of 'incorporation', where the newly acquired foreign text jostles for position in its unfamiliar host culture. Here lie the potential threats posed by translation. I quoted in Chapter 1 Steiner's warning that the individual translator can be consumed by their labours and the voice of another drown out forever their own creative impulse. What Steiner envisions as the fourth stage in his model of translation is something like 'an equal and opposite reaction'; he admits himself that the movement he seeks to describe is hard to pin down, but it implies the reciprocity of mutual transfer, a re-crossing of the linguistic

---

[60] 'Ausencia y memoria en la traducción poética', p. 376.
[61] Steiner, pp. 312–13.    [62] Steiner, p. 314.

divide, when what has been plucked from the heart of the original language takes root in the receptor language:

> The translator, the exegetist, the reader is *faithful to* his text, makes his response responsible, only when he endeavours to restore the balance of forces, of integral presence, which his appropriative comprehension has disrupted. Fidelity is ethical, but also, in the full sense, economic.[63]

Something of this process of mutual enrichment and reciprocity might be found in Marías's notion of 'ausencia' ('absence'). The translator experiences the poem as an absence in his own tongue and hopes to both appropriate it and make it new.

> El traductor, al encararse con su tarea, siente el texto original como una ausencia. Lo que cuenta para él y para su labor es la ausencia de ese texto en su lengua, en la llamada lengua receptora, y por ende en el sistema de pensamiento de dicha lengua. El traductor no reproduce, no copia, no calca, entre otras cosas porque no está en su mano hacerlo, porque no se halla capacitado para ello. Plasma siempre por vez primera una experiencia única, irrepetible e intransferible; crea en su lengua lo que en su cabeza se encuentra en otra lengua. Y digo 'en su cabeza' en lugar de 'en el texto original' muy a conciencia, pues ese texto por sí solo, dentro del ámbito de la traducción, no es nada: es como un rumor de olas que ningún poeta escucha.[64]

> (When he confronts his task, the translator feels the original text like an absence. What matters for him and for his undertaking is the absence of that text in his language, in what is called the receptor language, and by extension in the thought system of that language. The translator does not reproduce, copy, or calque, because, among other things, it is not in his hands to do so, because he does not have the capacity to. He gives expression always for the first time to a unique, unrepeatable, and untransferable experience; he creates in his language that which in his head exists in another language. And I say 'in his head' rather than 'in the original text' very deliberately, because that text in itself, within the field of translation, is nothing: it is like a murmur of sea waves which no poet can hear.)

Marías is arguing that the experience of reading a poem in a foreign language can be like the small acts of discovery and inspiration that he also experiences when writing in his own. He has always stated that he writes 'con brújula' ('with a compass') rather than a map. In other words, he writes his novels without a set plot outline or determined cast of characters in mind. Instead, he lets inspiration and intuition guide him as the work unfolds. Hence he has described the sensation he often has that writing allows him to discover and reveal areas of human experience that

---

[63] Steiner, p. 318.
[64] 'Ausencia y memoria en la traducción poética', p. 378.

he had not consciously contemplated before. He is trying to turn what might seem like his particular relationship to creative process and practice into a more universal argument for the creativity of translation. Whether or not he succeeds in convincing the many practitioners and theorists who have worked in this area is less important for our present purposes than noting the fact that translation—as he experiences it—can be compared to original inspiration.

A logical progression from his argument is that there are as many potential versions of the original poem as there are minds to interpret and translate it:

> unas seguirán determinados criterios y otras otros distintos, a veces opuestos; unas serán mejores y otras peores, unas conmoverán más y otras menos, pero ninguna dejará de ser creación literaria, ni aun la más literal, ni tampoco se podrá acusar a unas de ser menos 'fieles' que otras. Todas lo serán por igual, no al texto original tal vez, que, como antes dije, no es nada en sí, sino al recuerdo que de dicho texto se haya impuesto en cada una de ellas.[65]

> (Some will follow certain criteria and others different, on occasion even contradictory criteria; some will be better and others worse, some will be more moving and others less, but none of them will stop being a literary creation, not even the most literal; nor can some be accused of being less 'faithful' than others. They will all be equally faithful, not perhaps to the original text, which, as I said before, is nothing in itself, rather to the memory of that text which has been left in each of them.)

Yet, instead of leaving his reader with the feeling of overwhelming vertigo that would normally accompany such a relativistic statement, Marías claims that 'el quién traductor' ('who is doing the translating') becomes the crucial factor when one is seeking an equivalent adequacy between text and original. How this rigorous, even elitist, interpretation has played out in his subsequent activities as a translator will be the subject of comment in Chapters 3 and 5 of this study. How it has affected his attitudes as a critic and editor of translated works is an altogether more complex and nuanced matter which I shall discuss in the light of his second significant essay on Translation Theory, 'La traducción como fingimiento y representación'.[66]

There, he offers a gloss on a debate that has been raging since the first writings on the subject of translation—over whether to naturalize foreign elements. If in his first essay he had argued that translation was in its own way a creative art, then in his second, he hopes to show that it closely resembles other mimetic literary forms. Thus, he asks, when a reader picks up a Spanish translation of Dickens or Flaubert (doubtless chosen for

---

[65] 'Ausencia y memoria en la traducción poética', p. 380.
[66] 'La traducción como fingimiento y representación', in *LF*, pp. 383–92.

their emblematic status at the heart of the Western canon) what is it that allows that reader to suspend disbelief enough to enjoy a work that is a logical impossibility? According to Marías, the answer is that the reader enters into a fictive pact in much the same way as a theatre audience suspends disbelief for the duration of a performance. While knowing that the actor on stage is not in fact Hamlet or that the painted backdrop is not in fact the walls of Elsinore (to take one example), the audience consents to believe so for the purposes of fiction:

> podríamos decir que desde tiempo inmemorial se simula, *se hace como* que [la obra] sigue siendo la misma. Es por esta razón por la que, a mi modo de ver, se podría comparar la actividad de traducir con cualquiera de los modos habituales de representación, tanto de los consagrados por siglos de tradición como de los más modernos, pues todos ellos precisan de convenciones semejantes para su existencia.[67]

> (We could say that since time immemorial we pretend, *we act as though* [the work] were still the same. It is for this reason that, in my view, one could compare the act of translation with any of the other customary representational modes, as much those established by centuries of tradition as more modern ones, since all of them rely on similar conventions for their existence.)

In much the same way, readers of a translation require the text they are confronted with to demonstrate its otherness but, paradoxically, to scan as if it were written in their language:

> El lector de una traducción, para entrar en el juego, para poder cumplir con su parte en la convención establecida entre él y el traductor, no debe percibir continuamente que se trata de eso, de una traducción: para olvidarlo, para poner en suspenso esa idea, ha de leer con tanta facilidad y naturalidad como está acostumbrado a hacerlo en su propia lengua; pero a la vez, y a fin de poder creer que está leyendo en verdad a Dickens, es decir, a fin de que esta lectura resulte verosímil, no puede recorrer el texto traducido sin notar en él 'algo' distinto e inequívocamente ajeno a lo que está acostumbrado a leer en los textos escritos originalmente en su lengua. Tiene que advertir 'algo' que, sin tampoco recordarle de continuo que se encuentra ante una traducción, le permita al mismo tiempo adivinar, intuir ese original que, como acabamos de ver, no puede conocer de otro modo.[68]

> (The reader of a translation, in order to enter into the game, to be able to keep his side of the bargain established between him and translator, must not perceive continually that that is what he is reading, a translation: in order to forget it, to put that idea on hold, he must be able to read the text with as much ease and naturalness as he usually does in his own language; but at the same

[67] 'La traducción como fingimiento y representación', p. 385.
[68] 'La traducción como fingimiento y representación', pp. 389–90.

time, and in order to believe that he is actually reading Dickens, that is to say, for that reading experience to seem plausible, he cannot go through the translated text without finding in it 'something' different and unmistakeably alien to that which he usually reads in texts written originally in his language. He has to notice 'something' that, without continually reminding him that he is reading a translation, allows him at the same time to intuit that original which, as we have just seen, he cannot get to know through any other means.)

What that 'algo' might be or how it might be described is one of the most vexed questions in all of Translation Theory. Marías cites Benjamin's conjecture that the act of translation allows the reader to see in the slippage between two languages the common ancestry of language itself. That formulation appears to inform Steiner's observation that the 'translator enriches his tongue by allowing the source language to penetrate and modify it. But he does far more: he extends his idiom to the hidden absolute of meaning'.[69] How this glimpse might be had and this paradox resolved in practice is through the conservation of an otherness that makes tangible the sense of the mystery of translation. In formulating this response, Marías was doubtless drawing on his opinions about Spain's cultural life at this juncture: if there was one thing it needed, it was an openness to the world beyond its narrowed and inward-looking borders. But he was drawing also on the translation theories of Ortega, whose suggestion it was that 'al traducir, procuremos salir de nuestra lengua a las ajenas y no al revés' ('when translating, let us try to reach out from our language towards others and not the other way around'):

> Es cosa clara que el público de un país no agradece una traducción hecha en el estilo de su propia lengua. Para esto tiene de sobra con la producción de los autores indígenas. Lo que agradece es lo inverso: que llevando al extremo de lo inteligible las posibilidades de su lengua transparezcan en ella los modos de hablar propios al autor traducido.[70]

> (It is clearly the case that the reading public of a country do not appreciate a translation written in the style of their own language. For that they have quite enough with the production of their home-grown authors. What the reading public are grateful for is the opposite: that by pushing the expressive possibilities of their language to the limits of intelligibility, the translated author's particular idiom will shine through it.)

To achieve this, the translator must be given a degree of linguistic freedom, certain room for manoeuvre within the porous boundaries of his own tongue.

---

[69] Steiner, p. 67.
[70] José Ortega y Gasset, 'Miseria y esplendor de la traducción', in *Obras completas*, 12 vols (Madrid: Revista de Occidente, 1946–1983), V: *1933–1941* (1947), pp. 431–52 (p. 452).

What this issue immediately throws up in 'La traducción como fin-gimiento y representación' is the controversy surrounding the battles that Spanish was (and is) fighting against linguistic cannibalization from English. Although the movement of Marías's thought is understandable, inasmuch as such controversy raged then just as it does today, his exclusive focus on English—the language from which he was translating—hints at another, perhaps subconscious motivation. It is possible that, in addressing the touchy subject of linguistic incorporation from English, he was implicitly defending his own practice, or at least what he could see was an enticing path for his work. The year of his essay's composition, 1982, must have seen the initial throb of *ES*, the first of his novels to show the sustained influence of an author he had been translating, as we shall see in Chapter 6. He had already indulged a version of cultural incorporation by parodying Hollywood cinema and Victorian adventure novels in his first two works. The possibilities offered by a creative dialogue with authors he had translated must have seemed endless. Nevertheless, he concedes that the fears of those who lament the insidious creep of English into Spanish are real. He lists examples of ludicrous calques from English that are becoming common mistakes, among them the redundant use of the prefix 'auto' before reflexive verbs—'autoconsolarse' ('to self-console one-self'), 'autodefenderse' ('to self-defend oneself), even 'autosuicidarse' (to commit self-suicide'). Exasperating though these errors are, the outright rejection of linguistic flexibility and the tendency to translate so as to domesticate at all costs strikes him as counterproductively protectionist:

> Esta postura es en mi opinión... tan perjudicial para el castellano—o para la lengua de que se trate—como la opuesta, y creo que conduce a largo plazo a un empobrecimiento grave de la lengua que se quiere preservar. Las lenguas se enriquecen por innumerables causas, pero no cabe duda de que una de ellas es el contacto y la permeabilidad a los usos y dicciones de otras lenguas, a su vez en permanente evolución.[71]

> (This stance is in my opinion... as prejudicial for Castilian—or for any language—as the opposite extreme, and I believe that in the long term it leads to a serious impoverishment of the language that one is trying to preserve. Languages enrich themselves by innumerable means, but there is no doubt that one of them is contact with and permeability to the customs and diction of other languages, which are themselves constantly evolving.)

He concludes by returning to the idea of competence. Just as the actor on stage will persuade the audience to believe in his character through quality of performance, so the translator who renders a Dickens novel that

[71] 'La traducción como fingimiento y representación', p. 391.

reads simultaneously and paradoxically as English and Spanish will do so only through the flexibility of his linguistic and literary ability.[72] In this he is echoing Nabokov's stricture that the translator 'must have as much talent, or at least the same kind of talent, as the author he chooses'.[73] Nabokov, like Ortega and Steiner, believed that very few translations fulfil the exacting standards he had in mind, and here too Marías concurs with his illustrious forerunners.[74]

Hence, we can see that three significant points emerge from an analysis of Marías's most substantial essays on Translation Theory. Firstly, he has ensured that his practical experience of the translator's art is underpinned by theoretical insight. Secondly, he sees a meaningful equivalence between the translation of poetry and autonomous artistic creation. Thirdly, he believes in literary incorporation and interlingual cross-fertilization through translation that foregrounds the otherness of the original text. Moreover, his stance on translation is unapologetically elitist. Only the most versatile practitioners will shiver the linguistic boundaries of their own tongue or produce works of art through poetic translation. Since the early 1980s he has largely maintained this stance, albeit with added caveats and an increased awareness of the market forces in the publishing industry that work against the conscientious translator. What undoubtedly helped Marías to gain this enhanced understanding was his move into commissioning and editing translations for his Reino de Redonda press. From the turn of the twenty-first century onwards, when his publishing venture first took off, he has published a succession of articles bemoaning both the exploitative conditions under which translators are forced to work and the sloppiness that is too often the result. It is to an examination of Marías's articles on translation and the Spanish language that I devote the final section of this chapter.

A thought-provoking starting point is a pair of articles written in the mid 1990s, 'Un mistero incognoscible' and 'Lección de lengua'. In the first of these he describes his reaction to a photograph of himself printed alongside a magazine interview, one in which—in his words—he looked like 'un killer', using the English term rather than any of the Spanish alternatives he might have chosen—'asesino' ('assassin'), 'criminal' ('murderer'), 'homicida' ('murderer'), even 'sicario' ('hired assassin').[75] Several weeks later, in 'Lección de lengua', he answers the criticisms of a reader who had suggested that his use of the English term was gratuitous, given

---

[72] 'La traducción como fingimiento y representación', p. 392.

[73] Vladimir Nabokov, 'The Art of Translation', in *Lectures on Russian Literature*, ed by Fredson Bowers (London: Harvest, 1981), pp. 315–21 (p. 319).

[74] 'The Art of Translation', *passim*; Ortega, pp. 438, 448–9; Steiner, 416–17.

[75] JM, 'Un misterio incognoscible', in *MS*, pp. 205–7 (p. 205).

that Spanish has several synonyms that would have conveyed his meaning just as well. While conceding that the practice of needlessly importing foreign terms is indeed irritating, Marías explains that the English word 'killer' has a nuance of uncontrolled savagery that none of the Spanish terms convey, hence his decision to use it. He even wonders whether his compatriots might follow suit and Hispanicize the term into 'quíler', just as they have done with the English term 'leader' ('líder' in Spanish) or the German 'werra' ('guerra' in Spanish, ['war']). He adds that linguistic usage is subject to the shaping effects of a community of native speakers whose lexical choices have an ineluctable democratic force:

> Las lenguas varían continuamente, se mezclan, se permean unas a otras, y así se enriquecen. No hay que ser muy purista. Nadie decide sobre ellas, sino que serán siempre ellas mismas las que incorporen o rechacen los neologismos a través de sus hablantes. Esos hablantes tienen además oído, y transforman a su gusto y conveniencia lo que les llega de fuera pero les es útil.[76]

> (Languages vary continually, they mix, they permeate one another, and by doing so they enrich themselves. There is no need to be very purist. Nobody can make decisions over them, rather the languages themselves will always be the ones to incorporate or reject neologisms through their speakers. Besides which, those speakers have ears, and they transform according to their taste and convenience what they receive from outside but find useful.)

However, what his other articles on poor translation practice and the declining standards of spoken Spanish illustrate is his ambivalence in the face of linguistic change. While at times open to the possibilities offered by incorporation of words and grammatical structures from English, at others he displays a conservative resistance to that same process. In an interview conducted in 2000, he espoused the view that incorporation and linguistic cross-fertilization were two of the most important legacies offered by translation. Anxious to determine the limits of the process Marías had in mind, the interviewer asked him whether Spanglish would qualify as linguistic cross-fertilization:

> This, I'm afraid, has nothing to do with what I was talking about before. No 'incorporation' here, not in any real sense. It's just an artificial mixture apparently due only to laziness. Spanglish could never be an enrichment of either English or Spanish. Rather both would be abolished by it.[77]

Clearly, in his view incorporation should be left in the hands of the best translators and authors, among whom he includes himself. It is

---

[76] JM, 'Lección de lengua', in *MS*, pp. 247–9 (p. 249).
[77] Matthew Perret, 'Telling Stories', *The Broadsheet*, 93 (2000), 30–1 (p. 30).

important to note that in this and other regards, he is far from being a postmodernist. (He believes, for example, in a thoroughgoing distinction between high art and low culture: 'Hablando del canon, me parece que lo que sí que hay que hacer es mantener la idea fundamentada de que no todo es igual, de que hay obras de arte y hay obras a secas' ['Talking about the canon, I think that what we should try to do is maintain the well-founded idea that not everything is equal, that there are works of art and just works'].)[78] By contrast, incorporation through the production of calques in bad translations or through the lazy use of Spanish by public figures—politicians and journalists the main offenders—will not do. And yet, Marías is perfectly aware that the ultimate arbiter of linguistic change is the population of native speakers, against whom it is almost impossible to legislate. In spite of which, that awareness has not stopped him from trying.

A representative sample of his articles on the Spanish language from 1996 to 2007 reveals his exasperation at the declining standards of its usage: provoking his ire have been its pronunciation on television; its decline in comparison to a less tainted Mexican Spanish; efforts to make it 'less sexist'; the inability of politicians to convey ideas through it or speak it correctly; the relentlessness with which Spanish journalists calque it with English.[79] Nor do translators escape his opprobrium. Some are unable to recognize the names of foreign cities and supply their Spanish equivalents—Belén for Bethlehem, Nimega for Nijmegen, Colonia for Cologne.[80] He upbraids others for their inability to recognize false friends, translating the English adjective 'embarassed' as 'embarazado' ('pregnant'), 'law court' as 'corte' ('the court of a monarch'), 'actually' as 'actualmente' ('currently'), 'the buildings collapsed' as 'los edificios se colapsaron' ('the buildings were brought to a standstill'), 'to ignore' as 'ignorar' ('to be unaware of').[81] However, Marías shows a reluctance to acknowledge that this kind of translationese can become part of the natural process of linguistic renewal. To take his final example, the verb 'ignorar', as a test case, it is clear that as a result of consistent misuse, the word's semantic field has in fact shifted to include the English active meaning of ignore: it is now

---

[78] Michael Pfeiffer, 'Javier Marías', in *El destino de la literatura: Diez voces* (Barcelona: El Acantilado, 1999), pp. 107–24 (p. 118).

[79] JM, 'Lección pasada de moda', in *MS*, pp. 310–12; 'Malas hablas', in *A veces un caballero* (Madrid: Alfaguara, 2001), pp. 22–4 (this article collection hence referred to as *AVC*); 'Navío recadero', in *AVC*, pp. 75–7; 'Todas las farsantas son igualas', in *AVC*, pp. 291–4; 'Decir feamente nada', in *DNA*, pp. 210–12; 'Hundidos en una ciénaga', in *LNVD*, pp. 15–17.

[80] JM, '¿Mande?', in *DNA*, pp. 114–16.

[81] JM, 'Fastidiosos y muy embarazados', in *HMC*, pp. 45–7; 'Se colapsaron tributos actualmente', in *EOOL*, pp. 188–90.

used regularly to mean just that in the pages of *El País* as well as by many of Spain's leading writers.[82]

Lest his criticisms should seem like truculence, he is clearly well aware of the factors that have contributed to this situation. In 1997 he wrote the article 'Intermediarios literarios' in celebration of the translators whose contribution to Spanish letters too often goes unsung and, more importantly, unrewarded. He reveals that a translator can expect to receive 0.5 per cent of profits from sales of the books he or she produces, a beggarly sum that is sometimes reduced even further by unscrupulous editors who insist that the work be done for a flat fee with no entitlement to royalties. And this in spite of the fact that it is thanks to translators that Spaniards can read 'a unos cuantos genios además de a Borges, Valle-Inclán y Cervantes' ('a few geniuses besides Borges, Valle-Inclán and Cervantes').[83] Five years later the situation had not improved, attested to by his piece 'Píseme el cogote, jefe' (April 2002), in which he describes the fate of an unnamed translator who had the 'temerity' to ask his or her editor for the royalty payments to which their contract entitled them, only to be sacked on the spot and their reputation rubbished across the industry.[84] A further five years on and the burden of his song remains the same. If anything the situation had got slightly worse by the time he was writing 'El comino de nuestra lengua' (January 2007). Some publishing houses had by then stopped paying translators by the page and were instead doing so by the word, further reducing their meagre income by 20 per cent. Bidding wars, instigated by editors putting translations out to tender, had introduced the harshest realities of market economics into an environment where quality control was very much a thing of the past:

> Esto equivale a premiar al que tiene en menos su tarea, al que—en consecuencia con el ridículo precio acordado—se tomará las molestias mínimas y entregará una chapuza, al que no se sentirá obligado ni a consultar el diccionario en caso de duda, ni tendrá reparo en cambiar o suprimir los pasajes que no entienda bien.[85]

> (This amounts to rewarding he who has the least regard for his job, he who—as a result of the ludicrous price agreed—will take the least possible trouble and deliver a dog's dinner, he who won't feel obliged to consult a dictionary in cases of doubt, or think twice about changing or cutting out passages he doesn't understand properly.)

---

[82] One of Marías's contemporaries to use 'ignorar' in its new sense of 'to ignore something deliberately' is Almudena Grandes. See her *El corazón helado* (Barcelona: Tusquets, 2007), pp. 69, 535.

[83] JM, 'Intermediarios literarios', in *Seré amado cuando falte* (Madrid: Alfaguara, 1999), pp. 168–70 (p. 170). This article collection hence referred to as *SACF*.

[84] JM, 'Píseme el cogote, jefe', in *HMC*, pp. 203–5.

[85] JM, 'El comino de nuestra lengua', in *DNA*, pp. 300–2 (p. 301).

When good translators are not allowed to earn an acceptable wage for their efforts and when critics and readers accept the substandard products brought out by the publishing houses, the outlook from Marías's point of view is bleak.[86]

I suggested above that his role as publisher and editor of translations for the Reino de Redonda series appears to have had a significant role to play in fuelling his renewed interest in both the plight and inadequacies of some translators. In another of the pieces where he decries the quality of contemporary translation, he cites yet another example of egregious error:

> Esas mentes dementes se molestan de vez en cuando en poner notas a pie de página, y explican, ufanas, que a una madre a la que sus hijos llaman Pussy (en los años veinte y de clase alta), en realidad la están llamando 'minino, chochete'.[87]

> (Those crazed minds occasionally take the trouble to put footnotes at the bottom of the page, and explain proudly that when her children call an old woman Pussy (in the 1920s and among the upper classes), what they are really calling her is 'puss, fannykins'.)

This unusual nickname features in one of the novels Marías commissioned for translation for the Redonda series, *The House* by Richmal Crompton.[88] Evidently, he sent the novel out for translation and received back a version containing this extraordinary blunder. The published version of *La morada maligna* is credited to Panteleimón Zarín, a nonexistent person. The latter is a compound of two names that feature incidentally in *NET*, where the novel *Three Pairs of Silk Stockings* is mentioned in passing. Its author, Panteleimon Romanov, and translator, Leonide Zarine, have been spliced together to create a compound name.[89] It seems most likely that Marías received back a version of *La morada maligna* from his translator that he then had to edit himself or send out for more work. He must have withdrawn the original translator's name from the cover and replaced it with this fantastical creation as a way of expressing his displeasure. The latter was no doubt particularly acute because he goes

[86] He had started the process of providing honest assessment of poor translators in 2001 by advising his readers against a new version of Conan Doyle's Sherlock Holmes stories by Juan Antonio Molina Foix. Although not identifying him by name, Marías describes 'las nuevas traducciones de la Editorial Valdemar' ('the new translations published by Editorial Valdemar') which, in his words, 'parecen hechas por Moriarty *himself*' ('look like the work of Moriarty *himself*'). Those new translations were the work of Molina Foix. See 'Cuando no es triste la muerte', in *HMC*, pp. 69–72 (p. 69).

[87] JM, 'Productos podridos', in *DNA*, pp. 27–9 (pp. 28–9).

[88] Richmal Crompton Lamburn, *The House* (London: [n.p.], [1926]), p. 56. See also *La morada maligna*, p. 94.

[89] *NET*, p. 255.

out of his way in his editorial role to ensure that his translators are treated fairly. Writing in 2008 on the subject of his Redonda editions, he revealed that 'a los ocasionales traductores les pago el máximo y, si lo desean, la mitad por adelantado, pues no en balde fui yo traductor en su día y habría deseado ese trato para mí' ('I pay the occasional translators the maximum going rate and, if they want, half up front, no wonder since I was once a translator in my day and I would have wanted that treatment for myself').[90]

Clearly Marías is fighting the good fight, though with a limited likelihood of success. His views on translation are unambiguous and reflect a deep conviction that Spain's cultural borders should be open to outside influence. However, that influence should not be allowed to swallow up indigenous linguistic practice simply through laziness. On his election to the Real Academia, whose authoritative dictionary is one of the custodians of the Spanish language, he suggested that he would be 'muy atento a los anglicismos innecesarios' ('very much on the look out for unnecessary Anglicisms').[91] We should await developments on that front. It is in the next chapter that I shall examine how all of this theory meets practice in the case of Marías's *Tristram Shandy*.

[90] JM, 'Esta absurda aventura', *El País*, Babelia section, 23 August 2008, p. 23.
[91] García, A., and Rojo, J. A., 'Javier Marías entra en la Academia', *El País*, 30 June 2006, p. 49.

# 3

## Sterne Challenges

One piece of information that critics, scholars, and journalists consistently deploy to sum up Javier Marías's career as a translator is that, in 1979, he won the Premio Nacional de Traducción for his version of Sterne's *The Life and Opinions of Tristram Shandy, Gentleman* (1759–1767; hence *TS*).[1] For many of them, this fact seems to prove that he is a gifted translator. How could the situation be otherwise? The twentieth century offers prominent examples—Beckett, Borges, Cortázar, Nabokov, Pound—of writers who moved confidently between languages either in their own work or when translating. The passively endorsed belief that if someone writes well in their mother tongue, they must be a good translator, receives further unexamined corroboration. None of the aforementioned critics has troubled to ask whether the jury that awarded him the Premio Nacional was right to do so. His translation of *TS* is excellent, as I aim to show; my point is merely that Marías's translations have yet to receive adequate critical analysis.[2] Luis Pegenaute is unique in having devoted any substantial attention to Marías's Sterne translations in three articles on the tardy reception of *TS* in Spain.[3] He discusses what might seem an incredible anomaly surrounding the latter's publication history in Spanish, a language into which it was not translated until 1975. At that point, like long-awaited buses, three versions arrived in four years—Marías's being the last, in 1978. When it comes to the translations themselves, regrettably, Pegenaute's approach is more impressionistic than analytical. The main purpose of this chapter is

---

[1] See, for example, Cuñado, p. 64; Logie, p. 67; Christina Patterson, 'In search of lost time', *The Independent*, 28 July 2006, Arts and Books Review section, pp. 20–1.

[2] For Marías's version, see Laurence Sterne, *La vida y las opiniones del caballero Tristram Shandy. Los sermones de Mr Yorick*, trans. with notes by Javier Marías, 2nd edn (Madrid: Alfaguara, 2000). Page references in brackets in the text refer to this edition.

[3] Luis Pegenaute, 'The Unfortunate Journey of Laurence Sterne Through Spain: The Translations of his Works into Spanish', *The Shandean*, 6 (1994), 24–53; 'Las primeras traducciones de Sterne al español y el problema de la censura', *Livius*, 1 (1992), 133–9; 'Sterne Castles in Spain', in *The Reception of Laurence Sterne in Europe*, ed. by Peter de Voogd and John Neubauer, The Athlone Critical Tradition Series: The Reception of British Authors in Europe, 2 (London: Thoemmes, 2004), pp. 234–46. All three pieces cover much the same ground, though the latter two contain less detail, hence why I shall quote exclusively from the first.

thus to undertake much-needed analysis of Marías's Sterne translation, focusing on several key areas. Firstly, what are likely to have been the causes of *TS*'s tardy reception in Spain? Secondly, how does Marías confront the task of translating as difficult and idiosyncratic a work as *TS*? What criteria does he follow in relation to naturalization of foreign elements—forms of address, punctuation, cultural norms? Thirdly, I offer a comparison and textual analysis of translated passages of *TS*, examining how Marías tackles the novel's many and varied difficulties. My discussion will also be tailored to highlight those aspects of *TS* that Marías would later use in his own Shandean novel, *NET*.

Before discussing any of these things, however, a few words on *TS* the novel. The task of summarizing as digressive and haphazard a work as *TS* is not easy and appears doomed to fail in any of several ways. The narrator Tristram Shandy sets out to record his 'life and opinions', starting with his conception, and, in the course of the eighty volumes he at one stage promises the reader, hopes to reach the present moment at which he writes. As he observes, his progress is ponderous at best:

> I am this month one whole year older than I was this time twelve-month; and having got, as you perceive, almost into the middle of my fourth volume – and no farther than to my first day's life – 'tis demonstrative that I have three hundred and sixty-four days more life to write just now, than when I first set out.[4]

His text enacts one of the difficulties of autobiographical writing, in that time passes inexorably while the writer writes to catch up. Part of his problem stems from a febrile and endlessly associative memory that will not allow him to stick to one strand of the divergent narrative flow. From this aberration stems much of the novel's humour and enjoyment:

> The reader is more pleasured than perplexed by the narrative chaos that results from Tristram's digressive swerves and meanders, and the eccentricity of the book, like the eccentricity of its characters, seems less an aberration from any retrievable norm than a beautifully appropriate adaptation to a world of pure contingencies.[5]

By writing his first sentence then 'trusting to Almighty God for the second'[6], Tristram displays a faith in divine benevolence as well as indifference

---

[4] *TS*, 4.13.341. I quote from Melvyn New's Florida edition of *TS*, giving references in brackets in the form (Volume number. Chapter. Page number). See Laurence Sterne, *The Life and Opinions of Tristram Shandy, Gentleman*, ed. by Melvyn New and Joan New, 3 vols (Gainesville: University of Florida Presses, 1978–1984).

[5] Fred Parker, *Scepticism and Literature: An Essay on Pope, Hume, Sterne, and Johnson* (Oxford: Oxford University Press, 2003), p. 190.

[6] *TS*, 8.2.656.

to the conventions of a linear narrative. And so, while much of the first four volumes is taken up with the day of his birth, we learn far more about the cast of eccentrics who fill the Shandy household on this fateful day than we do about the narrator. As his mother lies upstairs in labour, Walter, his father and an inveterate theorizer, plans for the future education of his heir. Doctor Slop, who is nominally in attendance as a physician, spends most of the time downstairs talking to the local parson Yorick, Tristram's Uncle Toby, and Corporal Trim—Toby's servant and confidant. Their conversation, the reading of a sermon, a treatise on invitro baptism, the exact terms of Mrs Shandy's lying-in arrangements, and the moment of conception itself are just a few of the digressions through which Tristram trips up any attempt to get on with narrating his life. For the remainder of the novel, we follow Uncle Toby's attempts to recreate in his back garden the siege of Namur, and his 'amours' with the Widow Wadman; Tristram's travels in Europe; the frustration of Walter's attempts to bring up a son according to his carefully wrought theories; the interpolation of folk tales; numerous dedications; black, blank, and marbled pages. In short, an endless series of more and less pertinent digressions, culminating with the cock and bull story that draws the novel to a close.

## STERNE NOT QUITE IN SPAIN

The summer of 1763 found Laurence Sterne in the French town of Bagnères-en-Bigorre. He had intended that this small resort in the Pyrenean foothills should be his starting point for a brief trip across the frontier into Spain, land of his beloved Cervantes. Ever desirous of new material for the ongoing *TS*, he anticipated spending 'a week in that kingdom, which is enough for a fertile brain to write a volume upon'.[7] Misfortune was to intervene, however, and prevent him from setting foot on Spanish soil. A sufferer from tuberculosis since a severe attack while an undergraduate at Jesus College, Cambridge, he was forced to abandon any idea of crossing the Pyrenees when the thin mountain air caused his lungs to haemorrhage.[8] If the subsequent reception of his works in the Iberian Peninsula is any indication of the welcome he might have received, it is better for him that ill health scuppered his plans. As we have already seen, no attempt was made to translate *TS* into Spanish until as late as

[7] *Letters of Laurence Sterne*, ed. by Lewis Perry Curtis (Oxford: Clarendon Press, 1935), p. 198.
[8] Ian Campbell Ross, *Laurence Sterne: A Life* (Oxford: Oxford University Press, 2001), pp. 298–9.

1975, and a Portuguese translation had to wait until 1986.[9] The first Spanish version of *A Sentimental Journey* presented to censors in 1799 was rejected on the basis that, 'Neither delight nor pleasure can be obtained from reading it as it is merely constituted by a collection of incoherent trivialities'.[10] Though the censor in that instance had found nothing in *A Sentimental Journey* to offend the ecclesiastical authorities, he disliked it on aesthetic grounds that sufficed to prevent its publication. I wish to examine some of the possible reasons why Sterne could not reach a Spanish audience.

It would be wrong to assume that the England in which *TS* first appeared was unanimous in its praise of this latest literary novelty. Getting his work between hard covers was no easy matter for Sterne who had to take out a considerable loan in order to finance the private printing of the first two volumes in late 1759. A parson with a parish in Sutton near York, he was hampered by his distance from London, the hub of all that was then fashionable in England. His astuteness in striking a distribution deal with a renowned London bookseller, coupled with bare-faced self-promotion, ensured that he recouped his initial outlay with room to spare. His self-promotion included asking an actress friend to write to David Garrick, the famous actor whose influence on public taste Sterne hoped would secure *TS*'s success, a letter fulsomely recommending his book:[11] of course, he dictated the letter himself, but the ruse worked—Garrick liked the novel and, when they met later in 1760, he and Sterne became firm friends. That first edition of *TS* was published anonymously, with many reviewers referring to the author as Tristram Shandy. Sterne's most recent biographer, Ian Campbell Ross, notes that reviews of the first two volumes were initially positive and did not decry as immoral the bawdy content of several of its scenes: 'What happened to change the generally benign, as well as enthusiastic reception the book received was the revelation that its author was a clergyman'.[12] What was acceptable from a private citizen was not to be tolerated from a man of the cloth, and reviewers began to mention Sterne's vocation when registering their disapproval of the novel's sexual content. Such criticism dogged each of the successive instalments in which *TS* appeared and contributed to its waning popularity.[13]

[9] 'The Unfortunate Journey of Laurence Sterne Through Spain', pp. 24–53; Philippe Humblé, 'A tradução de *Tristram Shandy*', *Ilha do desterro*, 17 (1987), 63–75.
[10] 'The Unfortunate Journey of Laurence Sterne Through Spain', pp. 25–6.
[11] Ross, p. 214.    [12] Ross, p. 222.
[13] *TS* was published in two-volume instalments, with the exception of the last, volume nine, which appeared alone. Volumes one and two appeared in December 1759, three and four in January 1761, five and six in January 1762, seven and eight in January 1765, and volume nine in January 1767.

Whereas in Britain reviewers contented themselves with registering their disapproval of Sterne's liberties, Spain had by the mid eighteenth century honed a system of censorship that sought to ensure undesirable material never fell beneath the eyes of readers. According to Richard Herr, conservative opposition to Enlightenment thought during this period meant that the Inquisition was particularly active in rooting out prohibited or dangerous foreign texts. Even when the latter had been printed outside Spain, they could not be distributed until they had received the permission of an official censor. Operating through a network of Church and State oppression, the Inquisition was ruthlessly efficient. Calvin, Cervantes, Dante, Defoe, Erasmus, Luther, and Petrarch all found their names on the Index of prohibited works.[14] Given such a climate, Sterne's bawdy farce stood no chance. In the opinion of one scholar, 'coartó sin la menor duda este puritanismo... las posibilidades de renovación literaria, sobre todo las del teatro y la novela' ('This puritanism undoubtedly hampered... the chances of literary renewal, above all those of the Spanish theatre and novel').[15] Censors concentrated their efforts particularly on the French frontier, perceived to be among the most likely entry points for banned books. It was also the most likely route *TS* would have taken into Spain. Although popular in France, *TS* was still being read there in English and a partial translation of the novel had to wait until 1776, several years after the initial hype had subsided. Two eighteenth-century English novelists whose work did make it over the frontier, Fielding and Richardson, were in fact translated from French versions of their works. In their case, what probably allowed their work to find favour were the 'máximas preciosas para la instruccion [*sic*] de la juventud de ambos sexos' ('precious maxims for the instruction of young people of both sexes'), which were used as *Pamela*'s selling points in a Madrid newspaper advertisement.[16] Without more detailed research, we must accept that, on balance of probabilities, the scurrilousness of Sterne's writings, the late arrival of a French translation, and lack of any self-evident morality all discouraged their publication in Spain in the late eighteenth century. Sterne was known to at least one of Spain's nineteenth-century novelists but why his omission from the canon should have taken nearly two centuries to remedy is a question beyond my competence to answer. In his essay on Dickens, Galdós bemoaned the fact that the subtleties of Sterne's humour—or indeed any humour—would be lost on his compatriots,

[14] Richard Herr, *The Eighteenth-Century Revolution in Spain* (Princeton: Princeton University Press, 1958), pp. 201–7.
[15] *Historia de la Edición y de la Lectura en España 1472–1914*, ed. by Víctor Infantes et al. (Madrid: Fundación Germán Sánchez Ruipérez, 2003), p. 279.
[16] See Ada M. Coe, 'Richardson in Spain', *Hispanic Review*, 3 (1935), 56–63 (p. 57).

whose reading habits still ran only to pot-boilers: 'A los que de modo tan exclusivo buscan en la lectura de novelas la provocación y el estímulo de sus sentimientos adormecidos, no les mandéis leer una novela inglesa. No sabrán reír con Sterne, ni llorar con Richardson, ni horrorizarse con Poe' ('Don't ask those who so exclusively seek through reading the provocation and stimulation of their numbed feelings to read an English novel. They won't know how to laugh with Sterne, or cry with Richardson, or be horrified with Poe').[17] So it was that José Antonio López de Letona had the honour of putting his name to the first Spanish translation of *TS*, published by Ediciones del Centro in 1975. According to Pegenaute, that distinction ought to have fallen to Francisco Luis Cardona who announced the imminent publication of his version of *TS* in 1943:[18] the edition seems never to have appeared, if it existed at all. Ana María Aznar produced Spain's second *TS* translation in 1976, publishing it through Clásicos Universales Planeta. Alfaguara published Marías's version in 1978, along with a selection of four of Sterne's sermons, a move simply intended to differentiate his edition from those already available.[19] While I do not intend to devote any attention to Letona and Aznar's translations, it is worth asking what was it about the literary climate of mid-1970s Spain that suddenly made *TS* as indispensable as three translations in four years would suggest. Were publishers making up for lost time or were there more identifiable cultural trends within which we might place *TS*?

Among the reviewers of Letona's first Spanish translation of *TS* was José Luis Giménez-Frontín, the man whom Marías would later succeed in the post of lecturer by decree at Oxford.[20] In his view *TS*

> is one of those literary figures that I have most frequently heard about in the intellectually initiated circles of this country, but until now I had not been able to gather any proof that any of my interlocutors or informants had ever read it, to the extent that I had even suspected its very existence.[21]

---

[17] Benito Pérez Galdós, 'Carlos Dickens', in his *Ensayos de crítica literaria*, ed. by Laureano Bonet (Barcelona: Península, 1999), pp. 116–22 (p. 117).

[18] 'The Unfortunate Journey of Laurence Sterne through Spain', pp. 29–30.

[19] It was Claudio Guillén, in his role as chief editor of the Clásicos Alfaguara series, who commissioned Marías to translate *TS* after the latter had expressed his interest in the project. Links between the Marías and Guillén families stretch back before Javier's birth. We recall that Jorge Guillén, Claudio's father, helped Julián Marías secure his first visiting lectureship in the United States. This is not to suggest that any degree of nepotism was involved: Guillén would have been foolish indeed to employ a translator he did not think was up to the job, especially when *TS* presents challenges with which a flat-footed linguist would be simply unable to cope.

[20] Giménez-Frontín would also produce an autobiographical work out of his experiences in Oxford. See José Luis Giménez-Frontín, *Woodstock Road en julio: Notas y diario* (Iruña-Pamplona: Pamiela, 1996). It owes much, if not too much, to Marías's novel *TLA*.

[21] See 'The Unfortunate Journey of Laurence Sterne through Spain', pp. 37, 49.

Fascinating as this insight is, as much for what it tells us about Giménez-Frontín's anxiety at not being among the 'initiated' as for what it says about Spanish intellectual circles in the mid 1970s, it is disappointingly short on detail. What is certain is that *TS* was much discussed by Spanish intellectuals at this time. I wish to suggest some of the reasons why this may have been the case.

As we saw in Chapter 2, Benet's *La inspiración y el estilo* (1966) argued against politically committed literature and defended the writer's intellectual freedom in ways that resonated with Marías and other members of his generation. Carmen Martín Gaite echoed Benet's pleas in *La búsqueda de interlocutor* (published in September of the same year) and dedicated the title essay to him—'Para Juan Benet, cuando no era famoso' ('For Juan Benet, when he wasn't famous'). There she covers much of the same ground, defending the idea that the best novels are those written by individuals who have contemplated in private the horrors of the human condition; that novels written to criticize social pressures rather than out of personal enjoyment are dead before they are born; that writing should be fun:

> ¿Quién tiene presente finalidad alguna cuando se lanza a un juego? Se habla luego de finalidades para justificarlo, pero solo [*sic*] se juega porque ilusiona y divierte, porque aquel terreno supone riesgo y porque en él se prueban la emoción y la zozobra. Es el motivo de las empresas lúdicas, entre las que, desde luego, no vacilo en incluir la literatura, como fenómeno absolutamente gratuito que es, aunque hoy día se ponga tan terco empeño en embutirla dentro de los uniformes del deber y la obligatoriedad.

> No se me oculta que estoy tocando un punto peliagudo al sacar a relucir un concepto tan teñido de proscripción como es el de juego, y ya me parece oír los acentos escandalizados de quienes, esgrimiendo las tópicas salvedades de 'literatura de evasión' y 'literatura de compromiso', van a negar para muchos casos la licitud de mi afirmación, que mantengo, a pesar de todo, atribuyéndole una validez general: en cualquier caso de nuevo empeño literario, encontraremos juego en su raíz.[22]

> (Who has in mind any purpose at all when they embark on a game? One talks afterwards of purpose to justify it, but really one plays only because it's exciting and fun, because the game's territory entails risk and because there one feels anticipation and anxiety. They are the reasons behind all ludic enterprises, among which, of course, I don't hesitate to include literature, like the completely gratuitous phenomenon that it is, although in this day and age so obstinate an insistence is deployed in trying to shoehorn it into the uniforms of duty and obligation.

---

[22] Carmen Martín Gaite, *La búsqueda de interlocutor y otras búsquedas* (Madrid: Nostromo, 1973), p. 23.

It hasn't escaped my notice that I am touching a thorny issue by bringing up a concept as tainted with proscriptions as the notion of game is, and I believe I can already hear the scandalized tones of those who, brandishing the hackneyed provisos of 'escapist literature' and 'committed literature', will deny in many cases the legitimacy of my statement, one which, in spite of all, I stand by, attributing to it a universal validity: in any case of new literary endeavour we will find play at its root.)

Her insistence that play lies at the heart of literary endeavour adds to the weight of opinion that was seeking to distance Spanish letters from the po-faced seriousness of the Franco era. A literary culture that had the ability to smile could look to few better antidotes than Sterne's ludic masterpiece. As we have seen, Goytisolo was among the writers who drew attention to the funereal gravity that blighted Spanish fiction under Franco. Can it be any coincidence that his novel *Juan sin tierra* (1975) owed a debt to *TS* that he was quick to acknowledge?[23]

The belated translation and reception of Sterne on the Iberian Peninsula coincided with a renaissance of interest in Sterne in Anglophone academic circles. Even in Sterne's lifetime, *TS*'s star began to wane and interest in it fell away from the heights of enthusiasm with which it had first been greeted. Subsequent revelations over the amount of material Sterne 'borrowed' from Robert Burton's *The Anatomy of Melancholy* (first edition 1621) further helped to undermine the former's credibility. Whereas prominent writers, among them Dickens, Hazlitt, Joyce, and Woolf defended his legacy vociferously, academic appreciation had, until the second half of the twentieth century, been conspicuous by its absence. Such were the depths to which opinion of Sterne had sunk by the early twentieth century that F. R. Leavis felt able to dismiss his contribution to the English novel in a brief footnote.[24] According to Melvyn New, *TS*'s most recent and conscientious editor, the revival of interest in Sterne could be attributable to our growing awareness that art which draws attention to what we do not know may be salutary:

> Because every fiber of our being cries out to resolve the painful (threatening) mysteries surrounding us, the artist whose work embodies a countervailing tendency has much to show us. Sterne's increasing reputation, which has grown perhaps more than that of any eighteenth-century author in the past half century, strongly suggests that modern readers and writers alike feel an

---

[23] For a fuller discussion of Sterne's influence on Goytisolo, see Abigail E. Lee, 'Sterne's Legacy to Juan Goytisolo: A Shandyian Reading of *Juan sin tierra*', *Modern Language Review*, 84 (1989), 351–7.

[24] F. R. Leavis, *The Great Tradition: George Eliot, Henry James, Joseph Conrad* (Harmondsworth: Peregrine, 1962), p. 11.

urgent need to understand and cultivate Sterne's antirationalism as this most rational—and murderous—century draws to a close.[25]

Four decades before, John Traugott cited the learned editing of *TS* by James Aiken Work as a necessary antidote to the long period in which the novel was too easily dismissed as trivial.[26] Undoubtedly modern readers and academics have found in Sterne what some like to call postmodernism 'avant la lettre'—the self-conscious display of the artifice of narrative. This renewed enthusiasm for Sterne in Anglophone circles seems to have coincided tellingly with attention in Spain. What this renaissance of interest meant in practice was that the now definitive Florida edition of *TS* came out a matter of months after Marías's Spanish version.[27]

## MARÍAS'S SHANDY: TEXTUAL APPARATUS AND THE 'NOTA SOBRE EL TEXTO'

I alluded above to the impressionistic approach Pegenaute took when he assessed the three versions of *TS* that appeared in Spain in the 1970s. Perhaps because of the restrictions on space imposed by academic journals, he offers no direct textual comparisons to substantiate the claim that, of the three versions, Marías's is the superior. In his view, Letona's translation displays 'incompetence' while Aznar's 'contains a far smaller number of both covertly and overtly erroneous errors, even if these two kinds of errors still prove to be very numerous'. Marías's, by contrast, endeavours to preserve the rhythm of Sterne's prose by making small alterations in syntax; his version likewise retains the eccentric punctuation of the original, and eschews cultural adaptation to Spanish norms.[28] There is a striking similarity between Pegenaute's claims and Marías's 'Nota sobre el texto' (xli–xlv): all three points are made by the translator himself. It is difficult to see how else Pegenaute arrived at these conclusions since he offers no examples to illustrate his argument. His article does suggest familiarity with the textual notes to Marías's edition since he observes that '[he] has decided to juxtapose the two different Spanish meanings of certain English puns even if he loses some naturalness', but again does not offer an actual example.

[25] Melvyn New, *Tristram Shandy: A Book for Free Spirits* (New York: Twayne, 1994), p. 11.
[26] John Traugott, *Tristram Shandy's World: Sterne's Philosophical Rhetoric* (Berkeley: University of California Press, 1954), p. xii.
[27] He worked from the aforementioned Work edition, alongside that of Graham Petrie who had edited *TS* for the Penguin Classics series in 1967.
[28] 'The Unfortunate Journey of Laurence Sterne Through Spain', pp. 41–4.

My analysis of Marías's translation is based on close textual reading: I quote passages from *TS*, in English, and then describe how the translator has confronted the particular challenges presented by that extract. Providing a representative selection from a novel as long and diverse as *TS* is no easy matter. The challenges a translator of Sterne faces include rendering Sterne's frequent innuendo and occasionally opaque vocabulary; the rhythm of sentences (on which humour or pathos often rest), and the shifts in register from smutty dialogue to high-flown, religious or scientific rhetoric must also be considered.

Before going on to discuss topics of greater interest, I must make some general remarks about the features of Marías's *TS* edition. Background material includes an Introduction by Andrew Wright, a chronology of Sterne's life, a select bibliography, and the translator's note.[29] Wright appears to have written his introduction especially for the Spanish edition, as I have not found it elsewhere: he is, moreover, the first name on Marías's list of those he thanks for their help with the edition.[30]

To set his translation apart from those too recently written by Letona and Aznar, he offers four translated sermons from the first volume of *The Sermons of Mr Yorick*. The decision was perhaps also intended to help the reader observe the parallels between Sterne's pulpit oratory and the prose rhythms of *TS*, parallels to which John Traugott draws attention in his study of Sterne's rhetoric.[31] A textual note[32] reveals that Marías was familiar with Traugott's study and would explain why he reproduces almost verbatim the latter's claim in his translator's note.[33] The glossary[34] includes rhetorical terms, obscure vocabulary, and the wealth of military terminology for which explanations are often supplied in English-language editions of the novel.

Marías cannot help indulging in some gentle Shandyism of his own in the translator's note:

Si ahora soy yo quien se interpone entre el texto y el lector paciente (el impaciente hace ya rato que, con bastante buen criterio, estará disfrutando de *Tristram Shandy*) es, al menos en parte (quiero creerlo), por el bien de ambos: no me guía otra intención, lo juro, que la de restarle obstáculos al primero y ahorrarle al segundo ciertos engorros con los que, si es demasiado curioso o

---

[29] The bibliography is in many ways far from 'selecta', and includes some recherché writings on Sterne, including Virginia Woolf and William Hazlitt. It would appear to be testimony to the considerable amount of research Marías undertook in order to grapple adequately with *TS*.

[30] 'Note sobre el texto', p. xlv.

[31] Traugott, *Tristram Shandy's World*, p. xiv.

[32] *La vida y opiniones del caballero Tristram Shandy*, p. 631.

[33] *La vida y opiniones*, p. xliii.   [34] *La vida y opiniones*, pp. 711–18.

está ávido de información, puede tropezarse a lo largo de la presente edición.[35]

(If it is now me who intervenes between text and patient reader [the impatient reader will, with pretty good reason, have started *Tristram Shandy* some time ago] it is, at least in part [I would like to believe], for the good of both: I am not guided, I promise, by any intention other than to spare the former a few obstacles and spare the latter some hassles across which, if he is too curious or eager for information, he might stumble in the course of the present edition.)

His awareness (or hope) that some readers will have long since lost interest in his edition's scholarly apparatus counterpoints Tristram's rebuke to those who read 'more in quest of the adventures, than of the deep erudition and knowledge which a book of this cast, if read over as it should be, would infallibly impart'.[36] In the chapter just quoted, Tristram insists that 'Madam', the careless female reader he has embedded in *TS*, look over the previous chapter again for proof that his mother was not a papist. While she returns to pay her penance, the rest of his readership continues, creating a situation in which the novel is read at different paces and in parallel by different readers.

Apologetic though Marías's opening gambit is, he does have useful information to impart. He first tackles the subject of fidelity to the original English, bemoaning the 'lamentable y generalizada tendencia de los traductores a *castellanizar* los textos extranjeros de tal forma que cualquier vestigio de su condición de obra inglesa, o francesa, o alemana, queda borrado' ('lamentable and widespread tendency among translators to *hispanize* foreign texts in such a way that any vestige of their nature as English, French or German works is lost').[37]

Rather than a text full of 'inoportunos casticismos' ('unfortunate Castilianisms'), he wants to 'posibilitar la *adivinación* del texto inglés por parte del lector español' ('to make it possible for the Spanish reader to *intuit* the English text'), the realization of the practice he was to defend four years later in 'La traducción como fingimiento y representación', as we have already seen. According to Pegenaute, Marías consulted Letona's translation and found 'absurd' the latter's decision to transpose British cultural references for Spanish equivalents.[38] His translation practice, by contrast, was founded on Ortega's belief that: 'Sólo cuando arrancamos al lector de sus hábitos lingüísticos y le obligamos a moverse dentro de los

---

[35] *La vida y opiniones*, p. xliii.    [36] *TS*, 1.20.65.
[37] *La vida y opiniones*, p. xliii.
[38] 'The Unfortunate Journey of Laurence Sterne Through Spain', p. 34.

del autor, hay propiamente traducción. Hasta ahora casi no se han hecho más que pseudotraducciones' ('Only when we tear the reader away from his linguistic habits and force him to move among those of the author, only then is translation really happening. Until now there have hardly been anything other than pseudotranslations').[39]

To give some examples of what this means in practice in his version of *TS*, the refusal to naturalize foreign elements for a Spanish audience becomes evident in the first chapter, where the phrases 'los humores' ('the humours') and 'espíritus animales' ('animal spirits') warrant notes about English eighteenth-century medical theory. '¡Por D—!' elicits the explanation that blasphemy was considered more sinful on the eighteenth-century British ear than it will appear to the modern Spanish reader. We also see the following as early as the second chapter, during Tristram's discussion of the 'HOMONCULUS': '[It] is a being of as much activity,—and, in all senses of the word, as much and as truly our fellow-creature as my Lord Chancellor of England'.[40] Marías translates 'my Lord' using the Anglicism 'milord' and provides a textual note to the effect that 'el Canciller de Inglaterra'[41] 'es el equivalente... del Ministro de Justicia'[42] ('is the equivalent... of the Minister for Justice'). He provides the Spanish reader with enough information to understand the reference while not shying away from the title's cultural specificity. A more obvious example is offered by Marías's use of the English titles 'Mr' and 'Mrs' for Tristram's parents. What Marías's practice insists upon is otherness, but one leavened by the kind of rigorous footnoting that Nabokov believed was an essential component of all genuine translation. As Venuti has noted, '[t]ranslation is always ideological because it releases a domestic remainder, an inscription of values, beliefs, and representations linked to historical moments and social positions in the receiving culture'.[43] Although inadvertently drawing attention to the implicit belief systems of Spaniards at the end of the 1970s, Marías's translation is also challenging his readers to absorb something entirely new.

Curiously enough *TS* presents what might be the acid test of a Spanish translator's determination to retain the foreignness of an alien text. The passages that present such a test are, of course, those in which Sterne paraphrases Cervantes. In the course of his chapter on sleep[44] Tristram has occasion to paraphrase Sancho Panza's blessing:

---

[39] 'Miseria y esplendor de la traducción', pp. 448–9.   [40] *TS*, 1.2.3.
[41] *La vida y opiniones*, p. 6.   [42] *La vida y opiniones*, p. 630.
[43] Venuti, 'Translation, Community, Utopia', p. 498.   [44] *TS*, 4.15.

y bien haya el que inventó el sueño, capa que cubre todos los humanos pen-
samientos, manjar que quita la hambre, agua que ahuyenta la sed, fuego que
calienta el frío, frío que templa el ardor y, finalmente, moneda general con
que todas las cosas se compran, balanza y peso que iguala al pastor con el rey
y al simple con el discreto.[45]

(long live the man who invented sleep, the cloak that covers all human
thoughts, the food that takes away hunger, the water that chases away thirst,
the fire that warms the cold, the cold that cools the heat and, in short, the
universal coinage that can buy anything, the scales and weights that make
the shepherd the equal of the king and the fool the equal of the wise
man.)[46]

Sterne glosses rather than reproduces the words verbatim and so Marías,
rather than restore the original Cervantine Spanish, translates the gloss:
' "God's blessing, said *Sancho Pança*, "be upon the man who first invented
this self-same thing called sleep—it covers a man all over like a cloak" '[47]:
'Que Dios bendiga' dijo Sancho Panza, 'al hombre que inventara el
sueño,—que cubre a los hombres de la cabeza a los pies como si fuera un
manto'.[48] He follows the same criteria when translating Yorick's last words.
Tristram narrates the death of the local parson in chapter twelve of the
first volume, the reader having only been introduced to him in the previous chapter. Like Sterne, Yorick is a country clergyman too given to high
spirits to gain advancement in the church. On his death bed, he despairs
of ever finding preferment: 'I might say with Sancho Pança, that should I
recover, and "Mitres thereupon be suffered to rain down from heaven as
thick as hail, not one of 'em would fit it [his head]" '.[49] He adapts Sancho's
doubts over his wife's suitability to reign as queen: 'tengo para mí que,
aunque lloviese reinos sobre la tierra, ninguno asentaría bien sobre la
cabeza de Mari Gutiérrez'.[50] Marías once again rejects the idea of restoring
the original Spanish: 'que podría decir, con Sancho Panza, que si me reco-
brara y el cielo consintiera en que desde allí llovieran Mitras como si fuera
granizo espeso, ninguna le sentaría bien'.[51]

The remainder of Marías's 'Nota sobre el texto' is devoted to discussion
of the notes he has provided at the end of the volume. Far from revelling
in the research that produced them, he encourages the casual reader to

[45] Miguel de Cervantes Saavedra, *Don Quijote de la Mancha*, ed. by Francisco Rico, 2nd
edn, 2 vols (Barcelona: Instituto Cervantes, 1998), I, 1180.
[46] Miguel de Cervantes Saavedra, *The Ingenious Hidalgo Don Quixote de la Mancha*,
trans. by John Rutherford (London: Penguin, 2003), p. 945.
[47] *TS*, 4.15.347.        [48] *La vida y opiniones*, p. 254.
[49] *TS*, 1.12.34.        [50] *Don Quijote de la Mancha*, I, p. 94.
[51] *La vida y opiniones*, p. 29.

ignore them: breaking off to consult notes interrupts the novel's rhythm, rhythm he has tried so painstakingly to maintain in his Spanish:

> Confieso, en cambio, que al mismo tiempo hay en la traducción algunas infidelidades notorias (tales como la adición o supresión de un adjetivo, por ejemplo), que, sin embargo, no pertenecen al orden del capricho; están justificadas por una cuestión de ritmo, esencial en la novela de Sterne, y, sin estas ligeras libertades, dicho ritmo podría haberse visto gravemente alterado o trastocado al verter el texto al castellano.[52]

> (I confess, however, that at the same time my translation contains some obvious infidelities [such as the addition or subtraction of an adjective, for example], which, nevertheless, are not simply the product of caprice; they are justified by considerations of rhythm, essential to Sterne's novel, and, without these minor liberties, the aforementioned rhythm could have ended up being gravely upset or disrupted by its passage into Castilian.)

He claims furthermore that 'lo esencial de *Tristram Shandy*... no está en las notas, sino en el texto' ('the heart of *Tristsam Shandy*... is not in the notes but in the text').[53] Joaquim Mallafrè had to ask himself how much of *TS*'s difficult or obscure content to explain through potentially cumbersome notes when producing his 1993 Catalan version.[54] By his own account, he did not wish his translation to seem like 'an archaeological object of study, displayed in the pantheon of the illustrious dead'.[55] His brand of leaving the reader to do the work borders on the cavalier, especially when he remarks that 'some pieces of information can be found in easily available guides or encyclopaedias'. What he maintains above all, however, is the need to let Sterne's text flow with the humour that pervades it. I shall discuss Marias's notes in more detail when examining his translation of *TS*'s jokes.


## TRISTRAM'S OPENING GAMBIT

I now offer more detailed textual analysis, starting with Tristram's unforgettable opening gambit. To provide his reader with all the information necessary from which to form an opinion of his character, Tristram takes the proposition to its logical extreme and starts his autobiography with his conception. As we shall see, sex in the Shandy household is a purely functional affair, dispatched without enthusiasm on the first Sunday of

---

[52] *La vida y opiniones*, p. xliii.    [53] *La vida y opiniones*, p. xliv.
[54] Joaquim Mallafrè, 'Sterne in Catalan: Notes on Translation', *The Shandean*, 9 (1997), 109–21.
[55] 'Sterne in Catalan', p. 110.

every month. Walter Shandy, Tristram's father, makes a point of winding the clock on the same day that he performs his marital duty, such that his wife begins to associate the two—the first of many Lockean associative acts that generate much of the novel's comedy: she cannot hear the clock being wound or copulate with her husband without the parallel activity popping into her head. On the occasion of Tristram's conception, she asks, at an inopportune moment during coitus, whether Walter has wound the clock. Tristram attributes some of his misfortune to his father's distraction from the task in hand at this critical juncture.

> I wish either my father or my mother, or indeed both of them, as they were in duty both equally bound to it, had minded what they were about when they begot me; had they duly consider'd how much depended upon what they were then doing; - that not only the production of a rational Being was concern'd in it, but that possibly the happy formation and temperature of his body, perhaps his genius and the very cast of his mind.[56]

He couches his retroactive parental rebuke in language that oscillates between conversational familiarity—'minded what they were about'—and philosophical terminology—'rational Being'. Until the semicolon, the first sentence is structured in such a way as to delay the revelation of what Tristram's grievance is. Marías's version replicates this effect by forcing Spanish syntax: 'Ojalá mi padre o mi madre, mejor dicho ambos, hubieran sido más conscientes, mientras los dos se afanaban por igual en el cumplimiento de sus obligaciones, de lo que se traían entre manos cuando me engendraron'. The gap between 'conscientes' and its preposition 'de' does not sit easily on the Spanish ear, but the effect of delaying the revelation is crucial to the humour of Tristram's first words to us. Disjunction between man and wife is hinted at immediately since it is Tristram's first impulse to think of his copulating parents as separate entities. Marías translates his rectification 'or indeed' as 'mejor dicho', emphasizing the impression that Tristram is striving for the best formulation of the idea he can muster. The sense of duty that surrounds sex Marías renders as 'mientras los dos se afanaban por igual en el cumplimiento de sus obligaciones', where the emphasis falls on toil. There is irony implicit in 'por igual': despite the mutuality it implies, this is an encounter in which neither party has invested much passion, as Mrs Shandy's impertinent question attests. In contrast to the formality of 'cumplimiento' and 'obligaciones', Marías translates 'minded what they were about' as 'lo que se traían entre manos', with its sense of 'what they were up to'. He displays sensitivity to register again when giving the grand-sounding 'begot' as the

---

[56] *TS*, 1.1.1.

equivalent 'engendraron'. He notes the importance of the rhythm of the clause beginning 'that not only': 'que no sólo estaba en juego la creación de un Ser racional sino que también, posiblemente, la feliz formación y constitución de su cuerpo, tal vez su genio y hasta la naturaleza de su mente'.[57] The pause Sterne inserts—'concern'd in it, but that possibly'—Marías inserts by use of twin commas around 'posiblemente'. What the pause allows is the small crescendo of listed attributes that might have been affected by the conditions surrounding his conception, the final emphasis of which Marías gives as 'y hasta la naturaleza de su mente'.

> And being somewhere between fifty and sixty years of age, at the time I have been speaking of, - he had likewise gradually brought some other little family concernments to the same period, in order, as he would often say to my uncle *Toby*, to get them all out of the way at one time, and be no more plagued and pester'd with them the rest of the month.[58]

Tristram's careful tread around a delicate topic once more provides the humour. We note also that Sterne is aware of how rhythm affects the delivery of jokes—the skills of the orator in the pulpit and in private.[59] The hiatus created by 'in order', separated by commas from the rest of the phrase, acts as a moment in which the penny drops; what those 'little family concernments' are dawns on the reader. Though Marías cannot replicate the effect absolutely, he appreciates that the pause is there for rhetorical effect: 'había asimismo ido trasladando a las mismas fechas, de manera gradual, algunas otras pequeñas obligaciones domésticas'. By inserting the adverb 'asimismo' between the auxiliary verb 'había' and the past participle, he is forcing Spanish syntax to do that which it never normally does but which English does far more naturally. The effect is immediately one of strangeness to the Spanish reader, reinforcing the firm principle Marías was to state several years later in 'La traducción como fingimiento y representación'. More immediately in this instance, it alerts us to the fact that syntax is being forced in order to drag out the revelation of the punchline even further. The reader then glimpses what seems likely to be Walter's indirect speech: 'como le decía a menudo a mi tío Toby, quitárselas de encima todas a la vez y no tener que andar jorobado y pendiente de ellas durante el resto del mes'. The rest of *TS* confirms this early impression: this is a man who will always use two

---

[57] *La vida y opiniones*, p. 5.    [58] *TS*, 1.4.6.
[59] James Boswell, Johnson's great biographer, reportedly remarked that Sterne was 'the best companion I ever knew'. When fame eventually found him, Sterne became a fixture in fashionable London dining circles where his wit and good conversation made him a highly desirable guest. See Ross, pp. 41, 257–8.

words—'jorobado y pendiente'—when one will do. He thinks sex burdensome, hence Marías's 'quitárselas de encima'. Such measured language applied to sex, combined with the oddly gradual 'había ido trasladando', captures the deliberation with which Walter imbues all his actions.[60] In fact, his endeavours to bring order to the world of sex are those of a man who mistrusts both it and womankind. On hearing of his brother Toby's unfortunate encounter with the Widow Wadman, he rails: 'que la totalidad de los males y desórdenes del mundo, fueran de la clase y naturaleza que fuesen, desde la caída inicial de Adán hasta la de mi tío Toby (inclusive), se debían siempre, de una u otra forma, al mismo apetito desenfrenado'.[61]

## ASYSTEMIC HUMAN REACTIONS: TOBY AND WALTER

The two brothers' contrasting reactions to the revelation of sexual desire offer substantial insights into their respective characters. Whereas Walter

> from a little subacid kind of drollish impatience in his nature, whenever it befell him, he would never submit to it like a christian; but would pish, and huff, and bounce, and kick, and play the Devil, and write the bitterest Philippicks against the eye that ever man wrote.[62]

Uncle Toby

> on the contrary took it like a lamb – sat still and let the poison work in his veins without resistance – in the sharpest exacerbations of his wound (like that on his groin) he never dropt one fretful or discontented word – he blamed neither heaven nor earth – or thought or spoke an injurious thing of any body, or any part of it; he sat solitary and pensive with his pipe – looking at his lame leg – then whiffling out a sentimental heigh ho! which mixing with the smoak, incommoded no one mortal.[63]

For Marías there seems little option but to translate Walter's 'subacid kind of drollish impatience...' as literally as possible: 'una especie de impaciencia extravagante, bastante graciosa y un poco agria'. It appears that the sequence of actions with which Walter displays his displeasure are a

---

[60] *La vida y opiniones*, p. 9.
[61] *La vida y opiniones*, p. 573. The Widow Wadman had been anxious to ascertain the extent of Toby's groin injury, sustained at the Battle of Namur, with a view to the possibility of his fathering her child. Ever the innocent, Toby imagines that she shares his interest in the exact disposition of the battlefield and it falls to the more worldly Trim to disabuse him. The revelation precipitates the end of all relations with the Widow Wadman.
[62] *TS*, 8.26.709.        [63] *TS*, 8.26.710.

mixture of the human and the animal: humans pish whilst we might expect a horse to bounce and kick: 'sino que renegaba, y bufaba, y amenazaba, y pataleaba, la mandaba al Diablo, y escribía contra los ojos, las más amargas filípicas que jamás haya escrito hombre ninguno'.[64] Although 'play the Devil' might be paraphrased in English as 'act up', Marías turns the phrase into a curse, which is perhaps not the most successful solution.

In his version of Toby's response, Marías is able, through the Spanish use of double negatives, to heighten the impression that Toby could (literally, as we shall see) never hurt a fly: 'no culpó ni al cielo ni a la tierra;—ni pensó o dijo nada injurioso de nadie ni de ninguna de las partes del cuerpo del susodicho nadie'. In fact 'se lo tomó como un corderillo', where the diminutive augments the effect of the English 'lamb'. Toby's ever-present physical props, whether his pipe or stick, provide telling physical detail in descriptions of the man who Hazlitt described as 'the finest compliment ever paid to human nature':[65] 'se sentó, solitario y pensativo, con su pipa entre los labios;—se miró la pierna lisiada,—y a continuación exhaló un sentimental ¡ayayay! que al salir mezclado con el humo, no incomodó a ningún mortal'.[66] Once again Marías has caught the rhythm and balance of the sentence with the insertion of commas providing key rhetorical pauses.

The idiosyncrasy and unfathomability of human behaviour were of great interest to Sterne. In the view of Thomas Keymer, he had become aware that eighteenth-century novelists were prone to hubristic claims about their ability to scrutinize human actions.[67] More specifically, Keymer identifies Samuel Richardson as the principal target of Sterne's satire. Tristram's minute observation of human gesture—Toby looking over his pipe[68] or rubbing his nose[69]—is thus best thought of as parodying Richardson's belief that by observing his characters at close quarters, he is able to reveal inner turmoil through the interpretation of gesture:

---

[64] *La vida y opiniones*, p. 515.
[65] *The Collected Works of William Hazlitt*, ed. by A. R. Walker and Arnold Glover, 13 vols (London: Dent, 1902–1906), VIII (1903), 106–32 (p. 121).
[66] *La vida y opiniones*, p. 516.
[67] Thomas Keymer, *Sterne, the Moderns, and the Novel* (Oxford: Oxford University Press, 2002). Christopher Ricks is of the same opinion: 'But all the same the limits of a novelist's (and indeed any man's) knowledge and power are wittily and resolutely insisted on. The novelist, like the rest of us, is committed to the idea of getting to know people, but he must not get too confident about his ability to know what makes so-and-so tick'. See his 'Introductory Essay', in Laurence Sterne, *The Life and Opinions of Tristram Shandy, Gentleman*, ed. by Melvyn New and Joan New, rev. edn (Harmondsworth: Penguin, 2003), pp. xi–xxxii (p. xviii).
[68] *TS*, 3.40.281.    [69] *TS*, 3.33.260.

Richardsonian replays of this kind take on a more critical edge, in ways that seem to challenge the pretensions of circumstantial realism to disclose inward psychological truth as well as outward material fact (a key plank in a theory of fiction claiming to reveal – as Warburton, for one, had said of it –'the recesses of the Human Mind').[70]

A textual note in Marías's translation[71] reveals his awareness that Richardson is the target of Sterne's barbs. Walter, the inveterate systematizer, is one of the vehicles through which such parody is achieved, since he takes all his learning from the printed page:

> In truth, there was not a stage in the life of man, from the very first act of his begetting, - down to the lean and slipper'd pantaloon in his second childishness, but that he had some favourite notion to himself, springing out of it, as sceptical, and as far out of the high-way of thinking, as these two which have been explained.[72]

With one of his most striking and effective passages, Sterne describes Walter's systematization of every stage of the life of man. Regrettably for Marías's Spanish readers, he does not realize that Walter's tendency to think of man in general terms is what is in play here. Instead, Marías mistranslates 'man' to mean 'this man' (Walter Shandy)—'no hubo un sólo momento de la vida de este hombre'.[73] From this initial mistake, a cascade of errors follows: 'desde el mismísimo instante en que fue engendrado—hasta que durante su segunda infancia se convirtió en una especie de delgado arlequín enzapatillado'.[74] Sterne's alliterative and affectionate evocation of old age thus begins to seem like a needless, direct insult to Walter. We might even take issue with the word 'arlequín' since 'pantaloon' is surely being used in its generic sense of a foolish old man, rather than a particular character type from late eighteenth-century drama.

And yet, while Walter may be the vehicle for parody, it is precisely through him that Sterne brings his readers up short, slicing through their too-readily-formed opinions. If, as Tristram maintains, reading should be like a conversation, then the description of Walter we are about to examine is a riposte to our insensitive appreciation of his text. Readers must be tamed as well as flattered.

The unfortunate incident involving a sash window and Tristram's genitalia would, we might expect, send Walter Shandy into a depthless despair,

---

[70] Keymer, p. 43.     [71] *La vida y opiniones*, p. 52; note at p. 640.
[72] *TS*, 2.19.170.
[73] This is not the only occasion on which we find Marías mistranslating the word 'man' or 'men' when used generically. He would appear to have something of a blind spot over it.
[74] *La vida y opiniones*, p. 125.

were it not for the fact that Tristram reminds us to take nothing for granted:

> As many pictures have been given of my father, how like him soever in different airs and attitudes, - not one, or all of them, can ever help the reader to any kind of preconception of how my father would think, speak, or act, upon the untried occasion or occurrence of life. – There was that infinitude of oddities in him, and of chances along with it, by which handle he would take a thing, - it baffled, Sir, all calculations.[75]

This appears to be one of the rare moments at which Tristram is in earnest: no irony undercuts the assertion at the last minute, and aside from the final address to yet another inscribed reader—'Sir'—his tone is flatly matter-of-fact. Marías translates in much the same vein: 'Aunque ya he hecho numerosísimas descripciones de mi padre en los más variados estados de ánimo y actitudes...'. Beyond the alliteration of 'ánimo' and 'actitud', matching that of 'airs and attitudes', his version is correctly prosaic—'Aunque ya he hecho'—being the simplest way of conveying Sterne's meaning. He neatly avoids the need for three verbs in the conditional tense by turning 'would think, speak, or act' into a nominal phrase: 'a la hora de intentar imaginar anticipadamente sus reacciones (de pensamiento, palabra u obra)'. When it comes to the figurative 'by which handle he would take a thing', Marías again translates literally, retaining the image of Walter approaching a new subject with the zeal and deliberation of a man whose learning is found exclusively in the obscure tomes over which he pores: 'Sus peculiaridades, y en consecuencia los mangos por los que podía asir un determinado acontecimiento, eran incontables:—hasta el extremo, señor, de que todo cálculo sería en vano'.[76]

In Tristram's world, an aspect of a man's character that partially explains his eccentricities is his 'hobby-horse'. The phrase itself presents the translator with a quandary. Joaquim Mallafrè, *TS*'s Catalan translator, explains his reasoning:

> There is a key-word in *TS*, 'hobby-horse', which has several Catalan equivalents. But the link with a horse, meaningful in Sterne (see especially *TS*, 1.24) and the derivatives ('hobby-horsical', 'hobby-horsically') could be easily lost in translation or result in a clumsy solution. I chose *cavall de batalla*, which keeps the sense of a favourite topic, without missing the 'horsical' allusion. A minor addition (*de cartró*), when the word first appears, conveys the original allusion to a toy-horse.[77]

---

[75] *TS*, 5.24.456.    [76] *La vida y opiniones*, p. 338.
[77] 'Sterne in Catalan', p. 115.

Marías opts for 'caballo de juguete', hobby horse's literal meaning, which is that of a children's toy rocking horse. Another option would have been the Castilian equivalent of Mallafrè's 'cavall de batalla'—'caballo de batalla'—which conveys the idea of a favourite topic but which Marías probably rejected on the basis that it was not silly enough: he must have wanted to evoke the image of grown men riding the 'camino real' on toy horses. His choice does also leave the difficulty of the adverbial and adjectival phrases derived from 'hobby-horse' that pepper *TS*: 'besides what [Trim] gained HOBBY-HORSICALLY, *Non hobby-horsical* per se';[78] 'the generous (tho' hobby-horsical) gallantry of my uncle *Toby*'.[79] In both cases,[80] Marías uses variations on 'caballuno', or 'caballunamente', relying on his readers to recall the earlier way in which 'caballo de juguete' was being employed. It is thus to the distinct hobby horses that they ride that we can attribute Walter and Toby's starkly contrasting reactions to love and womankind. Where Walter seeks erudition in books and systematizes, Toby wishes for no other distraction than his elaborate battle reconstructions in the company of Corporal Trim.

At the same time as warning novelists not to push their claims to omnipotence beyond the worlds of their own invention, Sterne strives to explore the mystery of human emotional responses. Why physical gestures—what we see as opposed to what we hear—should have so rapid and rich an effect on the nervous system is a question that interests him greatly. By way of illustration, he offers two contrasting responses to the death of Bobby, Tristram's older brother. The first, that of Walter, is purely verbal, whereas the second, Corporal Trim's, is an affecting mixture of rhetoric and the physical gesture. Parker says of the first that

> As Walter enthusiastically strings together his favourite classical topics of philosophical consolation in a great declamatory anthology, carried away by the energy of his own performance, he loses touch altogether with the reality of death, his nominal subject.[81]

Corporal Trim meanwhile goes below stairs to break news of Bobby's death to the Shandy household staff, all of whom appear indifferent until, that is, he delivers the following performance:

> -"Are we not here now;" - continued the corporal, "and are we not" – (dropping his hat plumb upon the ground – and pausing, before he pronounced the word) – "gone! in a moment?" The descent of the hat was as if a heavy lump of clay had been kneaded into the crown of it.[82]

---

[78] *TS*, 2.5.109.        [79] *TS*, 3.22.243.
[80] *La vida y opiniones*, pp. 82, 179.
[81] Parker, *Scepticism and Literature*, p. 193.        [82] *TS*, 5.7.432.

Trim illustrates his point—little more than a hackneyed truism—with a gesture that strips the platitude of its tired veneer and renews its meaning: 'Nothing could have expressed the sentiment of mortality, of which it was the type and fore-runner, like it'. This is a supremely artistic moment: a sentiment and its illustration through gesture coalesce to provoke the sympathy of each of the servants. Marías captures the sense of uniqueness—at that time no better illustration of death could be imagined—by translating 'Nothing' as 'ningún otro objeto': 'Ningún otro objeto podría haber expresado el sentimiento de la mortalidad como aquél, su símbolo y su presagio'.[83]

Many contemporary reviewers of *TS* wondered why Sterne, who had so great a gift for this kind of pathetic scene, indulged it only sparingly. One such anonymous reviewer wrote that *TS* contains 'some pathetic touches of nature, which compels us to wish the author had never stooped to the exhibition of buffoonery'.[84] The years after his death saw the appearance of anthologies of the sentimental scenes culled from his works that sought to slake the late eighteenth-century thirst for sensibility.[85] Many of them, like the one we are about to examine, featured Uncle Toby whose kindly nature has already been noted. Tristram recalls a moment from his childhood, his uncle's benevolence in releasing out of the window a fly that had pestered him. Why this particular configuration of sentiment and gesture should have so affected him is again a mystery. As a writer all he can hope is to recreate that impression for his reader:

> I was but ten years old when this happened; - but whether it was, that the action itself was more in unison to my nerves at that age of pity, which instantly set my whole frame into one vibration of most pleasurable sensation; - or how far the manner and expression of it might go towards it; - or in what degree, or by what secret magick, - a tone of voice and harmony of movement, attuned by mercy, might find a passage to my heart, I know not; - this I know, that the lesson of universal good-will then taught and imprinted by my uncle *Toby*, has never since been worn out of my mind.[86]

Marías's version of this passage offers insight into the translator's need to clarify and interpret as he progresses. He must first decide what the subject of the verb 'set' is, which could be 'the action itself' or 'my nerves'; he opts for the latter—'que al instante hicieron vibrar mi esqueleto con una sensación placentera'. He finds it necessary to clarify 'might go towards it',

[83] *La vida y opiniones*, p. 320.
[84] *Laurence Sterne: The Critical Heritage*, ed. by Alan B. Howes (London and New York: Routledge, 1995), p. 139. For further examples see pp. 69, 141, 167.
[85] See, for example, Laurence Sterne, *The beauties of Sterne: including all his pathetic tales, & most distinguished observations on life* (London: C. Etherington, 1782).
[86] *TS*, 2.12.131.

where 'it' is the overall effect of Toby's gesture, and supplies the verbal phrase 'me conmovieron': 'o hasta qué punto fueron el ademán y la expresión de mi tío los que me conmovieron'. Sterne's sentence is suspended through three speculative sub-clauses (and their attendant clarifications), each of which begins with a different indirect question, variation Marías also supplies—'hasta qué punto…en qué grado…por qué magia oculta'. To bring the sentence back round to its starting point, he sums up this trium- virate of questions as 'todo eso es algo que yo no sé': 'lo que sí sé es que la lección de buena voluntad universal dada y grabada en mi ánimo aquel día por mi tío Toby nunca, desde entonces, se ha borrado de mi mente'.[87] The 'tono de voz' and 'armonía de movimientos imbuidos de misericordia' are reproduced rhythmically by the alliteration in 'dada y grabada'. Again Marías uses a hiatus in rhythm around 'desde entonces' to give the final clause the weight that the English is afforded by the comma after 'Toby'.

For all this, however, there are moments when Sterne abandons words and resorts to direct visual representations. From the actual drawing out of the shape cut through the air by the flourish of Trim's stick to the black page of mourning for Yorick, *TS* plays with the physical appearance of text as no other novel had ever done. Keymer regards such recourse to the visual as a sign of desperation on Tristram's part:

> Far from connecting Tristram with his reader's conception, as he complains in his transposed preface, the 'tall, opake words' (3.235) to which he entrusts his life and opinions sturdily thwart communication. In this context there is an undertow of desperation to his most celebrated moments of resort to the visual: the black page for Yorick's death in the first instalment, the blank one for Widow Wadman's beauty in the third, and between the two, the marbled page that stands for the work as a whole.[88]

Needless to say, Marías's edition preserves each of Sterne's eccentric inno- vations: black, blank, and marbled pages are all present, as is the jump in pagination to denote the missing chapter twenty-four of the fourth vol- ume;[89] even the cross sign Dr Slop makes before falling from his horse is in the Spanish text.

## THE CHALLENGES OF HUMOUR

Among Tristram's unusual requests to his readers (though this time character- ized exclusively as male) is that they should provide the portrait of the Widow Wadman, lest his endeavours be insufficient to represent her beauty:

[87] *La vida y opiniones*, p. 98.     [88] Keymer, p. 75.
[89] *La vida y opiniones*, pp. 264–75.

To conceive this right, - call for pen and ink – here's paper ready to your hand. – Sit down, Sir, paint her to your own mind – as like your mistress as you can – as unlike your wife as your conscience will let you – 'tis all one to me – please but your own fancy in it.[90]

It is not difficult to detect one prominent aspect of Sterne's character behind these words; a man never happier than when admiring a woman other than his wife, he establishes a rakish camaraderie with male readers through the reference to infidelity. In his version Marías begins with, 'Para hacerse usted una idea adecuada de ella', translating the sense entirely, though he might have used the verb 'concebir' to retain the pun on conception that resonates from the novel's first line. The Spanish polite form of address—'Usted'—provides the nuance of distance that English must supply by other means: 'pida pluma y tinta;—aquí, bien a mano, tiene usted listo el papel.—Tome asiento, señor, y píntela o descríbala a su entero gusto:—tan parecida a su querida como le sea posible,—tan distinta de su mujer como le permita la conciencia'.[91] Note again the ease with which Marías renders the balance of 'as like your mistress as you can—as unlike your wife as your conscience will let you', using verbs which take indirect object pronouns in each clause.

By the sixth volume and its request to draw the Widow Wadman readers will have long since lost hope that Tristram is about to knuckle down to the task of conventionally narrating his life. Amidst all the chaos of promised chapters that never appear, missing pages, and impromptu French travelogue, Tristram on the one hand encourages his readers to sit back and enjoy the ride while on the other seems to have a perversely accurate picture of his novel's overall structure:

My mother, you must know, - but I have fifty things more necessary to let you know first, - I have a hundred difficulties which I have promised to clear up, and a thousand distresses and domestic misadventures crouding in upon me thick and three-fold, one upon the neck of another, - a cow broke in (to-morrow morning) to my uncle *Toby*'s fortifications, and eat up two ratios and half of dried grass, tearing up the sods with it, which faced his horn-work and covered way.[92]

Such feints heighten the effect of what has come to be known as Shandyism. In submitting his imagination to the mind's associative efforts—following his own bastardized version of Locke's theory—he takes delight in the haphazard results. It is only in the later volumes, by which time

[90] *TS*, 6.38.566.     [91] *La vida y opiniones*, p. 414.
[92] *TS*, 3.38.278.

Sterne had realized that his tuberculosis was going to kill him sooner rather than later, that a hint of desperation enters Tristram's urge to supply the best that his life and opinions have to offer: the Widow Wadman's amours with Uncle Toby. In the above extract, the humour derives from the realization that what appears to be Tristram's exaggeration could in fact be true: he could indeed have hundreds or thousands of anecdotes to share with us. The disruption of ordinary narrative time is an innovative way of presenting the muddle the narrator has created—'(to-morrow morning)'. Marías's version of this passage effectively generates the impression of tasks piling up by stacking descriptive clauses before the main subject of the sentence is revealed:

> tengo encima, además, todas apelotonadas y triplicadas, pisándose el cuello las unas a las otras, mil calamidades y desventuras domésticas que narrar: - una vaca penetró (mañana por la mañana) en las fortificaciones de mi tío Toby y se comió dos raciones y media de hierba seca, y, al hacerlo, arrancó el césped que cubría su hornabeque y su camino-cubierto.[93]

He resists any temptation to make sense of this temporal impossibility and retains the joke for the Spanish reader.

On the subject of translating *TS*'s humour Joaquim Mallafrè asserts, with some justification, that 'a joke in need of being explained is a poor joke indeed'. It is for that reason, he maintains, that he chose not to supply textual notes elucidating the frequent double entendre and word play that pepper the novel. Regrettably, by its very nature, double entendre is not always translatable: words that in one language have sexual or comic connotations may not have them in another whilst, by the same token, attempts at translating double entendre may turn it into single entendre whereby the subtly implied secondary meaning is foregrounded too prominently. Marías worried that he had fallen into the latter trap in this passage from *TS*, in which Walter, Toby, and Trim discuss exactly how it was that Mrs Bridget and Trim splintered a bridge on the mock-up battlefield to fragments:[94]

> - ¡Sí, en efecto!, decía mi padre: - en refriegas de este tipo, hermano Toby, es muy fácil romperse un miembro. - - Y así, con el permiso de usía, fue cómo el puente, que, como usía sabe, era muy ligero, se hundió entre nosotros haciéndose añicos.[95]

The word Marías translates as 'miembro' is the English 'limb', the sexual connotations of which are not far to find. However, his textual note

---

[93] *La vida y opiniones*, pp. 204–5.    [94] *TS*, 3.24.248.
[95] *La vida y opiniones*, p. 183.

reveals anxiety that he has turned a subtle joke into a rather clunking one: 'el doble sentido...no resulta, pues tan evidente y descarado en inglés como en castellano; es más velado y menos perceptible'.[96] We might also note in passing that Marías uses 'con el permiso de usía' and 'como usía sabe' to translate 'your honour', the courtesy title Trim confers on most of his interlocutors. His remarks usually open with 'an' please your worship'. An earlier textual note reveals the reasons for this translation: 'he optado por *usía*, trato que en castellano daban los militares de menor a los de mayor graduación, como es el caso de Trim con el tío Toby'.[97]

And yet, there are other moments when language conspires almost miraculously to help the translator. *TS* ends with the discussion between Obadiah and Walter as to whether or not the town bull, property of the latter, is infertile. Obadiah took his cow to the bull on the same day he married one of the Shandy servants, despite which, though his wife is now the mother of a healthy child, his cow shows no signs of producing offspring. He begins to remonstrate with Walter when Mrs Shandy interrupts them:

> L—d! said my mother, what is all this story about? -
> A COCK and a BULL, said Yorick – And one of the best of its kind, I ever heard.[98]

Marías clarifies the English by making Spanish readers aware that 'a cock and bull story' is a popular term—rendered as 'una Fábula'—for a tall tale:

> - ¡S—r!, dijo mi madre; pero, ¿qué es toda esta historia? -
> - Ni más ni menos que una Fábula: sobre una POLLA y un TORO, dijo Yorick; - y es una de las mejores que en su género he oído jamás.[99]

His textual note explains—'se le añade otro [sentido] por una de esas coincidencias milagrosas del lenguaje: *polla*, en castellano, es también *la gallina que pone huevos o que empieza a ponerlos*, como es el caso metafórico de la mujer de Obadiah';[100] I need not spell out what 'polla' is more often taken to mean in Spanish.

From this textual analysis we can see that Marías is a sensitive translator of the varied textual difficulties presented by *TS*. I am aware that so selective and brief a discussion can only provide a glimpse into what is a monumental achievement. What perhaps best sums up that achievement is

---

[96] *La vida y opiniones*, p. 658.    [97] *La vida y opiniones*, p. 646.
[98] *TS*, 9.33.809.    [99] *La vida y opiniones*, p. 575.
[100] *La vida y opiniones*, p. 707.

the delicacy and sensitivity of the translation in passages where pathos or humour depend on the rhythm, deferrals, and diction of a sentence. In the next chapter I examine how Marías took the Shandean precedent and adapted it in writing an autobiographical novel that he too wanted to be guided by digression and the pure contingency of his associative memory.

# 4

# Following the Precedent:
# Marías's Shandean Novel

In 1989, the editors of the *Revista de Occidente* decided to devote their July/August issue to Spain's young writers. Among those who took the opportunity to showcase their work was Javier Marías. He chose his previously unpublished short story 'Un epigrama de lealtad'[1], in which he drew on what was fast becoming his literary fixation—the life of John Gawsworth. Immediately preceding the story itself is a short preface, entitled 'Los reconocimientos', where Marías endeavoured to fill in his literary background. The editors of the *Revista de Occidente* evidently asked each young contributor to situate their work and attitudes within a canonical context, as a similar introduction can be found before each of the contributed pieces. As we have already seen, Marías felt considerable ambivalence towards Spanish literary heritage, and had decided to serve his literary apprenticeship translating literature in English into Spanish. Ironically, he argues in 'Los reconocimientos' that his apprenticeship, and specifically the task of translating Sterne, have brought him full circle. By following the influence that Cervantes and *Don Quijote* had on Sterne, he believes he has followed 'el recorrido que ha hecho la propia herencia de Cervantes y que seguramente toca todos los países occidentales menos España precisamente' ('the route taken by Cervantes's legacy itself and that undoubtedly encompasses all Western countries with the very exception of Spain').[2] That Marías is deliberately ignoring the manifold ways in which Galdós made use of Cervantes's legacy ought not to surprise us when we recall that he had spent his formative years under the wing of Benet whose antipathy for Galdós knew no bounds.[3] Steiner wrote that:

---

[1] JM, 'Un epigrama de lealtad', *Revista de Occidente*, 98–9 (1989), 162–9.
[2] JM, 'Los reconocimientos', *Revista de Occidente*, pp. 162–3 (p. 162).
[3] For an indication of Benet's low opinion of Galdós, see his 'Sobre Galdós', in *Artículos: Volumen 1 (1962–1977)* (Madrid: Pluma Rota, 1983), pp. 89–99. In conversation with Inés Blanca, Marías went on record as agreeing with Benet's dismissal of Galdós: 'Si él opinaba que Galdós era un latazo, lo decía. Y a mi modo de ver lo opinaba con considerable razón' ('If he thought Galdós was a pain in the backside, he would say it. And from my point of view, he was quite right to think that'). For interview text, see the following URL: http://www.javiermarias.es/PAGINASDEENTREVISTAS/javierybenet.html (accessed 2 November 2008).

Translation is made metamorphosis of the national past. All tongues and lit-
eratures are treated as a common store of being from which we may draw at
will in order to countermand the errors, the lacunae of reality. An English
Flaubert, an Italian Rabelais, a French Edward Lear—these are fantastications.
But...such fantastications are given substance in the act of translation.[4]

We might well wonder whether Marías's *TS* has, in his mind, become an
oddly inverted example of Steiner's vision: *TS* is a way of accessing Cervantes's legacy cleansed of the baggage of theorizing on national character
that dominated his reception by Galdós, Unamuno, and Azorín at the
turn of the twentieth century.[5] His refusal to acknowledge the contribution of his fellow countrymen could strike one as indicative of the 'extranjerizante a ultranza' attitude he had been so anxious to avoid in the mid
1970s before he began his career as a translator. Nevertheless, Marías
maintains that it was the privileged reading and rewriting of Sterne that
allowed him to appreciate Cervantes's contribution to the European
novel. It is in Cervantes that he sees the fusion of literary styles that he was
then hoping to emulate—the fusion of the noble style (epitomized by
Browne, Conrad, James, Propertius, and Proust) with 'lo cómico, lo bufo,
la farsa...inseparable de lo más grave y conmovedor' ('the comic, the
humorous, farce...inseparabale from what is most serious and moving')
(to be found in Constant, Dinesen, Gogol, Jonson, and Molière).[6]

It is important for readers of Marías to recognize how much he feels his
translation career has defined him as a writer. He was not content to limit
his horizons to the Spanish or even Hispanic worlds that would have
provided his more natural literary heritage and instead looked to literature in English. Yet, rather than content himself with the worn-on-the-
sleeve cosmopolitanism that irritated many of the opponents of the
'Novísimos' generation, Marías turned his rejection of Spanish heritage
into an opportunity: an opportunity for serious engagement with the
wider Western canon through translation of some of its choicest morsels.
In 'Los reconocimientos' he asserts that his version of *TS* 'es, sin duda, *mi
mejor obra*' ('is, without doubt, *my* best work'), epitomizing the way in
which he believed himself to have appropriated the models and forerunners he had translated. In the above-quoted list of writers who possessed
the particular stylistic traits he hoped to emulate are four whose works he
had by then translated into Spanish. Though he would later claim that

---

[4] Steiner, *After Babel*, p. 359.
[5] I am aware that this description of Galdós's and Unamuno's interest in Cervantes is
not exhaustive or fair; rather I am putting the case as Marías may have seen it in the 1970s
when his antipathy towards his homeland (and the discussion of its national vices) was at
its most violent.
[6] 'Los reconocimientos', pp. 162–3.

some writers had a more 'contagious' effect on him than others, there can be no doubt that translating Browne, Conrad, Dinesen, and Sterne had given him, he felt, privileged access to their styles, ideas, and insights in ways that simply reading them would not have done.

The purpose of this chapter is to determine precisely how Marías later used the example offered by Sterne in his own fiction. What we find on examining Marías's subsequent novels is that he waited nearly twenty years before fully engaging with *TS*. The result was his Shandean novel, *NET* which this chapter shall examine in detail. Quite how much material *TS* and *NET* share has not yet been appreciated, though, in a paper on contemporary digressive narrative in Spain, Grohmann has noted some of their similarities.[7] Central to my discussion is the contention that, because of his translation of Sterne, Marías felt that he had earned the right to use *TS* as a literary precedent. For that reason, when quoting from *TS* in this chapter to illustrate comparisons between it and *NET*, I quote from Marías's Spanish text.

## PAYING HOMAGE TO STERNE

Two months after 'Un epigrama de lealtad' appeared, Marías published an article where he repeated the claim that his *TS* translation was his best work to date. Furthermore, his enthusiasm for Sterne remained undiminished, despite the ten years that had elapsed since he won the Premio Nacional de Traducción. As its title, 'Mi libro favorito', suggests, Marías was seeking to provide a definitive response to the request so often made of writers that they name their favourite work of literature. All writers, were they being honest, he claims, would choose one of their own works, since these are 'los que un autor lee más veces, con mayor detenimiento, paciencia, afán, comprensión e indulgencia' ('those an author reads most often, with most care, patience, eagerness, understanding and indulgence'). They do so because 'Escribir es, en suma, la forma más perfecta y apasionada de leer' ('Writing is, in short, the most perfect and passionate form of reading').[8] He continues by evoking the habit—indulged by many writers during childhood—of copying out their favourite poems, so as to appropriate them for themselves. Copying out the poem, Marías believes, is 'la mejor manera de leerlo, la más cabal, la más alerta, la más segura' ('the best way of reading it, the fullest, the most alert, the most reliable').

---

[7] Alexis Grohmann, 'Literatura y errabundia', in *Antes y después del* "Quijote", ed. by Robert Archer et al. (Valencia: Biblioteca Valenciana/Association of Hispanists of Great Britain and Northern Ireland, 2005), pp. 373–81.

[8] 'Mi libro favorito', in *LF*, pp. 398–401 (p. 398).

It soon becomes clear how these remarks relate to the topic under discussion—his favourite book. He is in the unusual situation of having both read and 'copied out' *TS*, his favourite novel: 'además de leerlo, también lo he escrito' ('as well as reading it, I've also written it'):

> Ahora bien, si digo que *Tristram Shandy* es mi libro preferido, no se me escapa que lo es justamente *porque* lo traduje, porque todas y cada una de las frases, de las palabras que lo componen... no sólo pasaron ante mi vista, sino por mi cuidadoso entendimiento, y por mi vigilante oído, y luego por mi propia lengua (quiero decir el castellano, no la húmeda), y finalmente fueron reordenadas y plasmadas sobre el papel por mis laboriosos y fatigados dedos.[9]

> (However, if I say that *Tristram Shandy* is my favourite book, it has not escaped me that this is precisely *because* I translated it, because every single one of its sentences, of the words that compose it... not only passed before my eyes, but also through my understanding and my vigilant ear, and then over my own tongue (I mean Castilian, not the wet one), and were finally reordered and expressed on paper by my diligent and weary fingers.)

Note the care with which he enumerates each painstaking stage of the translation process, giving the sentence a final epic twist with the transferred epithets 'laboriosos y fatigados' applied to his fingers. Evidently he still thinks of translating *TS* in terms of a heroic struggle, partly because, as he later confesses, he remains in awe of his own achievement: among all the works he has either written or translated, it is the only one that, 'pese a saber que lo he hecho, hoy en día me considero incapaz de hacer' ('despite knowing that I have done it, nowadays I think of myself as incapable of doing it').[10] Marías's favourite work is '*Tristram Shandy* en mi versión o según ella' ('*Tristram Shandy* in my version or according to my version').[11]

It is his favourite work 'por el placer que cualquiera de sus páginas proporciona' ('for the pleasure that any of its pages gives'), but more importantly because he and Sterne have collaborated on the final version.[12] He had to rethink and re-imagine in Spanish every word of the text; hence, his assertion that the translator—the rewriter par excellence—is the most privileged of readers. His experience of this favourite book was thus unique, in that he had never collaborated in the creation of his other best loved works (among which he lists *Adolphe* by Constant, *Madame Bovary*, and *Heart of Darkness*) in quite the same way: 'ninguno, por último, se apoderó de mi prosa, me hizo ponerme literalmente en la piel del autor, del otro, pensar como él, hablar como él, decir lo que él como

---

[9] 'Mi libro favorito', p. 399.     [10] 'Mi libro favorito', p. 401.
[11] 'Mi libro favorito', p. 400.     [12] 'Mi libro favorito', p. 401.

lo dijo él' ('none, finally, took hold of my prose, made me get inside the author's skin, the skin of another, think like him, talk like him, say the things he says in the way that he says them').[13] It is no surprise that Marías, an author with a long-standing interest in literary ghosts, should have chosen to describe Sterne's influence on him in terms that recall possession or haunting. Nor is it a surprise that he should draw attention to the qualitatively different experience of enjoying a book as a reader and feeling the full force of literary influence through translation.

In later summer 2004, a further fifteen years later, Marías went to pay homage to the writer he had taken such pains to translate into Spanish and, in the process, test the veracity of Virginia Woolf's tongue-in-cheek assertion 'That men have ghosts; that ghosts revisit the places where life ran quickest; that Sterne therefore haunts no churchyard, but the room where *Tristram Shandy* was written—all this may be taken for granted'.[14] He had just finished the second volume of his ongoing novel *TRM* and needed to rest. He decided to return to Britain and stayed in the city of York. From there, he took an excursion to Coxwold, Sterne's Yorkshire parish, where he saw both the author's grave and Shandy Hall, the home in which most of *TS* was written. In the event, Sterne's ghost did not put in an appearance. Rather, as Marías wrote of the house that has been converted into a museum:

> En ella, shandianamente, varios ancianos – uno por estancia-, asaltan al visitante y, le guste a uno o no, le explican cuanto en cada una hay de explicable. En el despacho, recuerdo, no hubo forma de imaginar al escritor ante su escritorio, porque su silla la ocupó todo el rato el anciano perorador de turno, rico en disquisiciones y digresiones.[15]

> (There, in true Shandean fashion, several elderly people – one per room – accost the visitor and, whether he likes it or not, explain as much as there is to be explained about each room. In Sterne's study, I recall, there was no way of imagining the writer at his desk because his chair was occupied the whole time by the elderly speechmaker of the moment who was rich in tangents and digressions.)

'El cadáver jovial'—the article where he wrote up his Shandean pilgrimage—opens tellingly with his memory of when and where he was while translating *TS*: 'no en balde pasé un par de años remotos—de 1975 a 1977, vivía entonces en Barcelona—traduciendo su gran obra' ('it was not

---

[13] 'Mi libro favorito', p. 400.
[14] *The Essays of Virginia Woolf*, ed. by Andrew McNeillie and Stuart N. Clarke, 6 vols (London: The Hogarth Press, 1986–2011), IV: *1925–1928*, ed. by Andrew McNeillie (1994), p. 1924.
[15] JM, 'El cadáver jovial', in *EOOL*, pp. 272–4.

in vain that I spent a couple of now long-gone years—from 1975 to 1977, I was living then in Barcelona—translating his great work'). Perhaps prompted by the visit to Sterne's study, Marías betrays an awareness that writing happens in a certain time and place. The incongruity of two men separated by language, country, and two centuries of history, who never-theless spent years poring over the same text, cannot fail to strike the alert reader. The collapse of the intervening time and space demonstrates how printed texts can establish fragile yet tangible affinities between human beings who would otherwise have been irrevocably divided. Marías had already dwelt on this subject at length in his Shandean novel, *NET*, and his visit to Shandy Hall brought the point home once more, when he could see for himself the desk and chair that Sterne had occupied two centuries before.

Several things are clear from 'El cadáver jovial': his esteem for Sterne is great; the memory of how difficult he found the *TS* translation remains vivid despite the twenty-five years that have elapsed; he regards him as the true inheritor of Cervantes's legacy; above all, perhaps, issues of literary posterity are uppermost in his mind since he dwells at length on the farci-cal indignities meted out to Sterne's corpse after death. Despite being buried with all due ceremony in London in 1768, his corpse ended up on a Cambridge University dissecting table where it was to be used in an anatomy lesson: the grave-robbers' ruthless but lucrative trade not sparing even one of the most famous men in England. Not before the physician's knives had set about this latest specimen, one of the people in attendance, who had met Sterne not long before, recognized the illustrious author and managed to halt proceedings. Though his body was returned to its resting place, his head had by this time become detached, meaning that when, in 1969, the Laurence Sterne Trust sought to return his remains to Cox-wold, a search of the surrounding earth was needed before skull could be reunited with torso.

In the event, Sterne's desire to die laughing, like his beloved Cervantes, could not have been better fulfilled since there is a strong element of farce to this shambolic saga. However, the defiling of his grave did offer a Shan-dean twist to the familiar topos of the writer no longer in control of his legacy after death. Auden's reminder that 'The words of a dead man/Are modified in the guts of the living' falls some way short of the horrors of Sterne's immediate posthumous fate and yet, as Marías has had ample opportunity to observe, it is not only dead writers who suffer that indig-nity.[16] Following publication of his Oxford novel, *TLA*, Marías was given

---

[16] W. H. Auden, 'In Memory of W. B. Yeats', in *Collected Poems*, ed. by Edward Men-delson, rev. edn (London: Faber and Faber, 1991), pp. 247–9 (p. 247).

a stark demonstration of how, even in his own lifetime, his works, once published, escape his control. It was the reception and misreading of *TLA* that provided the inspiration for *NET*, a novel, I contend, in which he drew heavily on Sterne's Shandean precedent, reworking its tropes, gestures, and even manner. The Shandean trope he exploited most obviously in *NET* was digression. Several reviewers, myself included, mentioned in passing that Marías's novel, coming as it did from a writer who had translated *TS* into Spanish, appeared to owe much to the digressive precedent set by Sterne.[17] The author even drew attention to the parallel in an interview published in 2000:

> This book [*NET*] is probably the one that owes the most to *Tristram Shandy*. I learned a lot from translating Sterne's novel, about how to use and shape time. In fact, time is all important in novels, much [more] so than in other art forms. In the novel, you can play with it, change it, make it go slower or faster, you can even make it stop altogether if you want. Both *Tristram Shandy* and *Don Quijote* are erratic, digressive books playing against linear time.[18]

His claim in the text that 'este es un libro de incisos, sólo que se avanza también con ellos' sounds distinctly like Tristram's claim that 'mi obra es digresiva, y también progresiva,—y es ambas cosas a la vez' ('my work is digressive, and it is progressive too,—and at the same time').[19]

Weaving the digressions loosely together is one thread of narrative unity, inasmuch as the majority of the anecdotes that make up *NET* concern the ways in which the strife that surrounded publication of *TLA* came to impinge on the author's everyday existence. *TLA* provoked consternation among some of his former colleagues in Oxford University's sub-faculty of Spanish, who believed themselves to have been caricatured in its pages. Their reactions, which ranged from indifference to annoyance, vexed him particularly since he imagined that, of all people, they were best placed to discern the distinction between autobiography and fiction. He later reached agreement with Elías and Gracia Querejeta for them to adapt *TLA* for the screen, only for the resulting film to bear little resemblance to his text.[20] So angry was he with the result that he pursued

---

[17] Gareth Wood, 'The Dark Backward and Abysm of Time', *The London Magazine*, June/July 2004, pp. 105–7 (p. 106).

[18] Paul Ingendaay, 'Interview with Javier Marías', *Bomb*, 73 (2000), <http://bombsite.com/issues/73/articles/2345>, pp. 150–8 (accessed 2 November 2008).

[19] *La vida y opiniones del caballero Tristram Shandy*, p. 62.

[20] For an unconvincing defence of the film see Dona Kercher, 'Children of the European Union, Crossing Gendered Channels: Javier Marías's Novel, *Todas las almas*, and Gracia Querejeta's Film, *El último viaje de Robert Rylands*', in *Cine-Lit III: Essays on Hispanic Film and Fiction*, ed. by George Caballero-Castellet and others (Corvallis: Oregon State University Press, 1997), pp. 100–12.

and won a case against them for breach of contract.[21] A visit to Oxford prior to filming also revealed that two bookseller acquaintances were already hopeful of playing the bookseller couple from the novel.

Since publication of *TLA*, Marías had continued to search for information on Gawsworth, whose literary fame and subsequent descent into obscurity he had charted. That search led him to the anthologies of ghost stories prepared by him in Britain between the two World Wars. There Marías encountered many gem-like stories by authors whose memory had all but faded from view, despite the reputations they enjoyed in their own era. When he decided to anthologize and translate some of those stories for the collection *Cuentos únicos* (1989), he sought out biographical data with which to introduce the authors: the task proved far more difficult than he could have imagined, and reinforced his growing awareness—epitomized by Gawsworth—that literary posterity is fickle in its favours. Such was the basis for the Shandean *NET*, a companion volume to his Oxford novel, *TLA*, which had itself not been free from references to Sterne. Readers of the novel will recall the scene depicting dinner at high table, during the course of which the narrator has to listen to one of his companions (Halliwell by name) give him chapter and verse on the subject of a cider tax levied in the mid eighteenth century. The narrator gives the dates when the tax was in force as 1760–1767—the publication dates of *TS*.[22] Given Marías's background, we might already suspect him of substituting the real dates for others from the mid eighteenth century that are closer to his heart. We might also see that suspicion confirmed on examining 'Por fin nos envidian', one of the journalistic pieces he wrote shortly after his return from Oxford, in which he railed against the 'lumbrera económica que sólo se dignará hablar del tema sobre el que un día lejano versó su tesis doctoral, a saber: cierto impuesto con que, entre 1762 y 1765, fue gravemente gravada en Inglaterra la producción de sidra *(sic)*' ('Economics whiz who will only deign to talk about the subject on which in days gone by he wrote his doctoral thesis, namely: a certain prohibitive tax which, between 1762 and 1765, was levied in England on cider production').[23] Perhaps he wanted to point to the Shandean absurdity of the situation and gave the careful reader this hint as to his meaning. Halliwell, after all, later exclaims: '¡Sterne mencionó el impuesto en uno de sus sermones!' ('Sterne mentioned the tax in one of his sermons!').[24] Such

---

[21] The legal wrangles over the case, which Marías first won in 1998, came to an end in March 2006 when Spain's Supreme Court ordered the Querejetas to pay 36,000 euros in compensation and remove all reference to Marías's name from the credits of the film.

[22] *TLA*, p. 56.

[23] JM, 'Por fin nos envidian', in *VF*, pp. 381–4 (p. 381).

[24] *TLA*, p. 65; JM, *All Souls*, trans. by Margaret Jull Costa (London: Vintage, 2003), p. 46.

coincidences between the narrator and author of *TLA* remind us of Marías's desire to capture a version of self through writing. However, rather than narrate *NET*—his 'falsa novela' ('fake novel')—through an anonymous Spanish academic, Marías narrates the novel himself. Whether that means we should hence regard the novel as autobiographical is not easy to say. How much of *NET* is autobiography and does it matter?

## AUTOBIOGRAPHY OR NOT?

To what extent *NET* is autobiography is difficult to pin down for several reasons. When the novel was first published, Marías refused to undertake the punishing round of press interviews that would normally accompany publication of the work of such a high-profile writer. He explained the decision four years later in an interview with Hilario Pino on the program *Cara a cara*:

> El motivo para hacerlo con *NEDT* fue que al ser yo el narrador en esa novela o falsa novela como efectivamente la llamé, pues había algunos elementos un poco demasiado personales y yo no me sentía capacitado para por ejemplo hablar con un periodista de cosas sobre las que uno puede escribir en el silencio de la habitación, de cosas un poco personales pero no hablar en público y ese fue el principal motivo.[25]

> (The reason for doing so with *NEDT* was that with me being the narrator of that novel or fake novel, as I in fact called it, well there were some elements that were a little too personal and I didn't feel able, for example, to talk with a journalist about things which one can write about in the silence of one's room, about slightly personal things but not speak in public and that was the main reason.)

He goes on to point out that many journalists took his decision as a sign of arrogance or indifference. But if his reluctance stemmed from the personal, self-revelatory nature of the text, by May 2005 he appeared to have changed his mind: '[ese libro] no permitía sin embargo saber mucho más sobre mí a quien lo leyera de lo que sabía antes de leerlo, a pesar de que hay algunas cosas que sí se pueden saber' ('[that book] nevertheless didn't allow whoever read it to know much more about me than they did before starting it, in spite of the fact that there are a few things that can be found out from it').[26] This anomaly is perhaps best explained by the time that had elapsed: what at the time seemed too laceratingly personal, when viewed with hindsight, did not provoke the same defensive response.

---

[25] Interview with Hilario Pino. www.javiermarias.es/main.html (accessed 2 November 2008).
[26] Pittarello, *Entrevistos*, p. 25.

The assumption that the novel is to be treated as purely fictional has led at least one critic up the garden path. Amélie Florenchie calls the reference to the world expert on Gawsworth, Steve Eng of Nashville, Tennessee, 'una alusión clara a "Tlön, Uqbar, Orbis Tertius"' ('a clear allusion to "Tlön, Uqbar, Orbis Tertius"').[27] While it might be the complex allusion she imagines, there is also the possibility that Steve Eng is in fact simply from Nashville, Tennessee; this is indeed the case. If purely fictional interpretations are liable to come up against such stumbling blocks, Marías appears to enjoin caution to readers who would stress the novel's autobiographical aspects: 'Es una falsa novela en la medida en que el narrador soy yo, por lo menos se llama Javier Marías y cuenta algunas cosas que son indudablemente ciertas, otras estaría por ver' ('It is a fake novel inasmuch as the narrator is me, at least he's called Javier Marías and he describes some things that are undoubtedly true, others we'll have to wait and see');[28] 'Let's say the narrator is someone with my own name, and some of the things I am telling are true, or all of them are true and presented as such'.[29] These potentially contradictory responses given in interviews only a year apart hint that what the author was seeking was to record a version of the self governed more by fidelity to novelistic or artistic 'truth' than historical fact. He had long harboured the ambition to 'abordar el campo autobiográfico, pero sólo como ficción' ('to approach autobiographical territory, but only as fiction'), as the essay 'Autobiografía y ficción', written two years before *TLA*, reveals. There he spoke of his desire to write a novel in which the balance between fiction and autobiography was delicately poised, such that the author, 'al presentar su texto como ficción pero no hacer nada para ficcionalizarlo, lo que quizá está haciendo es indicar ambas cosas a la vez' ('when presenting his text as fiction but doing nothing to fictionalize it, perhaps what he's doing is suggesting both things at the same time').[30] Five years later he would suggest that all writers 'desean íntimamente verse tratados' ('privately want to be treated') as 'personajes de ficción' ('fictional characters'), demonstrating that this desire was not fleeting, rather a lasting tenet of his theory of fiction.[31]

Behind this assertion is the belief he shares with Aristotle that mimetic art can offer more penetrating insight into the human condition than

[27] Amélie Florenchie, 'Marías en clave borgeana', in *Cuadernos de narrativa: Javier Marías*, pp. 155–68 (p. 167).
[28] Interview with Juan Cruz. For text see the following URL: http://www.javiermarias.es/PAGINASDEENTREVISTAS/entrevistaCSD.html (accessed 2 November 2008).
[29] Paul Ingendaay interview. www.javiermarias.es/main.html (accessed 2 November 2008).
[30] JM, 'Autobiografía y ficción', in *LF*, pp. 70–8 (p. 78).
[31] JM, *Vidas escritas* (henceforth *VE*), p. 15.

other structures of thought:[32] 'sé que al escribir o al contar historias e inventar personajes he sabido o reconocido o he pensado cosas que sólo en la escritura pueden saberse o reconocerse o pensarse' ('I know that when writing or telling stories and inventing characters I have learned or recognized or thought things which can only be learnt, recognized, or thought through writing').[33] He goes on, in the essay just quoted, to explain his 'pensamiento literario' ('literary thinking'), a way of thinking that 'puede contradecirse y no está sujeto a razonamiento ni a argumentación ni a demostraciones' ('can contradict itself and is not tied to reason or argument or proof').[34] Such thought patterns enable Marías to produce fiction that is driven by the exploration of ambiguity in human motive, speech, and behaviour. Benet could be thought to have predicted the evolution in Marías's work that would lead him into just this territory. The former argues in *La inspiración y el estilo* that the writer who has achieved stylistic maturity will eventually tire of expressing the sensations and ideas that are man's common currency. When this happens the writer will reach into 'una oscura zona de su razón en que las ideas... no se hallan claramente perfiladas' ('a dark area of his reason in which his ideas... are not clearly delineated'), seeking through his or her writing the better to express, though not to solve, enigmas that reason alone cannot fathom.[35] The result is often a striking metaphor, one that the reader may 'comprender' ('comprehend'), yet not 'entender' ('understand').[36] By this, he means that such metaphors do not make literal sense (reason alone cannot decipher them) and yet they have meaning on an emotional level beyond literal language. Marías uses exactly those two verbs to elucidate the contradictory meanings of Lady Macbeth's phrase 'a heart so white' from which he took the title of *CTB*.[37] Tellingly, another of the metaphors Benet uses to illustrate his argument in *La inspiración y el estilo* is 'the dark backward and abysm of time', which he translates as 'la negra espalda y abismo del tiempo'. Marías acknowledged in the essay 'La negra espalda de lo no venido' (1996) that it was Benet who first alerted him to this enigmatic Shakespearean utterance that was to provide *NET* with its title. Grohmann also makes an excellent case for seeing Marías's quest for a distinctive, individual style in the context of his mentor's views:

---

[32] For a discussion of Aristotle's conception of mimesis, see Stephen Halliwell, *The Aesthetics of Mimesis: Ancient Texts and Modern Problems* (Woodstock [Oxfordshire]: Princeton University Press, 2002), pp. 177–206.
[33] 'Contar el misterio', in *LF*, p. 122.
[34] 'Contar el misterio', p. 123.
[35] *La inspiración*, p. 201.
[36] *La inspiración*, p. 199.
[37] JM, 'Shakespeare indeciso', in *LF*, pp. 363–8 (pp. 363–4).

Th[e] synthesis and interaction of imagination and style, or style conceived broadly enough to encompass the workings of the imagination, as it is understood in Benet's *La inspiración y el estilo*, is central to comprehending Marías's writing: his loose, digressive, errant style is the voice or vehicle of his imagination, blocking the conscious 'gestalt' need for precise visualization and rational planning and foresight, whilst providing the latter with the necessary freedom to invent.[38]

In a later essay, 'Incertidumbre, memoria, fatalidad y temor' (delivered as a lecture in 1972, published in 1976), Benet expands on his idea that the best writing will be accomplished by a writer who surrenders him- or herself to the exploration of ambiguity. When a writer realizes that through conventional reason and language, participation in 'la empresa del saber' ('the task of knowledge') can be no more than slight, 'es posible que elija su campo, para dirigirse en lo sucesivo... en la dirección opuesta a la del saber' ('he might then choose his field, to proceed from then on... in the opposite direction from certainty'). Once the writer has found 'la ciencia' ('learning') wanting as a means of understanding his or her 'entorno' ('surroundings'), they will concentrate on the hinterland that exists beyond demonstrable truth:

> De ese mundo de claroscuro, de esas fugaces impresiones de lo incierto, de ese telón de fondo que trasciende al saber, es de donde extraerá su mejor inspiración. No en balde al perder esa absoluta confianza en la ciencia, una buena parte de su experiencia se desarrollará en la zona fronteriza entre las luces y la sombra, al asumir con su vida el papel a que le arrastran sus propias convicciones.[39]

> (From that world of chiaroscuro, from those fleeting impressions left by uncertainty, from that backdrop that transcends knowledge, is from where he will extract his greatest inspiration. It is not in vain that in losing that absolute faith in learning, a large part of his experience will develop in the hinterland between the light and darkness, in taking on in his life the role towards which his own convictions drag him.)

Again, in that essay Benet draws his best examples of ambiguous literary language from Shakespeare.

I do not seek to claim that Benet and Marías are unique in having highlighted this fruitful ambiguity. Marías is quick to acknowledge both his debt to Benet and the fact that 'pensamiento literario' has a long history. Two notable precedents are offered by John Keats and Thomas de Quincey. The former endeavoured to clarify in a letter to his brothers what kind of thought process great writers were able to sustain that others could not:

---

[38] *Coming Into One's Own*, p. 101. See also pp. 80–4, 95, 99–101.
[39] Juan Benet, 'Incertidumbre, fatalidad y temor', in *En ciernes* (Madrid: Taurus, 1976), pp. 43–61 (p. 51).

what quality went to form a Man of Achievement especially in Literature & which Shakespeare possessed so enormously: I mean *Negative Capability*, that is when man is capable of being in uncertainties, Mysteries, doubts, without any irritable reaching after fact & reason.[40]

Likewise, in his essay 'On the Knocking at the Gate in *Macbeth*', de Quincey sets out how he came to understand the effect produced by the referred-to knocking. The knocking begins immediately after Macbeth has murdered Duncan and his wife has smeared the servants' faces with blood to implicate them in the crime. After years scrutinizing his only half-formed impressions, de Quincey concluded that the knocking represents emotionally and symbolically the reassertion of everyday concerns following the descent into almost supernatural evil, thereby heightening the horror of the murders. He arrived at his solution, however, solely by 'relying on my own feeling'. In fact, he exhorts his reader

> never to pay any attention to his understanding when it stands in opposition to any other faculty of his mind. The mere understanding, however useful and indispensable, is the meanest faculty in the human mind, and the most to be distrusted.[41]

From as early as *EMT*, where the central essay is an analysis of a scene from *Julius Caesar*, Marías has found Shakespeare's plays pregnant with inspiration. Just as he draws a distinction between the authors who influenced him through his translation of them and those who did not, he believes that some authors are more 'fertile' than others. While Conrad, Sterne, and Browne had a 'contagious' effect on him through translation, Yeats or Dinesen did not.[42] Bernhard, Kafka, Beckett, and Joyce 'serían autores que desde mi punto de vista, por mucho que a uno le entusiasmen, tienden a esterilizar' ('would in my view be authors who, however much one might like them, tend to have a sterilizing effect'). He singles out Joyce as a writer whose most emblematic work, *Ulysses*, 'lleva incorporado el gesto del genio' ('carries in it the conspicuous display of genius'), where, 'el propio autor está diciendo "fíjense ustedes en esto"' ('where the author himself is saying "look at this"').[43] By contrast, Shakespeare is 'un

[40] *The Letters of John Keats 1814–1821*, ed. by Hyder Edward Rollins, 2 vols (London: Cambridge University Press, 1958), I, 193.

[41] *The Works of Thomas de Quincey*, ed. by Grevel Lindop et al., 21 vols (London: Pickering and Chatto, 2000–3), III: *Articles and Translations from the* London Magazine, Blackwoods Magazine *and Others 1821–1824*, ed. by Frederick Burwick (2000), pp. 150–4 (p. 150).

[42] See Appendix ('Eight Questions for Javier Marías') in JM, *Voyage Along the Horizon*, trans. by Kristina Cordero (San Franciso: Believer Books, 2006), pp. 175–82 (p. 177).

[43] Sol Alameda, 'Javier Marías: el éxito europeo de un indeciso', *El País Semanal*, 10 November 1996, pp. 58–64 (p. 62).

autor fértil, que invita, no te paraliza' ('a fertile author, one who invites creativity, does not paralyse you').

Shortly after *CTB* was published, Marías explained how it had gained its title in the essay 'Shakespeare indeciso'. As had been the case with *EHS* and *TLA*, Marías had finished *CTB* before deciding what to call it.[44] If he did so 'pese a lo gastada que está la palabra inicial' ('despite how tired the first word has become'), it was because he realized that Lady Macbeth's words to her husband remained a mystery to him: 'My hands are of your colour, but I shame/To wear a heart so white'.[45] A reader whose attention alights on this enigmatic utterance, even one well versed in Shakespeare, is likely to find that they have not understood it as well as they imagined. The same goes for other phrases highlighted by Marías, including Othello's 'It is the cause' speech, and Prospero's phrase 'the dark backward and abysm of time', both of which echo through *NET*. Crucially, he maintains that he is most aware of Shakespeare's ambiguity when trying to translate him.[46] Samuel Johnson sniffily complained in his famous *Preface* that Shakespeare's language is occasionally underdeveloped:

> It is incident to him to be now and then entangled with an unwieldy sentiment, which he cannot well express, and will not reject; he struggles with it a while, and, if it continues stubborn, comprises it in words such as occur, and leaves it to be disentangled and evolved by those who have more leisure to bestow upon it.[47]

One suspects that Marías celebrates rather than bemoans this space at the fringes of Shakespeare's language, that it has given him food for thought and freedom to invent. He confirmed this suspicion in an interview published in late 2006: 'Shakespeare leaves many paths unexplored, many things just announced, strong images unexplained—these invite you not to follow him but to be inspired'.[48] We find in *NET*, however, he is adamant that, even though metaphorical language can widen or renew our understanding of the human condition, it can neither transcend it nor console us.

To return to the question of whether or not it matters if Marías is 'telling the truth' in *NET*, I would argue that it does not. As Susan Sontag remarks of another fictional autobiography which draws heavily on *TS* (*Memórias póstumas de Brás Cubas* [1880] by Machado de Assis):

[44] See Elide Pittarello, 'Prólogo: Gente en el tren', in JM, *El hombre sentimental*, Prologue by Elide Pittarello (Madrid: Espasa Calpe, 1994), pp. 9–21 (p. 10); *NET*, p. 292.

[45] 'Shakespeare indeciso', in *LF*, pp. 363–8 (pp. 366–7).

[46] 'Shakespeare indeciso', p. 363.

[47] *The Yale Edition of the Works of Samuel Johnson*, ed. by Arthur Sherlo, 18 + vols. (New Haven and London: Yale University Press, 1958–), VII: *Johnson on Shakespeare* (Part 1 of 2) (1968), p. 73.

[48] 'Javier Marías: The Art of Fiction No. 190', p. 33.

quite different ideas of decorum apply to a narrative constructed in the first person and to one in the third person. To slow down, to race ahead, to skip whole stretches; to comment at length, to withhold comment—these done as an 'I' have another weight, another feel, than when said about or on behalf of someone else. Much of what is affecting or pardonable or insufferable in the first person would seem the opposite if uttered in the third person, and vice versa... There are registers of feeling, such as anxiety, that only a first-person voice can accommodate. And seems natural in a text written in the first person, but amateurish in an impersonal, third-person voice.[49]

Thus we should look to the ebb and flow of *NET*, its changes of tone, digressions, and suppressions to fathom its meaning. Given that the novel represents a version of Marías's self conceived as a textual construct, we should look to the manner rather than the matter of the telling: 'es el contar y no el cuento lo que aquí está en juego' ('the telling and not the tale are what matter here'), as Pittarello reminds us.[50] Central to that manner is deliberate mimicry of Sterne's Shandean model and it is to this aspect of *NET* that I now turn.

## SHANDEAN AUTOBIOGRAPHY: LIFE AND TEXT ENTWINED

Sontag says of fictional autobiographies in the Shandean vein that they 'tend to be autumnal undertakings: an elderly (or, at least, loss-seasoned) narrator, having retired from life, now writes'.[51] Although the Marías we see in *NET* is not at the end of his life, the tone modulates between humour and a melancholy which bespeaks the grief and suffering he or those close to him have endured. He describes his final meetings with his mother and with Benet— scenes that are among the most affecting in all his fiction; three prominent recurring backdrops are the First and Second World Wars and Spanish Civil War: either he is recounting his father's betrayal and subsequent imprisonment, Wilfrid Ewart's time in the trenches, or Hugh Oloff de Wet's mercenary activities both in Spain and on the Western front during the Second World War. The novel betrays an underlying awareness that the twentieth century has seen much loss of life and a diminution of the value we set on it. The phrase 'y qué, si no hubiera nacido nunca nadie' ('so what, if no one had ever been born') echoes throughout like a jaded refrain.

---

[49] Susan Sontag, 'Afterlives: The Case of Machado de Assis', in *Where the Stress Falls* (London: Vintage, 2003), pp. 30–40 (pp. 31–2).

[50] Elide Pittarello, '*Negra espalda del tiempo*: instrucciones de uso', in *El pensamiento literario de Javier Marías*, pp. 125–34 (pp. 128–9).

[51] Sontag, 'Afterlives', p. 31.

Whilst he did not retire from public life during the writing of *NET* and, in fact, kept up with his weekly press column, the novel does make clear reference to the solitude Marías requires to produce substantial fictional works. Like Tristram Shandy, he seems intent on recording a textual version of the self that transcribes his consciousness as closely as words ever can. His textual voice 'va llenando estas páginas un día tras otro a lo largo de las muchas horas en que nadie sabe de mí ni me ve ni me espía, y así parece que no he nacido'('is slowly filling these pages day by day during the long hours that nobody hears from me, sees or spies on me, so that it seems as if I had never been born')[52] where an explicit equivalence is drawn between the physical voice of the man, Javier Marías, and his writing. Or, as Pittarello puts it:

> Así transforma los signos de la página en los sonidos de la voz, devolviendo simbólicamente el discurso del textual cuerpo que lo produce, donde el acto verbal (o enunciación) y su producto (o enunciado) se dan y se pierden al mismo tiempo.[53]

> (In this way he transforms the signs on the page into vocal sounds, symbolically returning the discourse of the textual body that creates it, where the verbal act (or enunciation) and its product (or enunciate) take place and are lost at the same time.)

Tristram Shandy offers similar glimpses of the private world he inhabits while writing. They range from his throwing his wig in the air after accidentally burning a finished page to discussing 'ese asma maligno que cogiste patinando con el viento de cara en Flandes' ('the vile asthma thou gattest in skating against the wind in Flanders')—the tubercular attacks that Sterne suffered with greater regularity as he grew older and which he also inflicted on his creation.[54] By referring often to the particular date when he is writing, Tristram gives the reader chance to observe the passage of time from one autobiographical instalment to the next. In his first such reference, he gives the date as 'hoy mismo, 26 de marzo de 1759, día lluvioso, entre las nueve y las diez de la mañana' ('this very rainy day, 26 *March* 1759, and betwixt the hours of nine and ten in the morning').[55] Over two years later, Tristram is writing his fifth volume and describing Doctor Slop, 'y en el día de hoy (10 de agosto de 1761) aún estoy pagando parte del precio de la reputación de este señor' ('and I am this day [*August* the 10th, 1761] paying part of the price of this man's reputation').[56] And

---

[52] *NET*, p. 114.
[53] Elide Pittarello, 'Haciendo tiempo con las cosas', in *Cuadernos de narrativa: Javier Marías*, pp. 17–48 (p. 28).
[54] *La vida y opiniones*, pp. 256, 485.
[55] *La vida y opiniones*, p. 55.     [56] *La vida y opiniones*, p. 333.

almost exactly five years after that, having just begun his final volume, Tristram writes of his father's prophecy for the future behaviour of his son: 'Y heme aquí sentado ante una mesa este 12 de agosto (el de 1766), con un coleto púrpura, un par de zapatillas amarillas y la Cabeza al descubierto (ni peluca ni sombrero)' ('And here I am sitting, this 12th day of August, 1766, in a purple jerkin and yellow pair of slippers, without either wig or cap on').[57] Following Tristram's example, Marías refers to one particular day on which he is writing: 'Es desazonante que en el día de hoy, 8 de noviembre del 97, esté aquí en Madrid la tinta que distraída o solemnemente dejó correr Wilfrid Ewart' ('It is troubling that today, the 8th of November '97, the ink that Wilfrid Ewart absently or solemnly traced should be here in Madrid').[58] That reference, appearing as it does on page 260, can be compared to the work's final date of completion of March 1998—five months later—to catch a glimpse of writing as also the passage of time.

Moreover, as Pittarello remarks, the reminder of the author's physical presence behind the narrative serves to reinforce his mortality: 'el sujeto empírico que se dice en la actualidad del discurso marca el comienzo puntual del tiempo que remite a su destino mortal' ('the empirical subject who describes himself as in the now of the discourse marks the exact starting point of the time left before his mortal end').[59] Tristram Shandy becomes increasingly aware of time's relentless march as his autobiography progresses, the more so since Sterne inflicts on him the same tuberculosis that would cut short his creator's life. Sontag and Keymer both point to the ways in which Sterne and his successors exploit the comic incompleteness of autobiography; by its very nature, autobiography can never tell a full story because the author's death, so often seen in Western art as a defining moment, must necessarily be left unwritten.[60] Marías reflects at length in *NET* on the tendency for a person's final moments to be seen to define them. The prolonged digression on Wilfrid Ewart's demise encapsulates the futility of attempts to make a life and death cohere or make narrative sense: 'lo inmediatamente anterior a lo último o a la catástrofe no tiene por qué ser siempre significativo ni encerrar interés alguno ('there is no reason why what immediately precedes the final deed or the catastrophe should always be significant or even especially interesting').'[61]

Though he does not restate in *NET* what it was that first alerted him to this aspect of the modern mindset, he wrote in 1986 that an essay by

[57] *La vida y opiniones*, p. 534.     [58] *NET*, p. 260.
[59] '*Negra espalda del tiempo*: instrucciones de uso', p. 129.
[60] Keymer, *Sterne, the Moderns, and the Novel*, p. 114–16; Sontag, p. 31.
[61] *NET*, p. 209.

Rafael Sánchez Ferlosio had shown him that the manner in which a life, film, or novel end has a disproportionate effect on our judgement of them: 'más o menos de acuerdo con la tradicional e ilusa idea de que, "al final resplandece siempre la verdad"' ('more or less in line with the traditional, naive idea that "the truth will out in the end"').[62] Marías's own lengthy reflections on whether or not we are right to attribute transcendent importance to a person's final moments—as if these latter might provide an insight that their life has not yet yielded—may well stem from the realization that his death will ultimately elude his pen.

Tristram reacts with both humour and desperation to the realization that his autobiography will not catch up with the present moment of writing:

> That Tristram is progressively ailing as he writes, losing his life even as he endeavours to write it, gives urgency to what might otherwise seem a merely playful meditation on the impossibility of fixing the self (or the memories and opinions that constitute a self) in serial print.[63]

Keymer offers an excellent overview of the successive warnings that Tristram sounds about his ability to finish the text. From his initial promise to keep writing 'durante los próximos cuarenta años, si es que la fuente de la salud se complace en bendecirme durante tanto tiempo con vida y con buen humor' ('these forty years, if it pleases the fountain of health to bless me so long with life and good spirits'), he admits with disappointment, three volumes later, that despite being a year older than the same time twelve months before, his autobiography is still stalled on his first day of life.[64] In the same volume he promises the reader another two volumes within the year, 'a menos que esta maldita tos me mate en el entretanto' ('unless this vile cough kills me in the mean time').[65] By his final instalment, Tristram has completed the identification between his life and the work: 'el Tiempo se desvanece con demasiada rapidez: cada letra que escribo me habla de la velocidad con la que la Vida sigue a mi pluma' ('Time wastes too fast: every letter I trace tells me with what rapidity Life follows my pen').[66] Marías similarly conflates his consciousness and the work he is writing. What he calls the 'relato'—the textual version of lived experience—is inexorably entwined with his consciousness since 'Su final . . . coincidirá con el mío, dentro de algunos años, o así lo espero' ('Its

---

[62] JM, 'Lo que no ocurre', in *PP*, pp. 162–6 (p. 164). I have not succeeded in identifying the Ferlosio essay to which Marías refers.
[63] Keymer, p. 116.
[64] *La vida y opiniones*, pp. 62, 250–1.
[65] *La vida y opiniones*, p. 297.        [66] *La vida y opiniones*, p. 543.

end…will coincide with mine, some years from now, or so I hope').[67] Moreover, the written version of the self is a form of death, since it freezes what would otherwise be a dynamic human life that is subject to contingency and change: 'yo mismo me estoy enterrando con este escrito y en estas páginas, aunque nadie las lea, no sé qué es lo que estoy haciendo ni por qué lo hago' ('I too am burying myself with this text and in these pages, I don't know what it is I'm doing or why I'm doing it').[68]

Marías's concern that any attempt at mimetic representation through language is 'una mera ilusión o quimera' ('a mere illusion or chimera')[69] also meets Sontag's expectation of how fictional autobiography ought to be introduced by the narrator:

> most fictional autobiographies of any stylishness or depth also start with an explanation, defensive or defiant, of the decision to write the book the reader has just begun—or, at least, a flourish of self-deprecation, suggesting an attractive sensitivity to the charge of egotism. This is no mere throat-clearing, some polite sentences to give the reader time to be seated. It is the opening shot in a campaign of seduction in which the autobiographer tacitly agrees that there is something unseemly, brazen, in volunteering to write at length about oneself—exposing oneself to unknown others without any evident interest (a great career, a great crime) or without some documentary ruse, such as pretending that the book merely transcribes existing private papers, like a journal or letters.[70]

In fact, Marías's opening chapter is a radical rejection of the usefulness of the task he is about to undertake. Just as Sterne doubted the efficacy of language in holding on to meaning, for Marías, words deform speech and thoughts by their very nature because they retain only slender traces of the sense with which the speaker or thinker hoped to invest them: 'cualquiera cuenta una anécdota de lo que le ha sucedido y por el mero hecho de contarlo ya lo está deformando y tergiversando' ('anybody can relate an anecdote of something that happened to them and the simple act of telling it already distorts and twists it').[71] Hence, '"Relatar lo ocurrido" es inconcebible y vano, o bien es sólo posible como invención' ('"To tell what happened" is inconceivable and futile, or rather only possible as invention').[72] In spite of which he will 'alinearme aquí con los que han pretendido hacer eso alguna vez o han simulado lograrlo, voy a relatar lo ocurrido o averiguado o tan sólo sabido' ('align myself with those who have at one time tried to do so or have pretended to manage it, I am going to tell what happened or was discovered or simply known').[73] He presents himself as

---

[67] *NET*, p. 12.     [68] *NET*, p. 73.     [69] *NET*, p. 10.
[70] Sontag, 'Afterlives', p. 32.     [71] *NET*, p. 9.     [72] *NET*, p. 10.
[73] *NET*, p. 11.

though he were the passive voice that merely transmits 'los elementos de este relato' ('the elements of this story'),[74] 'porque en el fondo no los guía ningún autor aunque sea yo quien los cuente, no responden a ningún plan ni se rigen por ninguna brújula' ('because in the end no author is guiding them, even though I am the one telling them; they don't correspond to any plan nor are they guided by any compass'):[75]

> De dónde viene lo que se sabe y adónde lleva lo que se hace importa sólo como cruce accidental de circunstancias, recogidas por una voz que no es la del autor (el escritor que crea voluntariamente una obra), aunque sea la de Javier Marías.[76]

> (Where what is known comes from and where what is done leads matters only as an accidental crossover of circumstances, gathered together by a voice which is not that of the author (the writer who voluntarily creates a work), even though it belongs to Javier Marías.)

Out of this nihilism and pessimism about what literature can achieve grows a narrative in which Marías will act as 'una forma inesperada de posteridad' ('a kind of unexpected posterity')[77] for the host of writers, among them Ewart, Hugh Oloff de Wet, Gawsworth, and Shiel, whose works have left ghostly traces of their passage through the world. Of a volume of Ewart's, he remarks:

> Algo tiene de incongruente, algo tiene de irónico y quizá mucho de injusto la perduración de este volumen o de cualquiera de los objetos que nos sobreviven, y que son casi todos los que nos rodean y nos acompañan y están a nuestro servicio, simulando su insignificancia.[78]

> (There is a touch of incongruity, a touch of irony, and perhaps plenty of injustice in the continued existence of this volume or of any of the objects that survive us, and which are nearly all of those that surround and accompany and serve us, feigning their insignificance.)

His deliberate understatement and tentative tone resist the temptation to provide a full-blown lament for the authors who wrote or owned the books Marías possesses. By understating his horror at the human mortality so easily mocked by the inanimate objects that survive us, he registers the fact that writing makes him aware of just that fact: 'Contar es lo que más mata y lo que más sepulta, lo que fija y dibuja y hiela nuestro rostro o el perfil o la nuca' ('Telling the tale is what kills fastest and buries deepest, what fixes and traces and freezes our face or profile or the nape of the neck').[79] Words are static, fix a single version of events that will certainly

---

[74] *NET*, p. 11.     [75] *NET*, p. 12.
[76] Pittarello, '*Negra espalda del tiempo*: instrucciones de uso', p. 128.
[77] *NET*, p. 15.     [78] *NET*, p. 260.     [79] *NET*, pp. 72–3.

have been more complex than the final text can accommodate: 'Lo que se le atribuye en una ficción a uno tiene en cambio poco o ningún arreglo, no hay vuelta de hoja ni enmienda' ('What's attributed to you in a work of fiction remains by contrast largely or completely irrevocable, there is no going back or chance for amendment').[80] If this conclusion appears to negate Marías's faith in the dynamism of metaphorical literary language, that is because it does. Even though language can offer metaphorical representations of man's fate as an interval between the impenetrable oblivion before birth and after death, it cannot transcend that fundamental fact. By becoming the 'fantasma' ('ghost') for Gawsworth and others Marías remains aware that his hopes for posterity are as illusory as theirs:

> Este simulacro [el fantasma] que sabe de los muertos y los vivos, conociendo ambas dimensiones de su tiempo, se configura como el intérprete adecuado de la literatura, la cual 'no cuenta lo consabido sino lo sólo sabido y a la vez ignorado. O en menos palabras: sin poder explicarlo, cuenta el misterio.' ... Pero en *Negra espalda del tiempo* el misterio envuelve también la vida real y quien la e-voca, re-presenta o resucita acude igualmente al arte ilusorio de la imaginación.[81]

> (This simulacrum [the ghost] who knows of the dead and living, having experienced both dimensions of his time, takes shape as the ideal interpreter of literature, that which 'does not relate well-worn truths rather only what he knows and at the same time remains unaware of. Or put more succinctly: without being able to explain, he relates the mystery' ... But in *Dark Back of Time* the mystery also surrounds real life and the person who e-vokes, re-presents, or resuscitates it resorts equally to the illusory art of the imagination.)

Among Marías's further Shandean habits is the physical appearance of *NET*. Just as Tristram supplies black, blank, and marbled pages, Marías's text is full of the drawings, maps, photographs, and family portraits that offer more concrete proof of the past existence of his dead brother Julianín, his mother, Gawsworth, Will the porter (who had featured in *TLA*), Shiel, and Ewart than any number of words could do. As we saw in the last chapter, Keymer interprets such recourse to the visual on Tristram's part as an act of desperation, an attempt to escape the pitfalls of 'tall, opake words'.

Another way in which Tristram hopes to avoid those pitfalls is to make his writing into a conversation. To that end, he addresses his readers in a variety of guises, sometimes even asking them to read the text at different paces or to repeat passages they have already read. As early as the fourth chapter of his first volume, Tristram divides his readers into the curious and the incurious: whilst the former will be all ears to hear about Tristram's conception, the latter he advises 'que se salten el resto de este capítulo'

---

[80] *NET*, p. 72.
[81] Pittarello, '*Negra espalda del tiempo*: instrucciones de uso', p. 130.

('that they skip over the remaining part of this chapter'), on the basis that it will not interest them.[82] Marías too encourages some readers to skip a section of his novel—that in which he replicates the background information on Gawsworth supplied in *TLA*—only to withdraw the permission a few lines later:

> Quienes ya hayan leído esas páginas en aquella novela podrán saltárselas—creo—sin sentirse estafados (siempre gusta saltarse páginas y casi nunca es posible) y quienes no las conozcan podrán leerlas ahora sin tener que desembolsar un céntimo más para hacerse con ellas, aunque seguramente la reproducción no va a ser íntegra y puede que incluya acotaciones o comentarios intercalados, de forma que no sé si a la postre harán bien en saltársela quienes ya se dispusieran alegre y frívolamente a ello.[83]

> (Those who have already read those pages in that novel can skip them—I believe—without feeling cheated (it's always nice to skip pages and it's hardly ever possible) and those who have yet to encounter them can read them now without having to spend a cent more to get their hands on them, although undoubtedly the reproduction isn't going to be word-for-word and might include some annotations and interspersed comments, so that I'm not sure if those who were already joyfully and frivolously preparing to jump ahead would be wise to do so.)

One suspects that the vast majority of readers who continued to read in linear fashion, ignoring the invitation to skip ahead, are indirectly flattered by the barbed adverbs Marías uses to describe readers who too readily jumped forward in the text. That his rebuke is no more than tongue-in-cheek is confirmed by his next, self-deprecating remark: 'Claro que también podrían saltarse todas las páginas, estas, sin muy graves consecuencias' ('Obviously all the pages can be skipped, these pages, without any especially serious consequences').[84] He emphasizes that his text is a fragile object, at the mercy of a reading public who might withdraw its attention at any moment.

Despite inscribing numerous readers into his text, according to Keymer, Sterne found the conversational mode most easily realized between one instalment of the novel and the next, due to the opportunity afforded by responding to reviews:

> Reception acts most obviously on the text in Tristram's allusions to reviews of preceding instalments, to which reviewers could then respond when reviewing the next, thereby perpetuating a genuinely conversational dynamic that peaks with the fourth instalment, when both the *Critical* and *Monthly* reviewers pick up and play on Tristram's idea of meanings left 'to be settled by/The REVIEWERS OF MY BREECHES'.[85]

---

[82] *La vida y opiniones*, p. 8.        [83] *NET*, p. 152.
[84] *NET*, p. 152.        [85] Keymer, p. 102.

Because the reception of *TLA* is *NET*'s guiding narrative thread, Marías takes the opportunity to respond to many of those who had offered their opinion of the earlier novel. By promising that *NET* will also have a sequel, he has also created the as yet unrealized potential for the kind of dialogue— response and counter-response—that Keymer describes in *TS*:

> Es tanto lo que ha saltado desde la novela [*TLA*] a mi vida que ya no sé cuántos folios necesitaré para contarlo, no bastará con este volumen ni quizá tampoco con el segundo previsto, porque han transcurrido ocho años desde que publiqué esa novela.[86]

> (So much has leapt from the novel [*All Souls*] into my life that I no longer know how many pages I'll need to tell the tale, this volume won't be enough nor even perhaps will the second I'm planning, because eight years have passed since I published that novel.)

Ironically enough, it was at the hands of Jorge Herralde, Marías's publisher at Anagrama, that *TLA* and its author suffered their harshest treatment. (Although Herralde remains unnamed in *NET*, the narrator hints that his surname begins with 'H' and, given the very public rift that grew between them in the 1990s, there can be no doubt who the mysterious 'H' is.) Marías describes how the two men thrashed out the terms of the publishing contract in negotiations he considered exploitative, if not underhand. He eventually agreed to 'condiciones leoninas e inaceptables' ('one-sided and unacceptable conditions')[87] out of misplaced loyalty to an editor whom he regarded as a paternal figure.

However, instead of writing up the episode as a crude settling of scores, Marías turns it into a brilliantly self-conscious piece of literary gamesmanship. He begins the interpolated chapter on Herralde, and the financially disadvantageous contract he persuaded Marías to sign for *TLA*, with a discussion of the shoddy treatment Hermann Melville received at the hands of Harper & Brothers of New York. The latter having offered Melville miserly financial terms to publish his latest work, *Pierre, or the Ambiguities*, he, surprisingly, accepted 'la mezquina oferta sin que se sepa bien el motivo' ('their miserly offer without his reasons being clear'); those last words 'sin que se sepa...'[88] are purely for artistic effect—Marías is about to tell us why he acquiesced:

> Aplazó sin embargo la entrega definitiva de la novela, la reabrió e insertó tres capítulos algo postizos en los que dibujó una amarga sátira del mundo literario en que se veía obligado a sobrevivir y ajustó ficticiamente las cuentas a sus editores y detractores, sobre todo a uno de éstos llamado Duyckinck.[89]

---

[86] *NET*, p. 253.      [87] *NET*, p. 287.
[88] Literally these words mean 'without it being known'.      [89] *NET*, p. 284.

(He nevertheless delayed the final delivery of the manuscript, set to work on it again and inserted three somewhat tacked-on chapters painting a bitter satire of the literary world in which he was forced to earn his crust, and fictitiously settled a score with his publishers and detractors, in particular one of the latter named Duyckinck.)

And all becomes clear. Though Marías lacked the chance to follow Melville's example at the time of *TLA*'s publication, he seized the next that presented itself of responding in kind to Herralde's shoddy treatment of him: he writes an interpolated chapter on his miserly editor, the ostensible subject of which is another set of interpolated chapters Herman Melville used to get his own back on his miserly editors. The sleight of hand is worthy of Sterne himself.

Sterne's difficulties with his bookseller, Thomas Becket, were of a different nature but still managed to find their way into *TS*. It was during his stay in France that Sterne's difficulties came to a head. Always a spendthrift and with the added burden of maintaining his family on their travels abroad, he sent a succession of letters from Southern France to Becket, his London bookseller, importuning him to send on the latest royalties payments earned from the sale of *TS*'s fifth and sixth volumes. Unfortunately, Becket was unable to satisfy Sterne's immediate financial need because copies of *TS* were not flying off the shelves with the speed, or in the numbers, they once had. Rather, its popularity had waned, and the print run of four thousand sets of the aforementioned fifth and sixth volumes wildly overestimated the amount of reader interest. True to form, Sterne sees the funny side of a difficult situation; one he fictionalizes by having Tristram chastise himself for failing to curb the incessant digressions that are hindering the serious business of telling his story:

> ¿No te basta estar ya en deuda, y tener todavía diez carretadas de tus volúmenes quinto y sexto por vender,—sin vender aún? ¿Ni haber agotado ya prácticamente todos los recursos de tu ingenio buscando el medio de deshacerte de ellos?[90]

> (Is it not enough that thou art in debt, and that thou hast ten cart-loads of thy fifth and sixth volumes still—still unsold, and art almost at thy wit's ends, how to get them off thy hands.)

Despite the waning interest in *TS* and failing health, Sterne was able to produce one further instalment, albeit one that consisted only of the single ninth volume, breaking his pattern hitherto of producing volumes in pairs. There can be little doubt that the quality and inventiveness of *TS*

---

[90] *La vida y opiniones*, pp. 484–5.

fall away in the later volumes, above all, perhaps, Tristram's travels in Europe, which become frankly tedious.

Marías promises that *NET* will have at least a second instalment[91] but has hitherto remained more measured in approach. Since 1998, far from allowing *NET* and its sequels to absorb all of his creative energy, he has pursued other projects, most importantly *TRM*. Nonetheless, as originally conceived, he evidently intended *NET* to remain a perpetual work-in-progress, updating itself as new events unfolded, and narrating them with the same artful artlessness of the Shandean narrator:

> Algún tiempo ha de pasar todavía hasta que hable más claro esa voz o letra y yo pueda contar lo que cuenta, alguna distancia he de tomar con acontecimientos recientes y por eso prefiero esperar un poco y hacer una pausa, aún es todo demasiado cambiante.[92]

> (Some time yet will have to pass before that voice or writing speaks more clearly and I can tell what it tells, I need to put some distance between me and recent events and for that I prefer to pause and wait a while, everything is still too unsettled.)

Marías uses prominent polysyndeton, coupled with the polyptoton 'contar...cuenta', 'Algún...alguna', to create an air of lethargy. By connecting clauses with the weakest of conjunctions—'y'—he creates the impression that fatigue has undermined his ability to link ideas in more sophisticated fashion. The polyptoton suggests a similar apathy towards elegant variation: where before synonyms would be employed, now the narrator is tired. Likewise the threefold clarification of 'alguna distancia he de tomar...prefiero esperar un poco...hacer una pausa': it is as if his gift for precision has temporarily deserted him. As we saw above, Marías manages to conflate his physical voice with the text he produces, much as Tristram does. When examining the passage just quoted, we do well to remember Marías's earlier assertion that written texts do not tire because 'no padecen el esfuerzo de emitir sonido y oírse' ('don't suffer the effort of emitting sound and hearing themselves'). He, by contrast, is the man of flesh and blood whose physical characteristics were described in the novel's opening chapter.[93] He has tired of the 'esfuerzo' required by long bouts of writing, writing that often takes place in the early hours of the morning. We might well ask what the effect is of providing so vivid and immediate an insight into the world of the writer. If, as seems clear, Marías is anxious that his readers should know just how arduous the writer's task is, why does he do it when, by his own admission, he sees no particular benefit arising from the task? I hope to provide an answer to that question in the final section of this chapter.

---

[91] *NET*, p. 253.      [92] *NET*, p. 387.      [93] *NET*, p. 14.

## THE HOBBY HORSE: BOOK COLLECTING AND
## MARÍAS'S WORLD BEFORE HE KNEW IT

Tristram Shandy would have it that what determines a man's particular world view more than anything else is his hobby horse. Walter Shandy is an obsessive systematizer who looks continually into the obscure tracts that chance throws into his path. On finding a sermon hidden inside Stevinus, Walter remarks that: 'Siempre he tenido una fuerte propensión, dijo mi padre, a examinar detenidamente aquellas cosas que, por extraños azares y predestinaciones (como en el presente caso), se cruzan en mi camino' ('I have ever a strong propensity, said my father, to look into things which cross my way, by such strange felicities as these').[94] Marías too shares this partiality for rare volumes, sniffing out works by Gawsworth, Shiel, de Wet, and Defoe, the covers of some of which are reproduced in the text as supporting props to the literary anecdotes and digressions. His hobby horse does prove psychologically revelatory, in the same way as Walter's search for the cold science of ancient lore runs alongside a deep mistrust of, and desire to control, his passions. The figure of Gawsworth provides an unsettling mirror for Marías's hobby horse since, as he had written in *TLA* and repeats in *NET*, one of Gawsworth's less destructive vices was 'el coleccionismo malsano de libros' ('an unhealthy obsession with book collecting').[95] Thus, not only was Gawsworth another compulsive collector of books, his spectre also foreshadows the literary oblivion that Marías fears—the thought that one day he might end up 'corriendo su suerte idéntica' ('sharing his exact same fate').[96] In life, both men have haunted London's second-hand bookshops, knowledge on which Marías drew when writing 'Un epigrama de lealtad'; there he imagines the vagrant Gawsworth in later life scrutinizing the shop window of Bertram Rota and seeing one of the books he once owned now priced beyond what he could ever afford.

Excessive drinking undermined Gawsworth to such an extent in later years that he was unable to hold down a job and, as a consequence, fell into penury. Marías says that the dark back of time encapsulates 'todo lo que se malogró' ('all that came to nothing'):[97] it would be hard to find a better example than Gawsworth's of a life that promised much, only to deliver little. Wilfrid Ewart too, he who in the England of his day, '"No necesita[ba] presentación ante el público lector"' ('Need[ed] no introduction to the reading public'),[98] fell into the most complete obscurity after

---

[94] *La vida y opiniones*, p. 103.        [95] *NET*, p. 158.        [96] *NET*, p. 169.
[97] See interview with César Güemes at the following URL: http://www.javiermarias.es/PAGINASDEENTREVISTAS/JornadaNov98.html (accessed 4 November 2008).
[98] *NET*, p. 175.

death, despite the books he wrote. Collecting rare volumes by such authors allows Marías to glimpse traces of the past, while reminding him of the vanity of all human wishes at self-perpetuation through objects.

One person to spot Marías's hobby horse and mock his conspicuous pride in his foraging abilities was Benet. The two friends engaged in some gentle sparring over the figure of de Wet, an airman and spy, who later in life turned his hand to sculpture, Gawsworth's death mask being among his works. Marías had challenged his mentor to scour his considerable Civil War library in search of information on this elusive figure; it was alleged that de Wet had flown planes for the Republican side. Benet, having proved himself equal to the task, throws down the gauntlet in return:

> A ver gran sabueso de los Baskerville, Arsenio Lupin de las letras, a ver, Joven Marías, ¿no presumes de que no hay libro que se te resista por inencontrable que sea? Ahí te quiero yo ver con este Oloff de Wet que parece el nombre de un perfume; a ver si eres capaz de traernos por aquí un ejemplar de ese *Cardbord Crucifix* del que nos sales ahora con que estabas tan al cabo de la calle.[99]

> (Well, we'll see, great hound of the Baskervilles, Arsène Lupin of letters, we'll see, Young Marías, don't you claim there's no book that you can't find no matter how elusive? I want to see you there with this Oloff de Wet that sounds like the name of a perfume; let's see if you can manage to bring us a copy of this *Cardboard Crucifix* that you've just been boasting you knew so much about.)

Note the care with which Marías reproduces the speech rhythms and mock-paternalistic tone that Benet adopts towards him. One of the books by de Wet that Marías eventually presents to Benet—'con un movimiento de pulgar e índice como si fueran naipes' (with a flick of forefinger and thumb as if they were cards') (his reputation intact)—has the added curiosity that its previous owner has left within its flyleaf several newspaper reports on de Wet's trial for espionage at the hands of the Nazis. Just as Yorick's sermon on the death of *Le Fever* excites interest as an artefact because it contains the preacher's hand-written annotations, Marías observes that second-hand books are no longer just the texts themselves but have the added curiosity value of the annotations and comments their previous owners have left on their pages.[100]

But literary posterity has handed down far more to Marías than a collection of dusty old volumes. It has secured for him a fantastical realm and its attendant kingship. And yet, he does not introduce the subject with the fanfares and pomp that ought to accompany a coronation. Instead, in the midst of a long digression in which he imagines what the 'negra espalda del tiempo' might contain, he lets slip that Redonda has a new king:

> puede que en esa dimensión o tiempo resida y sestee ese reino entero que a
> veces aparece en los mapas y otras no figura, como corresponde a un lugar
> que existe y a la vez es imaginario, the Realm of Redonda, the Kingdom of
> Redonda con su aristocracia intelectual de falsos nombres españoles y sus
> cuatro reyes, y que tras la abdicación en mi favor del tercero yo sea el cuarto
> de esos reyes desde el 6 de julio del 97, King Xavier o todavía King X mien-
> tras esto escribo y también con ello el albacea literario y el legal heredero de
> mis predecesores Shiel y Gawsworth, o Felipe I y Juan I.[101]

> (perhaps it is in that dimension or time where the Realm of Redonda, the
> Kingdom of Redonda resides and slumbers, that entire dominion which
> sometimes appears on maps and sometimes does not, as befits a place that is
> at once real and imaginary, with its intellectual aristocracy of fake Spanish
> names and its four kings, and it may be that, following the abdication of the
> third in my favour, I have been since the 6th July 1997 the fourth monarch,
> King Xavier or still King X while I write this, and with it literary executor and
> legal heir to my predecessors, Shiel and Gawsworth, or Felipe I and Juan I.)

When repeating one hundred pages earlier the fear that underlies his fascination with Shiel and Gawsworth—that 'acabaría corriendo su suerte
idéntica'[102]—he had subtly revealed that Redonda had a new ruler. Far
from articulating his trepidation at the prospect of literary oblivion, his
words hint at a more direct emulation: 'más ahora que nunca, cuando
resulta que soy ahora lo que fueron Shiel y Gawsworth' ('more so now
than ever, when it turns out that I have become what Shiel and Gawsworth were'). As the later date—July 1997—reveals when compared to
the date at which Marías was writing page 260 of *NET*—November
1997—the transfer of sovereignty must already have taken place. Marías
had been 'crowned': 'Es difícil resistirse a perpetuar una leyenda, más aún
si uno contribuyó a extenderla' ('It is hard to resist perpetuating a legend,
all the more so if one helped to prolong its life').[103] One imagines that Jon
Wynne-Tyson's abdication of the Redonda throne in Marías's favour was
among the 'acontecimientos recientes'[104] that persuaded him to break off
this first instalment of *NET*. He needed time both to reflect on what had
just happened and to allow further events to unfold before he could incorporate them into the world of the novel. It would at least explain why he
leaves this coup de théâtre to the penultimate chapter and provides little
in the way of details of his accession.

While Tristram's hobby horse brings him no such rewards, as readers
we are given ample opportunity to observe it. Were a reader of *TS* to try

---

[101] *NET*, pp. 365–7.     [102] *NET*, p. 253.
[103] *NET*, p. 253.        [104] *NET*, p. 387.

to define Tristram's particular obsession, two of the first things to come to mind might be digressions and, as we saw in the last chapter, the precise circumstances of his prenatal existence. As well as Mrs Shandy's ill-timed enquiry concerning the clock, a decisive factor in Tristram's upbringing was the premature death of his brother Bobby, whose demise made Walter all the more determined to ensure that his second-born son should receive an education founded on the finest tenets of pedagogical theory: 'Yo era la última apuesta de mi padre:—había perdido definitivamente a mi hermano Bobby' ('I was my father's last stake—he had lost my brother *Bobby* entirely').[105] Marías too explores decisive events that shaped the family environment into which he would be born: the betrayal and imprisonment his father suffered after the Civil War, and the death, two years before his birth, of his brother Julianín.

We learn of his father's betrayal in a digression that grows out of the difficulty Marías experienced when trying to prove that the events of *TLA* were not autobiographical:

> Lo que yo no podría ni puedo es demostrar que los hechos de la novela *no* me sucedieron a mí en mi vida, como es siempre imposible demostrar que *no* se ha hecho algo o cometido un delito si se parte del supuesto contrario, y esto bien lo han sabido los dictadores.[106]

> (What I could not, nor can I, do is prove that the novel's events had *never* happened to me in my life, just as it is nearly always impossible to prove that you have *not* done something or committed some crime if the opposite is assumed to be the case, a lesson all dictators have learned well.)

From the light-hearted denials that *TLA* caricatured any member of Oxford's academic staff, the tone darkens: 'en la propia España sin ir más lejos, esa fue la política judicial del franquismo nada más terminar la guerra y en el tiempo largo' ('in Spain itself, without going further afield, such was Franco's judicial policy both immediately after the war and in the longer term').[107] Everyone who lacked a conspicuously good service record on the Nationalist side was vulnerable to denunciation and the list of potential accusers—'Un vecino, un enemigo, un rival, un envidioso, un amigo' ('a neighbour, an enemy, a rival, an envious colleague, a friend')[108]— is worrying in its range and ordinariness. How many of each do all of us know? Franco's justice system laid the burden of proof at the door of the accused, not the accuser, making fair trials almost impossible. As often happens in *NET*, remarks of a general nature alight sooner or later on a subject close to the narrator's heart: 'Y eso le sucedió al hijo menor de María Aguilera de Marías, mi padre, a quien se imputó, entre otras cosas

[105] *La vida y opiniones*, pp. 329–30.     [106] *NET*, p. 28.
[107] *NET*, pp. 28–9.     [108] *NET*, p. 29.

imaginativas, haber sido durante la guerra...' ('And that is what happened to María Aguilera de Marías's youngest son, my father, who was accused, among other imaginative things, of having been during the war...').[109] That he was later able to beget and rear the son who narrates the novel we are reading clearly suggests that the trumped-up claims of which his father was victim did not stick. Rather than continue in a sombre vein, Marías sees the humour in a potentially precarious situation that had a happy outcome. He admits, tongue in cheek, that he feels 'inconsolable envidia' ('undying envy') that his father should have been accused of something so patently absurd as being an 'acompañante voluntario del bandido Deán de Canterbury' ('willing companion of the bandit Red Dean of Canterbury'). There follows a digression on the subject of this English warrior cleric, one that need not concern us here since it only serves to confirm Marías's insatiable curiosity. The point is in fact that:

> Pero por su involuntaria compañía y causa yo estuve a punto de no nacer, habida cuenta de que el paredón solía ser en 1939 el más repetido y común destino de los denunciados por las amistades patrióticas y precavidas, y si mi padre no pasó de la cárcel fue por suerte y por tenacidad de mi madre—aún no sabían que se casarían—y no por falta de inquina en sus dos delatores. Y qué, si no hubiera nacido.[110]

> (But because of the Red Dean and his unwilling companionship I could easily never have been born, given that in 1939 the firing squad was what most commonly and most often awaited those denounced by their patriotic and cautious friends, and if my father went no further than prison it was down to luck and my mother's tenacity—they didn't yet know that they would marry each other—and not for any lack of ill will on the part of his two accusers. So what, if I'd never been born.)

We need again to be sensitive to modulations of tone: from the ironic opening, with its play on 'voluntario'/'involuntaria', we move to a bitter historical fact—'el paredón solía ser...'—and from there to the sarcasm of 'las amistades patrióticas y precavidas' where the alliterative 'p' sounds could be the narrator spitting the words out. By exploring the disposition of the world into which he was born, Marías may be evoking Shandean subject matter, but the tone is more nuanced than Sterne's.

He concludes the digression into his father's imprisonment with the following disillusioned account of the modern world's overanxiety to bury the past:

> Hay demasiados que nacen y es como si no hubiera ocurrido y no hubieran nunca existido; son tan pocos de los que se conserva memoria y hay tantos

[109] *NET*, p. 29.    [110] *NET*, p. 30.

que mueren pronto como si el mundo no tuviera paciencia para asistir a sus
vidas o hubiera prisa por desprenderse de ellos, el esfuerzo baldío y los pasos
diminutos sin huella o sólo para el recuerdo afilado de quien enseñó a darlos
y cometió el error o realizó el esfuerzo, como un lujo costoso y superfluo que
se expulsa de la tierra como si fuera vaho y ni siquiera se permite poner a
prueba. Y qué, si no hubiera nacido nunca nadie.[111]

(Too many people are born and it's as if it had never happened and they had
never existed; there are so few of whom any memory is retained and there are
so many who die young, as if the world lacked the patience to witness their
lives or was in a hurry to get rid of them, the vain effort of the diminutive
footsteps that left no traces or only in the sharp-edged memory of the person
who taught the feet to step and made the mistake or the effort, like a superfluous and costly luxury that is expelled from earth as if it were a breath and
not even allowed to test its mettle. So what, if no one had ever been born.)

Only 'quien enseñó a dar [los pasos diminutos]' bucks this trend towards
indifference. The figure immediately called to mind when thinking of who
teaches us to walk is a parental one. That parental figure suffers a 'recuerdo
afilado', a phrase Marías adapted from Browne, for whom 'our sorrows are
not kept raw by the edge of repetitions' (see Chapter 7). A relentlessly
retentive memory not blessed with the ability to forget would constitute a
torment in the eyes of Browne and Marías; it is just such a memory that
parental figures possess. The narrator expresses the same sentiment, though
with slight variations of phrasing, later in the novel, during the narrative of
Wilfrid Ewart's last day of life.[112] There it is the 'recuerdo hiriente de quien
se molestó en enseñar [los pasos diminutos]' ('lacerating memory of the
person who bothered to teach [the tiny footsteps]') that characterizes the
parental figure and distinguishes him or her from the indifferent mass of
humanity. On the third occasion that the thought recurs, Marías has
focused on his mother as the person who specifically suffers this memorial
torment and the 'pasos diminutos' belong to Julianín, the brother who
predeceased him. He illustrates in the process how infrequently he—and,
by extension, others—think in truly abstract terms. The threefold repetition of this image removes successive layers of abstraction until narrator
and reader come to a simultaneous realization of what underlies Marías's
beliefs. In this instance, his distaste for modern tendencies to bury the past
and move inexorably forward can be traced to an awareness that his mother
suffered considerable grief over an event that to the rest of the world could
hardly matter less. This revelation is artistically satisfying for the reader
because it suggests a moment of clarity, though not order, in what is the
otherwise chaotic associative flow of the narrator's mind:

[111] *NET*, pp. 30–1.     [112] *NET*, pp. 235–6.

Se teje este material filtrado en una una [*sic*] red de sutiles y casuales asocia-
ciones gobernadas por unos procesos más o menos inconscientes, que se
desarrollan en una libertad de la que la creatividad artística los dota.[113]

(This material is woven together in a web of subtle and chance associations
governed by processes that are more or less subconscious, and that develop
in a free environment bestowed by artistic creativity.)

As mentioned above, Tristram's brother Bobby died young, leaving Tristram
alone at the mercy of Walter the compulsive systematizer. No such definitive
consequences can be traced back to the untimely death of Julianín, only the
wistfulness Marías sometimes caught in his mother's eyes while she looked at
her dead child's portrait: 'mi madre se quedaba en ocasiones con la vista fija en
el cuadro, no con pena sino como si reviviera y quisiera decirle algo' ('my
mother would sometimes stay still with her gaze fixed upon the picture, not in
grief rather as if she were reliving the past and wanted to say something to
him').[114] Again, the digression on Julianín grows out of what appears at first a
chance remark. Discussion of Wilfrid Ewart's demise having exhausted itself
without anything resembling a conclusion in sight—which is precisely the
point—Marías wonders: 'Qué sentido tiene el paso por el mundo callado de
quienes no tienen tiempo ni de acostumbrarse al aire, y todavía Ewart escribió
y luchó y vivió treinta años, qué habría sido de él más adelante' (What sense is
there in the silent passage through this world of those who don't even have time
to get used to the air, and even Ewart wrote and fought and lived for thirty
years, what would have become of him in the future').[115] Although these are
questions, they are pointedly not framed by the punctuation symbols we
would expect. It is as if Marías expected these enquiries to elicit no response
because the answers are in every sense unknowable. He lists two friends' children who died in infancy—those of Aliocha Coll and Juan Benet—before
mentioning his own dead brother. He appears to grapple not with undefined
grief, rather with the series of imponderables that having an older brother he
never knew opens up: 'Es extraño pensar que hubo alguien tan próximo a mí
como un hermano a quien no he conocido' ('It's strange to think that there was
someone as close to me as a brother whom I never knew'):

No puedo saber cómo habría sido Julianín ni cómo me habría llevado con
ese hermano desconocido y previo a mi nacimiento, si me habría protegido
o mangoneado desde sus seis años de diferencia más fuertes y expertos.[116]

(I cannot know what Julianín would have been like nor how I would have
got on with this brother who was both unknown and prior to my birth, if

[113] Alexis Grohmann, 'La errabundia de *Negra espalda del tiempo*', in *Cuadernos de
narrativa: Javier Marías*, pp. 135–44 (p. 140).
[114] *NET*, p. 266.     [115] *NET*, p. 264.     [116] *NET*, p. 266.

he would have protected me or bossed me around with his six years of advantage over me in strength and skill.)

Like Gawsworth, Conan Doyle, and the host of departed of whom Marías has no direct memory, Julianín exists now only through portraits and the objects on which he left his mark.[117] In the absence of their owners, it is easy for such objects to become 'testigos y metáforas y emblemas' ('witnesses and metaphors and emblems').[118] To regard them in this way is not to sentimentalize them, though for him and his brothers Julianín's toys were 'reliquias casi intocables' ('almost untouchable relics'). It is merely a small human gesture that seeks to prevent the absolute death of someone too obviously no longer present in person. It falls to the maternal figure, with her 'recuerdo afilado', to remember what the rest of the world would so easily forget.

## EVOKING THE DEAD: 'THE EYE ... HAS THE QUICKEST COMMERCE WITH THE SOUL'

Of course, in *NET*, Marías recalls several of his dead, going against what he sees as the modern tendency to denigrate or forget them. Among the friends he had lost, Benet in particular had been victim of cowardly defamation, following his death from a brain tumour on 5 January 1993. Their mutual friend Vicente Molina-Foix pulled no punches the following day in attacking the Spanish literary establishment for its failure formally to reward Benet while it still had the chance.[119] During an act of homage that took place on 23 February at Madrid's Círculo de Bellas Artes, Marías alluded to the fact that Benet provoked 'mucha animadversión en algunos medios'; he could hardly have expected to be proved right in so squalid a fashion so soon after. Barely two months after Benet's death, a spokesperson for the Partido Popular in Castilla y León's regional assembly, José Nieto Noya, unleashed a storm of controversy by calling the writer 'discutido, discutible e insoportable' ('disputed, disputable, and insufferable').[120] What Marías saw as a tendency to defile the memory of writers while their corpses were still warm, was continuing to exercise him in 1996, while *NET* was taking shape: 'Es algo que me subleva. Parece como si el muerto fuera culpable de haberse muerto. La gente borra rapidísimamente, pero yo no lo hago ni quiero hacerlo' ('It's something that infuriates me. It seems as if the dead person were guilty for having died.

[117] *NET*, pp. 268–9.    [118] *NET*, p. 269.
[119] Vicente Molina-Foix, 'Primera página', *El País*, 6 January 1993, p. 28.
[120] Aurelio Martín, 'El PP de Castilla y León dice que está abierto al homenaje a Juan Benet', *El País*, 17 March 1993, p. 31.

People erase all traces far too quickly, but I don't do it and nor do I want to').[121]

In evoking his departed friend, Marías concentrates particularly on Benet's physical gestures as observed and remembered. Sterne too was aware that the eye 'mantiene un comercio más vivo con el alma', and, as we saw in the last chapter, illustrates the point with Trim's dropping of his hat during his announcement of Bobby's death.[122] Hence Marías recalls the occasions on which Benet would ostentatiously take out in public the moustache comb that his protégé had bought for him as a mocking, mystery gift, only for Benet to guess at the first opportunity what the intended present was:

> Se lo vi utilizar a menudo en los años siguientes, de vez en cuando lo sacaba en una reunión en presencia mía y se repeinaba el bigote con delicadeza un ratito, haciéndose el distraído, sin duda para restregarme aquel brillante triunfo deductivo suyo.... Muy propio de él este disfrute recurrente y retrospectivo.[123]

> (I often saw him use it in subsequent years, he would occasionally take it out at a gathering in my presence and meticulously preen his moustache for a while, pretending to do it absently, no doubt to rub my nose in that brilliant deductive triumph of his... So typical of him that reiterated and retrospective enjoyment.)

Marías does not appear to share Sterne's wariness of literary renderings of human behaviour that claim accurately to fathom character or motivation. And yet, one of the reasons why he can state with such certainty that this is the case is because Benet has been deprived by death of the ability to contradict Marías's statement. His life is no longer dynamic and hence is, at least partially, susceptible to being narrated. The intrusion of this sudden certainty in a narrative that abounds in adverbs expressing doubt heightens the poignancy of the memory and reinforces the finality of Benet's demise.

Marías's last vision of his mentor alive is similarly etched into his memory:

> Él salió a la puerta a despedirnos ya tarde, y la última visión es por tanto la de su figura larga en lo alto de los escalones de entrada de su chalet de El Viso, con la sonrisa aún puesta de la risa pasada como un rastro suave y adormecedor antes del sueño, la larga figura en penumbra recortada contra la luz de dentro diciéndonos adiós con la mano y no con el pensamiento.[124]

---

[121] Interview conducted by Javier del Castillo. Text available at the following URL: http://www.javiermarias.es/PAGINASDEENTREVISTAS/Tribunafeb96.html (accessed 4 November 2008).

[122] *La vida y opiniones*, p. 320.     [123] *NET*, pp. 326–7.     [124] *NET*, p. 217.

(He came out to the door to say goodbye, it was late by now, and so my last image of him is that of his tall silhouetted figure standing at the top of the stairs leading up to his house in El Viso, the smile still lingering from his recent laughter, like a slim, somnolent trace on the face of someone who's falling asleep, his tall frame outlined in shade against the light coming from inside the house, waving goodbye with his hand but not in his mind.)

Whether 'true to the facts' or not, this last sight of his friend is retrospectively tinged by the knowledge that he was to die soon after. His 'sonrisa' which is 'como un rastro suave y adormecedor antes del sueño' anticipates the more lasting sleep into which he was soon to slip. His figure silhouetted against the light of the doorway also suggests the passage from one world to the next: doors and gateways have a longstanding metaphorical value as indicators of such transitions. All the more poignant, then, that this scene, which has, through the retroactive effect of memory and literary evocation, acquired a certain artistic aptness, should find Benet 'diciéndonos adiós con la mano y no con el pensamiento'.

## WOUNDED THIGHS

Marías's final vision of Juan Benet is seared into his memory precisely because it was the last chance he had of observing his friend in life. By reworking the description with artistic skill, reconfiguring its aspects so that they hint at the unforeseen parting, he conveys to the reader something of its poignancy. While such attention to the scene's universal or communicable elements is what we would hope the best novelists capable of, we should, nonetheless, not underestimate his achievement, nor how affecting the description is. Later in *NET*, Marías quotes Dinesen's observations on the necessity of re-imagining a story for it to become communicable:

> sólo si uno es capaz de imaginar lo que ha ocurrido, de repetirlo en la imaginación, verá las historias, y sólo si tiene la paciencia de llevarlas largo tiempo dentro de sí, y de contárselas y recontárselas una y otra vez, será capaz de contarlas bien.[125]

(only if you are capable of imagining what happened, of repeating it in your imagination, will you see the stories, and only if you have the patience to carry them for a long time within you, telling and retelling them to yourself over and over again, will you be able to tell them well.)

Part of this process of artistic fashioning concerns the deployment of apt illustration or description: 'la constante jerarquización a que somete a las

---

[125] *NET*, p. 370.

cosas del mundo, el esfuerzo y el cansancio que supone discernir hasta en los menores detalles: un color, un gesto, un diálogo' ('the constant process of ranking the objects in the world, the effort and fatigue that it means to distinguish even in the smallest details: a colour, a gesture, a dialogue').[126] One such image in *NET* is the 'cicatriz de un muslo', a scar an ex-lover had sustained on her thigh, to which the narrator's memory returns periodically. To say that this image has a more humorous correlative in the shape of Uncle Toby's wound does not seem to me a huge leap of faith, given the wealth of Shandean parallels with which Marías has so evidently peppered *NET*.

When first mentioned, the 'cicatriz' ('scar') jars on the reader because, appearing as it does in a list of otherwise abstract nouns, its specificity seems out of place:

> Y además uno olvida siempre demasiados instantes, también horas y días y meses y años, y la cicatriz de un muslo que vio y besó a diario durante largo tiempo de un tiempo conocido y perdido. Olvida uno años enteros, y no necesariamente los más insignificantes.[127]

> (And besides one always forgets far too many moments, even hours, days, months, and years, and the scar on a thigh that one saw and kissed daily for a long time in a period once known and now lost. One forgets entire years, and not necessarily the most insignificant ones.)

Talking in the third person, Marías rejects the idea that human beings can reach a stable narrative of self, given the fallibility of our memories. What is the status of that narrative, what we think of as the trajectory of our lives, if we have forgotten swathes of our own past? We have already seen how Marías tentatively describes an abstract parental figure afflicted with a too-accurate memory, only to reveal later that he has his mother and her grief at the death of Julianín strongly in mind. A similar trope is in operation here, with his would-be abstract example turning out to be an intimate memory. We have to wait for over one hundred pages before we learn that the 'cicatriz enorme e injusta' scarred the thigh of an ex-lover: 'Yo olvidé la cicatriz enorme e injusta que vi y besé a diario no durante dos sino durante tres años, en tiempos todavía más viejos y en una ciudad distinta que tampoco era la mía, la cicatriz de un muslo' ('I forgot the huge, unjust scar that I saw and kissed daily not for two but three years in even older times and in a different city that wasn't mine either, the scar on a thigh').[128] Once readers have seen confirmed their earlier suspicion that the image had particular personal resonance for Marías, they realize also that in his mind it forms a complex synecdoche of everything that he

---

[126] JM, 'Contagio', in *LF*, pp. 49–50 (p. 49).          [127] *NET*, pp. 10–11.
[128] *NET*, p. 123.

wishes he had not forgotten. Because the memory had slipped his mind, only for him to be reminded of it by a friend, the scar evokes both the woman who bore it and the slippage at the edges of memory: 'cómo puede ser que durante años haya desaparecido de mis atesoradas visiones esa cicatriz que me fue familiar e hice mía' ('how can it be that for years the scar that was so familiar and that I made my own should have disappeared from my treasured visions'). That he should have first committed the scar to memory, only for it then to vanish, begs the question how many more such instances might there be. He recalls the tact and tenderness with which his lover first told him of her scar, 'como diciéndome: "Escucha, ven, mira, en mí hay esto y quizá prefieras no llegar a verlo"' ('as if she were saying to me: "Listen, come here, look, I have this thing and you may not want to see it"').[129] Despite the kisses he lavished on this blemish to prevent it from making his lover self-conscious, he manages to poison the nobility of even that gesture: the subsequent failure of the relationship retrospectively tarnishes what he would like to think of as his higher sentiments or better nature:

> Lo vi, y lo vi luego a diario hasta que sin duda dejé de verlo cuando pasaba la vista por ello porque mis ojos lo pasaban por alto aunque allí siguiera suave y quemado, y si lo besaba era ya sin darme cuenta y sin mérito—si es que eso puede tenerlo.[130]

> (I saw it, and then I saw it every day and no doubt I stopped seeing it when my eyes ran over it because my eyes ignored it although there it remained, smooth and burnt, and if I kissed it, it was by then without realizing and without merit—if something like that can have merit.)

The difficulty he experienced in accepting the end of the relationship—brilliantly expressed as 'como si me hubiera quedado prendido en su tela de araña que ella ya no tejía'—contrasts with her indifference. He wonders whether she even spares him a thought these days, supplying her extempore as a series of inconsequential musings: '"vivió aquí conmigo una vez un joven, era madrileño, me pregunto qué habrá sido de él, hace ya tanto tiempo"' ('"a young guy once lived here with me, he was from Madrid, I wonder what's happened to him, it's all so long ago"').[131]

Because the thigh is not usually seen when a person is clothed, the fact that Marías's lover needed to warn him of what he was about to see operates as a tender euphemism for the greater intimacy they must have shared. It is also a reminder of Uncle Toby's wound sustained on the battlefield of Namur, the extent of which Widow Wadman is so anxious to ascertain. Scarred thighs have a long history in literature, not least in the story of Venus and Adonis from Book X of Ovid's *Metamorphoses*. More

---

[129]  *NET*, p. 124.      [130]  *NET*, p. 124.      [131]  *NET*, p. 125.

generally, the image hints at the vulnerability that underlies emotionally and sexually charged relationships, the way that such intimacy leaves us open to harm. With that in mind, it is ironic that, though his lover bore this physical scar, it was the narrator who suffered 'largos años de estéril y ensimismado esfuerzo y de soliloquios o despedidas sobrantes que no contestaba nadie' ('long years of fruitless, self-absorbed effort and of monologues or superfluous goodbyes that no one answered').[132]

## 'APAGA LA LUZ, Y LUEGO APAGA LA LUZ'

Having examined two images that acquire wider metaphorical significance through Marías's treatment of them, I wish to examine two further sights observed by the narrator. The task is made easier in this case because they always appear in close proximity to one another and are clearly linked in the narrator's mind. The first are the 'faroles' observed from his window in the early morning—the street lights that remain lit after dawn has broken. The second are the man and woman waiting at the bus stop who appear three times in the novel and whose lives he imagines in vivid detail. Marías's responses to these images offer a commentary on the enterprise of writing fiction, one that goes some way to answering the question of why the novel exists at all. Far from believing *NET* to be of transcendent importance, Marías lays greater emphasis on the futility of his—or indeed any—artistic endeavour. The novel as a whole celebrates the serendipity that has brought Marías into ghostly contact with so many writers and lives that had hitherto remained dark to him. However, it refuses to be anything more than stoically aware of its own futility. Whereas Tristram Shandy claims to believe that:

> El verdadero shandismo...ensancha el corazón y los pulmones, y como todas las demás afecciones que participan de su naturaleza, obliga a la sangre y a otros fluidos vitales del cuerpo a correr libremente por sus correspondientes conductos y hace que la rueda de la vida gire alegremente durante mucho tiempo.[133]

> (True *Shandeism*...opens the heart and lungs, and like all those affections which partake of its nature, it forces the blood and other vital fluids of the body to run freely thro' its channels, and makes the wheel of life run long and cheerfully round.)

*NET* is on the other hand like the 'faroles'—no more than a chance to observe the passing between two periods of darkness.

---

[132] *NET*, p. 124.        [133] *La vida y opiniones*, p. 297.

To explain why I believe the 'faroles' to be emblematic of the novel, I must first explain that for the author they provide an image of time's benevolence. According to Marías, 'el respetuoso tiempo' ('respectful time') allows humans the chance to observe the significant shifts in the perpetual flux of our existence, flux that we would otherwise erroneously divide into 'ilusorios límites' ('illusory limits').[134] As we have seen, he rejects the idea that human lives have either coherence or structure. In fact, his one explicit reference to *TS* in this most Shandean of texts is to refute King William's theory—as reported by Trim—that '"cada bala llevaba su propia esquela"' ('"every bullet has it's [*sic*] billet"'), which strikes him as playing too easily to human needs for finite, straightforward narrative.[135] Time nevertheless concedes a moment of contemplation between the end of one sequence (be that a life or a time period) and the beginning of the next; even though as human beings we have a tendency to load such moments with retrospective significance, they should not be confused with coherence or narrative. As we have seen, Marías catches himself doing just that when describing his final meeting with Benet, despite concluding from Ewart's death that 'lo inmediatamente anterior a lo último o a la catástrofe no tiene por qué ser siempre significativo ni encerrar interés alguno' ('that which comes before the end or the catastrophe does not always have to be significant nor be especially interesting').[136] The 'faroles' that burn long after their light has been superseded by the advancing day are the metaphorical representation of time's benevolence: 'son el testimonio respetuoso y benigno de que existió lo que ya ha cesado' ('give respectful and benign testimony to the existence of what has now gone').[137]

Marías's Shandean insistence on his physical presence behind the novel we read means that he is able plausibly to evoke the specific scene outside the windows while he writes in the early morning. Except that he is not alone in observing them:

> Yo las veo y los veo a veces desde mis balcones en mañanas de insomnio o de despertar traicionero o de arriesgada y vencida farra, faroles decimonónicos enclavados en el muro con sus bombillas ya inútiles, pasan junto a ellos hombres y mujeres con apresurados tacones que dejaron hace rato sus camas...[138]

> (I see them sometimes from my balcony during insomniac mornings or when a treacherous awakening or reckless and spent carousing find me still up, nineteenth-century streetlamps hanging from the wall, their bulbs now useless, while passing by go men and women with hurried heels who left their beds a while ago...)

---

[134] *NET*, p. 142.     [135] *NET*, pp. 244–5; *La vida y opiniones*, p. 504.
[136] *NET*, p. 209.     [137] *NET*, p. 147.     [138] *NET*, pp. 143–6.

These hypothetical figures are quickly individualized as people waiting for the bus—a woman who has just had a one-night stand[139] and a man whose debts are mounting and who fears his wife may abandon him any day.[140] Marías imagines the former with a wealth of pitiful detail, capturing the transitory consolations and ultimate disappointments of her sexual conquests: 'no volverá a ver al joven que le arrancó ese vestido sin ningún cuidado más por ser joven que por desear quitárselo, se irá cuando se despierte sin dejar una nota y hasta es posible que le robe algo' ('she will never see again the young man who carelessly tore off that dress, more because he was young than because he especially wanted to tear it off her, he'll go when he wakes up without leaving a note and it's even possible that he'll steal something from her on his way out').[141] With great economy, he sketches her character through the company she keeps; the kind of woman who picks up a young buck to fulfil her needs, relying on the fact that he will be so flattered by the offer that he will not stop to think. The price she pays is in the items he will steal the following day: not quite paying for sex but sadly close to it. The male stranger at the bus stop is introduced with the following evocative sentence:

> Mira el hombre los faroles y piensa en la mujer que se levanta más tarde y siguió soñando o fingiéndolo impacientada mientras él se preparaba para salir al mundo y se preparaba el café en medio del amanecer oscuro, ella en él no estará pensando. [142]

> (The man looks at the streetlamps and thinks of the woman who gets up later than him and went on sleeping or pretending to sleep while he got ready to face the world and made himself coffee in the midst of the gloomy dawn, she won't be thinking of him.)

Marías uses anacoluthon—'piensa en la mujer…ella en él no estará pensando'—to emphasize the disjuncture between them. Once again, the devil is in the detail; on this occasion, the woman who would rather feign sleep than talk to him captures the domestic dysfunction that underlies all the man's fears.

Julian Barnes's essay, 'Justin: A Small Major Character', provides an indication as to what Marías achieves by including these two apparently inconsequential figures, who are only ever seen from a distance. Barnes explores the role played in *Madame Bovary* by Justin, the local lad who runs messages for the heroine and, ultimately, gives her access to the poison that kills her. Barely noticed by the reader Justin is nevertheless instrumental at key points in the novel, facilitating Emma's adultery and helping

---

[139] *NET*, p. 146.        [140] *NET*, p. 147.
[141] *NET*, p. 146.        [142] *NET*, p. 147.

her to endure its disappointments when they arrive; he falls quietly in love with her and grieves more than any other character at her death. The danger of critical approaches that make nuanced artistry seem cumbersome is something of which Barnes is all too aware: 'To string [Justin's] appearances together inevitably has the effect of making Flaubert's use of him seem more obvious and less delicate than it is; though it won't make it seem less brutal'.[143] Nonetheless:

> Justin's brief erotic tragedy goes unnoticed in the wider world. He is an echo of her, that perfectly placed bit of kindling which makes Emma's story blaze the brighter. To change the metaphor: if *Madame Bovary* were a mansion, Justin would be the handle to the back door; but great architects have the design of door-furniture in mind even as they lay out the west wing.[144]

With similar hopes of avoiding analysis that bleeds the life from its subject, I want to suggest that the anonymous pair at the bus stop provide a comparable commentary on the narrator of *NET*. It is important to remember that their appearances are always linked with the metaphor of time's benevolence and the 'faroles', the chance to observe the moment of transition from light into darkness. We might also remember that Marías is not working from genuine data. Whether or not he did see two such people from his window early one morning is a moot point. He is free to envisage their lives in whatever way he chooses and decides to give each of them a stay of execution. The woman's one-night stand becomes, over the subsequent occasions we meet her, a more stable relationship;[145] the man's gambling debts and the threats hanging over him never take concrete form.[146] By the novel's final paragraph, the fusion between Marías's consciousness, the image of 'faroles', and the strangers in the street is complete:

> Aparto la vista un momento de los balcones para sacudirme la noche larga y también la duda y acaso ser de nuevo uno solo; y al volver a mirar el autobús ha llegado y se ha llevado a sus pasajeros. Miro las incongruentes luces todavía encendidas bajo el sol que avanza haciéndolas insignificantes; y sin embargo son ellas el tiempo respetuoso y benigno que quiere dejar constancia de lo que ya ha cesado: hasta que la soñolienta mano de algún funcionario repara en el despilfarro y apaga la luz, y luego la apaga. Y aun así los pasajeros ahí siguen, y aun así la luz no se ha apagado.[147]

> (I turn my eyes away from the balcony for a moment to shake off the long night and also the doubts and perhaps just to be me alone again; and when I look back, the bus has arrived and taken away its passengers. I watch the

[143] Julian Barnes, 'Justin: A Small Major Character', in *Something to Declare* (London: Picador, 2002), pp. 289–302 (pp. 295–6).
[144] 'Justin: A Small Major Character', p. 302.
[145] *NET*, pp. 281–2, 401–2.     [146] *NET*, pp. 280–1, 402–3.     [147] *NET*, p. 404.

incongruous lights still burning under the rising sun that is making them
insignificant; and yet the lights are benign, respectful time that wants to leave
a record of what has now ceased: all until the drowsy hand of some civil servant notices the waste and puts out the light, then puts it out. And even then
the passengers are still there, and even then the light is still not out.)

The final affirmation of this fleeting permanence is tied up with Marías's
consciousness and his ability to register that consciousness. Even though
they have gone, they are still present in his mind's eye, just like the 'relato'
that will only die with him.[148]

## CONCLUSION

That Marías should have chosen to follow Sterne's precedent in *NET*
demonstrates several things. The first is that, despite the twenty years that
intervened between his translation of *TS* and his fullest fictional engagement with Sterne, he still felt the latter's influence strongly enough to
rework Shandean gestures, tropes, and preoccupations in his own *NET*.
Second, we might see the reasons for his decision as growing out of his
and Sterne's shared suspicion of narrative that seeks to lay grand claims to
insight and order. *NET*, like *TS* before it, is a novel which represents
Marías's attempts to give narrative coherence to chaotic, serendipitous,
and inexplicable events while not losing sight of their chaos, serendipity,
and inexplicability. Narratives of this kind, because they are all that
humans have to make sense of a world that so often resists classification,
can aspire only to communicate the workings of an evolving consciousness in all its searches after meaning.

[148] *NET*, p. 403.

# 5

# Competing with Illustrious Forerunners: Browne, Borges, and Bioy Casares

## INTRODUCTION: FAULKNER AND BORGES

We saw in the first chapter of this study that Marías regards the Argentine writer Borges as a rival. Although happy to recognize his admiration for Borges's short stories, his comments on Borges the translator are less complimentary, and the latter's version of *The Wild Palms* warrants only a withering aside in the introduction to *Si yo amaneciera otra vez*.[1] In the present chapter I will be drawing direct comparisons between Marías's rendering of the fifth chapter of Sir Thomas Browne's *Hydriotaphia* and that produced by Borges in collaboration with his life-long friend Adolfo Bioy Casares. As a starting point, however, I wish to examine whether there is any substance to the claim that Borges translated Faulkner 'bastante mal' ('pretty badly').[2] By doing so I wish to determine whether Marías's claim is an opportunistic smear on an undoubtedly illustrious forerunner or a sound verdict on a poor piece of work. Challenged by Juan García Ponce to justify his assertion, Marías explained that: 'Si Borges no tradujo muy bien a Faulkner no fue por sus argentinismos, sino por su conocimiento imperfecto del inglés... por sus frecuentes antojos y por su falta de aliento novelístico' ('If Borges didn't translate Faulkner particularly well it wasn't because he used too many Argentine idioms but instead because of his imperfect grasp of English... his frequent caprices and lack of novelistic staying power').[3] In his study of Borges the translator, Efraín Kristal offers another reason why the Spanish language may require a better version of *The Wild Palms*, explaining that, 'Borges often

---

[1] He recognized his admiration for Borges's short fiction in an interview with Jaime Bello León in May 1997. Jaime Bello León, Entrevista con Javier Marías', *La Brújula*, 67–8 (1997). www.javiermarias.es/main.html (accessed 4 November 2008).

[2] *Si yo amaneciera otra vez*, p. 14.

[3] JM, 'Nuestra o suya y mía', in *AVC*, pp. 96–8 (p. 98).

removes gory or distasteful details from his translations, especially when they diminish another aspect of the literary work', adding in a footnote that '[i]n his translation of William Faulkner's *The Wild Palms*, Borges removes the episode of the abortion, perhaps for similar reasons'.[4] This is a substantial claim and deserves to be investigated, especially as Kristal implies that *The Wild Palms* could be aesthetically improved by the removal of its abortion scene. Nabokov called such tampering by omission a 'step to Hell', condemning the translator who 'is as ready to know less than the author as he is to think he knows better'.[5] More importantly for our purposes, this explanation would corroborate Marías's claim that Borges wrote a flawed version of Faulkner. Those familiar with the novel will recall that it comprises two juxtaposed stories separated by ten years in time and told in alternating chapters. The first (entitled 'The Wild Palms') is that of the doomed romance between Harry Wilbourne and Charlotte Rittenmeyer: doomed because she has left her husband, fallen pregnant, and persuaded Wilbourne (a not quite fully trained doctor) to perform an abortion, which has gone wrong, leaving her haemorrhaging internally. The second (entitled 'Old Man') concerns the fate of a prisoner in a Mississippi jail who is enlisted into the effort to rescue stranded villagers when the region's giant flood defences fail in the face of the swollen Mississippi river. As the novel opens, Wilbourne and Charlotte arrive at a rented coastal cottage, with the latter appearing unwell and, it transpires, bleeding from her vagina. The narrative then flashes back to the start of their affair, leading up to their elopement and eventually the failed abortion. 'The Wild Palms' thread of the novel ends with Wilbourne arrested and charged with causing Charlotte's death, as well as facing the wrath of her estranged husband.

From this brief synopsis, it is clear that *The Wild Palms* would be a strange, not to say inexplicable novel without the abortion scene around which the entire action of one half of it revolves. Were it the case that Borges had managed to translate Faulkner's novel without this central piece of information, it would be a remarkable feat and a very different reading experience from the original English. Unsurprisingly, Kristal is wrong in his description of Borges's translation and we will need to examine the latter more closely to assess its viability.

While Borges does not remove the abortion scene from *The Wild Palms*, there are two instances where more graphic phrases from the description of the act itself are missing or softened. For example, when Charlotte is

---

[4] See Efraín Kristal, *Invisible Work: Borges and Translation* (Nashville: Vanderbilt University Press, 2002), pp. 119, 185.
[5] 'The Art of Translation', p. 315.

nerving Wilbourne for the task (whose hand is shaking so violently he is afraid even to begin), she makes the following conciliatory observation: "'All right. We'll wait a minute. It's simple. It's funny. New, I mean. We've done this lots of ways but not with knives, have we? There. Now your hand has stopped"'.[6] A piece of dialogue that in Borges's version is rendered as follows: 'Bueno. Esperaremos un minuto. Es sencillo. Es gracioso. Nuevo, quiero decir. Ahora. Tu mano está quieta'.[7] Clearly the sentence beginning 'We've done...' has been omitted from his version, a decision we would understand if the Argentine translator were indeed endeavouring to avoid causing offence. However, *The Wild Palms* was issued almost simultaneously in 1939 in the United States and the United Kingdom, by Random House and Chatto & Windus respectively. What we find on examining the UK edition of the novel is that the sentence that, according to Kristal, Borges removed for reasons of propriety is also missing from the Chatto & Windus UK edition.[8] Comparison of other apparent omissions or censorship of Faulkner's original can also be attributed to the fact that he was using the UK edition that had been 'cleaned up' for British readers. These include the editing of the following speech by the character McCord, reproduced in the original American text and Borges's version: "'Sweet Jesus,' Mc Cord said. "Holy choriated cherubim. If I am ever unlucky enough to have a son, I'm going to take him to a nice clean whore-house myself on his tenth birthday"';[9] 'Dulce Jesús—dijo McCord—Dulces querubines. Si me toca la desgracia de tener un hijo ...'.[10]

Again we find that the UK edition censors McCord's speech after the comma and trails off with '...' just as the Borges version does.[11] Further examples include the censorship of expletives—*'males and females but without the pricks or cunts'* becomes '...but without their sex' and in Borges 'pero sin sexo', 'Shit!' becomes 'Hell!' and in Borges '¡Demonio!'.[12]

[6] William Faulkner, *Novels 1936–1940* (New York: Library of America, 1990), p. 644.

[7] William Faulkner, *Las palmeras salvajes*, trans. by Jorge Luis Borges, 3rd edn (Buenos Aires: Editorial Sudamericana, [1940] 1949).

[8] William Faulkner, *The Wild Palms* (London: Chatto & Windus, 1939), p. 203.

[9] *Novels 1936–1940*, p. 589.

[10] *Las palmeras salvajes*, p. 135. Juan Benet drew attention to the suppression of this passage in his prologue to Borges's translation of *The Wild Palms*. He also comments rather ambiguously that 'me veo obligado a transcribir las citas del texto traducido por Borges, por carecer de otra edición' ('I find myself forced to quote from Borges's translation, there not being any other edition'), suggesting perhaps that his opinion of the Argentine's work was not especially high. See Juan Benet, *Una biografía literaria* (Madrid: Cuatro, 2007), pp. 83–91 (p. 85).

[11] *The Wild Palms*, p. 128.

[12] *Novels 1936–1940*, p. 529; *The Wild Palms*, p. 46; *Las palmeras salvajes*, p. 54. *Novels 1936–1940*, p. 564; *The Wild Palms*, p. 93; *Las palmeras salvajes*, p. 100.

However, I stated above that there are two possible instances where Borges could be thought to have edited Faulkner for reasons of propriety. We have seen that the first of these was not his doing at all, rather a function of the censored edition he was using, but the second does provide (tentative) evidence to support the suggestion that Borges tempered the more graphic elements in Faulkner's prose: 'Do you think I would let that bloody bungling bastard that never even finished hospital poke around in me with a knife'; '¿Crees que yo iba a permitir que ese bastardo chambón que ni siquiera acabó su práctica me anduviera con un cuchillo?...'.[13] Charlotte's attempted deflection of blame away from her lover moves towards the same degree of implicit graphicness as her earlier efforts to reassure him immediately prior to the procedure. We might detect Borges doing his best to avoid such explicitness by translating 'poke around in me' with the non-specific, even euphemistic 'me anduviera'.

What we have seen is therefore that Kristal's explanation for the deficiencies of *Las palmeras salvajes* does not fit the facts. Although he appears to have been unaware that Borges was working from a censored early edition of Faulkner's novel, his assertions do not stand up to scrutiny even when that has been taken into account. We must seek an alternative explanation for Marías's criticisms of *Las palmeras salvajes*. He levelled the serious charge that the work of Borges suffered because of its author's 'conocimiento imperfecto del inglés' ('imperfect grasp of English') and the following section of this chapter will seek to test that claim. To do so, I have selected passages from Faulkner's novel that are notable for their linguistic difficulty, either due to the use of colloquialisms or complex verbal constructions, and compared the original English with Borges's Spanish. I also kept in mind that the sense of a stable source text was undermined in this instance because the Argentine was working from a censored edition and I have ascertained that the original English is the same in both the US and UK first editions of *The Wild Palms*.

An example of a colloquialism in American English can be found late in the novel when the wife of the doctor who begins to treat Charlotte at the beach house rebukes her husband for his puritanical reaction to her plight: '"Suffer fiddlesticks," the wife said. "You're mad because he used a scalpel without having a diploma. Or did something with it the Medical Association said he mustn't"'; 'Pagar el demonio—dijo la mujer—. Te has enloquecido porque ha usado un bisturí sin tener diploma, porque ha hecho algo que la Facultad de Medicina prohibe'.[14] The Spanish shows a deficiency in

---

[13] *Novels 1936–1940*, p. 690; *Las palmeras salvajes*, p. 271.
[14] *Novels 1936–1940*, p. 691; *Las palmeras salvajes*, p. 273.

Borges's command of English: 'to be mad' in American English (obviously) means 'to be angry' rather than the literal (and incorrect) translation he has supplied 'te has enloquecido', which means 'to go insane'. A second colloquialism or piece of slang Borges was evidently unable to translate appears in another of McCord's speeches. The latter criticizes Wilbourne's plan for he and Charlotte to leave the city behind and set up home in an isolated Utah mining community, a place that McCord warns will not have 'a railroad or a telephone or even a decent can'. Bizarrely, in Borges's version this becomes 'sin ferrocarril o teléfono y ni siquiera una cucaracha' ('without a railroad, phone or even a cockroach').[15] None of the dictionaries of Spanish slang I have consulted suggest that 'cucaracha' is a colloquial term for a toilet, which is what the original English means. Instead 'cucaracha' is a slang term for a priest. Peter France warns against assessing a translation on the basis of semantic accuracy alone, arguing that 'doing justice to the values and/or formal qualities of the original' is equally if not more important. He does concede, however, that 'there is, arguably, an implicit pact between translator and reader that the basic elements of signification will be rendered with a reasonable degree of accuracy'.[16] Borges, it seems, falls at that first hurdle. The substitution of cockroach for toilet (or perhaps 'bog' in British-English slang) is not only wrong on a literal level, it also makes no sense to include that most hated of creatures in a list of desirable characteristics in the community to which Wilbourne is moving.

If these examples suggest that Borges's grasp of English left much to be desired, two final passages will suffice to draw this appraisal of *Las palmeras salvajes* to a close. In the first case, a complex verbal construction trips the Argentine up:

> "Oh you bloody ass," she said. She came to him. "Stand up. We're going to eat it. Stand up like a man." He rose, she put her hard arms around him, wrestling him against her with restrained savage impatience.

> —¡Oh, no seas imbécil!—le dijo ella. Se le acercó—. Párate. Vamos a comerlo. ¡Arriba como un hombre!

> Se levantó contra ella con salvaje impaciencia contenida.[17]

The translation here is a simple misrepresentation or misreading of the English. Where in the English Wilbourne is the passive recipient of Charlotte's fierce passion—as he is throughout the novel—Borges has made him uncharacteristically and inexplicably active, either through

---

[15] *Novels 1936–1940*, p. 584; *Las palmeras salvajes*, p. 128.
[16] *The Oxford Guide to Literature in English Translation*, ed. by Peter France (Oxford: Oxford University Press, 2000), p. 8.
[17] *Novels 1936–1940*, pp. 568–9; *Las palmeras salvajes*, p. 107.

carelessness or an inexplicable desire to change Faulkner's meaning. Borges fares no better when it comes to translating Faulkner's ear for the speech rhythms of the South, on this occasion a prison guard from the Mississippi jail: '"Well, your partner beat you. He's free. He's done served his time out but you've got a right far piece to go yet"'; 'Bueno su socio le ganó. Está en libertad. Ya ha cumplido su condena, pero a usted le queda un buen trecho que andar'.[18] By comparison with the original, the Spanish falls flat and staid, attempting none of the verbal idiosyncrasies of popular speech.

Hence we can see that the criticisms Marías levelled at Borges the translator are justified when it comes to *Las palmeras salvajes*. In spite of this the Spaniard has not yet tried, nor is he likely now to try, to supersede Borges's Faulkner. The case of Sir Thomas Browne is different, however, because Marías did seek to better the version of the fifth chapter of *Hydriotaphia* that the Argentine produced in collaboration with Bioy Casares, as well as extending the range of works available by Browne in Spanish. It is my view that of all the authors Marías translated into Spanish and who find echoes in his work, Browne is the one whose influence has been most consistent and long-lasting. I therefore devote the following three chapters to discussion of Marías's Browne translations and their subsequent influence on his fiction.

Like Sterne, Browne was a writer who had received little attention in the Spanish-speaking world before Marías translated him. The first writer to translate Browne into Spanish was Borges, who tackled two extended quotations from *Religio Medici* and *Hydriotaphia* or *Urn-Burial* in his 1923 essay 'Sir Thomas Browne'. In 1944, four years after *Las palmeras salvajes* appeared, he and Bioy Casares published in *Sur* their collaboratively produced translation of the fifth chapter of *Hydriotaphia*, a piece of prose long considered among the finest in English.[19] Marías went several steps further, translating *Religio Medici*, Browne's meditation on religious faith; the whole of *Hydriotaphia*, his treatise on ancient burial rites; and 'On Dreams', one of Browne's miscellaneous tracts in which—as the title suggests—he considers diverse aspects of dreaming. Marías published them together in a single volume in 1986 through Alfaguara, then again under his Reino de Redonda imprint in 2002. In the meantime, a further Spanish translation of Browne had appeared by Daniel Waissbein, who translated a selected edition of *Pseudodoxia Epidemica* under the title *Sobre errores vulgares* in 1994.

---

[18] *Novels 1936–1940*, p. 549; *Las palmeras salvajes*, p. 80.
[19] Sir Thomas Browne, 'Quinto capítulo de la "Hydriotaphia"', trans. by Jorge Luis Borges and Bioy Casares, *Sur*, 111 (1944), 15–26.

In view of the limited exposure Browne had received in Spanish, we might well ask how Marías came across his work.[20] Despite citing Browne on numerous occasions in prefaces, interviews, and articles, Marías has never put in print how his interest developed. Lacking any other source of information, I asked Marías myself by letter. He answered:

> Creo que la primera vez que oí hablar de Browne fue en la Universidad, pero sin consecuencia. Luego, quizá Juan Benet me recomendó su lectura (no fue sino hasta más tarde cuando supe del entusiasmo de Borges y Bioy por él).[21]

> (I believe that the first time I heard about Browne was at university, but without me following it up. Then, perhaps Juan Benet recommended I read him (it wasn't until later that I learned of Borges and Bioy's liking for him).)

Given Benet's interest in the 'grand style' he was more than likely a reader of Browne, and it is telling that his recommendation seems to have been the decisive factor in guiding Marías's choices as a translator.

The vague reference to Borges and Bioy Casares in Marías's letter leaves it unclear whether the fact that two such illustrious predecessors had already translated Browne spurred him on or held him back. Brief examination of the prefatory remarks to his editions of Browne reveals that, while working on his version of *Hydriotaphia*, he did indeed consult Borges and Bioy's translation of the fifth chapter; he thought it 'tan hermosa como inexacta' ('as beautiful as it is inaccurate').[22] By taking on projects that Biorges (as Borges and Bioy were dubbed by their friend Rodríguez Monegal) had already attempted, Marías is, whether consciously or not, acknowledging a debt of influence.[23] More importantly, he is also hoping to surpass the achievement of a writer—Borges—whose reputation in the twentieth century is comparable to that of Federico

---

[20] We might also well ask what had first attracted Borges and Bioy Casares to Browne. The matter is not cleared up by Bioy Casares's recently published memoirs of his long-lasting collaboration with Borges, though he does say that 'Entre los mejores momentos de mi vida están las noches en que anotamos *Urn Burial*, *Christian Morals* y *Religio Medici* de sir Thomas Browne' ('I count among the best moments in my life the nights on which we annotated Sir Thomas Browne's *Urn Burial*, *Christian Morals* and *Religio Medici*'). See Adolfo Bioy Casares, *Borges*, ed. by Daniel Martino (Barcelona: Destino, 2006), p. 29.

[21] Private letter dated 24 April 2006. Reproduced by permission of the author.

[22] JM, 'Nota del traductor', in Sir Thomas Browne, *La religión de un médico y El enterramiento en urnas*, trans. by Javier Marías (Barcelona: Reino de Redonda, 2002), pp. 9–15 (p. 15). All subsequent page references to Marías's translations of Browne, unless otherwise stated, refer to this edition.

[23] Jason Wilson, *Jorge Luis Borges* (London: Reaktion, 2006), p. 97. I will continue to use this hybrid name for the remainder of the discussion simply to avoid repeating Borges/Bioy. The reader should not take my decision to adopt this form as in any way disrespectful.

García Lorca or Gabriel García Márquez. Given that we have the opportunity to compare and contrast the different versions Biorges and Marías wrote of *Hydriotaphia*'s fifth chapter, I propose to seize it. I do so for three main reasons. First, by contrasting two versions, it will be easier to draw conclusions about their relative merits and distinctive conceptions of the original. Second, the famous fifth chapter has, my research indicates, been Marías's most fertile hunting ground for the Brownean quotations and echoes he incorporated into his own writings. For that reason and because the purpose of this study is to elucidate how Marías has made use of the works he translated, I thought it best to examine the fifth chapter in detail, rather than offer an overview of Marías's Browne translations. At the same time, I regret being unable to discuss in detail his versions of *Religio Medici* and 'On Dreams'. Third, my decision is determined by a matter of personal preference for close textual reading: the chance to examine how three highly-gifted translators tackled the challenges of one of the best prose passages the English language has to offer was too good to miss.

## TEXTUAL MATTERS AND BACKGROUND

Before beginning the analysis proper, some textual matters require clarification, as does the background to *Hydriotaphia*. Marías has published his Browne translations twice, once through Alfaguara, then through his own imprint, the Reino de Redonda press. An examination of the two editions reveals that he did not amend his translations at all. The only substantial differences in the later Reino de Redonda edition (apart from the usual 'Redondan Images' that appear as appendices in most of the volumes) are the addition of an English translation by Eric Southworth of Marías's 'Translator's Note' and the dedication, to W. G. Sebald:

> Este quinto volumen del Reino de Redonda está dedicado *in memoriam* a W G Max Sebald (1944–2001), Duke of Vértigo y amigo invisible, que escribió extraordinarias páginas sobre Sir Thomas Browne y encontró la muerte inesperada en un camino de Norfolk, no lejos de las enterradas y desenterradas urnas.[24]

> (This fifth volume in the Kingdom of Redonda series is dedicated *in memoriam* to W. G. Sebald (1944–2001), Duke of Vertigo and invisible friend, who wrote some extraordinary pages about Sir Thomas Browne and died unexpectedly on a Norfolk road, not far from the interred and disinterred urns.)

---

[24] *La religión de un médico*, p. 5.

As the dedication reveals, Sebald had been made a peer of Redonda (in 2000) and become what Marías calls an 'amigo invisible'—referring to the fact that, though the two men had corresponded and admired one another's work greatly, they had never met in person. Sebald's novel *The Rings of Saturn* contains several passages in which the narrator reflects on Browne, doubtless just one of the interests the two men shared.[25] It falls beyond the scope of the present study to elaborate further on what those interests might be, but a researcher seeking to map the points of contact between their fiction would not be short of material.[26] Another member of the Redondan court, Marius Kociejowski (appointed 'Poet Laureate in the English Tongue, or "Skelton"' in 1999), wrote of the relationship between Marías and Sebald that 'a brotherhood of artists exists more in spirit than it could ever do in fact, something critics should remember when writing of literary schools or movements'.[27] We would do well to agree.

Biorges and Marías used different editions of Browne when translating the fifth chapter. The former used Geoffrey Keynes's 1929 edition, whereas Marías consulted Keynes's 1964 edition, Charles Sayle's *The Works of Sir Thomas Browne* (London/Edinburgh, 1904–1907), C. A. Patrides's edition of Browne's major works (Harmondsworth, 1977), and Robin Robbins's *Religio Medici, Hydriotaphia* and *The Garden of Cyrus* (Oxford, 1972). In the following comparison of the two translations, I quote Robbins's text of *Hydriotaphia* for two reasons. First, Marías adopts Robbins's punctuation assiduously, thus making it easier to follow at least one of the versions being examined. Second, I find what Robbins calls his 'attempts to facilitate fluent reading, and to elucidate Browne's sometimes densely or tortuously expressed meaning' extremely successful.[28] Unless otherwise stated, therefore, any differences in capitalization of letters or punctuation in the Biorges version can be accounted for by the fact that they were using the 1929 Keynes text.

As to the background to *Hydriotaphia*, the following quotation tells us much of what we need to know:

[25] For Marías's reaction to Sebald's death, see his 'El amargo valor de algunos muertos', in *HMC*, pp. 196–8.

[26] Alexis Grohmann links Sebald's digressive aesthetic with that of Marías in his 'Literatura y digresión: la errabundia de *Negra espalda del tiempo*', in *Cuadernos de narrativa*, pp. 135–44 (p. 135).

[27] Marius Kociejowski, 'Intimate Distances', *Poetry Nation Review*, 29 (2002), 10–12, p. 11.

[28] See Robin Robbins, 'Introduction' in Sir Thomas Browne, *Religio Medici, Hydriotaphia*, and *The Garden of Cyrus*, ed. by Robin Robbins (Oxford: Clarendon Press, 2001), p. xx.

The immediate occasion of *Hydriotaphia* was the discovery in Norfolk of some forty or fifty urns, thought by Browne to have been Roman even as he recognized that some individuals "might somewhat doubt" whether they were not of a later provenance. Connected with funerary rites as these "sad and sepulchral Pitchers" were, they incited Browne to examine in detail a prodigious number of obsequial traditions drawn from his considerable experience and polymorphic reading. A treatise devoted largely to funerary habits is likely, I should have thought, to arouse at best expectations of a rebarbative dissertation, and at worst suspicions of a rather necrological obsession. Oddly enough, however, the tone of *Hydriotaphia* is not even remotely lugubrious, nor even—if one dares to use the word in this context—grave.[29]

Browne was a Norfolk physician and antiquarian who chose the opportunity offered by the unearthing of a collection of burial urns near Old Walsingham to discourse upon ancient burial customs. The first four chapters of *Hydriotaphia* are taken up by speculation on the provenance of the urns—are they Saxon or Roman?—and on burial customs more generally. The fifth and final chapter is where the treatise reaches its rhetorical and thematic pinnacle as Browne reflects on men's desire that future times should remember them. He wonders whether such hopes, however understandable they might be, are not empty consolations born of human vanity.

## TWO VERSIONS OF HYDRIOTAPHIA'S FIFTH CHAPTER

Now since dead these bones have already outlasted all the living ones of Methuselah, and, in a yard under ground and thin walls of clay, outworn all the strong and specious buildings above it, and quietly rested under the drums and tramplings of three conquests—what prince can promise such diuturnity to his relics, or might not gladly say. . .[30]

De Quincey claimed that this passage 'ha[s] no rival in literature', and it immediately presents the translator with several difficulties.[31] Browne uses conjunctions and interjections throughout *Hydriotaphia*, with the first word here, 'Now', presenting the quandary to the translator of whether or

---

[29] C. A. Patrides, '"The Best Part of Nothing": Sir Thomas Browne and the Strategy of Indirection', in *Approaches to Sir Thomas Browne: The Ann Arbor Tercentenary Lectures and Essays*, ed. by C. A. Patrides (London: Univesity of Missouri Press, 1982), pp. 31–48 (p. 34).
[30] *Religio Medici*, p. 126.
[31] *The Works of Thomas de Quincey*, XI, ed. by Julian North (2003), p. 38.

not, and, if so, how to translate it. Biorges opt for the obvious solution—'Ya que han durado'—conveying in Spanish the sense 'given that' or 'since'. Marías opts to start with 'Bien, ya que han durado',[32] as if 'Now' were Browne taking a deep breath before embarking on the rhetorical flights of the fifth chapter, an effect I find appealing. In this opening of Browne's chapter, he is intent on drawing attention to the longevity of the Walsingham urns, despite their fragility; they lie in quiet contrast to the more solid buildings that once stood above them. With this in mind, Biorges's choice of 'débiles tabiques' to translate 'thin walls of clay' emphasizes their flimsiness and seems preferable to the neutral 'paredes de barro'[33] chosen by Marías. Their survival is an affront to human ideas about our ability to perpetuate our own memories, with Browne framing the thought as a question.

Browne was not present at the unearthing of the urns: he merely transports himself imaginatively to the site to give himself material from which to work. With this in mind, Marías's translates 'strong and specious buildings' as 'cuantos resistentes y ostentosos edificios los cubrieron'.[34] Biorges write 'los soberbios edificios que los cubrían'. Note first that both translators have chosen to translate 'it'—where Browne is referring to the ground that covered the bones/urns—as 'los'—referring presumably back to 'los huesos'. As a way of clarifying the text for a Spanish reader, the change is not unwelcome, though it remains curious. Note also the differences in use of tense and article. The point here is that neither Browne nor anyone else can know whether buildings once stood above the urns, but if they did, they are no longer there; hence the idea of 'any and every' conveyed by 'cuantos', preferable to the flatter 'los'; Marías's use of the preterite is likewise more suitable than the imperfect tense because it better conveys the idea of the buildings demise in the dim and distant past. The adjectives Browne uses to characterize these buildings are also telling—'strong and specious'. Both translators have intuited that a tacit rebuke is being delivered here. The buildings were patently not strong because they no longer stand, and their apparent strength is an aspect of their speciousness, which I take to mean 'attractive but ultimately lacking in substance', a usage for which the *Oxford English Dictionary* lists a passage from one of Browne's miscellany tracts. Browne, however, is not a flat moralist, and the nuance has to be captured in passing, in a sub-clause inserted between the main clauses of his sentence. Biorges opt to capture the point with a single adjective, 'soberbios', which refers to both the splendour of the buildings and the

---

[32] *La religión de un médico*, p. 233.     [33] *La religión de un médico*, p. 233.
[34] *La religión de un médico*, p. 233.

unfounded pride their builders took in them. Marías conserves the irony implicit in 'strong' by translating it as 'resistentes', and opts for 'ostentosos' to retain the idea of a showiness that lacks foundation.

The last things to highlight in this opening paragraph are two differences in choices of nouns used by Marías and Biorges. For the evocative and indistinct 'tramplings', Biorges substitute the prosaic 'han reposado quietamente bajo los tambores y los caballos de tres conquistas', whereas Marías remains closer to the original with 'han reposado quedamente bajo los tambores y pisadas de tres conquistas', 'pisadas' being the steps of either man or beast. He also retains 'diuturnidad', a word derived from the same Latin root as Browne's 'diuturnity'. The root of 'duración', used by Biorges, is the Latin verb 'durare'.[35] Marías cites 'diuturnidad' in his prologue as one the 'palabras tan cultas, en desuso o dudosas' that he has nevertheless decided to employ in his translation. None of the Spanish dictionaries I have consulted lists 'diuturnidad' in its nominal form, though the adjective 'diuturno' does appear.

> Time, which antiquates antiquities, and hath an art to make dust of all things, hath yet spared these minor monuments. In vain we hope to be known by open and visible conservatories, when to be unknown was the means of their continuation, and obscurity their protection.[36]

In the second sentence quoted here we find an encapsulation of Browne's whole enterprise in the fifth chapter. Ostentatious physical monuments are subject to the ravages of time, such that, the harder man tries to prolong his existence through them, the vainer his attempts become. As Claire Preston points out, the vanity of such wishes extends to Browne's text as a whole: 'A work which enacts its own subject, *Urne-Buriall*, in arguing the fruitlessness of antiquarian enquiry offers a sparkling, finished array of recovered facts which only adds up to its own demolition'.[37] She puts the point rather strongly: *Hydriotaphia* has ultimate value as a spur towards the kind of Christian contemplation the text encourages. The polyptoton of 'antiquates antiquities' is the first of several instances where we find Browne using rhythmical, almost playful language to describe decay and waste; the most famous example being 'that duration which maketh pyramids pillars of snow, and all that's past a moment', where rhythm and alliteration belie the violence of what is being described. Marías retains the effect with 'deja las antigüedades anticuadas',[38] whereas

[35] For Biorges references, see 'Quinto capítulo', p. 15.
[36] *Religio Medici*, p. 126.
[37] Claire Preston, *Thomas Browne and the Writing of Early Modern Science* (Cambridge: Cambridge University Press, 2005), p. 139.
[38] *La religión de un médico*, p. 233.

Biorges convey the meaning without the sonority, 'que relega las Antigüedades'. Browne's indirect, understated description of time's wasting ability becomes, in Marías, 'tiene el arte de hacer de todas las cosas polvo'[39] and in Biorges 'resuelve en polvo todas las cosas'.

Also at issue here is the question of what 'hath yet spared' conveys to the English reader. 'Yet' acts as a temporal stay or as a contrastive, as if to say 'against all expectation'. That stay of execution, the fragment of time in which to contemplate the urns, is the space in which Browne develops his arguments, a hiatus on their shared path towards inexorable annihilation. Marías conveys the idea by inserting 'sin embargo' into the middle of the clause unobtrusively, something that placing it at either end would not have achieved: 'ha perdonado sin embargo estos monumentos menores'.[40] Biorges ignore the nuance and omit 'sin embargo' altogether: 'ha perdonado estos monumentos menores'. We observe a similar lack of precision in their translation of 'when to be unknown was the means of their continuation, and obscurity their protection'. They change the construction from a passive one to an active one—'deben su perduración a la ignorancia'—where the latter noun is too vague and could mean the ignorance of past peoples or a general state of ignorance, rather than the specific fact of being unknown. Although the point may be a minor one, to cast the urns in a passive role, as in Marías's 'cuando ser ignorados era el medio de perduración de éstos, la oscuridad su protección', seems a better solution.[41]

> If they died by violent hands, and were thrust into their urns, these bones become considerable; and some old philosophers would honour them, whose souls they conceived most pure which were thus snatched from their bodies, and to retain a stronger propension unto them; whereas they weariedly left a languishing corpse, and with faint desires of reunion.[42]

The quoted sentence is one of the denser in Browne's treatise; its correct reading depends on identifying the subject of 'they' in the final clause. Browne wishes to highlight the attitudes of some 'old philosophers' who idealize the lives of the heroes they investigate because, through reading about great deeds, they vicariously experience the adventures that a life of study has denied them. Although he is not moralizing, one wonders whether, given his repeated evocation of Judgement in the fifth chapter, he is not a man who sees a grounded spiritual life as a pressing need: he presents such philosophers as his mirror image, and yet, to judge from the

---

[39] *La religión de un médico*, p. 233.     [40] *La religión de un médico*, p. 233.
[41] For Biorges references, see 'Quinto capítulo', p. 15.
[42] *Religio Medici*, p. 126.

deployment of information in his own text, the thinker whose thoughts too often stray from the Christian path must be a figure far closer to home than he is admitting. Biorges have some difficulty rendering Browne's meaning—'almas con deseo de regresar, no como las que dejan, fatigadas, un cuerpo que declina, con el que ya no quieren reunirse'.[43] What is at issue here is whether Biorges have made it clear enough to whom Browne is alluding. In their version, the 'almas que dejan, fatigadas, un cuerpo que declina' could be a general comment and not the barbed remark Browne intends. The subject of 'they' in Browne is undoubtedly 'philosophers', the contrast Marías captures by using 'mientras que' to introduce them; in his version the human subject is clear 'mientras que ellos dejaban cansinamente un cadáver languideciente y con débiles deseos de reunión'.[44] The alliteration of 'left a languishing corpse', is transferred to 'cansinamente un cadáver' and 'débiles deseos de reunión'. He explained this translational mode in an interview conducted in October 1988:

> [La traducción] es también un arte basado en un sistema de compensaciones.... Por ejemplo, si renuncia a un adjetivo en un determinado momento, por alguna razón, dos o cinco líneas después puede probar a incluirlo, si no el mismo adjetivo, al menos el concepto que explicaba, e incorporarlo así a la traducción.[45]
>
> ([Translation] is also an art based on a system of give and take.... For example, if you have to leave out an adjective at a particular moment, for whatever reason, you can try to include it two or five lines later, if not the same adjective then at least the concept that it explained, and incorporate it that way into the translation.)

It seems that Marías is here applying the same criterion to the rhythmic effect of alliteration, if not in its exact original form, at least in the feel of the translated prose.

Biorges and Marías take contrasting approaches to the degree of doubt expressed in the hypotheticals Browne advances. Marías interprets the if-clause as an open condition and uses the preterite tense—'Si murieron'[46]—whereas Biorges use the pluperfect subjunctive to express a remote condition. Since the owners of these bones have been centuries in

---

[43] This is one of the few passages in their version in which Biorges depart from Keynes's punctuation. His version reads, 'whereas they weariedly left a languishing corps, and with faint desires of re-union'. Their choice of punctuation can be explained as a desire to mirror through the rhythm—the heavy caesura between verb and object in the sub-clause—the laboured progress of the departing soul.

[44] *La religión de un médico*, p. 234.

[45] Caterina Visani interview. www.javiermarias.es/PAGINASDEENTREVISTAS/entrevistaCaterinaVisani.html (accessed 4 July 2008).

[46] *La religión de un médico*, p. 233.

their urns—there is no doubt that they are dead—Marías's use of an open condition seems preferable. While not as important a consideration in this first example, the example below presents the hypothetical sugges-tions as even less pronounced: there seems even less doubt about what Browne puts forward as a possibility.[47]

> If they fell by long and aged decay, yet wrapped up in the bundle of time, they fall into indistinction, and make but one blot with infants. If we begin to die when we live, and long life be but a prolongation of death, our life is a sad composition: we live with death, and die not in a moment.[48]

Once again, the reader marvels at the inventiveness and sonority of prose that, were he or she obliged to explain its literal meaning, might prove more resistant to paraphrase than at first appeared. What is the 'blot' referred to? What do we understand by the 'bundle of time'? The latter seems to convey the layering and confusion of human history, though it may be an adaptation of the Biblical phrase 'the bundle of life', listed in the *Oxford English Dictionary* as a Hebraism derived from the First Book of Samuel.[49] The *Oxford English Dictionary* also lists a passage from *Pseu-dodoxia Epidemica* in which Browne uses 'bundle' in the same figurative sense of a collection or tying together: 'the subtilty of the Inquisitor shall not present unto God a bundle of calumnies or confutable accusations'.[50] Waissbein translates 'bundle' literally as 'hato de calumnias o acusaciones confutables',[51] just as Marías does, who opts for 'fardo del tiempo',[52] leav-ing to the reader the identical task of deciphering the enigmatic meaning. Biorges abandon literal translation to create their own metaphor of time as a network of avenues down which the souls of the dead are dragged, eventually becoming lost, and confused with children: 'aunque arrastra-dos por las avenidas del tiempo, se perderían, indistintos, y se confundirían con los niños'. The latter point leads us on to what 'one blot with infants' means, an answer to which may be found in Browne's frequent references to the annals of history and the lists of the dead, as imagined in God's possession on the Day of Judgement. Hence, those who have lived long but uneventful lives, make as little impact on such records as children—'but one blot'. Marías has faithfully followed this image sequence. Churl-ish though it seems to criticize Biorges for attempting to clarify the

---

[47] For Biorges references, see 'Quinto capítulo', p. 15.
[48] *Religio Medici*, p. 126.       [49] I Sam, 25. 29.
[50] *The Works of Sir Thomas Browne*, ed. by Geoffrey Keynes, 4 vols (London: Faber & Faber, 1964), II, 24.
[51] Thomas Browne, *Sobre errores vulgares o Pseudodoxia Epidemica*, trans. by Daniel Waissbein, 2nd edn (Madrid: Siruela, 2005), p. 71.
[52] *La religión de un médico*, p. 234.

meaning, their choice of metaphor—'las avenidas del tiempo'—is in my opinion parachronistic and, when it comes to 'se confundirían con los niños', unclear.[53]

As we have seen in this analysis thus far, Browne's meaning is intimately bound up with his prose's combination of simplicity and opacity. With this in mind, the straightforwardness of a phrase like 'If we begin to die when we live', might seem disarming. However, by conjugating those verbs in the first person plural, he makes the reader confront his words' meaning far better than if he were just to use infinitives or present participles. 'To live is to begin to die' has the air of a gloss and does not implicate the reader as much, or give him or her the same degree of participation, as the conjugated verbs, 'If we begin to die when we live'. It is as though, the reader's attention gained, he can resort to generalities—'long life be but a prolongation of death'—returning to the inclusive 'we' at the end of the sentence. Biorges opt not to convey the implied degree of participation, and use infinitives—'Si vivir es empezar a morir'. Marías does use the longer, more laborious form to preserve the effect outlined—'Si empezamos a morir cuando vivimos'.[54]

> If the nearness of our last necessity brought a nearer conformity unto it, there were a happiness in hoary hairs, and no calamity in half senses. But the long habit of living indisposeth us for dying, when avarice makes us the sport of death; when even David grew politicly cruel, and Solomon could hardly be said to be the wisest of men.[55]

This is the first of several examples where we find differences in Marías's and the Biorges version stemming from adjectival positioning. Whereas Biorges choose 'postrera necesidad' when translating 'last necessity', Marías decides to place the adjective after the noun. It would appear that in doing so, Marías wishes to maintain an air of detachment and distance. By placing the adjective before the noun, Biorges heighten the sense of Browne's emotional involvement in his text. The placing of the adjective after the noun also allows Marías to retain the alliteration of 'nearness... necessity'—'nuestra necesidad postrera'; alliteration he translates again later in the sentence when 'hoary hairs' become 'cabellos canos'.[56] Marías makes an unusual choice when translating 'half senses', his version of which is 'los demediados sentidos'.[57] The verb 'demediar', an archaism in Spanish, conveys the same idea of 'halved' or 'half' as Browne's English, while also steeping his grandiloquent idiom in similarly

---

[53] For Biorges references, see 'Quinto capítulo', p. 15.
[54] *La religión de un médico*, p. 234.    [55] *Religio Medici*, pp. 126–7.
[56] *La religión de un médico*, p. 234.    [57] *La religión de un médico*, p. 234.

recherché Spanish. Biorges translate 'half senses' as 'el embotamiento de los sentidos', where 'embotamiento' means 'dulling'.

In the penultimate paragraph of the fifth chapter, Browne sings a hymn to the knowledge of God attained by fortunate divines: 'the glory of the world is surely over, and the earth in ashes unto them'. In doing so, he makes us aware that people will confront death in different ways, depending on the depth of their spiritual life. Yet, as he acknowledges in the passage under examination, the very fact of life's persistence and reiteration through habit make death unpalatable even to those, like himself, whose spiritual life is strong. Thus we might say that 'conformity' takes on different forms, from anticipation to stoic forbearance. Biorges can be accused of sacrificing linguistic accuracy for succinctness of phrasing when translating this: 'Si la cercanía de nuestra postrera necesidad nos arrimara a la resignación'. Resignation is not the same as 'conformity', which Marías translates as 'conformidad' (234).[58]

> But who were the proprietaries of these bones, or what bodies these ashes made up, were a question above antiquarism, not to be resolved by man— nor easily perhaps by spirits, except we consult the provincial guardians, or tutelary observators.[59]

The linguistic point to be made here is a minor one, though it does reveal how much the translators were aware of Browne's uniqueness as an exponent of the English language. Biorges render 'antiquarism' as 'Arqueología'. As Preston points out, the discipline of Archaeology did not develop as a science until the eighteenth century:

> [T]he word itself [archaeology], although in use in the early seventeenth century, was roughly synonymous with ancient history, or the documentary records thereof, rather than with the study of material remains.[60]

In fact Browne's use of 'antiquarism' in *Hydriotaphia* is the only instance listed in the *Oxford English Dictionary*. Marías uses a similarly rare nominal form of the Spanish word 'anticuario'. None of the Spanish dictionaries I have consulted lists 'anticuarianismo',[61] a word whose meaning is plain from context but which, being a neologism, retains the air of newness and strangeness that Browne's readers experience. Browne is casting aside his enquiry into the provenance of the urns: 'What time the persons of these ossuaries entered the famous nations of the dead, and slept

[58] *La religión de un médico*, p. 234. For Biorges references, see 'Quinto capítulo', p. 16.
[59] *Religio Medici*, p. 127.     [60] Preston, p. 124.
[61] *La religión de un médico*, p. 235.

with princes and counsellors, might admit a wide solution'.[62] By 'wide solution' he presumably means his own doubts about whether the urns are Saxon or Roman. That wide span of time is associated in scope with the conjecture one might make as to 'what name Achilles assumed when he hid himself among women':[63] though educated guesses may be made, finding a definite answer is impossible and, in any case, the enquiry bears little fruit when seen alongside questions of Christian spirituality. Browne implies that the mysteries of each departed soul will never be captured by the arts of the enquiring mind. There is only one higher power privy to that information and, if nothing else, the urns should remind us of that.

> Vain ashes, which, in the oblivion of names, persons, times, and sexes, have found unto themselves a fruitless continuation, and only arise unto late posterity as emblems of mortal vanities, antidotes against pride, vainglory, and madding vices![64]

The urns' true role as *memento mori* bursts forth but the difficulty of translating one of Browne's favourite prepositions, 'unto', becomes immediately obvious. The *Oxford English Dictionary* lists no fewer than five instances where Browne's works provide examples of differing usage of the preposition, ranging from 'in relation to', denoting possession or fastening to something, 'down to', and 'all by oneself'. In the first instance here quoted, Biorges translate 'unto themselves' as 'en ellas mismas': 'han encontrado en ellas mismas una perduración inútil'. By contrast Marías translates it as 'para sí'.[65] The difference between the two versions would be that between 'found within themselves' and 'found for themselves'. Why I think that Marías's version is preferable is because he better conveys the idea of something the ashes have found that they lacked before. Browne perceives the ashes differently because time has bestowed status on them; from being vulgar objects in their own time, they have become echoes of things past and of lost people whose trace has now vanished. Biorges imply that the change has been wrought internally, not externally.

Once again the translators differ in their placing of adjectives. Biorges translate 'late posterity' as 'tardía posteridad' whilst Marías places the adjective after the noun. The same occurs with 'fruitless continuation' which Marías gives as 'perduración inútil' whereas Biorges give 'estéril continuación'. Given that Browne's thoughts are running along lines of

---

[62] *Religio Medici*, p. 127.      [63] *Religio Medici*, p. 127.
[64] *Religio Medici*, p. 127.      [65] *La religión de un médico*, p. 236.

heritage and ancestry—'names, persons, times, and sexes'—the idea of fruitlessness seems better conveyed by 'estéril'.[66]

If the predominant effect of the adjectival placement in the Biorges version is to heighten the level of emotional involvement with the subject, the following example confirms that impression:[67]

> And, therefore, restless inquietude for the diuturnity of our memories, unto present considerations, seems a vanity almost out of date, and superannuated piece of folly. We cannot hope to live so long in our names as some have done in their persons.[68]

Browne has reminded the reader that, according to Elias's prophecy, the world will last only six thousand years.[69] Thus it is that, even if men of his own era could perpetuate their memories through 'physical observatories', there is scant time left for those monuments to sing their glory. He acknowledges the success of some ancient heroes whose fame has lasted longer than any 'mechanical preservation' could have done. And yet, their fame is invariably associated with survival in the cultural memory bestowed by print: Methuselah and Hector are known because others have written of their deeds. Browne's connectives thus express progression in his argument—'And, therefore'. Marías translates them whilst Biorges ignore them. The result is a directness that does not pause for thought, one that seems more urgent. The Biorges version continues in that vein:

> Infatigablemente codiciar la diuturnidad para nuestra fama, es una vanidad ya tardía y una insensatez anacrónica. No esperemos perdurar tanto en nuestros nombres, como lo hicieron otros en sus personas.[70]

They have omitted altogether another of Browne's logical connectives—'unto present considerations'—perhaps because they find it redundant. Nevertheless it makes Browne's words sound more urgent, as does the negative imperative 'No esperemos' which, translated into English as 'Let us not hope', has a higher emotional charge than 'We cannot hope'. Marías's version of the same phrase retains Browne's neutral tone, 'No podemos esperar'.[71]

In the light of the above observations, I find unconvincing Kristal's claim that '[i]f Browne's *Urn-Burial* is a meditation on the stoic values

---

[66] For Biorges references, see 'Quinto capítulo', p. 17.
[67] See John Butt and Carmen Benjamin, *A New Reference of Modern Spanish*, 4th edn (London: Arnold, 2004), pp. 62–3.
[68] *Religio Medici*, p. 128.
[69] *Religio Medici*, p. 128. Robbins adds a note at p. 48 of his edition to the effect that Elias was a rabbinical commentator quoted in the Talmud.
[70] 'Quinto capítulo', p. 18.        [71] *La religión de un médico*, p. 236.

rewarded in the afterlife, Borges's translation articulates a quiet protest in the face of obliteration'.[72] The intensification of Browne's pleas for his readers to look to Christian salvation cannot be called 'a quiet protest in the face of obliteration' since they complement *Hydriotaphia*'s overall movement in every way.

> [A]nd, being necessitated to eye the remaining particle of futurity, are naturally constituted unto thoughts of the next world, and cannot excusably decline the consideration of that duration which maketh pyramids pillars of snow, and all that's past a moment.[73]

Mentioned above, in this quotation I wish to comment only on the different approach the translators take to the rhythm at the end of the sentence. Breaking with the Keynes punctuation that they generally follow, Biorges opt for a staggered rhythm: 'que hace de Pirámides pilares de nieve, y del pasado entero, un momento'. Keynes's version does not have the comma preceding the word 'moment' that the translators insert.[74] Marías produces a more rhetorically satisfying and elegant version, in which the verb-object-object-verb interplay is maintained: 'que hace de las pirámides pilares de nieve, y un instante de cuanto ya ha pasado'.[75] Note the use of 'cuanto' again to take in the idea of everything and anything that the past contains.

> There is no antidote against the opium of time, which temporally considereth all things: our fathers find their graves in our short memories, and sadly tell us how we may be buried in our survivors.[76]

The compilers of the *Oxford English Dictionary* list the above phrase as an instance in which opium is taken to mean a stupefying agent, one that dulls the senses. Even with this aid to understanding, the sentence's meaning is not abundantly clear. If time here acts as stupefying agent, one that 'temporally considereth all things', the result is man's fallible memory, both in a single lifetime and across generations. Biorges endeavour to clarify the ambiguous English and give 'que comprende todas las cosas'— 'which takes in or understands all things'—as their version. Although they are not translating accurately, the clarification is welcome. Marías favours a rigorous fidelity to the original English and writes 'que temporalmente considera todas las cosas'.

---

[72] Kristal, p. 93.          [73] *Religio Medici*, p. 128.

[74] *The Works of Sir Thomas Browne*, ed. by Geoffrey Keynes, 4 vols (London: Faber & Gwyer, 1929), IV, 45.

[75] *La religión de un médico*, p. 237.

[76] *Religio Medici*, p. 128. Robbins inserts an apostrophe after the final 's' of survivors to indicate 'the memories of our survivors'. I do not find this reading convincing and so do not include it.

Browne's ideas of metempsychosis and repetitious behaviour across generations have found their way into the work of both Biorges and Marías. Whereas Marías is accurate once more, Biorges subtly shift the emphasis of Browne's words when translating 'our fathers find their graves in our short memories'. Biorges render this as 'hallan sepulcro en la brevedad de nuestras memorias', where it is the brevity of human memory that causes the shortness of the memories of our fathers. What the text actually says is that our fathers are buried in our short memories. It is not that, were our memories longer, their fate would be better. The state of mortality means that all our attempts to perpetuate memory are doomed to disappointment. When the memory of our fathers is destined to fade, the brevity of their memory is poignant in itself, but making it longer would not remove the poignancy.[77]

> To be nameless in worthy deeds exceeds an infamous history: the Canaantish woman lives more happily without a name than Herodias with one. And who had not rather have been the good thief than Pilate?[78]

Kristal has the following to say when discussing the Biorges version of this passage (although we ought to note that his discussion of *Urn-Burial* barely acknowledges that the two men collaborated on the project):

> In the original Browne makes the poignant claim that "to be nameless in worthy deeds, exceeds an infamous history," which Borges subtly strengthens in 1944 translation by turning "nameless" into "anonymous," and "exceeds" into "is worth more," emphasizing human choice in confronting an "infamous history."[79]

Given that Browne is talking ostensibly about posterity—'Who knows whether the best of men be known?'—I do not believe that Biorges's alteration emphasizes choice in human affairs: that emphasis is already present in Browne. Whether or not posterity will preserve our names and celebrate our achievements is subject to forces that are beyond our control; all we may do is ensure that posterity has no reason to remember us for ill. A more fundamental question is how else Browne's phrase might be translated; the English phrase 'to be nameless' is synonymous with 'to be anonymous', hence the Spanish 'ser anónimo'; the verb 'exceeds' appears as a comparative, hence 'vale más que'. Marías chooses identical verbs to those used by Biorges: 'Ser anónimo en insignes hazañas vale más que una historia infame'.[80] In the second sentence of the quotation, we observe Biorges's sloppy use of tenses: '¿Quién no prefiere ser el buen ladrón, y no

---

[77] For Biorges references, see 'Quinto capítulo', p. 18.     [78] *Religio Medici*, p. 129.
[79] Kristal, p. 93.     [80] *La religión de un médico*, p. 238.

Poncio Pilatos?'. Browne uses a pluperfect conditional construction, 'had not rather have been', whereas the translators here use the present indicative, 'no prefiere ser'. The resulting question is ridiculous and suggests that author and reader might be in the habit of dressing up as either character for the purposes of role play. Needless to say, Marías faithfully follows Browne's tense sequence: '¿Y quién no habría preferido ser el buen ladrón que Pilatos?'.[81]

If by changing the verb tenses in the last example Biorges hoped to heighten the immediacy of the rhetorical questions Browne asks, they can be observed making identical efforts in the following passage:

> Who knows whether the best of men be known, or whether there be not more remarkable persons forgot than any that stand remembered in the known account of time? Without the favour of the everlasting register, the first man had been as unknown as the last, and Methuselah's long life had been his only chronicle.[82]

Once more it is Browne's hypothetical speculation in the pluperfect tense that Biorges bring forward into the conditional tense: 'Sin el favor del registro imperecedero, el primer hombre sería tan ignoto como el último, y la larga vida de *Matusalén* sería toda su Crónica'. The result is a greater immediacy that does not interfere with the meaning. Biorges provide an improvement on Marías's translation of 'Who knows whether the best of men be known'. Marías assumes, wrongly in my view, that Browne intends 'best of men' to refer to a single person: '¿Quién sabe si el mejor de los hombres es conocido'.[83] By contrast, Biorges realize that Browne has in mind the legions of dead men—'los mejores hombres'—whose deeds have not been recorded in our incomplete chronicle of the past.[84]

> Darkness and light divide the course of time, and oblivion shares with memory a great part even of our living beings.[85]

Browne turns to man's natural defences against the pain of mortality. The greatest of these is a fallible memory: 'oblivion shares with memory a great part even of our living beings'. Marías translates the phrase faithfully, picking up the nuance that Browne is seeking; even if our troubles appear insurmountable, we should remember that forgetting shields us: 'el olvido comparte con el recuerdo gran parte incluso de nuestros seres vivos'.[86] Biorges give the phrase a flat rendering and remove the augmentative

[81] *La religión de un médico*, p. 238. For Biorges references, see 'Quinto capítulo', p. 19.
[82] *Religio Medici*, p. 129.        [83] *La religión de un médico*, p. 239.
[84] For Biorges references, see 'Quinto capítulo', p. 19.        [85] *Religio Medici*, p. 130.
[86] *La religión de un médico*, p. 240.

'even of'; their version sounds like a commonplace: 'el olvido comparte nuestras vidas con el recuerdo'.[87]

Browne expands on his theme, in the following portentous lines.

> To be ignorant of evils to come, and forgetful of evils past, is a merciful provision in nature, whereby we digest the mixture of our few and evil days; and, our delivered senses not relapsing into cutting remembrances, our sorrows are not kept raw by the edge of repetitions.[88]

Biorges alter the deliberate weight and gravity given to the phrase by the repetition of the 'evils' in the first line: 'Ignorar los males futuros y olvidar los pretéritos'; whereas Marías maintains the effect: 'Ignorar los males venideros, y olvidar los males pasados'.[89] Biorges's version sounds more natural to the Spanish ear since the needless repetition of the noun in this clause is frowned upon in common usage. Marías once again opts to retain an effect that reminds Spanish readers of the original English lurking behind the text. Though the point is a minor one, Browne's prose depends on the weighting and rhythm given to clauses in each sentence. Biorges do not translate 'delivered senses', leaving it as 'exentos nuestros sentidos', perhaps because they are uncertain of what the phrase means or think it redundant. The idea of 'delivered senses' ties in with 'merciful provision': these are the ordinances of a benevolent Creator whose mercy allows man respite from pain. Marías translates 'delivered senses' as 'liberados sentidos', suggesting the idea of liberation from suffering. The phrase 'el filo de las repeticiones' is one that has recurred frequently in Marías's fiction, one of several borrowings from Browne. His translation of the complete phrase shows more flair than the Biorges version if only because he translates literally the figurative 'kept raw'. Biorges give the flat 'nuestros pesares no se eternizan bajo el filo de las repeticiones' whilst Marías retains the image of laceration: 'nuestras penas no se mantienen en carne viva por el filo de las repeticiones'.[90]

Of all the differences observed between Marías's fifth chapter and that of Biorges there are few that can be attributed to a failure of understanding. The following example is, however, an exception:

> But the most magnanimous resolution rests in the Christian religion, which trampleth upon pride, and sets on the neck of ambition, humbly pursuing that infallible perpetuity unto which all others must diminish their diameters, and be poorly seen in angles of contingency.[91]

---

[87] 'Quinto capítulo', p. 20.    [88] *Religio Medici*, p. 130.
[89] *La religión de un médico*, p. 240.
[90] *La religión de un médico*, p. 240. Biorges, 'Quinto capítulo', p. 21.
[91] *Religio Medici*, p. 133.

Browne's breadth of understanding across diverse fields of human knowledge produces the final image—'angles of contingency'. Both translators supply Browne's own textual note which explains that an 'angle of contingency' is the acutest of all angles. Likewise both translators find no better solution than 'ángulos de contingencia'. According to Mariano García's *Diccionario matemático*, 'contingencia' is indeed the Spanish for 'contingence'.[92] All other modes of perpetuity, be they pyramids, obelisks, or arches, offer limited scope for longevity when compared to the vast vista offered by salvation. It is not this image that caused Biorges problems of comprehension, however; rather it is 'sets on the neck of ambition', which they translate as 'cabalga en el lomo de la ambición'. Translated in this way, it is as though the Christian religion were championing the cause of ambition, riding on its back. Ambition is clearly seen as a negative force in Browne's theology since it stands in opposition to the quiet acceptance of forgiveness and the need for faith. Biorges have not understood, although Marías has, translating the phrase as 'y al cuello de la ambición se lanza'.[93] Marías's version retains precisely the image of Christian faith as like a pack of hounds bringing down ambition during a hunt.[94]

> And if any have been so happy as truly to understand Christian annihilation, extasis, exolution, liquefaction, transformation, the kiss of the Spouse, gustation of God, and ingression into the divine shadow—they have already had an handsome anticipation of heaven: the glory of the world is surely over, and the earth in ashes unto them.[95]

The final image eloquently demonstrates Browne's transformation of the ashes from emblems of mortal vanity to spurs to Christian contemplation. Biorges prove once again their reluctance to translate Browne's adverbs: the word 'truly' is lacking from their first sentence—'Y si algunos han tenido la dicha de comprender la iniquilación'—and the word 'already' is omitted from 'han tenido una hermosa anticipación del cielo'. As a result their version has a more direct tone, since here Browne's adverbs do not add greatly to his meaning, rather to the level of precision with which he writes. Neither translator supplies what would be the ideal translation of 'exolution', the release of the soul in mystical contact, which is 'desasimiento' in Spanish. Marías gets closer to the mark with 'liberación',[96] whereas Biorges supply the erroneous 'postración'.

---

[92] Mariano García, *Diccionario matemático* (New York: Dorman & Co., 1965), p. 8.
[93] *La religión de un médico*, p. 244.
[94] For Biorges references, see 'Quinto capítulo', p. 25.
[95] *Religio Medici*, p. 133.        [96] *La religión de un médico*, p. 244.

The above quotations cast into stark contrast Kristal's underdeveloped argument that:

> Browne's affirmation of Christian salvation over the illusions of wealth and power are transformed by Borges, in both the 1923 fragment and the 1944 translation, into the affirmation of ephemeral beauty.[97]

Kristal is anxious to gain insight into Borges's attitude to *Hydriotaphia* and, by extension, 'Tlön, Uqbar, Orbis Tertius', the story at whose conclusion the narrator retires to work on a Quevedian translation of *Hydriotaphia*'s fifth chapter (which he intends never to publish). The difficulty lies in making sweeping claims about a translator's attitude to a text on the basis of small fragments of the translation alone. Kristal seems to base the above claim on the selected quotations offered by Borges in the essay 'Sir Thomas Browne' published in *Inquisiciones* (1923). However, when extending that claim to the whole of the later translation, Kristal offers no evidence to substantiate it. A translator who does not translate selectively or inaccurately will be forced to express the opinions of his source text, however much his own views may differ from them. Though it may be the case that Borges has more interest in ephemeral beauty than Christian salvation, his translation of *Hydriotaphia*, which at every turn renders Browne's faith in Christian perpetuity, is not a place to find the evidence.

Having questioned Kristal's summation of Borges's attitude, what overall conclusions might we take from this comparison? First, assessed purely on the grounds of linguistic accuracy, Marías is a more meticulous translator. He called the Biorges version 'tan hermosa como inexacta',[98] a judgement which my own analysis does not contradict. Second, that accuracy takes the form of a greater sensitivity to rhythm and the weighting of clauses within a sentence. Given that, according to him, Browne's prose left an indelible mark on his own, it ought not to surprise us that Marías has a good ear for Brownean cadence. Third, Biorges produced a version of Browne the tone of which is far more yearning, earnest, and direct than the English.

In the following section of this chapter and the two that follow I analyse how Browne's works have found echoes in Marías's fiction. Having examined his translation of the fifth chapter in detail, we can suggest that he was struck by the weighting and cadence of phrase in Browne's prose. He also took care to translate literally Browne's striking metaphors. It becomes clear, when we examine how Marías has echoed Browne, that he was taken with the latter's ability to breathe new life into old thoughts

---

[97] Kristal, p. 93.     [98] *La religión de un médico*, p. 15.

through the use of striking or apt simile and metaphor. Elide Pittarello
has written, rightly in my view, that throughout his early career, Marías
has been 'tratando de inventar no algo inédito, sino algo distinto, a veces
tan sólo un detalle que recuerde cómo las palabras se relacionan siempre
con las cosas por un arbitrio de la voluntad' ('trying to invent not something unprecedented, but instead something different, sometimes only a
detail that brings to mind how words relate to things always through an
effort of will').[99] Marías's rejection of novelty and originality for their own
sake complements his interest in Browne who is a writer renowned more
for his manner than his matter. Both writers see their task not in exploring new ground but in reminding themselves and their readers of what
they think they already know.

## THE APOCRYPHAL FRAGMENT

The Marías and Biorges versions show one significant difference not mentioned above. I refer to the manuscript fragment Keynes supplied in his
1929 edition of the text which Biorges translated and partially included
in their 1944 *Sur* version. The interpolation begins:

> Large are the treasures of oblivion, and heapes of things in a state next to
> nothing almost numberlesse; much more is buried in silence than is recorded,
> and the largest volumes are butt epitomes of what hath been.[100]

Keynes is the only recent editor of Browne who regards the fragment as
belonging to *Hydriotaphia*. He prints it after the main body of the text on
the following page. As if to add to the confusion, by the time he edited his
1964 Browne edition he had changed his mind and the manuscript fragment is nowhere to be seen. None of the editions Marías consulted, which
included Keynes's 1964 edition, featured the interpolation, and it was for
that reason that he felt justified in asking Borges during a face-to-face
encounter in October 1983 whether he and Bioy had added an apocryphal fragment to their version of the fifth chapter. That exchange, which
took place in St Peter's College, Oxford, is recounted in Marías's article
'Borges: un fragment apocryphe de Sir Thomas Browne'.[101] Lytton

---

[99] 'Guardar la distancia', in Javier Marías, *El hombre que parecía no querer nada*,
pp. 11–31 (p. 15).
[100] *The Works of Sir Thomas Browne*, ed. by Geoffrey Keynes, 4 vols (London: Faber &
Gwyer, 1929), IV, 51.
[101] JM, 'Borges: un fragment apocryphe de Sir Thomas Browne', *Le Promeneur*, 58
(1988), 20–1 (p. 20); 'Falsificaciones literarias', in *PP*, pp. 185–90; 'El apócrifo apócrifo
(1988 y 1993)' in *LF*, pp. 402–9.

Strachey would have approved of this setting for so august an encounter. In his view, 'the most fitting background for [Browne's] strange ornament must surely be some habitation consecrated to learning, some University which still smells of antiquity and has learnt the habit of repose'.[102] In the event, however, Borges denied having added anything to Browne's text and placed any blame that might be due at Bioy Casares's door. Marías took the liberty of doubting the great writer's word and put his reluctance to speak the truth down to the fact that Pembroke College, Browne's old stamping ground, was only a stone's throw away.[103] As Marías subsequently discovered, however, neither Borges nor Casares had added a line to *Hydriotaphia*.

Since Biorges added the manuscript fragment to their translation, a succession of academics and writers have queued up to misattribute their insertion to impish artistic invention. After Marías's mistake came that of Cynthia Stephens who, in her article on Borges and metempsychosis, took it for granted that the passage was invented.[104] The editor of the Pléiade edition of Borges, Jean Pierre Bernès, was next to fall into the trap, repeating the claim in his notes on 'Tlön, Uqbar, Orbis Tertius'.[105] It took until the following year, when Daniel Waissbein published his selected translation of *Pseudodoxia Epidemica*, for any writer to point out in print the mistake Marías had made. By then the latter had written and not yet published his essay 'El apócrifo apócrifo' in which he recognized his earlier error. Marías, meanwhile, was put right by Francis Korn. She had been contacted by an unnamed translator, Waissbein in fact, and she it was who asked Bioy Casares in person, the latter confirming the fact that he and Borges had merely interpolated and edited a manuscript fragment from Keynes's 1929 edition of Browne's works. Waissbein for his part makes no reference to the source of his information and takes a certain joy in correcting Marías's mistake—'No hay tal falsificación. Se trata en cambio de un error de Marías, quien desconoce que el texto traducido existe en verdad' ('There is no such falsification. Instead it's a mistake on the part of Marías, who is unaware that the translated text really exists').[106]

---

[102] Lytton Strachey, 'Sir Thomas Browne', in *Books and Characters: French and English* (London: Chatto & Windus, 1922), pp. 31–44 (p. 44).

[103] According to Finch, Browne spoke during the inauguration ceremony of Pembroke College, having been a matriculated student at Broadgates Hall, Pembroke's previous incarnation, for eight months. See Jeremiah S. Finch, *Sir Thomas Browne: A Doctor's Life of Science & Faith* (New York: Henry Schuman, 1950), pp. 41–3.

[104] Cynthia Stephens, 'Borges, Sir Thomas Browne and the Theme of Metempsychosis', *Modern Language Studies*, 28 (1992), 268–79 (p. 268).

[105] Jorge Luis Borges, *Œuvres complètes*, ed. by Jean Pierre Bernès, trans. by Paul Bénichou et al., Bibliothèque de la Pléiade: 400, 2 vols (Paris: Gallimard, 1993), I (1993), 1569–70.

[106] *Sobre errores vulgares*, p. 385.

Marías published his 1993 essay detailing his exchange with Francis Korn in the 2001 edition of *LF* and reprinted it in the Reino de Redonda edition of his Browne translations.[107] The rivalry between the two most recent translators of Browne into Spanish is not difficult to detect, with Marías adding by way of 'descargo' and quoting from Korn's letter:

> 'el colega de Oxford', con todas las magníficas bibliotecas de esa Universidad a su disposición, 'tampoco podía encontrar el párrafo en cuestión' (yo había hecho mi traducción de Browne con anterioridad a mi estancia de dos años en esa ciudad).[108]

> ('the Oxford colleague', with all of the University's magnificent libraries at his disposal, 'couldn't find the paragraph in question either' (I had completed my translation of Browne prior to my two-year stay in that city).)

The exchange between Waissbein and Marías would not interest us were it not for the fact that it had one important practical upshot. Marías's continuous and repeated contact with his translations of Browne, brought about by his reflection on the interpolation and rectification of his error, meant that Browne's prose and ideas were never far from his mind over a considerable period of years. Before he was disabused, he also used the interpolation during his course on Translation Theory at Madrid's Universidad Complutense.[109]

What evidently intrigued Marías about the interpolation were the questions it raised over authorship: 'el fragmento apócrifo que reproducimos a continuación carece de paternidad, si bien tampoco puede decirse que sea anónimo' ('the apocryphal fragment that we reproduce below lacks an author, although nor can it be said to be anonymous').[110] The 'apocryphal' fragment disturbs what he sees as the delicate balance between fidelity and creativity that translation entails. As we saw when discussing his translation of Sterne, part of what he calls 'una de las paradojas irresolubles de la traducción' ('one of the insoluble paradoxes of translation') resides in how different from and yet identical to its original a translation is.[111] Adding to or suppressing any part of the original text disturbs that delicate collaborative equilibrium. Writing about the apocryphal fragment before he realized his mistake, he went on to say that, in the absence of clinching proof that Bioy Casares was responsible for the sleight of hand, the possibility remained that it could be attributed to the narrator

---

[107] The sudden proliferation of sources pointing out the true provenance of the 'apocryphal fragment' makes it all the more surprising that Efraín Kristal should have used the alleged interpolation as the cornerstone of his arguments on Browne in his study of Borges's career as a translator. Kristal, pp. 27, 91–3.

[108] *La religión de un médico*, p. 306.     [109] *La religión de un médico*, p. 299.

[110] *La religión de un médico*, p. 302.     [111] 'Mi libro favorito', p. 400.

of 'Tlön, Uqbar, Orbis Tertius'; the latter pledges at the end of the story to continue 'revisando... una indecisa traducción quevediana (que no pienso dar a la imprenta) del *Urn Burial* de Browne' ('revising... an indecisive translation in Quevedian style of Browne's *Urn Burial* [which I don't intend to publish]').[112] The irony of that would of course be immense, given that Borges's tale deals precisely with a world that exists only in print but which nevertheless begins to invade the world of the story.

However, as we shall see, Marías's real interest in both the apocryphal fragment and Browne more generally lies in the latter's facility for encapsulating commonplace thoughts in well-wrought phrases. Marías assimilated Browne's ideas and particular means of expressing them to such an extent that years later they remain part of his imaginative vocabulary: Browne's phraseology has become his principal touchstone when discussing memory, literary posterity, and the uncertainties of human history. That assimilation took time, nevertheless, and in the next two chapters I shall explore how Marías incorporated either overt or covert citation of Browne into his works. I start with the work he wrote while his Browne translations were still ongoing—*ES*—where I weave analysis of the Brownean citations into a wider discussion of that novel.

---

[112] Jorge Luis Borges, 'Tlön, Uqbar, Orbis Tertius', in *Obras completas*, I, pp. 431–43 (p. 443).

# 6

# Browne, *El siglo*, and the Depiction of Tyranny

## INTRODUCTION

In his famous Preface, Dr Johnson warned scholars of Shakespeare's work that

> his real power is not shewn in the splendour of particular passages, but in the progress of his fable, and the tenor of his dialogue; and he that tries to recommend him by select quotations, will succeed like the pedant in Hierocles, who, when he offered his house to sale, carried a brick in his pocket as a specimen.[1]

Rather than be like that pedant and try to discuss the echoes of Sir Thomas Browne in Marías's work divorced from their context, as far as possible I intend to develop such discussion within a wider treatment of the individual texts where they appear. In the next two chapters, I analyze *ES* (1983) and 'Cuando fui mortal' (1993) respectively, with a view to elucidating what they show us about how Marías has echoed, engaged with, and learned from the works of Browne; largely, but not exclusively, *Hydriotaphia*'s fifth chapter.

This chapter offers an examination of Marías's fourth novel, *ES*, with a view to examining how and why the author uses allusion and quotation as a means of characterizing the novel's protagonist. Discussion will focus on the engagement with Browne that *ES* develops through paraphrase and direct quotation in the text. Marías was working intermittently on his translations of Browne in the years 1982–1985[2] and he has been at pains to point out the influence of Browne's thought on his 1983 novel.

*ES* is the story of how its protagonist became an informer in the aftermath of a civil war that we can strongly associate with the Spanish conflict

[1] *The Yale Edtion of the Works of Samuel Johnson*, ed. by Arthur Sherlo, 18 + vols. (New Haven and London: Yale University Press, 1958–), VII: *Johnson on Shakespeare* (Part 1 of 2) (1968), p. 62.

[2] Marías confirmed this in a personal letter dated 24 April 2006.

that raged between 1936 and 1939. However, the novel gives no place names and does not name the country where it is set. We saw in Chapter 2 that Marías refused for the early part of his career to set his fiction in Spain or address issues pertaining to his homeland. *ES* offers an example of that reluctance taken to extremes. As Grohmann points out, there is only one indication in the entire novel of where its action is predominantly set: when the protagonist leaves his country to escape the civil war in which he will play no active part, he travels to Lisbon, from where he looks east back towards his homeland.[3] Although cagey on geographical detail, the novel is in fact a meaningful attempt to ask why a particular human being in a particular place might seek to inform on his fellow men and thus destroy them. It is as if Marías wanted the freedom to address this subject as a deeply personal conundrum but without the emotional clutter of national specificity.

Given that Marías grew up with the knowledge that an informer came within a hair's breadth of sending his father to the firing squad and scuppering all chances of his own birth, we ought not to be surprised that he should seek to understand and depict the 'delator' ('informer') in his work. We ought also to remember that Julián Marías was victim not just of the trumped-up allegations but of the lasting damage they did to his reputation and career. His son gave vent to his feelings on the ignominious treatment his father had endured at the hands of the Spanish state in an article, entitled simply 'El padre', that he wrote to mark his father's eightieth birthday.[4] It is one of the most impassioned he has ever written and he republished it unchanged in *El País* the day after his father's death on 15 December 2005.[5] One recurrent feature of Marías's thinking on the subject of betrayal, in evidence in 'El padre', concerns a fellow writer whom it would not be an exaggeration to describe as his bête noire. In no fewer than thirteen of his journalistic pieces Marías disparages the reputation of Camilo José Cela, the last Spanish writer to win the Nobel Prize for literature.[6] He accuses him directly and indirectly of, among other things, being a poor novelist, homophobic, excessively critical of Spain's young writers, and of plagiarizing the ending of James Joyce's 'The Dead'

---

[3] *ES*, p. 224. Grohmann, *Coming Into One's Own*, p. 58.
[4] JM, 'El padre', in *VF*, pp. 441–3.
[5] JM, 'El padre', *El País*, 16 December 2005, p. 36.
[6] See his 'Protoespañoles y antiespañoles', in *MS*, pp. 283–5 (p. 284); 'La edad del recreo', in *PP*, pp. 101–12 (p. 106); 'No pareces español', in *PP*, pp. 113–25 (p. 119); 'Esas máquinas mágicas', in *AVC*, pp. 335–8 (pp. 336–7); 'El estado de la sospecha', in *SACF*, pp. 43–5 (p. 44); 'Capulleo de verano', in *SACF*, pp. 276–8 (p. 277); 'Nuestros símbolos', in *VF*, pp. 260–2 (p. 262); 'El artículo más iluso', in *VF*, pp. 509–15; 'Contra la costurera y el decorador', in *LF*, pp. 128–34 (pp. 128–9); 'Monoteísmo literario', in *LF*, pp. 175–9; 'La comprometida situación del compromiso', in *LF*, pp. 200–4 (p. 201); 'Un país grotesco', *El País Semanal*, 10 September 2006, p. 110.

in *Mazurca para dos muertos* (1983).[7] The crux of Marías's antipathy towards Cela lies, however, elsewhere. To find it we must examine the articles 'El Padre' and 'El artículo más iluso' where he discusses the legacy of Franco's Spain and its problematic assimilation in the democratic era. He argues in both that while many Spaniards, including Cela, morally compromised themselves by collaborating with the dictatorial regime, others, like his father, did not: 'los hubo mejores... más rectos, o más dignos, o más resistentes, o más orgullosos, o más escépticos, o más asqueados, o más derrotados, no sé' ('there were others who were better... more honest, more honourable, stronger, prouder, more sceptical, more fed up or more defeated, I don't know').[8] The latter had to suffer the consequences of living on the wrong side of a vengeful and pitiless government that deprived them of employment, happiness, and in some cases even their lives. Cela, by contrast, 'se ofrecía como delator y luego recibía alguna condecoración franquista' ('offered his services as an informer and went on to be decorated by Franco'), also working as a censor for the newly-formed government.[9] He is the antithesis of Marías's dignified father. Well might he have written in the 1995 prologue for a new edition of *ES*, 'si me interesó este asunto fue en parte por una cuestión familiar' ('if I was interested in this subject it was in part because of an issue connected with my family').[10] That may be something of an understatement if the barely contained anger that bubbles beneath the surface of articles like 'El padre' and 'El artículo más iluso' is anything to go by.

Informers have subsequently reappeared in Marías's fiction, most notably in the short story 'Cuando fui mortal' (1993) and the novel *TRM*. And yet, *ES* still represents his most sustained attempt to provide a psychologically coherent portrait of this ignominious subject. As we saw in Chapter 4, Benet had suggested that a writer will produce original art once he or she forces their style to attack a subject which to them remains 'una oscura zona de su razón en la que las ideas... no se hallan claramente perfiladas' ('a dark area of his reason in which his ideas... are not clearly delineated').[11] That area of uncertainty in Marías's case surrounds the question of why one person would choose to exercise power cruelly over another. The reading of *ES* offered here examines precisely how Marías goes about answering that question, and building what I have just referred to as a psychologically coherent portrait of such a person. He uses allusion and citation of Browne, as well as other writers, in order to build this

---

[7] I have tried to show how Marías has echoed Joyce's story in his own fiction. See Gareth Wood, '"La nieve que cae": algunos antecedentes literarios y fílmicos de una imagen en *MBPM* de Javier Marías', in *Cuadernos de narrativa: Javier Marías*, pp. 125–34.

[8] 'El artículo más iluso', p. 515.        [9] 'El padre', p. 443.

[10] 'Prólogo a la edición de 1995', p. 11.        [11] *La inspiración*, p. 201.

portrait; he uses them above all to depict a sentimentalist and a tyrant whose final victim is none other than himself. Although strenuously disavowing Spanish issues at this stage in his career, *ES* confronts why an individual might end up offering an aggressive response to his inability to understand both himself and others. That question is central to an understanding of war and betrayal, both issues thrown up by the legacy of the Spanish Civil War.

Although *ES* is the story of how its protagonist, Casaldáliga, becomes an informer, we learn little of his actual career. Instead the novel alternates between two distinct voices, that of an omniscient third-person narrator who describes Casaldáliga's life until the age of thirty-nine, the age at which he became an informer, and his own first-person account, now retired and decrepit, of his final weeks of life. The odd chapters comprise Casaldáliga's narration, the even ones the voice of the omniscient narrator. There are nine chapters in total. I limit myself here to a description of his domestic situation after his retirement. What we glean from the chapters narrated in the first person by the moribund Casaldáliga is that he has had a successful career as both a judge and an informer. Having first offered his services to Coronel Berua at the end of the civil war, he has lived secure in the knowledge that he had a monopoly on the truth. The corrupt regime under which he worked provided the perfect cover for him to exercise control over the people around him either by judging their cases himself or denouncing them to destroy their reputations. His cousin and childhood sweetheart has borne him a son whom he has not publicly acknowledged but whom he has raised as his godson, el León de Nápoles, an opera singer. He has conducted affairs with his godson's wife and with Natalia Monte, Berua's niece. He receives his old colleague for lunch every Tuesday, living in fear of his possible reprisals against him. He plays dead occasionally in order to taunt the members of his close family with the fact that they are just waiting to inherit his wealth. His attention focuses on total control of his everyday environment, both people and objects, and increasingly on the lake by which he lives, wanting to capture its totality in one moment, the waters somehow taunting him with their mutability. He seems to get his wish where the lake is concerned: the narrative stops on a night when the waters are finally still, frozen by the low temperatures, and Casaldáliga anticipates the end of his life, scarcely able to believe that it is about to end for good.

Marías's maintained soon after completing *ES* that translating Browne into Spanish had profoundly influenced its gestation:

En el inicio de mis novelas suele haber una imagen, o una frase, o una situación aislada que sin embargo necesitan de algo que les dé cabida, que las alberge, para cobrar pleno sentido. Y creo que, en efecto, no son pocas las

ocasiones en que el edificio entero de una novela no tiene más misión ni más
razón de ser que las de arropar y posibilitar una oración, unos párrafos, unas
pocas páginas, que por sí solas serían impresentables o gratuitas o inanes o
harían sonrojar a su autor, y que en cambio, insertas en una complicada
estructura, quizá en boca de un personaje, resultan aceptables o necesarias o
reconocibles como verdaderas.[12]

(At my novels' inception there is usually an image, a phrase, or a particular
situation that nevertheless require something to accommodate them, that
will provide space for their full meaning to flourish. And in fact I believe
that, not infrequently, the whole edifice of a novel has no other mission than
to wrap up and make possible a phrase, a few paragraphs, a handful of pages,
which on their own would be unpresentable, gratuitous, inane, or make
their author blush, but which when they are inserted into a complex structure, perhaps in the mouth of a character, turn out to be acceptable, necessary or recognizable as true.)

He wonders whether these 'pocas páginas' ('few pages') were 'ya conteni-
das en un párrafo aislado de Sir Thomas Browne' ('were already contained
in a particular paragraph by Sir Thomas Browne'). Ten years later, he
claimed that:

veo más claras—y además me vienen a la memoria—otras huellas o influencias, en concreto de dos autores a los que había traducido poco antes y de
cuyo prolongado y simbiótico trato mi pluma no salió inmune: Joseph Conrad en su *Espejo del mar* y Sir Thomas Browne en su *Hydriotaphia*.[13]

(I can see more clearly—and also recall—other traces or influences, specifically those of two authors I had recently translated and from whose prolonged
and symbiotic company my pen did not emerge unscathed: Joseph Conrad
in his *Mirror of the Sea* and Sir Thomas Browne in his *Hydriotaphia*.)

He begins the prologue from which I have just quoted, 'Durante algunos
años creí que esta novela…era la mejor de cuantas había escrito y que
seguiría siéndolo durante bastante tiempo' ('For some years I thought that
this novel…was the best of all those I had written and would remain so
for a good while').[14] He continues that his opinion began to change when
he realized that the novel was selling poorly and had attracted few reviews
(apart from the attention of some colleagues in the literary magazine
*Ínsula* two years after its publication). Since 1988 he had put off publication of a new edition, 'inseguro como estaba de que la mereciera y
temeroso de su obligada relectura por mi parte' ('unsure as I was that it

[12] 'Desde una novela no necesariamente castiza', p. 69.
[13] JM, 'Prólogo a la edición de 1995', in *ES*, pp. 9–14 (pp. 13–14).
[14] 'Prólogo a la edición de 1995', p. 9.

deserved a second edition and fearful of having to read it again myself').[15] Having not plucked up the courage to reread the novel until 1994, his reservations principally concern its long, baroque sentences, rarefied vocabulary, and 'comienzo bastante arduo' ('fairly arduous beginning').[16] He states simply that, 'Hoy ya no escribo del mismo modo' ('I don't write this way anymore'), which is self-evident to anybody familiar with his subsequent work. And yet, we should not dismiss *ES* just because Marías has gone on to better things.

The only substantial accounts of *ES* yet published are those by Alexis Grohmann in a 2002 article and his study of Marías's novelistic development (published in the same year). The ground covered in each is largely identical and I quote from the latter on the basis that it is there that Grohmann develops his thoughts most substantially. His discussion focuses on *ES*'s stylistic virtuosity, virtuosity the author regards as showy and aggressive:[17]

> The reader's attention is repeatedly diverted from what is being written to the skill exhibited in writing it. His prose is self-indulgent in that it displays the author to advantage, somewhat ostentatiously exhibiting a certain virtuosity. Like the precious and rare style of baroque artists, it is an expression of aggression, an assertion of a certain independence.[18]

Grohmann examines the novel as a key stage in the development of Marías's style. *ES* represents, he claims, Marías's attempt to find a high style through adoption and imitation of features of seventeenth-century English prose, above all that of Browne. These features include the use of doublets (paired nouns or adjectives with synonymous meanings) and hypo- and parataxis, the better to depict realistically the unfolding of a character's thought. Grohmann argues quite rightly that these features, along with the use of aphorisms, have characterized all of his subsequent fiction. To that extent, I recommend his work on Browne's influence on Marías's prose style and my own analysis of *ES* should be thought of as complementing his findings.

Grohmann acknowledges openly that his interest in the novel is primarily stylistic: he wishes to trace a developmental trajectory where *ES* becomes an early, and possibly overambitious, attempt to write the kind of meditative prose that has marked his novels from *EHS* onwards. References to the novel's content are 'relegated in the discussion because', he believes, 'the content is subordinated to style'.[19] I therefore wish to

---

[15] 'Prólogo a la edición de 1995', p. 10.
[16] 'Prólogo a la edición de 1995', p. 12.
[17] *Coming Into One's Own*, pp. 78–83.
[18] *Coming Into One's Own*, p. 78.      [19] *Coming Into One's Own*, p. 57.

examine features of characterization and plot with a view to redressing the balance between Grohmann's discussion of purely formal characteristics and a richer engagement with the central protagonist. By examining the actual marriage of literary allusion, content, and form we may reach a richer understanding of what was Marías's most complex novel to date.

The final section of Grohmann's chapter on *ES* draws attention to Benet's belief that the acquisition of style is the greatest challenge a writer faces and the factor that will ultimately determine the longevity of his work. Implicit in the argument is the idea that Marías has been too eager to comply; that he has, to some extent, tried to run before he could walk. Grohmann is right to point to aspects of *ES* that foreground ostentatious display over their adequacy to purpose: principal among them are the abundant nautical similes, undoubtedly a product of Marías's then recent translation of Conrad, which are only tenuously connected to the plot and setting. However, as Benet and Grohmann acknowledge, the divorce of style from content is a critical approach which can prove problematic.[20] This is perhaps exemplified by the host of critics he quotes on seventeenth-century English prose, among them Stanley Fish, Morris Croll, whose argument is that Browne is a writer who foregrounds ostentatious display over any real content. Those arguments, advanced mainly in the 1950s and 1970s have been systematically rubbished by more recent criticism.[21] My own analysis of *Hydriotaphia*'s fifth chapter has shown that it is far from being a gratuitously showy piece of writing. Whereas Grohmann maintains that 'it would be misleading to say that *El siglo* is the story of an informer: the initial subject matter is transformed through its treatment', I wish to present the opposite viewpoint and foreground content over style.[22] He concludes that the marriage of content and style is incomplete because the former is subordinated to the latter.[23] And yet, in the midst of sound arguments about stylistic development, I believe Grohmann to have done the novel a disservice by failing to engage with what it is actually about. This discussion seeks to elucidate aspects of characterization and literary influence while focusing on matter rather than manner.

---

[20] *La inspiración*, pp. 175–6; *Coming Into One's Own*, p. 79.

[21] See, for example, Preston, *passim*; *Sir Thomas Browne: the World Proposed*, ed. by Reid Barbour and Claire Preston (Oxford: Oxford University Press, 2008); *'A man very well studied' new contexts for Thomas Browne*, ed. by Kathryn Murphy and Richard Todd (Leiden: Brill, 2008).

[22] *Coming Into One's Own*, p. 59.      [23] *Coming Into One's Own*, p. 83.

## ALLUSION AND QUOTATION IN *ES*

The opening chapter of *ES* introduces us to Casaldáliga in his own words. He focuses his description on the lake that stands outside his home and which he spends much of the day observing. It is as if he wants to track each of its changes, and yet the constantly shifting waters frustrate that desire, much to his annoyance. A life spent dominating the people around him through the power and fear he, as an informer, was able to inspire has left him with an unhealthy need to be on top of every aspect of his surroundings. Part of Casaldáliga's torment late in life is that he cannot relinquish that need for absolute control while also failing to see that the non-human world will never submit to him because it does not have a will to bend. The contemplative life is not for him because he has conditioned himself to interact with that world always on his own, aggressive terms. He recounts one particular day when the lake's waters changed to colours of yellow and crimson. A nearby factory was in flames, which were reflected in the water, producing noxious fumes, and perturbation in the man who was their solitary, obsessive watcher. He had interrupted his reading to stare out at the lake, the final sentence he had read echoing repeatedly through his mind—'*Con todo, este siglo no cambiará mis costumbres: sepa cada uno ir por su camino*' ('*In spite of all, this century shall not change my habits: let each man follow his own path*').[24] For the reader this is the first of many quotations that chance, or a more conscious process of self-fashioning, will bring to Casaldáliga's attention. The apparent resolution and decisiveness of Propertius's words is immediately juxtaposed with the opening of the next chapter, where the omniscient narrator informs us that Casaldáliga's path to his destiny has been anything but smooth:

> La mañana de agosto en que Casaldáliga decidió intervenir definitivamente en su destino y ofrecerse como delator estaba convencido de que su vida debía adquirir a toda costa la estructura dramática que hasta entonces, y pese a las circunstancias favorables habidas en los años previos, se le había negado de manera injusta e insistente.[25]

> (On the August morning on which Casaldáliga decided to make a decisive intervention in his own destiny and offer his services as an informer, he was convinced that his life needed at all costs to acquire the dramatic structure that until then, and despite the favourable circumstances that had presented themselves in the previous years, had been denied him unjustly and persistently.)

---

[24] *ES*, pp. 21, 29. Casaldáliga is reading elegy 25 from Book II of Propertius's *Elegies*.
[25] *ES*, p. 33.

This opening sets the pattern for the third-person chapters, all of which begin on the day in 1939 when Casaldáliga went to Berua's office to offer his services. Each chapter then leaps backwards in time to show how the protagonist has ended up in his present situation. What is striking about Marías's depiction of Casaldáliga's descent into tyranny is that it is not characterized by any grand scheme. Casaldáliga does not become a tyrant because of indoctrination by the ideologues of the Right, nor is he scarred by an abusive education. Rather we see him suffer a series of intimate failures that undermine his self-image at crucial moments in his development.

Was Casaldáliga's habit of taking lines from poems and applying their meaning to his own situation acquired in childhood? He grows up in an unnamed city in a household with only his father and their ayah for company. While he despises the latter for her rank odour, his father is an aloof presence, a man with whom the young boy barely exchanges a word except on their weekly Sunday walks in a local park. It is in the course of these that his father encourages him to find a unique destiny. Wondering what such a thing might be, he gradually concludes that his father's unique fate is to read French poetry every night, as he apparently does once his only child is in bed. Two couplets from different poems by Victor Hugo are given as examples of the alexandrines over which the 'afrancesado' dwells:

> Et l'esquif monstrueux se ruait dans l'espace./Les noirs oiseaux volaient, ouvrant leur bec rapace. O bien ('Or rather'): Qu'importe que mon corps se blesse et se meurtrisse!/Mon âme ira montrer à Dieu la cicatrice.[26]

Though a unity here is difficult to establish, the first couplet suggests impending misfortune, an uncontrolled vessel, and could be seen to anticipate later revelations about the father. The second hints at the father's bruised and battered soul, which can no longer appeal for comfort to anything other than a higher power. We will learn soon afterwards that Casaldáliga's father was in fact abandoned many years before by his wife and the mother of his only child. Since that devastating blow his mind has become enfeebled and fixated on the woman who did him such wrong. Grohmann contends that quotations have been chosen for their phonetic rather than conceptual function:

> [The foreign passages] seem to have been chosen for their sound and formal qualities on the level of the signifier, as when Casaldáliga regularly discovers his father reading his verses of Victor Hugo that he quotes. The sumptuous verses cited contribute to the grandiloquent style of the novel, but not to the characterization of the father.[27]

---

[26] *ES*, p. 37.
[27] *Coming Into One's Own*, p. 68.

While these verses may not characterize him in a concrete way, they act as a foreshadowing of what Casaldáliga will learn about his father; they act as a form of dramatic irony. His son moreover will have recourse to quotation when he wonders about what self-image his father retained in his unbalanced mind.

Important to note are the naïveté and even stupidity that characterize Casaldáliga for the whole of his early life. In a narrative mode that recalls the realist novel, Marías depicts the future tyrant as poorly equipped to assess the situations he encounters because he has so little dialogue with those around him; the latter are largely indifferent to him in any case. He falls back on artistic sources of comparison because he has no other barometer by which to measure behaviour, his own or other people's. His single guide are his father's repeated exhortations, never elaborated upon, to find his 'destino nítido e inconfundible' ('well-defined and unmistakable destiny') (one of the doublets so characteristic of Browne's style), such that all of Casaldáliga's initial attempts at finding it fall at the first hurdle: none of them is in the least unique.

Among the things we glean from the description of Casaldáliga's childhood and early life is that his maturation has coincided with the development of cinema. It is in the cinema that he begins to test his father's dull chosen fate alongside fictional representations of others' destinies. Whereas Grohmann has argued that Casaldáliga's first attempts at finding his destiny come when he decides to become an informer, the novel makes clear that he flounders in search of a destiny for a decade before deciding to become an informer; and it is his inadequacy twinned with misfortune that mean each successive role he tries does not fit.[28] Casaldáliga reaches the conclusion that his father must have chosen his—a nightly devotion to French poetry and solitude—because every other possible example had been used up. The abundance of other destinies in early films confirms him in this view:

> Y su descubrimiento del cinematógrafo... lo tranquilizó respecto al último impedimento o reserva para aceptar [la solución] del todo al comprobar allí que la imaginación de los hombres tenía capacidad ilimitada y nada escrupulosa para inventar, sin continencia alguna, entes de ficción cuyos destinos eran sin embargo intercambiables, poco nítidos, melodramáticos, escasamente memorables y, sobre todo—habida cuenta de la corta duración de las cintas—, muy fáciles de sobrellevar.[29]

---

[28] Alexis Grohmann, 'La nobleza literaria de Javier Marías' *Quimera*, 252 (2005), 61–6 (p. 63).
[29] *ES*, p. 49.

(And his discovery of the cinematograph…reassured him as to the final
impediment or reservation that was preventing him from accepting [the
solution] entirely, when he confirmed that human imagination had an
unlimited and utterly unscrupulous capacity to invent without the least
check fictional beings whose destinies were nevertheless interchangeable, ill-
defined, melodramatic, barely memorable and, above all,—bearing in mind
the short duration of the reels—very easy to endure.)

His responses to fiction point to an early affective deficiency; a boy starved
of love from an early age, his capacity to empathize appears stunted. Not
only that, he also applies his newfound scorn of fiction equally to literature, history books, and biographies: all works that appeal to the imagination are 'ficticias, delusorias e insustanciales' ('fictitious, delusory, and
insubstantial') and subject to 'tergiversación' ('distortion').[30] Once he has
solved the conundrum in relation to his own father, his anxiety in relation
to the quest subsides, believing that, if a 'destino nítido e inconfundible'
relies on only one distinguishing characteristic, then time will provide
ample opportunity for him to stumble upon it.

This certainty is shattered on the 'noche de San Juan' ('St John's
Night')—23–24 June—of his twenty-eighth year when he returns home
late to discover his father dead. The significance of the date should not go
unnoticed. In Spanish folklore the 'noche de San Juan' is associated with
amorous encounters and unrestrained passion. It is even hinted in *ES* that
Casaldáliga loses his virginity that night: 'su prima carnal…se había
empeñado en retenerlo a su lado por más tiempo del habitual exigiéndole
por mor de la fiesta algunas efusiones suplementarias bajo el entoldado de
fuegos' ('his carnal cousin…had insisted on detaining him a little longer
than usual by demanding he perform, in deference to the occasion, one or
two supplementary effusions beneath the canopy of fireworks').[31] Any
sense of affirmation or personal growth that this rite of passage might
foster in him is scuppered by the sight of his father's corpse. Next to him
is a gramophone Casaldáliga has never seen in the house before and the
score of Schoenberg's *Gurrelieder*. It is left to the despised ayah to reveal
the mystery behind this strange set up. She it is who tells Casaldáliga the
story of his absent mother, the woman whose departure twenty-seven
years before dealt his father a blow from which he never recovered and left
their son to grow up in a strained and affectionless household. The only
information that had reached his father of his mother's activities since her
departure was that she attended the première of *Gurrelieder* in her native
Austria twelve years after leaving them. Clinging desperately to this single
piece of knowledge, he has either read the score or listened to the piece

---

[30] *ES*, p. 40.    [31] *ES*, pp. 51–2.

every night for the last fifteen years, unbeknownst to his son who had always seen him settling down with a book of poetry as he bade him goodnight. Casaldáliga's refusal to engage with these revelations takes the form of a cold emotional detachment:

> Aquella mujer [el aya] le narraba sucesos, eventos, y expresaba de vez en cuando algún juicio dictado siempre por el sentido común. A Casaldáliga todo aquello, como el cinematógrafo, como la literatura entera y las biografías históricas, le parecía pobre e insuficiente, falaz y poco memorable.[32]

> (That woman [the ayah] was relating incidents, events, and occasionally expressing an opinion always dictated by common sense. It all seemed poor and insufficient, false and unmemorable to Casaldáliga, just like the cinematograph, the whole of literature, and historical biographies.)

Marías depicts a man who by his twenty-eighth year is capable of utter indifference when confronted with the knowledge that his mother had abandoned him as a child. He sees his life in coldly objective terms, as though it were the plot of a melodrama, one lacking verisimilitude at that. As readers we have a privileged viewpoint, one from which we see the irony in the fact that the Sunday walks with his father always ended at the bandstand, this another subtle reminder of music forming an invisible barrier between them. The narrator uses free indirect style to report Casaldáliga's words. He maintains, on finding his father's body, that 'Jamás había éste escuchado ningún tipo de música ni mostrado el menor interés por tal arte' ('Never had his father listened to any kind of music nor shown the least interest in that art').[33] Yet, the attentive reader can see the irony in his father choosing the metaphor of a musical score to illustrate his ideas on destiny:[34] he had said that Casaldáliga's 'destino' should be like the opening of a piece of music that forever identifies that composition as unique. By sharing these indications with the reader—indications that ought perhaps to provide Casaldáliga with a retrospective sense of coherence but which he misses—is Marías suggesting that his protagonist is inattentive, unobservant, and thus handicapped in his attempts to interpret the world?

What perturbs him more is the loss of the stable world view that he had cherished until his father's demise. 'Casaldáliga comenzó a sentir el aturdimiento de lo múltiple y amplio' ('Casaldáliga began to feel bewildered by the multiple and wide-ranging possibilities of things').[35] This leads him to contemplate the ambiguity in his father's constructed self-image. How did he see himself in relation to Waldemar, the protagonist of Schoenberg's *Gurrelieder,* who anticipates his grief in one of his love songs to Tove?

---

[32] *ES,* p. 67.     [33] *ES,* p. 57.     [34] *ES,* p. 41.     [35] *ES,* p. 72.

[Su padre] identificaba sus sufrimientos con los que recreaba en el lejano poema bárbaro de los Gurrelieder de Schönberg, los inconmensurables y blasfematorios padecimientos del rey Waldemar al haber perdido a la adorada Tove, y sentía como punzantes y propios el grito exultante Jetzt ist's meine Zeit! y el lamento lóbrego, luego, Unsere Zeit ist um!, viviendo así cada noche lo que va de exclamar '¡Ahora es mi tiempo!' a '¡Nuestro tiempo ha pasado!'...; si todo esto era así, y si su padre era sólo un desequilibrado para el sentido común de sus parientes y el aya, ¿quién entonces podría saber su destino?[36]

([His father] identified his sufferings with those he recreated in the far-off Barbarian poem of Schönberg's Gurrelieder, King Waldemar's vast and blasphemous sufferings on losing his beloved Tove, and experienced sharply as his own the exultant cry 'Jetzt ist's meine Zeit!' and the sombre lament of 'Unsere Zeit ist um!', that way living every night what goes from exclaiming 'Now is my time!' to 'Our time has passed!'...; if all this was the case, and if his father was nothing but mentally unstable according to the common sense of his relatives and ayah, who then could know his destiny?)

Marías explained in 1989 that in *ES* and *EHS* he had sought to explore characters who experience revelations that shake their world view. They experience 'un avatar en su vida, una circunstancia o suceso que de pronto les hace comprenderse a sí mismos, les hace ver su propia definición' ('an upheaval in their life, a circumstance or event that suddenly makes them understand themselves, makes them see their own definition').[37] In Casaldáliga's case, the revelation is not towards an affirmative self-definition, rather it shows him how unstable any self-image is. He will spend the rest of his life trying to keep the consequences of that revelation at bay.

Another of Marías's stated aims in relation to *ES* was the desire to marry, in a single subject, the two dominant modes of treating death in Western art—the burlesque and noble style. Examples of the latter that he gives are Browne's *Hydriotaphia*, Faulkner's *As I Lay Dying* or Broch's *Death of Virgil*; the burlesque tone is epitomized by Jonson's *Volpone* or some of Molière's comedies:

Lo más que puedo decir es que fui muy consciente de esos antecedentes y que, empezando por separar los dos tonos en las diferentes series de capítulos, mi intención era que en un momento dado acabaran mezclándose de manera casi osmótica, acabaran conviviendo, acabaran resultando imprescindibles el uno para el otro, casi uno solo.[38]

[36] *ES*, p. 58.
[37] Luis H. Castellanos, 'La magia de lo que pudo ser: entrevista con Javier Marías', p. 30.
[38] 'Desde una novela no necesariamente castiza', p. 68.

(The most I can say is that I was very conscious of those precedents and that, by starting by separating the two tones in the different chapter sequences, my intention was that at a particular moment they would end up blending into one another almost osmotically, end up coexisting, becoming essential to one another, nearly a single tone.)

Marías set himself similar aims when writing *EHS*, where he wished to fuse the narrator's memory of events with the present tense narrative, destroying the gap between experience as lived and as imagined.

By beginning the first-person chapter three with Casaldáliga playing dead to fool his household, Marías contrasts the dead father with the despotic, insecure son. By enquiring too closely what the effect of such juxtaposition is, we may remove its suggestiveness. Nevertheless it encourages the reader to make the causal link between a victim of fate's cruel twists and a despot who has conceived a need to control all aspects of his immediate environment, animate and inanimate. By alternating the viewpoint from which the story is told, Marías drip-feeds information, encouraging his readers to revise and renew their view of Casaldáliga's motivations and character as the novel progresses. From an ethical point of view, such a way of proceeding encourages us to view Casaldáliga not as a monster, rather as a conundrum. It is to his great credit that Marías is able to give voice to a character in which both burlesque and grandiloquent responses to death coexist and, more importantly, cohere. Thus the burlesque:

> Una de las escasas diversiones que me restan en esta situación tambaleante y cuasi yacente en la que me encuentro es fingirme muerto de cuando en cuando (no más de una vez por trimestre, para no abusar), como los viejos avaros de las comedias.[39]

> (One of the few bits of fun I have left in the doddery and quasi-recumbent position in which I find myself is to play dead from time to time (no more than once every three months, so as not to overdo it), like the greedy old men in plays.)

Now crippled by old age, his only chance of spying on his godson and his wife is by playing dead. 'Yo me divierto oyéndoles cuchichear, sobre todo porque eso me da ocasión de intuir el trato con que se obsequian a solas y de adivinar lo cursi de su vocabulario íntimo' ('I have fun listening to them whisper, mainly because it gives me chance to sense how they must speak to one another when they are alone and to guess at how cloying their private language must be').[40] Even a man who detests his fellow creatures must fuel his contempt, even when sending them to their deaths has been his life's work. Yet the paradox that taunts him, full of loathing

---

[39] *ES*, p. 79.     [40] *ES*, p. 80.

though he is, is that, since his post-war resolution, the only meaning he can find in his life is through the manipulation of others. He purports to despise his (god)son but cannot keep thoughts of him from his mind, principally because the bonds that unite them are mutual. He claims to have shaped his (god)son's avarice since birth, taught him to 'codiciar mis tesoros... por encima de las demás cosas' ('to crave my treasures... above all else'):

> Y al mismo tiempo que fuera del hogar compartido dictaba sentencias y decidía suertes, pronunciaba nombres y los separaba entre vida y muerte, también en casa, con otros métodos menos drásticos pero más sibilinos y más penetrantes, llevaba a cabo con aquel muchacho tan pedante y cilíndrico idéntica tarea de cinceladura, de fijación implacable según mi albedrío.[41]

> (And just as outside the home I would hand down sentences and decide fates, utter names and separate their owners between life and death, also within doors, using less drastic but more sibylline and incisive methods, I was carrying out on that pedantic and cylindrical boy an identical task of whittling, of implacable moulding according to my will.)

Even the moulding of another's character for bad creates bonds of dependence.

At the end of the chapter, Casaldáliga looks to the slopes of the Llama Azul, the mountain where he expects his body to lie after death. When that time comes he will no longer control his world, a thought that provokes a lament in noble style. He does not even know that adequate provision will be made for his corpse, whether the requisite ceremony will be observed when disposing of his mortal remains. Adopting the grand style with its wistful, melancholic tone, he even has the temerity to lament that loyalty is gone, bonds of duty having been replaced by financial contracts and considerations:

> Mas, ¿quién conoce el destino de sus huesos, o cuántas veces lo habrán de enterrar? ¿Quién posee el oráculo de sus cenizas, o sabe hasta dónde llegarán a esparcirse? ¿Quién intuye qué pisadas hollarán su tumba, o cuántas urnas serán volcadas? ¿Quién el tacto y forma de su calavera, o el humo pestífero de sus propias reliquias? ¿Quién el rictus postrero, o el dibujo del agujero en su frente? Yacen los restos de muchos hombres en las partes todas de la tierra entera, y nada es imposible tras la travesía del horizonte, donde al sol se hace burla sin que ya nos vea. Yo sé bien que en ese reino embozado podría el imán dejar de atraer al hierro, y el ave convertirse en madrastra de su propio nido, y el ruido de la ruina edificar con escombros. Y por eso procuran olvidarse ahora las ceremonias en los sacros bosques abandonados: todos ven-

---

[41] *ES*, p. 104.

eran el oro, vencida ya la piedad. La lealtad ha sido por el oro ahuyentada; por oro la justicia se vende, al oro sigue la ley, y luego va la moral no escrita. Pero nada cambia.[42]

(But who knows the fate of his bones, or how often he is to be buried? Who hath the oracle of his ashes, or whither they are to be scattered? Who can sense what footsteps will mark his tomb, or how many urns will be overturned? Who the touch and shape of his skull, or the pestiferous smoke of his own relics? Who the final rictus or the outline of the hole in his forehead? The relics of many lie in all parts of the earth, and nothing is impossible after the voyage over the horizon, where the sun is mocked since it can no longer see us. I know well that in that cloaked realm magnets could cease to attract iron, and the bird become stepmother to its own nest, and noise of ruin raise buildings with rubble. And because of that, efforts are now made to forget the ceremonies in the abandoned sacred forests: all worship gold, devotion already defeated. Loyalty has been chased away by riches; for riches justice is sold, justice obeys riches, and then goes unwritten morality. But nothing changes.)

Marías is quoting the dedicatory epistle Browne appended to *Hydriotaphia.* The themes of the dedication closely mirror those of the famous fifth chapter, as Leonard Nathanson has pointed out:

> The sense of the great heritage that outweighs any present or future possibilities and is in danger of being swept away; the transitoriness of human glory, decaying into nothingness unless transferred to the plane of memory and imagination which alone partakes of permanence—these haunting themes of the concluding chapter are emphatically foreshadowed in this dedication.[43]

When this passage is compared to its Brownean original, the departures become clear:

> But who knows the fate of his bones, or how often he is to be buried? Who hath the oracle of his ashes, or whither they are to be scattered? The relics of many lie, like the ruins of Pompey's, in all parts of the earth; and, when they arrive at your hands, these may seem to have wandered far, who, in a direct and meridian travel, have but a few miles of known earth between yourself and the Pole.[44]

Casaldáliga laments and fears the unknowability of future time. He presents his fears about a lack of adequate ceremony surrounding his

---

[42] *ES,* p. 105.
[43] Leonard Nathanson, '*Urn Burial*: The Ethics of Mortality', in *Seventeenth-Century Prose: Modern Essays in Criticism,* ed. by Stanley Fish (New York: Oxford University Press, 1971), pp. 440–61 (p. 443).
[44] Browne, *Religio Medici,* p. 91.

corpse as a consequence of inhabiting a world where certainty over the afterlife is gone. Browne can and does head off such fears with recourse to the Christian faith. Ceremony and man-made monuments pale into insignificance when seen alongside resurrection and eternal life. According to Nathanson, Browne reaches 'the crown of his art in offering the Christian solution to the fact of death'. Moreover, 'his presentation of the theme as an action of discovery contributes the pleasure and force of originality to what was, after all, the most familiar verity of the age'.[45] By contrast the godless Casaldáliga has nowhere to turn. He pictures the afterlife as beyond the horizon, a topsy-turvy world where natural laws no longer apply, in a series of paradoxical images that, as so often with Marías, the reader can 'comprender' without necessarily being able to 'entender'. Casaldáliga realizes that uncertainty over human fate breeds avarice, an excessive interest in the worldly and the transient. Marías has given him *Hydriotaphia*'s conclusion to speak, although with a subtle shift in emphasis: whereas Browne is 'as happy with six foot as the moles of Adrianus',[46] Casaldáliga's attention remains fixed on the wealth that he cannot renounce because he lacks any other sense of worth.

Marías's focus is skewed in order better to shape our view of Casaldáliga's character. His is the final lament and limited self-knowledge of a sinner whose own attachment to his wealth remains as strong as ever, not because he can spend it but because he can manipulate with it: 'el único campo en el que todavía puedo seguir sojuzgando y jugando con algunos humanos a mi absoluto antojo' ('the only area in which I can still carry on subjugating and playing with a few other human beings entirely on a whim').[47]

Grohmann claims meanwhile that the list of unanswered questions that Marías took directly from *Hydriotaphia*'s dedicatory epistle is used more for its rhythmical qualities than conceptual content: 'Again, the thought unfolded is possibly a by-product of the repetition, which suggests or insinuates itself from the second question onwards, as the figures obey rhythmical rather than conceptual considerations'.[48] In my view, only a reader who has ignored the actual meaning of the novel thus far could make such an assertion. Marías is endeavouring to explore the character and motives of the 'delator'. Having given us a glimpse of the burlesque treatment of death earlier in the same chapter, the quotation, paraphrase, and expansion of Browne's list of unanswered questions closes

---

[45] Nathanson, p. 453.      [46] *Religio Medici*, p. 133.      [47] *ES*, p. 90.
[48] *Coming Into One's Own*, p. 75.

Casaldáliga's reflections on his ability to influence the fate of others after death. The grandiloquent tone of Casaldáliga's fears stands in contrast to his actions towards his (god)son and the latter's 'mujer lasciva' ('lascivious wife'). It is here that Marías contrasts the two means of treating death: whereas the burlesque corresponds to the public sphere, to the scheming side of Casaldáliga's nature, Browne's grand tones are those of a man petrified by death's ultimate power over him. By pretending to be dead, Casaldáliga is anticipating what a world without him would be like, in such a way that it ends up being a harmless game designed to manipulate and mock the living. When in private, his treatment of the subject takes him into more personal, even pompous territory. Far from simply playing the 'sedulous ape' to Browne—as Stevenson feared he had done in many of his youthful writings—Marías intuited that his words, when given to a tyrant to speak, would sound like the affecting and grotesque lament they undoubtedly become.[49]

Marías uses Casaldáliga's responses and recourse to fiction as a means of characterizing him for the reader. Grohmann claims that

> The insertion of two verses of sonnets from Milton, in whose work the protagonist takes solace, seems again to obey a similar motivation, whilst (as in the case of the references to Browne) again providing an explicit link to seventeenth-century English literature and the preoccupation with style, a key to reading the novel.[50]

However, such a 'reading' of the novel does not seem to me to be a reading at all, given that Grohmann scarcely engages with the characterization of the central protagonist or plot, and claims elsewhere in his discussion of *ES* that 'this story [of an informer] becomes only an excuse, a pretext for stylistic experimentation'.[51] Isabel Cuñado also rejects Grohmann's formulation here, pointing out that *ES* is Marías's first treatment of themes that will recur in his fiction—'el padre encubridor de secretos familiares, la herencia de la condena histórica y la idea de que nada desaparece completamente' ('the father who covers up family secrets, the inheritance of historical guilt and the idea that nothing ever disappears completely').[52]

Let us examine the two references to Milton sonnets in the hope of drawing more satisfactory conclusions than that they are placed there

[49] Robert Louis Stevenson claimed to have played the sedulous ape to a succession of authors in his youthful writings, including Browne, Hazlitt, Lamb, and Montaigne. See Robert Louis Stevenson, *Memories and Portraits* (London: Chatto & Windus, 1887), pp. 59–60.

[50] *Coming Into One's Own*, p. 68.   [51] *Coming Into One's Own*, p. 59.

[52] Cuñado, *El espectro de la herencia: la narrativa de Javier Marías*, p. 95.

simply to remind us that Marías had been reading seventeenth-century English literature. Casaldáliga's first attempt at living out a unique destiny leads him to marry Constanza Bacio, whom he thinks is dying. Their marriage is devoid of affection and punctuated by sporadic musical games during the course of which the husband guesses the composer whose work his wife is playing on the piano. Casaldáliga's paltry musical knowledge is constantly exposed while his wife laughs at his ineptitude. At the conclusion of one such session, Constanza flees the room coughing uncontrollably, leaving in her wake a trail of spots of blood. Her husband takes this as confirmation of her terminal illness, and, chancing upon a score by Schoenberg while tidying the disarranged pile of sheet music, realizes that he is to live out the destiny that his father knew only in his imagination. The following passage anticipates Marías's interest in what he would eventually call the realm of 'lo que pudo ser' ('what might have been') or the 'negra espalda del tiempo':

> Pero Casaldáliga descubría ahora que tal vez la historia truncada y debida, la historia trazada por la cabeza insomne del progenitor y animada por su credulidad hasta una víspera de San Juan, no se había evaporado, tras su tachadura implacable y la desaparición del autor, en el reino inane y fantasmagórico de lo malogrado, sino que quizá solamente había aplazado su consumación.[53]

> (But Casaldáliga was discovering now that the truncated and unfulfilled story, the story dreamt up by his father's insomniac mind and encouraged by his credulity until one eve of San Juan, had not evaporated, after its implacable striking from the record and the disappearance of its author, into the inane and phantasmagorical realm of all that had come to nothing, rather it had instead perhaps only put off its consummation.)

This revelation also alters his response to the fiction he encounters. 'Aquella noche—las ventanas de la casa cerradas—comprendió que todo casaba como en el cinematógrafo tan despreciable' ('That night—the windows of the house shut fast—he understood that everything fitted just as it did in the loathsome cinematograph').[54] He realizes that he shares his destiny with the protagonists of so many films, plays, poems, and novels.[55] Rather than disconcert him, this realization acts as a comfort because it provides him with his uniqueness: unlike the characters in the fictions he so despises, he is aware of what the future holds; in short, he feels master of his own destiny. Casaldáliga intuits that human lives are lived again and again, that there is nothing new under the sun, and that the destiny his father lived out but imperfectly, and which he has seen so often

[53] *ES*, pp. 144–5.        [54] *ES*, p. 144.        [55] *ES*, pp. 148–9.

repeated in the fiction he reads and watches, is just one of many that circulate in the ebb and flow of human affairs:

> Nada escapa a las leyes tornadizas, contradictorias y complementarias del olvido y de la memoria, y de igual manera que las aguas de un lago permanecerán prisioneras hasta que no tanto una fuerza misteriosa y superior cuanto un simple accidente que no precise de ninguna fuerza las haga cambiar de carácter y condición, también los hombres están sometidos a la inercia descabezada y voluble de siglos acumulados sin su consentimiento ni su saber, y que, bostezantes y derrengados, marchitada ya su fantasía inventiva y reseca y exhausta su lengua facunda, les exigen una y otra vez la repetición de las mismas vidas y las mismas muertes, los mismos amores y los mismos crímenes.[56]

> (Nothing escapes the fickle, contradictory and complementary laws of forgetting and memory, and just as the waters of a lake will remain imprisoned until not so much a mysterious and superior force as a simple accident, which requires no force at all, makes them change their nature and condition, so too are men subject to the senseless and capricious inertia of centuries of time accumulated without their consent or knowledge, and which, yawning and exhausted, their invention spent, their eloquent tongue dry and weary, demand of them time and again the repetition of the same lives and the same deaths, the same loves and the same murders.)

The reference to the lake waters echoes or, in narrative time, foreshadows Casaldáliga's obsessive desire for control over the lake that lies next to his home. It is important to point out that the citation of Browne that follows in this passage must be attributed to the omniscient narrator rather than Casaldáliga himself. However, in citing Browne, the narrator comes closest to breaking the veil of complete anonymity and almost becomes a presence. His words stop just short of being a performative utterance since, in asserting the necessity of perpetual return and repetition, he nearly appears as a presence in the narrative. The coincidence of Browne having died on his birthday provides an elliptical means of introducing him into the narrative, as well as complementing the circularity being described. Given that it was partly the interest shown in Browne by Borges and Bioy Casares that persuaded Marías to read and translate him, we should note that the theme of metempsychosis is also a point of contact between Browne and Borges.[57]

> Y así, hoy hay alguien aquí condenado a decir, para mejor explicarse, las mismas palabras que hace casi tres siglos y medio escribió un médico londinense nacido un 19 de octubre para morir el 19 de octubre de setenta y siete años después: un médico de estilo paradójico, elegante y elíptico que sin

---

[56] *ES,* p. 146.
[57] See Stephens, 'Borges, Sir Thomas Browne and the Theme of Metempsychosis'.

188        *Javier Marías's Debt to Translation*

duda en aquel instante parafraseaba a su vez del Timeo o—quizá no tan lejos—del Eclesiastés: cada hombre no es tan sólo sí mismo; ... los hombres vuelven a ser vividos; el mundo es hoy como fue en tiempos remotos, cuando nadie había; pero ha habido alguien desde entonces que es el paralelo de ese nadie; que, por así decir, es su yo resucitado.[58]

(And so, today there is someone here condemned to repeat, the better to explain himself, the same words as those written nearly three centuries ago by a London doctor who was born one 19th October and died on another 19th October seventy-seven years later: a doctor possessed of a paradoxical, elegant, and elliptical prose style who at that moment was no doubt paraphrasing in his turn from Plato's *Timaeus* or—perhaps not so far away—from the Book of Ecclesiastes: every man is not only himself; ... men are lived over again; the world is now as it was in ages past, there was none then; but there hath been someone since that parallels him; who is, as it were, his revived self.)

Marías is quoting the sixth part of the first section of *Religio Medici*, Browne's first published work:

To see ourselves again, we need not look for Plato's year; every man is not himself; there have been many Diogenes, and as many Timons, though but few of that name; men are lived over again; the world is now as it was in ages past—there was none then, but there hath been someone since that parallels him, and is, as it were, his revived self.[59]

The major change in Casaldáliga's attitudes is from that of a cynic and an 'abúlico' ('apathetic man') to that of a sentimentalist. From the moment of his realization that he was destined to die the bereaved husband of a young wife cruelly plucked from him, he plays up to the role. Because his wife can only die once and Casaldáliga cannot rehearse his feelings in the realm of his day-to-day existence, he plays them out in fiction:

Siempre en silencio, en el silencio arraigado de su hogar conyugal, decidió perseverar en su espera, y así por ejemplo, la distraía y fortalecía leyendo y releyendo el soneto de Milton sobre su mujer difunta, y, sabiéndoselo de memoria, no dejaba de sentirse conmovido e identificado cada vez que llegaba a los versos finales, cuando al inclinarse la muerta soñada para abrazar al poeta ciego que nunca la había visto, I waked, she fled, and day brought back my night.[60]

(Always in silence, the entrenched silence of his marital home, he decided to persevere in his wait, and so for example, he would indulge and strengthen it by reading and rereading Milton's sonnet on his late wife, and knowing it off by heart, he never ceased to be moved by and see himself in the final lines, when as the dreamt-of dead woman leant over to embrace the blind

---
[58] *ES*, pp. 146–7.    [59] *Religio Medici*, pp. 7–8.    [60] *ES*, p. 152.

poet who had never set eyes on her, I waked, she fled, and day brought back my night.)

He sentimentally indulges the feelings of a bereaved husband in anticipation of their actual arrival. He even cries in the cinema when plot, heroine, and music coincide to 'suscitar las emociones más ramplonas y bajas de los espectadores' ('to arouse the audience's crudest and most basic emotions').[61] By introducing Milton's sonnet at this point, Marías is able to point to the failure of feeling that much sentimental behaviour actually indulges. Reluctant to confront the idea that all his apprehensions may be a misunderstanding, he neglects to ascertain from his wife, her family, or friends the veracity of the terminal illness that he assumes will curtail her life. His concern for her situation only reaches as far as its impact on him and the role he has chosen for himself. His wrought, self-fashioning use of literary texts here encourages us to wonder how much he manipulates or highlights the importance of some works that he comes across. The line from Propertius that 'fate' so conveniently put into his mind could not be a poorer summation of his life so far—'*Con todo, este siglo no cambiará mis costumbres: sepa cada uno ir por su camino*'[62]—the first thirty-nine years of which were spent stumbling from one disaster to another.

If we contrast Casaldáliga's recourse to fiction at this stage in his marriage to Constanza with the second occasion on which he seeks out Milton's poetry, this time in search of solace, the result is revealing. In the meantime his role as grieving husband has evaporated due to Constanza's robust health. Now in Lisbon with civil war raging across the border to the east, he cannot muster either the courage or the energy to return to participate in the conflict. As the years slip by, his daily round of the cafés and bars frequented by his exiled countrymen becomes a torment, his home now a claustrophobic reminder of his indolence, his wife utterly indifferent to him. Where before in Milton he had found a confirmation of his perceived role, recourse to his poetry now proves a source of mockery:

> Y si unos versos de Milton habían distraído y fortalecido la espera del advenimiento de su primer y sobreseído sino, ahora otra línea también famosa, la última del soneto sobre su ceguera, lo martirizaba mientras aguardaba, rondándolo con frecuencia como si fuera la aplicación de uno de esos castigos superfluos con los que sólo se busca una extraña equidad en cómputos insondables, la paz egoísta de quien los impone. No veía verdad en aquellas palabras: They also serve who only stand and wait.[63]

---

[61] *ES,* p. 153.     [62] *ES,* pp. 21, 29.

[63] *ES,* p. 236. The Milton sonnet is, like the quotations from Browne we have been examining, another example of a favourite poem that has remained part of Marías's creative imagination. He refers to it again in the article 'A los que están y sólo esperan', in *SACF,* pp. 286–8 and in *NET,* p. 19.

(And if some lines by Milton had indulged and strengthened his resolve in waiting for the consummation of his first, dismissed fate, now another famous line, the last in Milton's sonnet on his blindness, tormented him while he lingered, besetting him often, as if it were the application of one of those superfluous punishments with which only a strange equity is sought in unfathomable calculations, the selfish peace of their imposer. He saw no truth in those words: They also serve who only stand and wait.)

His failure to empathize comes to the fore once again. Despite his fellow countrymen fighting out a war across the border, he cannot conceive of the need to take part because the events themselves resemble fiction too closely.[64] His participation seems to him, 'como una ilusión sólo comparable a la descabellada idea de encontrarse de repente inserto en los vidriosos e indemostrables sucesos de un libro de Historia o en las intrigas trepidantes de un Joseph Bálsamo' ('like an illusion comparable only to the ludicrous idea of finding himself suddenly thrust into the glazed and unreal events of a History book or the fast-moving intrigues of a Joseph Balsamo').[65] Paradoxically, if at one moment he cannot imagine the war because it seems too unreal, at another it seems too daunting because he is aware that history is being written and 'nada se hace tan arduo como dotar de sentido nuevo a lo que ya ha recibido la indeleble marca de tinta y papel' ('nothing is as difficult as giving new meaning to something that has already received the indelible mark of pen and ink').[66] Nevertheless, the picture Marías paints is of a man who resorts to artistic models and precedents to fashion his self-image, whether his motivation is self-indulgence or self-flagellation. That tendency continues in the first-person narrative.

Casaldáliga's play-acting has a reprise in chapter seven. On this occasion noble style gives way to the burlesque, reversing the previous order. First comes a series of questions that recall the cadence and theme of the Brownean paraphrase earlier employed. He wonders who, after his death, will care for his mortal remains:

¿Quién retirará mi almohada, quién mis sábanas humedecidas? ¿Quién, incapaz de concebir la existencia sin mi presencia diaria, querrá seguir sin dilación mis pasos al contemplarme exánime? ¿Quién irá a visitar mi tumba, y me hablará solitario en lo alto de la Llama Azul tras haber ascendido por la pendiente y haberme mirado con amor y fatiga a través de la piedra inscrita?[67]

(Who will clear away my pillow, who my damp sheets? Who, unable to imagine existing without my daily presence, will want to follow in my footsteps without delay when they see my lifeless body? Who will visit my grave,

[64] *ES*, p. 225.      [65] *ES*, p. 230.      [66] *ES*, p. 226.      [67] *ES*, p. 241.

and talk to me alone high up on the Llama Azul having climbed the slopes and gazed at me lovingly and breathless through the inscribed stone?)

He acknowledges that these worries assail him when 'me noto muy débil y temeroso' ('I feel very weak and fearful').[68] Who will truly lament his death? The only way he has of finding out is by pretending to be dead. Natalia Monte, the only woman he has loved throughout his cruel life, has managed to pass all the tests he has set her. Her grief at his succession of fake deaths has seemed genuine, yet, as Casaldáliga says, 'no me basta' ('it's not enough for me').[69] His awareness of his own situation, seen through the prism of his reading, is considerable. 'Si tantas cosas que están en los libros ya me han ocurrido, no tendría nada de extraño que al final me encontrara en medio de una farsa moralista y clásica' ('If so many things to be found in books have already happened to me, it wouldn't be the least strange if now I found myself in the middle of classical moralist farce').[70] The predicament of the 'viejo avaro' ('old miser') of the moral farce is that he can manipulate those around him to try to discover what he wants to know, but can never be sure that he is not the victim of a double bluff. By employing underhand means, he cannot get straightfor-wardly at the truth. Now that he is dying, he wants to know 'cuánto de genuino hay en su [Natalia] amor por mí' ('how much truth there is in [Natalia's] love for me'), but, as he says—'los hábitos de esta vida son demasiado fuertes hasta para un moribundo, y no voy a traicionar mi carácter por ceder a un postrer antojo' ('the habits of a lifetime are too strong even for a dying man and I'm not going to betray my nature just for the sake of a final caprice').[71] Marías extracts pathos from this situa-tion, engaging our sympathy with Casaldáliga with the realization that, in his current state, the only person he is able successfully to victimize is himself. A lifetime spent choking the feelings he has long-since seen as weaknesses has left him bereft of sympathy and empathy even with his own emotional needs.

The final artistic mirror in which he sees himself is that of the 'canto místico' ('mystical song') el León de Nápoles sings repeatedly throughout Casaldáliga's final days. The latter's description of it displays all the bile and resentment of a man now forced into passivity but who refuses to surrender his aggression:

> Lo cierto es que por la mansión se extiende durante gran parte del día, por-tadora siempre de esa melodía afligida, ondulante, quejumbrosa y repetitiva, una voz impostada y ambigua, como de degenerado o hermafrodita, que todo lo invade y pringa con su pastosidad excesiva, que flota y avanza a

[68] *ES*, p. 242.     [69] *ES*, p. 247.     [70] *ES*, p. 247.     [71] *ES*, p. 249.

través de salas y corredores, que penetra sin misericordia en mis frágiles y ancianos oídos.[72]

(The fact is that throughout my mansion for large parts of the day can be heard, always carrying that grief-stricken melody, undulating, plaintive and repetitious, a projected and ambiguous voice, as though belonging to a degenerate or a hermaphrodite, which invades and smears everything with its excessive richness, floats and moves on through rooms and corridors, mercilessly penetrates my fragile and age-worn ears.)

First quoted in Latin, then translated two pages later, Casaldáliga believes the song depicts the final days of a tyrant—'*todos sus amigos lo han traicio-nado y se han convertido en sus enemigos*' ('*all his friends have betrayed him and become his enemies*').[73] Casaldáliga's fate is now to sit and listen to what he sees as taunts. Or is he seeking a last dose of our sympathy? The fact that Marías troubles to translate this final artistic mirror that Casaldáliga holds up ought to give the lie to Grohmann's claim that 'the foreign language insertions in the novel...are even more effective for the reader who does not comprehend their meaning'.[74] Instead the foreign passages, and Casaldáliga's use of and response to them, act as the markers to show how he attempts to fashion his self-image. Those attempts meet with varying degrees of success as he suffers the series of intimate humili-ations that will provoke him into tyranny. In recording the final months of his life, he monopolizes the truth and projects the image he wants of the pitiable yet defiant figure who fights on against his unloving family. It is Marías, however, who has played a last trick on his narrator.

El León de Nápoles, Casaldáiga's (god)son, is repeatedly singing the *Lamentations of Jeremiah*. The words lament the fall of Jerusalem. The symbolism of that fact should not escape us—a promised land gone bad, a fallen nation. Thus we return to the question of how to write about a nation's history (Spain's history) without repeating the mistakes of the past. How can Marías write a novel that will not have the didacticism of 'literatura comprometida' ('committed literature') at its core? It is here perhaps that the circularity of human affairs meets the particular depic-tion Marías has sought in *El siglo*. Marías's generation loathed covert or overt political commitment in art above all else, and yet here is Marías writing a novel the title of which implies a bold claim about its subject matter. The plot synopsis on the first edition of *El siglo* claims that it is 'en escorzo, la historia de un país' ('a foreshortened version of a country's history').[75] The author has always maintained an iron grip on the presen-

[72] *ES*, pp. 255–6.        [73] *ES*, pp. 256, 259.        [74] *Coming Into One's Own*, p. 69.
[75] The first edition of the novel was published by Seix Barral in 1983.

tation of his works and there is no reason to believe this synopsis will have been an exception: the photo on that same first edition is a photograph of São Vicente de Fora taken by his older brother Fernando. So in what ways does *El siglo* reflect on Spain in the twentieth century? Marías writes and allows the reader to watch the development of a man who responds to the opacity of his own soul and of those around him with aggression.

The word 'siglo' ('century') can also mean the 'vida y actividad de la gente' ('life and actions of people'), the everyday round of human life that exists alongside great narratives of history, as J. H. Abbott points out in his review of *ES*: '[el siglo] que viene a ser no sólo el siglo en que vive Casaldáliga, en que vivimos nosotros, sino *El siglo*, el mundo, la vida' ('[the century] that turns out to be not just the century in which Casaldáliga is living, in which we're living, but also *El siglo*, the world, life').[76] Casaldáliga in all his obsession with money, control over his legacy, and the physical reminders of his life is the antithesis of Browne's Christian stoic. Marías's novel is an attempt at answering the question of how such a man could exist in such a place at such a time. Further than that, neither he nor I are willing to go. Austin Warren has written of Browne that he possessed a speculative mind 'which delight[ed] to entertain conjectures and to ask unanswerable questions for the sake of the vistas they open'.[77] Marías may not have had a definitive answer to the question of human wrongdoing in *ES* but he was able to explore questions about how human beings manipulate their own self-image and lash out when faced with an unsympathetic, inscrutable world.

An attentive reading of the novel can suggest conclusions about aspects of characterization and Marías's creative imagination that have not been acknowledged in previous responses to the novel. I disagree with aspects of Grohmann's discussion of *ES*, but he is right to point to some of the novel's flaws. The use of quotation is excessive where the third-person narrator is concerned. Oblique reference is made to Pessoa in the chapter 'Lisboa', seeming to characterize the otherwise anonymous narrator, an effect I find undesirable.[78] Similarly nautical similes, though linked to the epiphany outside São Vicente de Fora, which abound in both third-person narrator and Casaldáliga's account, seem out of place as they do not grow organically from either the characters, setting, or plot of the novel.

---

[76] J. H. Abbott, 'El siglo', *Invitación a la lectura*, 8 (1990), 3.
[77] Austin Warren, 'The Styles of Sir Thomas Browne', in *Seventeenth-Century Prose*, ed. by Stanley E. Fish (New York: Oxford University Press, 1971), pp. 413–23 (p. 422).
[78] Reference is to the poem 'Acordar da cidade de Lisboa, mais tarde do que as outras'. See Fernando Pessoa, *Obras completas*, 11 vols (Lisbon: Ática, 1942–1974), II: *Poesias de Álvaro de Campos* (1944), pp. 98–102.

Their presence can, as Grohmann points out, undoubtedly be attributed to the fact that Marías had recently written his translation of Conrad's *Mirror of the Sea*.[79] The Herculean effort of rendering Conrad's tortuous prose and obscure naval vocabulary in Spanish stayed with Marías, who has stated that Conrad's autobiographical account is the hardest piece of translation he has ever done: '*El espejo del mar* me costó un trabajo endiablado, por los términos marinos y porque tiene una prosa enrevesada' ('*The Mirror of the Sea* was fiendishly hard work, due to the maritime terminology and because it's written in complex prose').[80] Perhaps he did not want the work to go to waste. The paucity of nautical simile in his subsequent fiction suggests that on reflection he did not endorse their profusion in *ES* either.

What we do note in the novels subsequent to *ES* is that Marías adopts the narrative voice of men whose profession brings them into daily contact with language, either as an interpreter (Juan Ranz and Deza), a ghost writer (Víctor Francés), a teacher (Deza when narrator of *TLA*), or as artistic manipulators of language (el León de Nápoles, Marías when narrating *NET*). Whether Marías felt he was forcing the use of quotation and allusion in *ES* is a moot point. Nevertheless, he made use in all his subsequent novels of narrators whose professional and personal preoccupations with language overlap and feed into one another. We can see the evolution of this shift in Marías's interview with Caterina Visani. Discussing *EHS* he acknowledged that he wanted a narrator 'que pudiese hacer una serie de observaciones y reflexiones no del todo vulgares' ('who could plausibly deliver a series of observations and reflections that were beyond the commonplace'), something that would have lacked verisimilitude had the narrator been a butcher.[81]

This shift in Marías's narrative voice has earned him the condemnation of more than one critic; Sebastian Faber notes with disapproval 'la casi total ausencia en estos mundos narrativos de elementos y conflictos socioeconómicos o de clase' ('the almost total absence from these narrative worlds of elements or conflicts either socioeconomic or of class');[82] Cecilia Dreymüller makes the claim that Marías's novels evoke with nostalgia '[e]l pasado franquista' ('the times of Franco's rule') because of the social position of the narrators and, what she sees as, their patronizing

[79] *Coming Into One's Own*, pp. 73–4.
[80] Alameda, 'Javier Marías: el éxito europeo de un indeciso', p. 62.
[81] Visani interview (http://www.javiermarias.es/PAGINASDEENTREVISTAS/entrevistaCaterinaVisani.html).
[82] Sebastian Faber, 'Un pensamiento que hace rimas: el afán universalizador en las novelas de Javier Marías', *Revista Hispánica Moderna*, 56 (2003), 195–204 (p. 202).

attitude towards women.[83] Neither claim seems to me to warrant a response.

However, rather than continue to examine the shift in Marías's fiction after *ES*, the next chapter will continue to examine how the author has drawn inspiration from the works of Browne. What we find is that *ES*, far from being an isolated case, represents only the first example of a lasting debt to the English prose writer.

---

[83] Cecilia Dreymüller, 'Las leyes del Mercado: acerca del fenómeno literario y editorial Javier Marías', in *Entre el ocio y el negocio: industria editorial y literatura en la España de los 90*, ed. by José Manuel López de Abiada et al. (Madrid: Verbum, 2001), pp. 83–92 (p. 86). Her assertions about Marías's sexism and nostalgia for Franco's dictatorship diverge so widely from both the content of his novels and his stated views that it is hard to believe that someone without a hidden agenda could seek to defend them.

7

# The Continuing Presence of Browne

## BROWNE AND RELICS

A continuity exists between the Brownean quotations that underpinned *ES* and Marías's subsequent works. Brownean images and cadence occur to him when certain subjects are uppermost in his mind: these include uncertainty over how posterity will remember him and others, the benevolence of a forgetful memory, memory's fallibility, snow as a simile of life's hardships, and uncertainty around the circumstances of one's own death. However, when such topics are in play, Marías does not always resort to metaphors inspired by Browne; nor do his echoes of Browne appear in groups or patterns that aid their identification. It would be more accurate to say that Browne's cadence and phraseology have become a habit of thought for Marías; quite simply, his Spanish version of Browne, most notably *Hydriotaphia*, have become one of his touchstones.

Browne dedicated his meditation on death and funeral practices to one of his oldest friends, Thomas Le Gros.[1] The dedicatory epistle sets out some of Browne's motives for having taken up his pen in pursuit of so unpromising a topic as ancient funerary rites. He explains that the unearthing in Old Walsingham of forty or fifty funeral urns two years previously had given him pause for thought:

> We were hinted by the occasion, not catched the opportunity to write of old things, or intrude upon the antiquary. We are coldly drawn unto discourses of antiquities, who have scarce time to comprehend new things, or make out learned novelties. But seeing they arose as they lay, almost in silence among us (at least in short account suddenly passed over), we were very unwilling they should die again, and be buried twice among us.[2]

Albeit that Browne, as Preston has recently shown, was very much engaged in networks of intellectual exchange and enquiry, he was not what we would think of as an archaeologist. She explains that 'antiquarianism' was

---

[1] As Jeremiah Finch writes of Le Gros, 'But his name would now be forgotten had it not happened that Browne dedicated to him a little tract entitled *Hydriotaphia: or Urn Burial'*. See Finch, *Sir Thomas Browne: A Doctor's Life of Science & Faith*, p. 179.

[2] *Religio Medici*, p. 92.

a science that found its material in books and among tracts of ancient lore, not at the bottom of muddied pits. She examines numerous instances in which Browne collaborated in the elucidation and classification of perplexing artefacts, unearthed by workmen on the estates of his wealthy friends; the archetypal example being a large fish bone, found miles from the sea and on land that revealed strata of fossilized vegetation.[3] Browne's enquiring mind, curiosity about the artefacts that chance threw in his way, and eagerness to examine them, resemble Marías's attitude towards literary posterity, the fickle finger of which passed so completely over John Gawsworth, the poet who was his obsession for several years. That *Hydriotaphia* has provided Marías with the stylistic means to describe the unpredictability of literary posterity is confirmed by two sources—the prologue to his anthology of interwar British ghost stories, *Cuentos únicos* (1989), and the 1990 essay 'Quinielas'. Most of the writers anthologized in *Cuentos únicos* have slipped into obscurity despite being considered, in their day, among the best practitioners of the short story form. Marías describes their descent into obscurity as if this were part of a natural law:

> Lo escrito y olvidado es incomparablemente más vasto que lo escrito y recordado, y hay páginas extraordinarias que nadie conoce porque quizá están en medio de tantas más desdeñables. No basta una imagen, una metáfora, una reflexión, un pasaje magníficos; no basta una sola página, ni siquiera—así parece—un cuento, un solo cuento.[4]

> (What is recorded and forgotten incomparably exceeds what is recorded and remembered, and there are extraordinary pages known to no one, perhaps because they sit between so many others more worthy of disdain. A striking image, metaphor, reflection, passage are not enough; a single page is not enough, nor even is—so it would seem—a short story, a single short story.)

A passage whose insights and phrasing cannot but recall Browne's question: 'Who knows whether the best of men be known, or whether there be not more remarkable persons forgot than any that stand remembered in the known account of time?'.[5]

In 1990, Marías published the essay 'Quinielas', in which he whimsically challenges Spain's literary critics to predict which of the then crop of home-grown writers would be remembered by posterity. The author begins by registering his dismay at the ease with which so many writers find almost complete oblivion:

---

[3] Claire Preston, *Thomas Browne and the Writing of Early Modern Science*, pp. 124–6.
[4] JM, 'Nota del traductor', in *Cuentos únicos*, trans. by Javier Marías and Alejandro García Reyes (Barcelona: Reino de Redonda, 2004), pp. 9–15 (p. 12).
[5] *Religio Medici*, p. 129.

Cuando uno hojea diccionarios de literatura o, aún más, índices de bibliote-
cas serias, produce verdadero pavor la cantidad de nombres muertos de los
que nadie sabe nada, salvo unos cuantos eruditos vivos de los que a su vez
todo se ignora. 'Más hechos hay sepultados en el silencio que registrados y
los más copiosos volúmenes son epítomes de lo que ha sucedido', dijo un
autor todavía hoy incierto, y sus afirmaciones se hacen abrumadoramente
verídicas si se aplican a la literatura.[6]

(When one flicks through dictionaries of literature or, even more so, the cata-
logues of good libraries, it really is terrifying the sheer quantity of dead names
about which no one knows anything, save for a handful of living authorities
about whom, in their turn, nothing is known. 'Much more is buried in silence
than is recorded, and the largest volumes are butt epitomes of what hath been',
said an author whose name even today remains uncertain, and his statements
become overwhelmingly true when applied to literature.)

Written at a time when he was still unsure of the authorship of the
interpolated fragment, it is nevertheless telling that the 'Brownean' echo
was still the best formulation he had yet come across of a commonplace:
that we know only a fraction of what we might know about the past. We
have only to look as far as the article 'El hombre que pudo ser rey'
(1985), Marías's first piece on Gawsworth, to see whose scent he had
been pursuing through the tomes of literary history: 'no existe ningún
libro ni, al parecer, artículo sobre J. G., y apenas si viene mencionado en
los más voluminosos y exhaustos diccionarios de literatura' ('there is not
a single book, nor apparently even article on J. G., and his name scarcely
features in the most sizeable and exhausted dictionaries of literature').[7]
That he should have linked the oblivion into which Gawsworth had so
nearly fallen with the potential fate of his own generation is unsurprising since, as stated above, it was this reminder of the fragility of literary
fame that partly drew Marías to Gawsworth in the first instance. His
recourse to Browne's insights had a further reprise in 2003 when he
quoted them in an article on Martin Scorsese's film *Gangs of New York*.
There, he registered his surprise that the historical events depicted in the
film—the widespread civil unrest that gripped the city in July 1863—
had apparently fallen out of the public consciousness, were no longer
discussed or remembered.[8] Such echoing demonstrates the extent to

---

[6] JM, 'Quinielas', in *LF*, pp. 172–4 (p. 172). The caveat inserted concerning the author's
identity can be explained by the fact that Marías had yet to realize his mistake over the Brownean attribution. On the page quoted, the author has inserted a footnote after the word 'incierto' ('uncertain'): 'Ya no: Sir Thomas Browne, a quien yo traduje y a quien debo tanto' ('no
longer uncertain: Sir Thomas Browne, whom I translated and to whom I owe so much').

[7] JM, 'El hombre que pudo ser rey', in *Pasiones Pasadas* (hence referred to as *PP*),
pp. 197–201 (p. 197).

[8] JM, 'Qué sería peor', in *EOOL*, pp. 92–4.

which Marías's thinking on literary posterity and oblivion have been shaped by Browne.

## 'CUANDO FUI MORTAL', GHOSTS, AND A FORGETFUL MEMORY

Given that Browne continued to provide Marías with well-phrased encapsulations of commonplace truths on the subject of memory, let us next examine his ghost story 'Cuando fui mortal' with a view to exploring its engagement with Browne. However, I do not limit myself to that aspect alone and analyse the story on its own terms and in the context of Marías's interest in ghosts, his use of the ghost story form, and his ideas about the role writing might play in dealing with the past.

Marías has done more than any other contemporary Spanish writer to renew the fortunes of the ghost as a vehicle for fiction. In the opinion of Cuñado,

> Ninguna otra obra española contemporánea está tan habitada por fantasmas y, por lo tanto, ninguna otra nos habla con tal continuidad y resonancia de la complicada y quizá irresoluble relación entre el pasado y el presente.[9]

> (No other contemporary Spanish oeuvre is so haunted by ghosts and, for that reason, no other talks to us so consistently and resonantly of the complex, perhaps insoluble relationship between the past and present.)

His first published work was a 'cuento de fantasmas' ('ghost story') entitled 'La vida y la muerte de Marcelino Iturriaga' (1968). It appeared in a now-defunct Barcelona newspaper without the author's knowledge, he having written it at the tender age of fourteen.[10] Moreover, his favourite film is Joseph Mankiewicz's *The Ghost and Mrs Muir* (1947), a love story between a young widow and the ghost of a sea captain who haunts the seaside cottage in which she lives.[11] He was also glowing in his praise of Pedro Almodóvar's 2006 film *Volver*, in which the protagonists are apparently haunted by the ghosts of their lost relatives.[12] In 1989 he published an anthology in Spanish of interwar British ghost stories, *Cuentos únicos*, some of which he translated himself, reissuing an extended version

[9] Cuñado, *El espectro de la herencia: la narrativa de Javier Marías*, p. 27.
[10] JM, 'Nota previa', in *MED*, pp. 9–12 (p. 11). Given that Julián Marías, Javier's father, published his journalistic pieces in *El Noticiero Universal*, the newspaper in which the story appeared, throughout the 1960s and beyond, it seems likely that it was he who sent it off for consideration. See Julián Marías, II, 164, 225, 292.
[11] JM, *Donde todo ha sucedido: al salir del cine*, ed. by Inés Blanca Muñoz (Barcelona: Galaxia Gutenberg, 2005), 62.
[12] JM, 'Por qué no vuelven', in *DNA*, pp. 198–200.

through his Reino de Redonda press in 2004; to both editions he mischie-
vously added a ghost story of his own, 'La canción de Lord Rendall',
published under the terribly British-sounding pseudonym James Den-
ham. To date Marías has written seven ghost stories, published in two
short fiction collections, *Mientras ellas duermen* (1990, with an expanded
edition in 2000) and *Cuando fui mortal* (1996).

As several critics have pointed out, ghosts interest Marías above all as
doubles for the writer.[13] In 1995 he explained that he felt a growing affinity with this favourite literary figure: 'alguien a quien ya no le pasan de
verdad las cosas, pero que se sigue preocupando por lo que ocurre allí
donde solían pasarle' ('someone to whom things are no longer really happening, but who continues to worry about what's going on in the places
where they once did'). Marías believes writers see strangely tangible
reminders of the selves they have left behind when reading what they once
thought or imagined. Far from believing that such testimony ensures
immortality through print, he offers a more pessimistic assessment of its
usefulness: a writer's words are merely 'ficticias cadenas' ('fictitious chains')
and 'intangibles palabras' ('intangible words').[14] However, it is precisely
the voice of a ghost that he had been trying to adopt for the narrators of
his fiction of the 1990s, as he revealed in conversation with Juan Gabriel
Vásquez in 2001.[15] These are narrators who revisit through their writing
traumatic events that they have yet to lay to rest, much as ghosts haunt
the places they once knew, to complete unfinished business. No longer
directly implicated in events, and powerless to alter the past, Marías's narrators nevertheless record their experiences in print.

Elide Pittarello gives an excellent description of Juan Ranz's obsessive
association of and return to traumatic events in the introduction to her
critical edition of *CTB* (2006). She summarizes the attitude of Marías's
traumatized narrators:

> Contadas todas en primera persona, estas historias se presentan como las
> aventuras excéntricas de individuos que dan nombres diferentes, pero anál-
> ogos, a lo que el logos no puede abarcar. Contra la práctica defensiva de
> conceptualizar el mundo a fin de dominarlo, ahí está la mezcla híbrida de
> memoria consciente y memoria onírica.[16]

[13] Critics to have drawn attention to this aspect of Marías's interest in ghosts include
Cuñado, pp. 29–31 and David Roas, 'Perdidos en Redonda: Javier Marías y lo fantástico',
in *Cuadernos de narrativa: Javier Marías*, pp. 217–30 (pp. 217–18).
[14] JM, 'Prólogo', in *VF*, pp. 19–24 (pp. 19–20).
[15] Juan Gabriel Vásquez, '"Tengo a veces la sensación de no estar ya vivo"', p. 15.
[16] Elide Pittarello, '"No he querido saber, pero he sabido": Javier Marías y "Corazón tan
blanco"', in JM, *Corazón tan blanco*, ed., with introduction and notes by Elide Pittarello
(Barcelona: Crítica, 2006), pp. 5–94 (p. 21).

(All told in the first person, these stories present themselves as the eccentric adventures of individuals who give different but analogous names to what their Logos cannot take in. In opposition to the defensive practice of conceptualizing the world in order to dominate it, we have their mixture of conscious and oneiric memory.)

In the following analysis of Marías's richest ghost story, 'Cuando fui mortal', I hope to elucidate a number of areas. Principal among these are the ways in which Marías's role as a translator of Browne and as an anthologizer of ghost stories affected the gestation of this tale. We shall examine too the question that Pittarello's description begs: what level of control do Marías's narrators exert over their texts? How much of their recreation of the past is the involuntary association of a traumatized memory and how much the conscious manipulation of their past for a supposed audience? Given the author's stated desire to adopt a ghost's viewpoint from the 1990s novels onwards, what might his ghost stories, and especially those narrated in the first person, tell us about the longer narratives? Despite a growing bibliography on Marías, no critic has yet answered this question.[17] Marías's first ghost story, 'La vida y la muerte de Marcelino Iturriaga', and 'Cuando fui mortal' have much in common; their points of contact and contrast reveal the development of Marías's artistic ambition and faithful return to the cherished literary staples of his childhood.

Marías discussed his beginnings as a writer with Paul Ingendaay in 2000:

> I started writing my own things when I was 12, 13, and I know why I did it: mainly because I had finished all the adventure novels, musketeer novels, and Dumas that I was reading at the time. Then I found out that I could write in order to read more of what I liked.[18]

He retained this habit of imitation, albeit in a more sophisticated form, until his twenties: as Grohmann has demonstrated, his first two novels, *Los dominios del lobo* and *Travesía del horizonte*, owe a great deal to mimicry and pastiche.[19] In 'La vida y la muerte de Marcelino Iturriaga', the eponymous

---

[17] Alicia Molero de la Iglesia contends that it is Marías's 'tendencia psicologista...la que mejor acogida tiene en sus cuentos, filtrándose a través de ella una conciencia por la que se vislumbra un sujeto creador muy próximo al de otras manifestaciones de su narrativa' ('psychologizing tendency...that finds itself most at home in his short stories, by filtering through it a consciousness behind which can be seen a creating subject which is very close to other manifestations of his fiction'); see her 'El narrador psicológico de Javier Marías', in *El cuento en la década de los noventa*, ed. by José Romera Castillo et al. (Madrid: Visor, 2001), pp. 257–66 (p. 265). Unfortunately, she offers this as the conclusion to an overview of his short story output and does not elaborate in specific detail. The present chapter seeks to do so more fully.

[18] For interview text, see Paul Ingendaay, 'Interview with Javier Marías', *Bomb*, 73 (2000), <http://bombsite.com/issues/73/articles/2345>, pp. 150–8 (accessed 2 November 2008).

[19] *Coming Into One's Own*, pp. 25–54.

narrator is a ghost who, after his physical death, surveys his conventional and uneventful life from the grave. He grew up living over a pharmacy, married more for convenience than love, had two children, put up with his warring parents-in-law, and died of a heart attack in his mid forties. Although Marcelino's spirit lives on, he remains trapped in his body and can only see the window of sky through the opening of his grave.

If we take it that in drafting his first short story Marías wished to mimic a form of writing he was enjoying at the time, I would suggest Poe's 'The facts in the case of M. Valdemar' to be a likely source. The premise of the spirit trapped within the extinct physical body—'sin respirar, pero viviendo; sin ojos, pero viendo; sin oídos, pero oyendo' ('not breathing but alive; without eyes, but able to see; without ears, but able to hear')—strongly resembles Poe's tale of the hypnosis experiment that proves horribly successful:[20] in Poe's tale M. Valdemar is kept alive after his physical death by a hypnotist who places him in a trance moments before he expires. M. Valdemar must then suffer the torment of being trapped in an extinct body until he manages to communicate his suffering to the hypnotist and is awoken, to death. Poe depicts the survival of consciousness beyond death as an unendurable torture, whereas what characterizes 'La vida y la muerte de Marcelino Iturriaga' is its benevolent vision of death: 'Veo a Esperancita cada mes y a los chicos cada dos, y esto es todo: esta es mi vida y mi muerte, donde no hay nada' ('I see Esperancita once a month, and the boys every other month, and that's all: this is my life and my death, where there is nothing').[21] He seems resigned to his fate, not tormented by memories of the past, and has settled into a comforting routine of visits and boredom: his wife visits him every month to place flowers on his grave. It appears that when Marías was first experimenting with the ghost story form, he realized its capacity to treat problems of existence and memory, while maintaining a benevolent view of death at a time, one might imagine, when mortality was first becoming a preoccupation for the young writer. In conversation with Pittarello, Marías tentatively suggested that a shift in his character from extrovert to introvert coincided with his becoming aware of death at the age of seven or eight.[22]

If we contrast this early treatment of death and memory in the light of Savater's discussion of the macabre, the result is revealing. Marías dedicated his anthology of interwar British ghost stories *Cuentos únicos*—'Para

---

[20] JM, 'La vida y la muerte de Marcelino Iturriaga', in *MED*, pp. 13–20 (p. 20); 'The Life and Death of Marcelino Iturriaga', in *While the Women Are Sleeping*, trans. by Margaret Jull Costa (London: Chatto & Windus, 2010), pp. 103–8 (p. 108).

[21] 'La vida y la muerte de Marcelino Iturriaga', p. 20; 'The Life and Death of Marcelino Iturriaga', p. 108.

[22] Pittarello, *Entrevistos*, pp. 16–17.

Fernando Savater, máximo merecedor y más seguro entusiasta de estas unicidades' ('For Fernando Savater, the most deserving and most assured enthusiast of these unique gems').[23] In *La infancia recuperada* (1976) Savater had examined the literary genres most read by children, exploring why those genres appeal to readers for reasons beyond sheer excitement.[24] In the chapter on the macabre, he asks what it is that makes ghosts, vampires, and werewolves simultaneously fascinating, attractive, and appalling. He explains how:

> Los sentimientos del lector hacia ellos son delicadamente ambiguos, algo así como un aterrorizado reconocimiento, una suerte de pavorosa simpatía. Por una parte, nuestra tranquilidad, nuestro orden y nuestra cordura exigen que sean destruidos, que se aplaste la amenaza que representan; pero por otro lado nos identificamos irrefutablemente con sus afanes y en nuestro fuero interno descubrimos que su desesperado ulular es nuestro himno secreto.[25]

> (The reader's feelings towards them are poised with delicate ambiguity, being something like a horrified recognition, a kind of fearful sympathy. On the one hand, our peace of mind, sense of order, and our sanity all demand that they be destroyed, that the threat they represent be quashed; but on the other, we irrefutably identify with their desires and in our innermost being we discover that their desperate howl is our secret hymn.)

That 'desesperado ulular' is one with which the reader cannot help but empathize since it concerns our ability to cheat death, our thirst for immortality:

> El cuento de terror se basa en proclamar que el zarpazo de la muerte sobre la realidad es algo a lo que jamás podremos hacernos del todo. Pero ¡qué feroces transformaciones sufren quienes se rebelan contra la necesidad! ¡A qué precio tan elevado pagan su atrevimiento subversivo![26]

> (The horror story is based on proclaiming that death's cruel blow to reality is something to which we will never be entirely reconciled. But what ghastly transformations await those who rebel against the inevitable! What a high price their pay for their subversive daring!)

Macabre stories are doubly unsettling because they place the reader in the position of at once wanting to destroy the supernatural evil while sharing

---

[23] *Cuentos únicos*, p. 9.
[24] Marías has also written that, in *La infancia recuperada*, Savater 'sin decirlo, bastante ha explicado sobre esta generación', referring to the rootedness of many writers of their generation in the reading they undertook as youngsters; see 'Desde una novela no necesariamente castiza', p. 58.
[25] Fernando Savater, *La infancia recuperada*, 10th edn (Madrid: Taurus, 2002 [1st edn 1976]), p. 184.
[26] *La infancia recuperada*, pp. 183–4.

the creature's thirst for immortality. This could not be more different from Marcelino Iturriaga, who has found in death the same kind of comfortable routines that dominated his life.

The ghostly narrator had, however, begun to fascinate Marías by the time he wrote 'Cuando fui mortal', to the point where 'cada vez me voy sintiendo más cercano a una de mis figuras literarias predilectas, el fantasma' ('I'm beginning to identify more and more with one of my favourite literary figures, the ghost').[27] The narrator of 'Cuando fui mortal' is the archetypal ghost who haunts the scenes of his past to survey unfinished business. He may not be ghastly in the obvious sense of haunting and tormenting the living, but he does partake in Savater's delicately poised ambiguity. He is immortal but at a tormenting cost that perhaps reassures the reader that an infallible memory, and infinite time to survey it, do not constitute a desirable destiny. It is here, as we shall see, that he incorporates one of Browne's pregnant metaphors to support his illustration of the point. Marías and his readers might be horrified at the prospect of annihilation, but the alternative, in this story at least, is to face a tormenting inability to act whilst retaining the integrity of our memory.

> En aquel momento recordé cómo era [Esperancita] la última vez que la vi con los ojos abiertos, y al hacerlo se me presentó claramente la escena que había ocurrido hacía un año en mi piso de Barquillo y, al mismo tiempo, toda mi vida.[28]

> (I remembered how she had looked the last time I saw her with my eyes open, and along with that scene, which had taken place a year ago in my apartment in Calle Barquillo, my whole life rose up before me too.)[29]

In this quotation from 'La vida y la muerte de Marcelino Iturriaga', Marcelino hints at, but does not elaborate upon, an infallible memory in the final sub-clause of the sentence. By contrast, it is this aspect of his predicament that most torments the narrator in 'Cuando fui mortal'. He is in an anomalous and unique situation. Following his physical death at the hands of a hit man, his spirit can roam freely over the scenes of his past, both those that he protagonized and those at which he was not physically present but which influenced the course of his life. Briefly, the facts of his life are as follows: he experienced 'una infancia sin sobresaltos o satisfactoria'[30] ('a childhood that was satisfactory or without surprises')[31]

---

[27] *VF*, p. 19.      [28] 'La vida y la muerte de Marcelino Iturriaga', p. 16.

[29] 'The Life and Death of Marcelino Iturriaga', p. 104.

[30] JM, 'Cuando fui mortal', in *CFM*, pp. 83–101 (p. 87). All further references are to this edition.

[31] JM, 'When I Was Mortal', in *When I Was Mortal*, trans. by Margaret Jull Costa (London: Harvill, 1999), pp. 43–55 (p. 45).

living with his mother and father, the latter a Republican sympathizer whose journalistic and academic career were curtailed in the climate of post-Civil War Spain.[32] The narrator particularly recalls one frequent visitor to the house, Doctor Arranz, who would give him a medical exam nearly every night. As a ghost the narrator learns that, far from being a family friend Arranz visited in order sleep with his mother: he had threatened to reveal his father's wartime activities to Franco's vengeful government, and the price of silence is unlimited access to his mother's sexual favours.

As an adult, the narrator marries a woman named Luisa, becomes an international businessman, and takes a lover, María. He takes great pains to hide his adultery from Luisa, believing that failure to do so would be inconsiderate and cruel. María breaks the rules they have devised by surreptitiously touching his hand when he and his wife are waiting in a crowded cinema queue. Although there was little danger of Luisa seeing the illicit contact, he punishes María by refusing to accept her phone calls, until she is reduced to ringing him at home, contravening their rules once more. His righteous indignation eventually gives way to routine and they resume their clandestine meetings at her flat. On his return from a business trip he discovers a message on his answer machine from María, saying only his name. Later, he falls asleep in bed, only to be woken by the blows of a metal object, blows that prove fatal; believing his killer to be his wife in revenge for the infidelity she must have just discovered, he thinks that in some way he has deserved it. Surveying the scenes of his life once more, however, from the objective point of a spirit, he is shocked to learn that his wife had taken a lover in her turn, ignorant of his dalliances.[33] Wife and lover had conspired to get him out of the way and hired a hit man to perform the task for them.

Unlike Iturriaga, the anonymous narrator of 'Cuando fui mortal' does not begin to reminisce immediately. Instead, he makes general remarks about ghosts, and how unaware the living are of their presence: 'las casas que habitamos están cambiadas y en ellas hay inquilinos que ni siquiera saben de nuestra existencia pasada, ni la conciben' ('the houses we lived in have changed and the people who live in them do not even know of our past existence, they cannot even imagine it').[34] He maintains that the second worst torment he must face is the repetition of every scene from his

---

[32] The parallels between the narrator's father and Julián Marías, the father of the author, form an interesting subtext in this story but will not be the subject of discussion.

[33] Azucena Mollejo is wrong to maintain, as she does in her discussion of 'Cuando fui mortal', that the decisive factor had been her discovery of his philandering; see her, *El cuento español de 1970 a 2000: Cuatro escritores de Madrid: Francisco Umbral, Rosa Montero, Almudena Grandes y Javier Marías* (Madrid: Pliegos, 2002), p. 179.

[34] 'Cuando fui mortal', p. 85; 'When I Was Mortal', p. 43.

past life, even those that his mortal memory had managed to suppress as too tedious to warrant recording:

> Todo es concreto y es excesivo, y es un tormento sufrir el filo de las repeticiones, porque la maldición consiste en recordarlo *todo,* los minutos de cada hora de cada día vivido, los de tedio y los de trabajo y los de alegría, los de estudio y pesadumbre y abyección y sueño, y también los de espera, que fueron la mayor parte.[35]

> (Everything is concrete and excessive, and the edge of repetitions becomes a torment, because the curse consists in remembering *everything,* the minutes of each day of each hour lived through, the minutes and hours and days of tedium and work and joy, of study and grief and humiliation and sleep, as well as those of waiting, which formed the greater part.)[36]

The rhythm of this sentence is important in conveying the impression of tedium. In the clause beginning 'los minutos', the insistence on the 'd' sound taps like a repetitious, insistent beat; in the second half Marías stretches the use of identical structures—'los de'—and the conjunction 'y'—'y pesadumbre y abyección y sueño', the polysyndeton forcing language to convey lethargy.

Valls, Turpin, and Cuñado have drawn attention to the phrase 'el filo de las repeticiones' as particularly apt when conveying the lacerating effect of infallible memory.[37] The reader familiar with Marías's Browne translations notices the following passage from the fifth chapter of *Hydriotaphia*:

> To be ignorant of evils to come, and forgetful of evils past, is a merciful provision in nature, whereby we digest the mixture of our few and evil days; and, our delivered senses not relapsing into cutting remembrances, our sorrows are not kept raw by the edge of repetitions.[38]

A comparison with Marías's translation of this sentence proves the point.

> Ignorar los males venideros, y olvidar los males pasados, es una misericordiosa disposición de la naturaleza, por la cual digerimos la mixtura de nuestros escasos y malvados días; y, al no recaer nuestros liberados sentidos en hirientes remembranzas, nuestras penas no se mantienen en carne viva por el filo de las repeticiones.[39]

---

[35] 'Cuando fui mortal', p. 86.

[36] 'When I Was Mortal', p. 44. I have modified Jull Costa's original here by restoring the Browne's English phrase 'the edge of repetitions', in place of her 'the razor edge of repetition'.

[37] Fernando Valls, 'Un estado de crueldad o el opio del tiempo: los fantasmas de Javier Marías', in *Brujas, demonios y fantasmas en la literatura fantástica hispánica*, ed. by Jaume Pont (Lleida: Universitat de Lleida, 1999), pp. 361–7 (p. 364); Enrique Turpin, 'La sutil omnisciencia del fantasma: "Cuando fui mortal" de Javier Marías', *La nueva literatura hispánica*, 2 (1998), 127–42 (p. 130); Cuñado, p. 110.

[38] *Religio Medici*, p. 130.　　[39] *La religión de un médico*, p. 240.

Browne is discussing the imaginative and physical consolations through which human beings keep at bay their horror at their failures and mistakes. He observes that human memory is one of our greatest buffers against hardship since its fallibility enables us to forget our sorrows. Browne's treatise on the burial urns is a deep meditation on man's need for, and ultimate folly in desiring, physical monuments to his existence. Rather than look to the physical realm for the assurance of long life, Browne exhorts his reader to look to the Christian faith. It is also in part a reflection on how physical objects become imbued with polyvalent meanings over time, much as books, cigarette holders, tie pins, and ashtrays have for Marías.[40] Ultimately, the urns become a *memento mori* for Browne, a reminder of man's doomed attempts to circumvent annihilation.

What Marías's borrowing demonstrates is how much Browne's works have become part of his imaginative vocabulary. That Browne's words should have returned to him a decade after he had completed his translation of *Hydriotaphia* makes us aware that he did and does consider his translations a continuing source of imaginative enrichment. He has made them his own, their insights belong now at least in part to him, and he feels that he has a greater right to them for having translated them into his native tongue. When casting around for inspiration on the subject of memory, repetition, and human folly, one suspects that Borges's Funes came to mind, but so did Browne. Browne also notes that those who have suffered a violent death are thought by some philosophers to retain a stronger link with the physical realm—'some old philosophers would honour them, whose souls they conceived most pure which were thus snatched from their bodies'.[41] This is the exact predicament of the ghost in 'Cuando fui mortal'.

The narrator then clarifies his assertion that repetitions are only the second worst torment with which he has to contend:

> Pero ya he dicho que eso es sólo lo segundo peor, hay algo más lacerante, y es que ahora no sólo recuerdo lo que vi y oí y supe cuando fui mortal, sino que lo recuerdo completo, es decir, incluyendo lo que entonces no veía, ni sabía ni oía ni estaba a mi alcance, pero me afectaba a mí o a quienes me importaban y acaso me configuraban.[42]

> (But, as I have already said, that is only the second worst thing, there is something far more wounding, which is that now I not only remember what I saw and heard and knew when I was mortal, but I remember it in its entirety, that is, including what I did not see or know or hear, even things

[40] See Elide Pittarello, 'Haciendo tiempo con las cosas', in *Cuadernos de narrativa: Javier Marías*, pp. 17–48.

[41] *Religio Medici*, p. 126; *La religión de un médico*, p. 234.

[42] 'Cuando fui mortal', p. 86.

that were beyond my grasp, but which affected me or those who were important to me, and possibly had a hand in shaping me.)[43]

Again the rhythm of the sentence is key to its impact and meaning. The increasing complexity and difficulty of the web of interconnections—the interconnectedness of all the people he ever knew and how their actions affected him—is expressed in the choice of verbs. Marías goes from the preterite tense—'vi y oí y supe'—to the less defined imperfect—'veía, ni sabía ni oía'. He then changes the type of verbs he has been using from trisyllabic to those with four or more syllables, an effect that slows the phrase and complements its meaning.

What the previously unimagined interconnectedness of human lives disturbs is the narrator's stable narrative of self:

[Uno descubre] que...sólo conoce un fragmento de lo que le ocurre, y que cuando cree poder explicarse o contarse lo que le ha sucedido hasta un día determinado, le faltan demasiados datos, le faltan las intenciones ajenas y los motivos de los impulsos, le falta lo oculto.[44]

([You discover] that...you only know a fragment of what happens to you and that when you believe yourself capable of explaining or recounting what has happened to you up until a particular date, you do not have sufficient information, you do not know what other people's intentions were or the motivations behind impulses, you have no knowledge of what is hidden.)[45]

The story represents an attempt to write in such a way as to express the links between events about which he has just learnt. He is careful to narrate those events as a set of discoveries. His nightly routine as a child is described in its reassuring, homely detail, only to be shattered by revelations about Arranz's hold over his parents. Likewise, he describes his death as he first interpreted it—his wife's revenge for his extramarital indiscretions—only to reveal that he has been the victim of a cold-blooded slaying, not a *crime passionnel*. Hence he develops strategies for representing his past other than a sequential narrative, relying instead on literature's capacity for enigmatic silences and focussing on two key points in his life—his childhood and marriage.

One of his first hints that his revised narrative of self will hinge on questions of infidelity comes in the quotation below. In order to illustrate his ideas about one's relatives and their unpredictable roles in one's life, he develops the simile of those relatives as actors who suddenly appear on stage:

[43] 'When I Was Mortal', p. 44.
[44] 'Cuando fui mortal', pp. 86–7. This passage, more than any other in 'Cuando fui mortal', reminds us that Marías's preoccupations as a writer had shifted considerably in the period when he was writing *CTB*. The narrator's words here echo Juan Ranz's awareness of the precarious twists of fate that led to him being born.
[45] 'When I Was Mortal', p. 44.

Tal vez se presentan disfrazados de Otelo o de Hamlet y hace un instante
fumaban un anacrónico cigarrillo imposible entre bastidores, y miraban un
reloj impacientes que ya se han quitado para aparentar que son otros.[46]

(Perhaps they appear as Othello or Hamlet and yet the previous moment
they were smoking an impossible, anachronistic cigarette in the wings and
glancing impatiently at the watch which they have now removed in order to
seem to be someone else.)[47]

His choice of Shakespearean characters is not accidental: Othello and
Hamlet are characters whose actions are defined by their responses to
imagined or actual infidelity. The ghost describes his predicament as 'el
estado de la crueldad' ('cruel state'), reminding the reader how much
human happiness relies on maintaining collaborative silence with those
closest to one: 'consideramos malvados a quienes no encubren ni ocultan
ni mienten, a quienes cuentan cuanto saben y escuchan, también lo que
hacen y lo que piensan' ('we consider as wicked those people who do not
cover up or hide or lie, those who tell everything that they know and hear,
as well as what they do and think').[48] The reader can see the irony in the
fact that Luisa shared his views and kept her own infidelities secret. And
it was she who took the ultimate step in removing him so that she could
continue her affair unhindered by his presence. Thus he is afforded a
totally objective panorama of the events, decisions, words, actions, and
infidelities that shaped the man he became. The ghost remains nameless
throughout the story, perhaps because he feels the fixed identity offered
by a name no longer has meaning for him. He also admits that he has
ceased perceiving time and that nothing can matter to him any more:

Yo no puedo hablar ahora de noches o días, todo está nivelado sin necesidad
de esfuerzo ni de rutinas, en las que puedo decir que conocí sobre todo la
tranquilidad y el contento: cuando fui mortal, hace ya tanto tiempo, allí
donde todavía hay tiempo.[49]

(I cannot speak now of nights and days, everything has been levelled out
without resort to effort or routine, a routine in which I can say that I knew,
above all, peace and contentment: when I was mortal, all that time ago, in
that place where there is still time.)[50]

And yet he is moved to recall particular scenes and aspects of the life he
led. His tale gives the lie to the fear that objectivity will provoke indifference. What he misses most are the routines that succeeded in giving an
appearance of uniformity to his life, the routines that he established in
order to make living bearable. In childhood those routines were externally

---

[46] 'Cuando fui mortal', p. 87.     [47] 'When I Was Mortal', p. 45.
[48] 'Cuando fui mortal', p. 87; 'When I Was Mortal', p. 45.
[49] 'Cuando fui mortal', p. 101.     [50] 'When I Was Mortal', p. 55.

imposed and included Arranz's repeated, reassuring visits—'el privilegio de un control casi diario y la mano del médico que tranquiliza y palpa bajo el pijama' ('the privilege of an almost daily check-up and the calming hand of the doctor slipping beneath your pyjama jacket').[51] Later in life he establishes his own domestic routines: his wife always at the airport to collect him on his return from business, the rest of the day spent sleeping and resting. There is even predictability about his visits to María: he usually sees her on the way home from work. What interests him above all in these separate but affectively similar scenarios are the routines that impose themselves with time and how they might reflect larger, more disturbing truths about the relationships that bind family members together.

In the brief essay 'Contagio' (1988), Marías describes an anomaly that faces many fiction writers (although he acknowledges that primarily he is talking about his own experience). They must constantly select and refine their detailed observation of the world around them—'el esfuerzo y el cansancio que supone discernir hasta en los menores detalles: un color, un gesto, un diálogo':

> No tiene prisa, pero aspira a contagiar su anomalía particular y a que lo que él ve deformado y muestra por vez primera sea, sin embargo, reconocido como propio por quien cae en la tentación de pasar sus páginas una detrás de otra.[52]

> (He is not in a hurry, but he aspires to infect others with his particular anomaly and to ensure that what he sees distorted and for the first time should, all the same, be recognized as their own by the person who falls into the temptation of turning over his pages one by one.)

He refers somewhat obliquely to how this is to be achieved—'[el novelista] tiene que disimular, y hacer saber de qué habla sólo cuando ya es demasiado tarde para que el lector pueda seguir pretendiendo ignorarlo' ('[the novelist] has to dissemble, and let the reader know what he is talking about only when it is too late for the reader to keep trying to remain unaware of it').[53] In other words, the writer must establish an internal coherence within his or her work that will convey the larger significance of those details he or she has taken such pains to select.

The 1992 essay, 'Errar con brújula' explores related themes. It describes his narrative practice of following the developing line of his fiction as he writes, as opposed to starting with a plan that must be followed. He again tackles the subject of telling details, attacking the idea that everything that appears in a text must be susceptible to explanation through one unifying theme:

---

[51] 'Cuando fui mortal', p. 88; 'When I Was Mortal', p. 45.
[52] JM, 'Contagio', in *LF*, pp. 49–50 (p. 50).
[53] 'Contagio', p. 50.

Barthes habló de *l'effet du réel* para denominar justamente aquellas cosas, detalles o episodios que se dan u ocurren porque sí, tanto en la vida como en las novelas, sin que tengan más significado o relación con una historia que la que el autor o el lector quieran hallarles con sus facultades asociativas.[54]

(Barthes talked about *l'effet du réel* to describe precisely those things, details, or episodes that, as much in life as in novels, happen just because, without their having any meaning or relationship to a story beyond what the associative capacities of author or reader can find in them.)

As readers of 'Cuando fui mortal' we learn more about the preoccupations that beset the narrator from details we associate with one another than from the narrative proper. The search for the telling and meaningful detail could seem arbitrary until we realize that the best writers can be those who create internal coherence to a work with a degree of subtlety that proves intellectually and artistically satisfying. That is exactly what we find in 'Cuando fui mortal', where Marías has his narrator make conscious or unconscious connections between his childhood and the adulterer he later became. Though the narrator does not draw moralizing conclusions where they would seem superfluous, his wistful tone leaves the reader wondering if he might have acted differently had he known then what he knows now. As he states in his opening remarks:

A menudo fingí creer en fantasmas y fingí creerlo festivamente, y ahora que soy uno de ellos comprendo por qué las tradiciones los representan dolientes e insistiendo en volver a los sitios que conocieron cuando fueron mortales. La verdad es que vuelven.[55]

(I often used to pretend I believed in ghosts, and I did so blithely, but now that I am myself a ghost, I understand why, traditionally, they are depicted as mournful creatures who stubbornly return to the places they knew when they were mortal. For they do return.)[56]

The fact that he starts his narrative with a belief that he has had to revise after death foreshadows the principal psychological movement of the story, in which revision and reassessment of his previously cherished narrative of self take place. He uses a third-person impersonal construction—'La verdad es que vuelven'—though the subject of the verb is obviously himself, registering the disjuncture he still experiences in relation to his predicament: in part he still thinks from the point of view of a living being. One might ask why it is that several of the scenes over which he is moved to dwell occur during sleep or on the threshold of sleep. Could it also be that he longs for the forgetting of sleep now that he is forced

[54] JM, 'Errar con brújula', in *LF*, pp. 107–10 (p. 109).
[55] 'Cuando fui mortal', p. 85.    [56] 'When I Was Mortal', p. 43.

constantly to remember his past failures? As Browne remarks in *Hydriot-aphia*, 'Darkness and light divide the course of time, and oblivion shares with memory a great part even of our living beings'.[57] To be denied sleep is to be denied the rest afforded the living. The narrator's first homely evocation concerns his nightly routine in the house where he grew up. It takes the form of a single, long sentence that moves from a general description of his childhood—'Me veo por ejemplo de niño a punto de dormirme en mi cama durante tantas noches de una infancia sin sobresaltos o satisfactoria' ('I see myself, for example, about to fall asleep in my bed on countless nights of a childhood that was satisfactory or without surprises')—to a more immediate recollection of the thought processes he experienced as a child:[58]

> el mango que por un momento parecía ir a clavarse en nuestra garganta para dar paso al alivio de recordar tras el primer contacto que era el doctor Arranz quien lo sostenía, su mano aseguradora y firme y dueña de objetos metálicos.[59]

> (the handle which for a moment, seems about to stick in your throat, a feeling that would give way to relief when I remembered, after the first contact, that it was Arranz holding the spoon in his reassuring, steady hand, mistress of metallic objects.)[60]

This last detail is a telling one in that it will recur in the form of the hand wielding the hammer that kills him. On second reading this passage yields the further retrospective irony that he felt privileged to receive such consistent, reassuring medical attention, little suspecting the real reason for the doctor's visits.

The narrator then provides a brief description of the two men who were his role models as a child. His father is described with sadness:

> mi padre el que menos reía, un hombre taciturno y apuesto con un poco de melancolía permanente en los ojos, quizá porque había sido republicano y había perdido la guerra, y eso debe ser algo de lo que uno no se recupera nunca, de perder una guerra contra los compatriotas y los vecinos. Era un hombre bondadoso que jamás nos regañaba a mí ni a mi madre y estaba mucho tiempo en casa escribiendo artículos y críticas de libros que firmaba con nombres supuestos porque era mejor que no usara el suyo.[61]

> (my father laughed the least, he was a handsome, taciturn man with a look of permanent melancholy in his eyes, perhaps because he had been a republican and had lost the war, and this is probably something you never recover

[57] *Religio Medici*, p. 130.
[58] 'Cuando fui mortal', p. 87; 'When I Was Mortal', p. 45.
[59] 'Cuando fui mortal', p. 88.     [60] 'When I Was Mortal', pp. 45–6.
[61] 'Cuando fui mortal', p. 89.

from, having lost a war against your compatriots and neighbours. He was a kindly man who never got angry with me or my mother and who spent a lot of time at home writing articles and book reviews, which he tended to publish under various pseudonyms in the newspapers, because it was best not to use his own name)[62]

The narrator is doing his best to recreate the childish reasoning that then reigned in his mind. His ingenuous explanation of why his father could not put his name to his journalistic output smacks of the euphemisms so often supplied to children, 'era mejor que no usara el suyo'. We judge that the narrator is supplying the explanations that prevailed when he was a child because the true explanation of the melancholy glimpsed in his father's eyes can be found closer to home. In recreating his childish reasoning, he more effectively conveys the sense of disillusionment that accompanied the revelations about his mother's enforced prostitution.

The contrasting potential role model is el doctor Arranz:

más jovial, un hombre zumbón con su hablar arrastrado, lleno de inventiva y frases, ese tipo de hombre que es el ídolo de los niños porque con las cartas sabe hacer juegos de manos y los divierte con rimas inesperadas y les habla de fútbol.[63]

(a jollier man, with a lazy, teasing way of talking, inventive and full of unusual turns-of-phrase, the kind of man children idolize because he knows how to do card tricks and comes out with unexpected rhymes and talks to them about football.)[64]

Once again the narrator resorts to a telling, impersonal third-person construction when describing what is evidently his attitude to Arranz, 'ese tipo de hombre que es el ídolo de los niños'. The reason for his reluctance to identify himself too closely with the family doctor emerges on the next page, where he describes the sexual encounters between his mother and Arranz. It is here that he highlights the first of the ironies, what from Marías's point of view constitute the points where the telling detail noticed by the reader should create an empathetic bond and highlight the situation's horror:

ahora sé que entonces mi madre y el doctor Arranz pasaban al dormitorio cuando ya era seguro que yo me había dormido tras ser tocado en el pecho y en el estómago por las mismas manos que la tocarían a continuación a ella ya no tibias y con más urgencia...y tras ser besado en la mejilla o la frente por los mismos labios que besarían luego—y la acallarían—el habla entre dientes y desenfadada.[65]

[62] 'When I Was Mortal', p. 46.
[63] 'Cuando fui mortal', p. 89.
[64] 'When I Was Mortal', p. 46.
[65] 'Cuando fui mortal', pp. 90–1.

(now I know that then my mother and Dr Arranz would go into the bedroom when they were sure I had gone to sleep after having been touched on the chest and on the stomach by the same hands that would then touch her, hands that were no longer warm, but urgent...and having been kissed on the cheek or the forehead by the same lips that would subsequently kiss the easy-going, low voice—thus silencing it.)[66]

We note that the 'habla entre dientes y desenfadada' belongs to Arranz, that his mother's lips are the subject of the verb 'acallar'. He feels the betrayal not just to have been on Arranz's side, in forcing his mother to prostitute herself, but on hers as well. He isolates his mother's lips and Arranz's hands as loaded with comforting associations for his childhood self and contrasts them with their acquired sexual function. He cannot avoid the revulsion of knowing that his mother's reassuring lips then became part of a sexualized figure.

While Arranz extracted the most degrading price for silence from his mother, his father would sit in the living room with the radio on so as to avoid hearing the noises made by the copulating couple next door. Where the pathos lies in this situation, for the narrator, is in the disruption it causes to what ought to have been the normal marital rites:

> El doctor se marchaba sin despedirse de él y mi madre ya no salía del cuarto, allí se quedaba aguardando a mi padre, se ponía un camisón y cambiaba las sábanas, él nunca la encontraba con sus bonitas faldas y medias.[67]

> (The doctor would leave without saying goodbye to him and my mother would stay in the bedroom, waiting for my father, she would put on a nightdress and change the sheets, he never found her there in her pretty skirts and stockings.)[68]

The implication is that shame motivates his mother's actions, as though she could not face her husband after submitting to the enforced adulterous caresses of their tormentor. The narrator has an eye for sordid detail: in this instance the soiled sheets that must be changed before the couple can occupy the bed together. Juan Ranz, the narrator of *CTB* (1992), worries that cohabitation will ruin the seductive allure of undressing his wife of her outdoor clothing: 'no quiero encontrármela bajo las sábanas en camisón o pijama, sino desnudarla desde su vestido de calle, privarla de la apariencia que ha tenido durante la jornada' ('I don't want to find her already under the sheets in her nightdress or pyjamas, I'd rather take off her street clothes, strip her of her daytime appearance').[69]

---

[66] 'When I Was Mortal', p. 47.      [67] 'Cuando fui mortal', p. 91.
[68] 'When I Was Mortal', p. 48.
[69] *CTB*, p. 113; JM, *A Heart So White*, trans. by Margaret Jull Costa (London: Harvill, 1995), p. 79.

His worries are of a piece with his fear that the future has suddenly become in all senses predictable. He wants still to be able to seduce his wife, and for her to seduce him.[70] In 'Cuando fui mortal', Arranz's demands deny the couple that minimal ritual. When it is later combined with the revelation that Arranz grows bored of his prize just as his mother 'empezó a marchitarse', we see the way in which the abusive arrangement has enforced a poignant disjunction:

> La edad de mi madre, en cambio, fue la edad en que empezó a marchitarse y a no reír, y mi padre a prosperar y a vestir mejor, y a firmar con su nombre los artículos y las críticas...y a salir por las noches con algunas entradas buenas mientras se quedaba mi madre en casa a hacer solitarios o a escuchar la radio, o poco después a ver la televisión, más conforme.[71]

> (My mother had by contrast reached the age that began to see her wither and no longer laugh, whilst my father started to prosper, dress better, and sign his articles and reviews with his own name...and go out at night with decent tickets in his pocket, leaving my mother at home alone playing patience or listening to the radio, or soon afterwards watching television, slightly happier.)

The description recalls the final words of Henry James's *Washington Square*—'Catherine, meanwhile, in the parlor, picking up her morsel of fancy-work, had seated herself with it again—for life, as it were'.[72] It suggests her participation in life's romantic aspects has vanished forever.

The story makes clear that the narrator's father's position was a precarious one because of his Republican sympathies. When his mother's forced prostitution ends, however, the narrator does not explain the fact in terms of the changing political climate. The upturn in his father's fortunes means that he must have lost the pariah status that made him so vulnerable to Arranz's threats. If he is now able to publish in the press, his position must have improved. And yet, the narrator does not present the information thus, preferring instead to draw attention to the coincidence with his mother's decline. For husband and wife, the roles have been reversed; now wife sits at home while husband flourishes, sharpening the impression that his mother and father were torn irrevocably apart by her selfless act. It is as if the increasing political freedom Spain enjoyed from the mid 1950s onwards were irrelevant to his family, where the damage had already been done.

---

[70] The reappearance of this motif in Marías's work may reflect a personal distaste for the stagnation of long-term cohabitation. See Pittarello, *Entrevistos*, p. 34.

[71] 'Cuando fui mortal', p. 93.

[72] Henry James, *Washington Square*, ed. by Brian Lee (Harmondsworth: Penguin, 1986), p. 220. Marías is an avid reader of James.

Marías has never been interested in drawing moralizing conclusions in his fiction, and 'Cuando fui mortal' is no exception.[73] However, the narrator's survey of his past clearly addresses unresolved tensions in his ability to assimilate those experiences. These tensions reveal themselves in ways that are artistically satisfying for a reader, who is tempted to ask what degree of self-knowledge the narrator has gained as a result. There is no question of this ghost mending either his ways or the past, since he is equally powerless to do either. Where his self-justification starts and stops in relation to Luisa and his marriage encourages us to observe those points of friction where the memory wishes to reassess and revisit past mistakes with a view to putting them to rest. Cuñado believes in this story,

> la transferencia de los papeles de culpable o de víctima entre el padre y el hijo, explorada dentro del marco del matrimonio en ambos textos [the other is *Corazón tan blanco*], se convierte en un eje central en la reflexión sobre la repetición de un destino fatal que se hereda a través de las generaciones.[74]

> (the transferral of the roles of aggressor and victim between father and son, explored in both texts through the frame of marriage, becomes a central theme in the reflections on the repetition of a fatal destiny inherited across generations.)

In my view, the situation is rather different. The narrator sees himself as markedly different from his father, to the point where he highlights his greater affinity with Arranz, as we shall see below. Part of the irony the narrator can now observe is how much his formative years were shaped by a man who was not his father. The narrator is conscious of how much culpability can be laid at his door in contrast to the blamelessness of his own father. His father, moreover, does not share the 'destino fatal'. We might wonder whether the narrator's growing realization that Arranz shaped his life means that his own demise was more deserved than he had previously recognized.

Having discussed the narrator's reappraisal of his childhood I shall now discuss the second set of domestic routines on which he focuses—those of his married life. Amongst them he highlights what used to happen when he returned from the business trips that his unspecified job obliged him to make: 'Vuelvo de un viaje y ella me espera en el aeropuerto, no hubo una vez en nuestro matrimonio en que ella no se llegara hasta allí a recibirme aunque me hubiera ausentado sólo durante un par de días' (I'm coming back from a trip and she's waiting for me at the airport, not once, all the time we were married, did she fail to come and meet me, even if I'd

---

[73] Marías has expressed his distaste for moral aims in literature on many occasions. See, for example, Pittarello, *Entrevistos*, p. 28.

[74] Cuñado, *El espectro de la herencia: la narrativa de Javier Marías*, p. 110.

only been away for a couple of days').[75] He has come to rely on his wife to provide him with this demonstration of her affection, just as he needs the rest of the following night's sleep to feel himself once more. Interestingly he adopts Luisa's viewpoint when making this statement:

> sabedora de que sólo necesitaría el sopor y el descanso de la noche inminente para recuperarme y al día siguiente ser el de siempre, un tipo activo y bromista que hablaba un poco entre dientes, una forma estudiada de acentuar la ironía que gusta a todas las mujeres.[76]

> (knowing that after that initial torpor and imminent night's rest, I would be fully recovered and that the following day, I would be my usual self, an energetic, jokey person who spoke in a rather low voice, in order to underline the irony that all women love.)[77]

His ability as a seducer is uppermost in his mind. The weapon in his seductive manner to which he draws attention is his habit of speaking slightly under his breath. Given that he has mentioned twice that Arranz had this habit, the narrator must be drawing attention to the fact that he has picked it up through mimicking the man who forced his mother into prostitution. Is he wondering what kind of influence Arranz had on him as a child? What is his attitude towards this potentially difficult revelation? Given his own sticky end, the victim of an adulterous wife's plotting, how appropriate is it that he should have picked up his seductive vocal habits from such a man?[78]

Like his parents before him, the narrator has played out an ironic disjuncture in his married life. As soon as he has recuperated after his travels, he lavishes his attention (sexual or otherwise) not on his wife but on his lover, María. Before describing the terms on which his adulterous relationship rests, in the course of which he is anxious to emphasize his care in ensuring Luisa never discovered his infidelity, he mentions that his visits to María would last 'tan sólo media hora o tres cuartos' ('only half an hour or three quarters of an hour').[79] This length of time is again identical to that

---

[75] 'Cuando fui mortal', p. 94; 'When I Was Mortal', p. 50.

[76] 'Cuando fui mortal', p. 94.

[77] 'When I Was Mortal', p. 50.

[78] Enrique Turpin suggests that the correct interpretation of 'Cuando fui mortal' relies on our realizing that Arranz is actually the narrator's father. The love affair between mother and family doctor would thus have been secretly devised by the adulterous couple (who did know one another before the Civil War began, we note) under cover of threats to the narrator's father; see Turpin, pp. 138–40. Such an interpretation, though it cannot be categorically dismissed, strikes me as unlikely for several reasons. First, given that the narrator sets down the absolute knowledge he has gained concerning his childhood, it would be strange if he had not had access to such maternal scheming. Second, the affinities between Arranz and the narrator are more habits than genetic inheritance; the narrator is disgusted at both himself and the power of nurture over nature in the formation of his personality.

[79] 'Cuando fui mortal', p. 95; 'When I Was Mortal', p. 51.

taken by Arranz when sating himself on the narrator's mother. For Arranz this earns him the rebuke, 'los médicos siempre van con prisa' ('doctors are always in such a hurry').[80] Again it is difficult to say precisely what effect the echoing is intended to achieve. Is he identifying himself deliberately with the rapist figure who tormented his parents in order better to understand his own death?

The narrator punishes María for her surreptitious advance towards him in the crowded cinema by cutting off all contact, until she is reduced to contacting him at home. He explains that he will sever all ties if she touches him again in his wife's presence—'Ni te lo [el teléfono] cogeré nunca más si vuelves a tocarme estando Luisa delante. Ni se te ocurra' ('And I'll never pick up the phone to you again if you ever touch me when Luisa is there. Don't even think of it').[81] His pride in righteous behaviour prompts him to include this scene, the effect of which is undercut immediately by the beginning of the next paragraph:

> Casi todo se olvida en la vida y todo se recuerda en la muerte, o en este estado de la crueldad en que consiste ser un fantasma. Pero en la vida olvidé y volví a verla un día y otro, de ese modo en que todo se aplaza indefinidamente para dentro de poco.[82]

> (You forget almost everything in life and remember everything in death, or in this cruel state which is what being a ghost is. But in life I forgot and so I started seeing her again now and then, thanks to that process by which everything becomes indefinitely postponed for a while.)[83]

We might suspect him of lamenting the fact that he did not stick to his guns and punish María by ending their relationship for good. Given that his account deliberately juxtaposes his own affair with his parents' torment, and the strain it put on their relationship, is he lamenting his ultimately empty gesture towards ethical behaviour? Or is it simply that all now seems vain, given that he could not have avoided or prevented his own death? The people who decided on his death thought they were killing an innocent man and had no compunction about doing so.

In *EHS* two (or more) competing versions of the events as remembered by the narrator intertwine in such a way as to make them difficult to distinguish. El León de Nápoles relies on his memory of the events of four years previously as much as on the dream he has had in the early morning of the day he sits down to write, which depicted those events in all their detail. The ghostly narrator in 'Cuando fui mortal' has been obliged to

---

[80] 'Cuando fui mortal', p. 91; 'When I Was Mortal', p. 48.
[81] 'Cuando fui mortal', p. 96; 'When I Was Mortal', p. 51.
[82] 'Cuando fui mortal', p. 96.
[83] 'When I Was Mortal', p. 52.

re-examine his past by the revelations to which death has given him access. Forced to reassess his attitudes to his upbringing, marriage, and even his death, he has no choice other than to inhabit the past, beset by the endless repetitions of scenes that prove him to have known only a fraction of what he thought constituted him as an individual. He nevertheless recreates his thought processes as they occurred to him then, sharpening the contrast between the ignorant mortal man who acted, as he saw it, out of the best intentions, and the ghost who has now to survey his own impotence in the face of events he could not control. Perhaps because we know what is coming, we are able to pick out the telltale signs that, taken individually, appear meaningless but, when taken together, become the herald of his death: his and Luisa's reticence on the journey back from the airport; María's message on the answer machine; Luisa's failure to provide anything more exciting than shop-bought cold meat for dinner; and the latter contrasted with her solicitousness in turning off the light to help him sleep—'Put out the light, and then put out the light!'[84]

Above all, the horror that besets the narrator is that of a disturbed narrative. Even at the moment of his death, he recalls that he placed his murder in a context that explained it and gave it coherence, justice. The motif at work here of a murder victim who is able to assess the justice of his own death between two blows to the head has a telling precedent in 'The Ghost' by Richard Hughes: the latter story was among those Marías chose for the anthology *Cuentos únicos* and its parallels with 'Cuando fui mortal' are clear from the opening lines:

> Me mató con la mayor felicidad: golpeándome la cabeza contra los adoquines de la calle. ¡Zas! ¡Dios mío, qué tonta había sido! Todo mi odio se desvaneció con aquel primer golpetazo. ¡Qué necia al armar todo aquel escándalo por haberle sorprendido con otra mujer! Y ahora eso era lo que me estaba haciendo, ¡zas! Ése fue el segundo, y después todo se oscureció.[85]

> La cosa negra cayó de nuevo y mató esta vez, y mi última conciencia en vida me hizo no oponer resistencia, no intentar pararla porque era imparable y

[84] William Shakespeare, *Othello*, ed. by E. A. J. Honigmann (London: Arden, 2003), p. 306. As well as the earlier evocation of *Othello* as an intertext for 'Cuando fui mortal', we note the recurrence of this Shakespearean image in *NET*, pp. 89, 143, 282, 404.

[85] *Cuentos únicos* (Redonda, 2004), pp. 185–92 (p. 187). The original English text of 'The Ghost' can be found in Richard Hughes, *A Moment of Time* (London: Chatto & Windus, 1926), pp. 140–5. (He killed me quite easily by crashing my head on the cobbles. *Bang!* Lord, what a fool I was! All my hate went out with that first bang: a fool to have kicked up that fuss just because I had found him with another woman. And now he was doing this to me – *bang!* That was the second one, and with it *everything* went out.) (p. 140).

quizá también porque no me pareció mala muerte morir a manos de la persona con quien había vivido con tranquilidad y contento, y sin hacernos daño hasta que nos lo hicimos. La palabra es difícil y se presta a equívocos, pero tal vez llegué a sentir que aquella era una muerte justa.[86]

(The black thing fell again and this time it killed me, and my last conscious thought was not to put up any resistance, to make no attempt to stop it because it was unstoppable and perhaps too because it didn't seem such a bad thing, to die at the hands of the person with whom I had lived in peace and contentment, and without ever hurting each other until, that is, we finally did. It's a tricky word to use, and can easily be misconstrued, but perhaps I came to feel that my death was a just death.)[87]

Marías wishes to undercut human habits of providing narratives retrospectively to fit events we cannot control. He intuits that our need for narrative acts as a barrier against unpalatable truths. Yet the narrator is forced to concede that in vain do human beings provide narratives for events that are out of their control. To return to Browne, I wonder if Marías has not taken 'el filo de las repeticiones' to mean more than just the repeated mistakes of an individual's life: 'Todo se recuerda ahora y por eso recuerdo perfectamente mi muerte, es decir, lo que supe de mi muerte cuando se produjo que era poco y era nada si lo comparo con la totalidad de mi conocimiento ahora, y con el filo de las repeticiones' ('Now I remember everything and that's why I remember my death so clearly, or rather, what I knew of my death when it happened, which was little and, indeed, nothing in comparison with all that I know now, given the constant edge of repetitions').[88] The narrator juxtaposes scenes from two generations of his family, featuring people whose ultimate fate was unhappy. Perhaps the realization that his parents had to endure political ostracism and sacrifice casts his own difficulties in a less-than-favourable light. Perhaps the 'hirientes remembranzas' ('cutting remembrances') remind the narrator of human misery across time, which he explores by suggesting ways in which his own actions may have been shaped by events and people of whose true nature he was not even conscious. We should remember that Marías had quoted Browne's remarks on circularity in human affairs in *ES*—'cada hombre no es tan sólo sí mismo;... los hombres vuelven a ser vividos; el mundo es hoy como fue en tiempos remotos, cuando nadie había'.[89] The nihilism of his final words expresses only his wish that things had been otherwise: he has lost above all the peace and contentment that ignorance afforded him. Nuanced story telling,

---

[86] 'Cuando fui mortal', p. 98.
[87] 'When I Was Mortal', p. 53.
[88] 'Cuando fui mortal', p. 96; 'When I Was Mortal', p. 52. As above, I have restored Browne's original English, modifying Jull Costa's version.
[89] *ES*, p. 147.

where readers are left to draw their own conclusions from a narrative that strategically, but never intrusively, places its own mirrors is the closest the narrator of 'Cuando fui mortal' can come to an understanding of his fate.

## FINAL ECHOES

The constraints of space in this study mean that I am unable to follow Browne's tracks any further through Marías's works. However, it is worth stating that the paragraph of *Hydriotaphia*'s fifth chapter from which he took 'el filo de las repeticiones' has been a fertile hunting ground for the Spanish writer. I reproduce part of it here:

> La tiniebla y la luz dividen el curso del tiempo, y el olvido comparte con el recuerdo gran parte incluso de nuestros seres vivos; apenas recordamos nuestras dichas, y los golpes más agudos de la pena nos dejan tan sólo punzadas efímeras. El sentido no tolera las extremidades, y los pesares nos destruyen o se destruyen. Llorar hasta volverse piedra es fábula: las aflicciones producen callosidades, las desgracias son resbaladizas, o caen como nieve sobre nosotros; lo cual sin embargo, no es un infeliz entumecimiento. Ignorar los males venideros, y olvidar los males pasados es una misericordiosa disposición de la naturaleza, por la cual digerimos la mixtura de nuestros escasos y malvados días; y, al no recaer en hirientes remembranzas, nuestras penas no se mantienen en carne viva por el filo de las repeticiones.[90]

In fact, Marías's quoted this lengthy passage as long ago as 1982 in the first piece he ever penned on Browne—an article entitled 'Los tesoros del olvido' which he wrote to mark the tercentenary of Browne's death. At that earlier date, having not yet published his own translation, he had been forced to rely on Biorges's Spanish version.[91]

In our earlier discussion of *NET* we saw that Marías adapted the metaphor 'el filo de las repeticiones' in order to describe the lacerating effects of memory suffered by parents who cannot but remember their dead children. There it became the 'recuerdo afilado' ('sharp-edged memory') or 'recuerdo hiriente' ('cutting memory')—a sharp blade that cuts with every fresh wave of remembrance.[92] He also adapts the metaphor to make the 'filo' into a whittling blade that shapes the past through our repeated imaginative recreations of it. The living replay in their minds the final day of a loved one, retrospectively colouring its events with nostalgia or seeing in them a false presage of what the future would hold: 'el anodino ayer se estiliza por el filo de las repeticiones, que lo veneran y cincelan y fijan ya

---

[90] *La religión de un médico*, p. 240.
[91] JM, 'Los tesoros del olvido', *El País*, 20 October 1982, p. 39.
[92] *NET*, pp. 31, 235–6, 271, 377.

para siempre porque de pronto ha adquirido la ominosa condición de víspera que en su hoy no tenía' ('the anodyne yesterday is stylized by the edge of repetitions, which venerate and carve and fix it now for ever because it has suddenly acquired the ominous status of previous day that on its today it lacked').[93] On the final occasion Marías employs the metaphor in the novel, his adaptation of its meaning remains. He denies that memory can ever recreate the past, just as words cannot recreate events; the 'filo' has become a blade that tries in vain to whittle a recreation of the past:

> Lo más que podría contar ese alguien son los hechos, y los hechos en sí no son nada, la lengua no puede reproducirlos como tampoco pueden las repeticiones reproducir con su filo el tiempo pasado o perdido ni resucitar al muerto que ya pasó y se perdió en ese tiempo.[94]

> (The most that person could ever tell would be the bare facts, and the facts in themselves are nothing, language cannot reproduce them just as the repetitions and their blade cannot reproduce time that has passed or been lost, nor breathe new life into the dead man who passed into or was lost in that time.)

Marías also puts Browne's characterization of the miserable life of man as 'nuestros escasos y malvados días', 'our few and evil days', in the mouths of Víctor Francés and Juan Deza, the narrators of *MBPM* and *TRM* respectively. The former imagines what role he has come to play in the life of Eugenio, Marta's newly motherless son, thinking of the events that will affect the child's life but of which he will have no memory: 'Este niño... nunca sabrá lo que ha sucedido, por qué ha acabado su mundo ni en qué circunstancias ha muerto su madre' ('This child... will never know what happened, he will never know why his world has ended nor the circumstances in which his mother died').[95] His thoughts extend from the particular to the general, from Eugenio to the whole of the human race, since we come to know only fragments of the life we might lead:

> no podemos estar más que en un sitio en cada momento, e incluso entonces a menudo ignoramos quiénes nos estarán contemplando o pensando en nosotros, quién está a punto de marcar nuestro número, quién de escribirnos, quién de querernos o de buscarnos, quién de condenarnos o asesinarnos y así acabar con nuestros escasos y malvados días.[96]

> (we cannot be in more than one place at once, and even then we often have no idea who might be watching us or thinking about us, who is about to dial

---

[93] *NET*, p. 210.    [94] *NET*, p. 396.
[95] *MBPM*, p. 81; JM, *Tomorrow in the Battle Think on Me*, trans. by Margaret Jull Costa (London: Harvill, 1996), p. 54.
[96] *MBPM*, p. 83.

our number, who is about to write to us, who is about to want us or seek us out, who is about to condemn us or murder us and thus put an end to our few and evil days.)[97]

Juan Deza, the narrator of *TRM*, shares his pessimism over the human condition, but imagines our inability to control our destiny from the point of view of the dead. When describing the night he sat up in Peter Wheeler's home to research Fleming, Orwell, the POUM, and Andreu Nin, he describes the inability of human beings to control what posterity will make of our reputations after death: a Brownean thought once more expressed in Brownean terms:

> Y es en mitad de la noche cuando más se asemeja uno mismo a esos hechos y a esos tiempos, que ya no pueden oponer resistencia a lo que se diga de ellos o a la narración o al análisis o a la especulación de que son objeto, igual que los indefensos muertos, aún más indefensos que cuando fueron vivos y durante mucho más tiempo, la posteridad es mucho más larga que los escasos y malvados días de cualquier hombre.[98]

> (And it is in the middle of the night that we ourselves most resemble those events and those times, which can no longer contradict what is said about them or the stories or analyses or speculations of which they are the object, just like the defenceless dead, even more defenceless than when they were alive and over a longer period of time too, for posterity lasts infinitely longer than the few and evil days of any one man.)[99]

In the second volume of *TRM*, he and Wheeler reflect at length on the Christian era and the consolation humans must have then drawn from anticipation of the Last Judgement—the thought that one day this supreme narrative act would right every injustice, pardon every guiltless victim: 'Qué enorme consuelo para la soledad absoluta creer que éramos vistos y aun espiados en todo instante a lo largo de nuestros escasos y malvados días' ('What an enormous solace to utter solitude it must have been to believe that we were seen and even spied upon at every moment of our few and evil days').[100] Browne's Christian faith and his belief that the world would end in the year 2000, a few short centuries after his own death, allowed him to

---

[97] *Tomorrow in the Battle Think on Me*, p. 55. Once again, I have restored Browne's English to this sentence. Jull Costa's original text reads 'few evil days'.

[98] JM, *Tu rostro mañana*, 3 vols (Madrid: Alfaguara, 2002–2007), I:*Fiebre y lanza* (2002), 141.

[99] JM, *Your Face Tomorrow*, trans. by Margaret Jull Costa, 3 vols (London: Chatto & Windus, 2005–2009), I: *Fever and Spear* (2005), p. 109. Once again, I have restored Browne's original English. Jull Costa's original reads 'few, evil days'.

[100] JM, *Tu rostro mañana*, II:*Baile y sueño* (2004), 164; *Your Face Tomorrow*, II: *Dance and Dream* (2006), p. 128. Once more I have restored Browne's English. Jull Costa's original reads 'few, miserable days'.

describe his generation as not afflicted with the same need for physical monuments and consolations for our demise that had beset peoples of the past:

> We whose generations are ordained in this setting part of time are providen-
> tially taken off from such imaginations; and being necessitated to eye the
> remaining particle of futurity, are naturally constituted unto thoughts of the
> next world, and cannot excusably decline the consideration of that duration
> which maketh pyramids pillars of snow, and all that's past a moment.[101]

Wheeler and Deza feel the acute lack of such certainty in a post-Christian
and morally ambiguous era; though both seem aware that their own
actions may not stand up to such scrutiny.

One final point at which we might see Marías echoing Browne's paragraph is in Deza's recurring description of himself as 'como nieve sobre los
hombros, resbaladiza y mansa'.[102] He uses the simile to describe the ease
with which his place at his wife Luisa's side may be occupied by another
man while he is in London working and she remains at their former home
in Madrid:

> Quién sabe quién nos sustituye y a quién sustituimos nosotros, sólo sabemos
> que sustituimos y se nos sustituye siempre, en todas las ocasiones y en todas
> las circunstancias y en cualquier desempeño y en todas partes, en el amor, la
> amistad, en el empleo y en la influencia, en la dominación, y en el odio que
> también mañana se cansará de nosotros, o pasado mañana o al otro o al otro.
> Sólo sois y sólo somos como nieve sobre los hombros, resbaladiza y mansa,
> y la nieve siempre para.[103]

> (Who knows who is replacing us and whom we are replacing, we only know
> that we are someone's replacement and that we ourselves are always being
> replaced, at all times and in all circumstances and in any endeavour and
> everywhere, in love and in friendship, in work and in influence, in domina-
> tion, and in the hatred that will also tire of us tomorrow, or the day after or
> the next or the next. All of you and all of us are just like snow on somebody's
> shoulders, slippery and docile, and the snow always stops.)[104]

I would tentatively suggest that the origin of this simile may be found in
Browne's description of the 'desgracias... resbaladizas, o caen como nieve
sobre nosotros' ('miseries [are] slippery, or fall like snow upon us').[105] They
fall like snow because snow falls gently; snow flakes melt or are brushed
aside, and are in any case quickly forgotten. Deza's fear is that he too will
suffer the same fate as Luisa brushes aside his memory and continues to
live a life apart from him. The transfer of the epithet 'resbaladiza' from

---

[101] *Religio Medici*, p. 128.      [102] *Fiebre y lanza*, p. 47; *Baile y sueño*, p. 246.
[103] *Baile y sueño*, p. 81.      [104] *Dance and Dream*, p. 59.
[105] *Religio Medici*, p. 130.

'desgracias' to the snow itself could be Marías reworking the simile in his own terms, supplying the further adjective 'mansa' to clarify Browne's characterization of the snow as a rapidly dismissed hindrance.

## CONCLUSION

I have shown over the last three chapters some of the ways in which Marías has both translated Browne and incorporated the latter's thought into his own fiction. My discussion might have focused, like that of Grohmann, on purely stylistic aspects. However, I have chosen what I believe to be the richer study of how Browne's unique formulations of ideas about circularity in human affairs, posterity, and memory became part of Marías's imaginative vocabulary. It is that incorporation of Browne's phraseology and metaphor that lies at the heart of what he gained by translating this master of the English language.

# 8

## Nabokov

*[handwritten annotation: "life & art — similarities with Marías:"]*

### INTRODUCTION

I pride myself on being a person with no public appeal. I have never been drunk in my life. I never use schoolboy words of four letters. I have never worked in an office or in a coal mine. I have never belonged to any club or group. No creed or school has had any influence on me whatsoever. Nothing bores me more than political novels and the literature of social intent.[1]

Thus did Vladimir Nabokov sum up his personal creed to a group of journalists on 5 June 1962. What is remarkable about it is that it could have been written by Javier Marías. The latter has never sought what Nabokov calls 'public appeal'; his journalism is unflinching in its criticism of Spain, whether its institutions or social habits. Asked in a 2006 survey who Marías thought his audience were, he replied, 'No escribo para nadie en particular, lo cual viene a ser lo mismo que escribir para cualquiera' ('I don't write for anyone in particular, which ends up being the same as writing for everyone').[2] By his own account, he does not use swearwords in his everyday speech and characters in his fiction who swear excessively are often depicted as ignorant, the archetypal example being Rafael de la Garza in *TRM*.[3] As for writing so that he could avoid the potential tyranny of the workplace, although Marías has held down several jobs—as a publisher, translator, and university lecturer—he has also said that one of the benefits of being a writer 'es que no se tiene uno que levantar muy temprano y no hay ningún jefe al cual rendirle cuentas' ('the good thing

---

[1] Vladimir Nabokov, *Strong Opinions* (New York: Vintage, 1990), p. 3.

[2] Alfonso Armada, '¿Para quién escriben? (I)', *ABC*, 8 January 2006, Cultural section, p. 6. We can see a continuity in this standpoint from an interview Marías gave in 1988 to Caterina Visani (http://www.javiermarias.es/PAGINASDEENTREVISTAS/entrevista CaterinaVisani.html), when he maintained that, 'Cuando escribo no pienso en un determinado lector, podría decirse que pienso en cualquier lector, no descarto a ninguno' ('When I write I don't have a particular reader in mind, you could say that I'm thinking of any and every reader, I don't rule anyone out').

[3] See interview with *Star* magazine 1993, at the following URL: http://www.javiermarias.es/PAGINASDEENTREVISTAS/cuestionario.html end of 1993 (accessed 26 October 2008). The interviewer asks Marías, '¿Acostumbra a decir tacos?' ('Do you usually swear?') to which he replies, 'No'.

is that you don't have to get up early and there's no boss you have to answer to').[4] While it could be said that Marías's early career was marked by an association with the 'Novísimos', he has acknowledged that link only begrudgingly.[5] Since then he has laid claim to no artistic affiliations whatsoever. Finally, as we have already seen, he has summed up his opinion on 'littérature engagée' with one word—'pésima' ('dreadful').[6]

Enquiring into the life of Nabokov, reading his fiction and the interviews he gave, the parallels that exist between his career and that of Marías are striking. I begin by comparing how each writer approaches or approached their role as a public intellectual. I am not suggesting that Marías has sought deliberately to mould his career on Nabokov's, merely that for biographical, artistic, and serendipitous reasons their lives, tastes, and trajectories have coincided in interesting ways. Although Marías claims not to understand why some of his readers have a burning desire to get to know him just because they have enjoyed one of his books—'me cuesta ver la relación entre esas dos cosas' ('I struggle to see the connection between those two things')—Nabokov is one author he has expressed regret at never having met:[7] 'Si hubiera estado Nabokov firmando libros en la Feria del Libro pues habría ido a que me firmara alguno, y le habría saludado encantado' ('If Nabokov had been signing books at the Feria del Libro then I would have gone along so that he could sign a few of my copies, and I would have been delighted to say hello to him').[8] It strikes me as telling that, despite his scepticism about the cult of personality that surrounds some writers, Nabokov is one author for whom he makes an exception. We might also note the sadness with which he describes hearing of Nabokov's death, a memory that remained vivid even as he wrote about it seventeen years later in the article 'Los muertos lejanos': 'Durante un viaje a Sevilla en 1977, y mientras desayunaba con la mujer que me acompañaba, los dos nos quedamos cabizbajos al descubrir en el diario que Vladimir Nabokov había muerto' ('During a trip to Seville, and while

---

[4] César Güemes, 'Puedo hacer muchas cosas, menos quejarme de cómo me trata la vida', *Jornada*, 18 November 1998. For the interview text see the following URL: www.javiermarias.es/PAGINASDEENTREVISTAS/JornadaNov98.html (accessed 26 October 2008).

[5] Luis H. Castellanos, 'La magia de lo que pudo ser: entrevista con Javier Marías', p. 24. Having acknowledged his affiliation with the phrase 'si me apuras' ('if you push me'), he continues, 'Luego cada uno ha ido por un lado distinto' ('But now each of us has followed a different path').

[6] Caterina Visani interview (http://www.javiermarias.es/PAGINASDEENTREVISTAS/entrevistaCaterinaVisani.html).

[7] Pfeiffer, 'Javier Marías', p. 108.

[8] Pfeiffer, p. 109. See also Juan Gabriel Vásquez, '"Tengo a veces la sensación de no estar ya vivo"', p. 15.

I was having breakfast with my female companion, we both bowed our heads when we read in the paper that Nabokov had died').[9]

Marías published versions of selected Nabokov poems in 1979, but he has by no means confined himself to this: interviews, novels, prologues, and Nabokov's autobiography have all fallen beneath his eyes. We can learn more also from 'La novela más melancólica: *Lolita* recontada', the brief retelling of *Lolita* that Marías wrote in 1992. To mark the one-hundredth anniversary of Nabokov's birth, Marías published *Desde que te vi morir: Vladimir Nabokov, una superstición* in which he collected all of the pieces he has written on Nabokov to date, amongst which are a biographical sketch, three essays, his 1979 poetry translations, and the afore-mentioned *Lolita* retelling.

## MARÍAS AND NABOKOV: AN UNCANNY CONVERGENCE

The literary careers of Nabokov and Marías epitomize the difficulties encountered by writers who inhabit two languages and cultures. As Marías points out in his biographical sketch, Nabokov felt frustrated by a critical establishment that wanted forensically to dissect his literary development: 'Le molestaba enormemente que le atribuyeran influencias' ('The attribution of influences on his work irritated him immensely').[10] Nabokov was not so much a giver of interviews as a writer of them: he insisted that the questions he was to answer be submitted before the face-to-face encounter took place so that he would have time to write out his answers in full. Pleading a lack of fluency in his spoken English, his habit of delivering fully-formed, written answers allowed him to keep his questioners at bay, or at least at one remove. Whether he found it easier to be dismissive on paper is a moot point; it is undoubtedly the case that his answers to interviewers' questions are often terse, bordering occasionally on the surly. In one typical exchange, he gives short shrift to his interviewer, A. Alfred Appel, Jr, who asks him about the Joycean antecedents of *Pale Fire*, to which he receives the following reply:

> Neither Kinbote nor Shade, nor their maker, is answering Joyce in *Pale Fire*. Actually I never liked *A Portrait of the Artist as a Young Man*. I find it a feeble and garrulous book. The phrase you quote is an unpleasant coincidence.[11]

---

[9] JM, 'Los muertos lejanos', in *VF*, pp. 458–61 (p. 459).

[10] Javier Marías and Felix de Azúa, *Desde que te vi morir*, p. 31. All subsequent references refer to this edition.

[11] *Strong Opinions*, pp. 70–1.

Corroboration, if it were needed, of Marías's observation.

By endeavouring to identify his literary forebears, critics hoped to place him within a given tradition, school, or movement, the better to see his work in a recognizable context. Nabokov bridged Europe and America in so complete a way that he could explore their interaction in many of his novels, perhaps most famously in *Lolita*. That fact did not help those who wished to situate him within either of those literary frameworks. Marías has likewise inhabited two literary worlds—the Hispanic and the English-speaking—such that Spanish critics have been reluctant to embrace a writer who appeared too anxious to highlight his credentials as an inheritor of British or American literary traditions.

In an article published in 1998, the novelist Eduardo Mendoza expressed surprise that Marías had not received the attention of the Spanish critical establishment that his talent deserved. Among the reasons Mendoza suggests by way of explanation is Marías's undefined place in the wider scheme of Spanish letters:

> no encaja [Marías] en ninguna de las corrientes al uso, aunque tampoco las combate ni las impugna; sus virtudes y sus defectos no se pueden calibrar en relación a los cánones de la prosa española, habría que inventar nuevos adjetivos para unas y otros; su mundo literario es, en cierto modo, cosmopolita (y utilizo este término a sabiendas de la connotación peyorativa que se le ha dado y se le da todavía en determinados contextos), pero no hay duda de que trabaja sobre la trama de la tradición y el lenguaje literario español, sin el mimetismo de mucha escritura actual, que parece prefabricada y, en muchos casos, mal traducida de otro idioma.[12]

> ([Marías] doesn't fit into any of the prevailing trends, although he does not oppose or contest them either; his virtues and defects can't be calibrated in relation to the rules of Spanish prose, new adjectives would have to be invented for both; his literary world is, in a sense, cosmopolitan (and I use the word fully aware of the pejorative connotations that have been, and continue to be, attached to it in certain contexts), but there can be no doubt that he is working on the fabric of tradition and Spanish literary language, while eschewing the mimicry which blights much contemporary writing, which seems prefabricated and, in many cases, badly translated from another language.)

In the 1970s and into the 1980s Marías saw himself as belonging to an iconoclastic generation whose mission it was to break free not only from a shared national past but also from a cumbersome literary heritage. As he himself acknowledged, however, a constant reaction against one's literary forefathers can eventually descend into wanton obscurantism.[13] He and

---

[12] Eduardo Mendoza, 'El extraño caso de Javier Marías', *El País*, 18 November 1998, p. 40.
[13] 'Desde una novela no necesariamente castiza', pp. 62–3.

the members of his generation had to occupy the territory that their upbringing and education had denied them. To put the point rather simply, they had to show the Spanish literary establishment what feats their worn-on-the-sleeve cosmopolitanism would allow them to achieve. Marías's reading, work as a translator, and experiences of foreign climes—most notably England and Oxford[14]—have helped him develop an individual voice in Spanish letters, one that other writers have tended to imitate rather than anticipate.[15] In spite of which, as late as 1995, he felt moved to bemoan the fact that the Spanish literary establishment still considered him a British writer who happened to write in Spanish.[16] The habits of Spanish literary criticism are not best suited to the discussion of his achievement since, as Mendoza points out, they involve a heavy reliance on categorization and description of trends. To observe this we have only to examine the myriad articles and studies published in the aftermath of Franco's death, in which Spanish critics, among them María Elena Bravo,[17] José María Martínez Cachero,[18] Abraham Martín-Maestro,[19] Gonzalo Sobejano,[20] and Luis Suñén,[21] sought to give a blow-by-blow account of the developing novelistic trends. If their studies have one

[14] In a revealing passage from his 'Diario de Zürich' (1997–1998) Marías wrote that because he grew up in the same city as the one in which he now lives, he is denied the sense of being feted and indulged when he returns to his home town. He says that 'Oxford y Londres son los extraños sustitutivos de ese sitio ideal que yo no tengo' ('Oxford and London are the strange substitutes for that ideal place that I lack'). See JM, 'Diario de Zürich', in *El pensamiento literario de Javier Marías*, pp. 11–28 (pp. 15–16).

[15] Alexis Grohmann is also of this opinion. He suggests that Marías's work 'ha engendrado o incidido en—o, como mínimo, allanado el camino a—toda una estirpe de obras publicadas recientemente' ('has brought about or influenced—or, at the very least, paved the way for—a whole line of recent works'). See 'La nobleza literaria de Javier Marías', p. 65. He goes on to mention *Sefarad* (2001) by Antonio Muñoz Molina, *Soldados de Salamina* (2003) by Javier Cercas, and *La loca de la casa* (2003) by Rosa Montero, to which I would add Muñoz Molina's *Ventanas de Manhattan* (2004) and Juan Manuel de Prada's *Desgarrados y excéntricos* (2001). In 2001, Marías lamented the reluctance of Spanish literary critics to draw attention to the unacknowledged borrowing Cercas and de Prada had made from his works. See Juan Gabriel Vásquez, p. 15.

[16] JM, 'Desplante y dominó', in *MS*, pp. 195–7 (p. 195).

[17] María Elena Bravo, 'Ante la novela de la democracia: Reflexiones sobre sus raíces', *Ínsula*, 444–5 (1983), 1, 24–5; 'Literatura de la distensión: el elemento policíaco', *Ínsula*, 472 (1986), 1, 12–13.

[18] José María Martínez Cachero, 'Diez años de novela española (1976–1985) por sus pasos contados', *Ínsula*, 464–5 (1985), 3–4.

[19] Abraham Martín-Maestro, 'La novela española en 1982 y 1983', *ALEC*, 9 (1984), 149–74 and 'La novela española en 1984', *ALEC*, 10 (1985), 123–41.

[20] Gonzalo Sobejano, 'Ante la novela de los años setenta', *Ínsula*, 396–7 (1979), 1, 22 and 'La novela poémática y sus alrededores', *Ínsula*, 464–5 (1985), 1, 26. Articles collected in Gonzalo Sobejano, *Novela española contemporánea 1940–1995* (Madrid: Mare Nostrum, 2003).

[21] Luis Suñén, 'Escritura y realidad', *Ínsula*, 464–5 (1985), 5–6.

thing in common it is the anxiety to construct a metanarrative of 'where the Spanish novel is heading' and to group authors.

The reluctance Marías and Nabokov share to ally themselves with any school, trend, or ideological standpoint is mirrored in their political views. Nabokov paints his political convictions with only the broadest of strokes, stating that, 'In home politics I am strongly anti-segregationist. In foreign policy, I am definitely on the government's side'.[22] He continues that his guiding principle is always to adopt the position most antagonistic to the Russian totalitarian state. In an earlier interview, he claimed to have been instinctively opposed to ideological coercion all his life;[23] that innate antipathy no doubt fed into his reluctance to ally himself with anything beyond the broadest liberal outlook either in politics or art. Marías's interventions in Spanish political life have always been as a critical observer rather than a tub-thumper for a particular party, although he did take the unusual step of admitting having voted for Spain's main socialist party—the PSOE—in the 2004 General Elections.[24] However, given the context of the article, which was written two years after those elections, he could hardly be accused of hoping to influence voters. He will not participate in state-run literary competitions because he believes that their decisions are often politically motivated and tainted by previous winners.[25] The decision to award the Premio Cervantes to Camilo José Cela in 1995 elicited this sarcastic reaction from Marías: 'Creo que el más oficial de los premios oficiales y el señor Cela se merecen mucho mutuamente' ('I think that that most official of official prizes and Mr Cela thoroughly deserve one another').[26] From his weekly newspaper column, first in *El Semanal* and then in *El País Semanal*, Marías's views have retained certain constants: opposition to ETA and to the increasing power of the state over the private individual, scorn for the Catholic Church in Spain, and contempt for George W. Bush, Tony Blair, and José María Aznar.[27] Among the things that exercise him most is the plummeting quality of debate at either end of the political spectrum, suggesting that he is driven by an awareness that democracy is the first and last value of the liberal state,

---

[22] *Strong Opinions*, p. 98.    [23] *Strong Opinions*, p. 64.

[24] JM, 'Decidir volverse loco', in *DNA*, pp. 248–50.

[25] See 'Diario de Zürich', pp. 15–16.

[26] For interview text, see the following URL: http://www.javiermarias.es/PAGINAS-DEENTREVISTAS/Tribunafeb96.html (accessed 27 October 2008).

[27] His opposition to ETA has also led Marías to throw his weight behind Fernando Savater, a personal friend and the leader of the intellectual and philosophical fight against Basque terrorism. See JM, 'Savater o ¿cómo que todo?', in *HMC*, pp. 30–2; on Bush, see 'Misterios de la imbecilidad', in *HMC*, pp. 118–20; on the Catholic Church in Spain, see 'Creed en nosotros a cambio', in *HMC*, pp. 317–19; on Blair, see 'Not forever England', in *SOOL*, pp. 254–6; on José María Aznar, see 'Cruzado de brazos', in *HMC*, pp. 23–5.

irrespective of his private political affiliations.[28] He is quick to remind his readers that it was not so long ago in Spain that the state held far more power than its citizens could comfortably countenance. The invasion of Iraq in 2003 appalled him because of the means employed by the US administration in trying to convince the world that Iraq posed an imminent threat to the West. In both the article 'Una añoranza preocupante' and a letter to the editors of *The Threepenny Review*, Marías expressed his dismay at recent statements made by Donald Rumsfeld, the then US Defence Secretary.[29] The latter had reversed the first principle of justice when claiming that the lack of evidence of the presence of weapons of mass destruction in Iraq did not prove they were not there.[30] The accused Iraq thus confronted the notoriously difficult task of proving that something is not the case, while facing the hostility of her accusers, who were already convinced of her guilt. Marías's evocation of Francoist judicial policy in *NET* reminds us that the principle of innocent until proven guilty is a moral and democratic good.[31]

The most striking parallel between Marías and Nabokov falls into the category of serendipity, though I suspect it did much to reinforce Marías's interest in the author he so admires. At the start of the tangled skein of events is, however, another parallel. Both men's lives were irrevocably affected by the advent of totalitarian regimes in their homelands. The Nabokov family fled the Crimea in the face of the advancing Red Army in 1919 for a period of exile that lasted the rest of Vladimir's life. After a period at Cambridge University and nearly two decades living in Germany, he fled Europe for America in 1940 to take up teaching positions at a succession of prestigious universities, among them Harvard, Wellesley, and Cornell. The persecution Julián Marías suffered in the aftermath of the Spanish Civil War meant he had to travel to the United States to deliver the university lectures he could not give in Spain. His family went with him, and Javier's earliest memories are of America. In fact, the Marías family stayed in the same apartment building that had housed Nabokov only a few years before, the same building that would house Javier thirty-three years later when he went to Wellesley as a visiting academic in 1984.[32] Which brings us to the serendipity: both men have taught at Wellesley College, Massachusetts, and both have delivered lecture courses

---

[28] JM, 'El desprestigio del desprestigio', in *DNA* pp. 102–4. See also Eric Southworth's observation that '"He's a radical liberal in the sense of J. S. Mill, believing in the dialectic as being something for the public good"', in Aida Edemariam, 'Looking for Luisa', *The Guardian*, 7 May 2005, Review section, pp. 20–3 (p. 20).

[29] JM, 'Una añoranza preocupante', in *EOOL*, pp. 20–2; JM, 'An Open Letter About Iraq' *The Threepenny Review*, 93 (2003), 35.

[30] *EOOL*, pp. 20–2.     [31] *NET*, pp. 28–9.

[32] Nabokov left Wellesley in 1947 for a permanent job at Cornell University.

on Cervantes's *Don Quijote*—Marías at Wellesley, Nabokov at Harvard. Although Marías could not have known that he would be invited to Wellesley—he did not engineer the situation—his decision to deliver a course of lectures on that particular book seems to me telling. Moreover, it could point to his attempts at self-fashioning in emulation of Nabokov, much as he translated works that Borges had already translated before him: complex acts of homage and literary one-upmanship. What we can say with certainty is that Marías was not recycling material he had already used while teaching at Oxford. As Eric Southworth recalls, there he taught courses on translation and the novel under Franco.[33]

## RESPONSES TO THE *QUIJOTE*: DIDACTICISM IN ART

Marías and Nabokov profess opposition to moral didacticism in art, perhaps because both had seen how powerless literature can be in the face of the armed totalitarian state. Whether or not Nabokov was consistent in applying this principle is a question answered by examining his response to *Don Quijote*. Marías notes in 'Vladimir Nabokov en éxtasis' that, 'El *Quijote* no lo entendió' ('He didn't understand the *Quixote*').[34] Antonio Muñoz Molina and Marías acknowledged their consternation at Nabokov's misinterpretation of the *Quijote* in an exchange of views on morality in art they maintained in the pages of *El País* in 1995. Their cordial disagreement was prompted by Muñoz Molina's article, 'Tarantino y la muerte', in which he attacked the casual depiction of sadism and torture in Quentin Tarantino's film *Pulp Fiction*.[35] Marías responded by defending the right of comic artists to explore those areas of human experience that would not normally be considered susceptible to humorous treatment.[36] Both agreed that a purely moral approach to criticism would lead to the dismissal of as great a work as *Don Quijote* because Cervantes's novel encouraged the reader to laugh at the beatings received by the deluded knight-errant.[37] And yet it was precisely on these grounds that

[33] Begoña Arce, 'Los fantasmas de Oxford', *El Periódico*, 18 November 2004, Libros section, p. 4.

[34] *Desde que te vi morir*, p. 32

[35] Antonio Muñoz Molina, 'Tarantino y la muerte', *El País*, 19 April 1995, p. 36.

[36] JM, 'Y encima recochineo', in *VF*, pp. 183–7.

[37] Like his late friend Sir Peter Russell, whose study *Cervantes* (Oxford: Oxford University Press, 1985) argued against Romantic readings of *Don Quijote*, Marías believes that the novel is intended to be humorous. Elsewhere he has written that 'quienes hablan del *Quijote* como de una obra realista no deberían volver a abrir la boca interpretativa'. See his 'El cadaver jovial', in *EOOL*, pp. 272–4 (p. 110).

Nabokov disliked *Don Quijote*, a reaction Marías considers 'puritana y simplista' ('puritanical and simplistic'), while Muñoz Molina calls his views 'injustas' ('unjust').[38] If Nabokov objected to the *Quijote* on the grounds that it was needlessly cruel and immoral, he criticized Dostoevski's *Crime and Punishment* because its morality was inconsistent with the doctrine of Christian forgiveness.[39] It seems that what he objected to in Dostoevski was the incorrect application of the very doctrine that the writer was trying to force on his audience in didactic fashion. He can hardly have thought, however, that Cervantes was advocating corporal punishment of the mentally unstable.

Paradoxically, in his most controversial work, *Lolita*, which deals with a middle-aged man's obsessive love for a twelve-year-old girl, Nabokov ridiculed the reader who might pick up the novel in search of moral lessons. He does so by inscribing within the text a rather literal-minded reader, Dr John Ray, Jr, into whose possession Humbert Humbert's confession has fallen. The former adds a 'Foreword', in which he extracts the following 'message' from Humbert's account of his twisted love for the young Lolita:

> for in this poignant personal study there lurks a general lesson; the wayward child, the egotistic mother, the panting maniac—these are not only vivid characters in a unique story; they warn us of dangerous trends; they point out potent evils. 'Lolita' should make all of us—parents, social workers, educators—apply ourselves with still greater vigilance and vision to the task of bringing up a better generation in a safer world.[40]

Nabokov repeated on numerous occasions his opposition to a literature that sought to improve its readers, although that opposition did not stop him from reading others' works in a moralizing spirit.[41]

Marías has also voiced his opposition to moral aims he regards as being beyond the remit of artistic endeavour. To date he has also been consistent in applying that principle to his response to others' fiction. Usefully for our purpose he formulated his view succinctly, using the depiction of crime in art as his example:

> The idea that literature should carry a message and strive to make us better human beings. I don't think literature has anything to do with that. One of

---

[38] See *VF*, p. 186; Antonio Muñoz Molina, 'Tarantino, la muerte y la comedia: una respuesta a Javier Marías', *El País*, 10 May 1995, p. 40.

[39] See Vladimir Nabokov, *Lectures on Russian Literature*, pp. 110–13. Nabokov objected to the moral equivalence Dostoevski implies between Raskolnikov, the murderer, and Sonya, the prostitute.

[40] Vladimir Nabokov, *Lolita* (London: Everyman, 1992), p. 5.

[41] *Strong Opinions*, pp. 3, 16, 22–3, 57.

the things that separates literature from the law is that judges only listen to facts, then find people guilty or not guilty. They don't get the whole story of what happened before, or how things came about, whereas in literature, you do see why things happened regardless of their moral value. And when you are witness to something, well it may not make a forgivable crime, but you realize how it came to happen, and maybe you understand its significance. That's what a novel should do, if it should do anything.[42]

Marías sees the value of literature as a medium in which judgement is perpetually deferred to allow uncluttered examination of human actions. This value in art is intimately connected with what he calls his 'pensamiento literario' ('literary thinking')—the ability of art to sustain contradictory truths in tension. Given the inscrutability of human intention as it develops, shifts, and backfires over time, for Marías, the best kind of fiction is that which allows his narrators to explore the grey areas around their actions.

## MARÍAS AS READER OF NABOKOV

Marías wrote the whimsical biographical sketches of famous writers that he would later collect as *Vidas escritas* under what he calls the 'alentadora y suave tiranía que sobre mí ejercieron [Javier Pradera y Fernando Savater]' ('encouraging and mild tyranny that [Javier Pradera and Fernando Savater] exercised over me').[43] In their role as editors of *Claves de razón práctica*, where these brief lives first appeared, Pradera and Savater evidently had to crack the whip to ensure that Marías came up with the necessary piece on time. Given this background, it seems unsurprising that he should have chosen to write about six writers—Conrad, Dinesen, Faulkner, Nabokov, Sterne, and Stevenson—whose work he had translated into Spanish. By doing so he could recycle the biographical research he had already undertaken at the time of translating their memoirs, novels, or poems. We find this idea confirmed by Marías's inclusion of a separate bibliography at the end of *Vidas escritas*, entitled 'Memoria personal' ('Personal memory') where he lists his own translations of each author, implying that these volumes have aided him in his task.[44]

In general terms, this information shows how thoroughly he researches given authors before translating their work. In the particular case of

[42] Paul Ingendaay, 'Interview with Javier Marías', *Bomb*, 73 (2000), <http://bombsite.com/issues/73/articles/2345>, pp. 150–8 (accessed 2 November 2008).

[43] JM, 'Prólogo', in *Vidas escritas: edición ampliada* (Madrid: Alfaguara, 2000), pp. 15–19 (p. 18).

[44] *Vidas escritas*, p. 283.

Nabokov, Marías's biographical sketch, 'Vladimir Nabokov en éxtasis', betrays ample familiarity with a considerable portion of the latter's oeuvre. It demonstrates, for example, that Marías had read *Strong Opinions*—an anthology of interviews and letters—from first page to last since it is there that many of the eccentric Nabokovian assertions he uses in his own text are to be found: Nabokov's claim to be 'tan americano como abril en Arizona' ('as American as April in Arizona'),[45] his judgement that *Finnegan's Wake* is 'literatura regional' ('regional literature'),[46] and his dismissal of Freud as 'el matasanos vienés' ('the Viennese quack').[47] Likewise, all of Nabokov's literary dislikes—of Camus, Lawrence, Lorca, and Mann,[48] Conrad,[49] Forster,[50] Faulkner, Pound,[51] Balzac,[52] and Sartre[53]—can be found along with the long list of everyday objects and phenomena that provoke his ire—bullfights, primitivist folk masks, hooligans, and jazz,[54] background music, bidets, insecticides, noisy motorbikes, swimming pools, transistors, and trucks,[55] circuses, nightclubs, and yachts.[56] Marías also quotes and translates from *Speak, Memory, An Autobiography Revisited*:

> Al parecer salvó goles cantados, y en todo caso prestó encarnación perfecta a la figura misteriosa y ajena de los guardametas más legendarios. Según sus propias palabras, era visto como 'un fabuloso ser exótico disfrazado de futbolista inglés, que componía versos en una lengua que nadie entendía sobre un país remoto que no conocía nadie'.[57]

> (Apparently he saved what looked like certain goals, and was the perfect embodiment of the strange, mysterious figure of the truly legendary goalie. In his own words he was seen as 'a fabulous exotic being in an English footballer's disguise, composing verse in a tongue nobody understood about a remote country nobody knew'.)[58]

Nabokov's novel *Pnin* appears twice in Marías's fiction as a novel either owned or being read by the narrator; in both cases the novel has been discarded or left behind. In *El hombre sentimental* we are told that, when he abandoned Berta for Natalia Manur, el León de Nápoles left a copy of *Pnin* amongst other books in the home they used to share. The

---

[45] *Desde que te vi morir*, p. 30.          [46] *Desde que te vi morir*, p. 31.
[47] *Desde que te vi morir*, p. 32; *Strong Opinions*, pp. 98, 71, 47.
[48] *Strong Opinions*, p. 54.          [49] *Strong Opinions*, p. 57.
[50] *Strong Opinions*, p. 95.          [51] *Strong Opinions*, p. 102.
[52] *Strong Opinions*, p. 118.
[53] *Desde que te vi morir*, p. 31; *Strong Opinions*, p. 175.
[54] *Strong Opinions*, p. 18.          [55] *Strong Opinions*, p. 150.
[56] *Desde que te vi morir*, p. 32; *Strong Opinions*, p. 158.
[57] *Desde que te vi morir*, pp. 30–1.
[58] JM, *Written Lives*, trans. by Margaret Jull Costa (Edinburgh: Canongate, 2006), p. 75.

associations el León has with those books are coloured by their role in her death.

> Con aquellas palabras concluía la carta de Noguer, aunque añadía un post scriptum en el que me preguntaba si deseaba recuperar esos libros míos que Berta cargaba cuando cayó por las escaleras; y meticulosamente, en cuartilla aparte, me incluía la relación, una cincuentena de títulos de los que sólo reconocí haber poseído o leído tres o cuatro o cinco: *La caída de Constantinopla, Comentarios reales, Wagner Nights, Nuestros antepasados, Pnin.*[59]

> (Noguer's letter concluded with those words, although he added a postscriptum in which he asked me if I wanted to come and collect the books of mine that Berta was carrying when she fell down the stairs; and meticulously, on a separate sheet, he included a list of fifty or so titles, of which I only remembered owning or reading three or four or five: *The Fall of Constantinople, Royal Commentaries of the Incas, Wagner Nights, Our Ancestors* and *Pnin.*)[60]

The presence of *Pnin* among el León de Nápoles's book collection is the first but not the last occasion on which we find Marías's characters reading Nabokov. Juan Ranz is another narrator we find reading *Pnin*. The day on which he has learned of his father's first wife, whose existence he had hitherto never suspected, he tells Luisa of his discovery. They are preparing for bed and he puts his novel to one side the better to concentrate on their conversation:

> Le quité de las manos el mando a distancia. Dejé en la mesilla de noche el libro que había tenido todo el rato entre las mías, sin leer una línea. Era Pnin de Nabokov. No lo he acabado y me estaba gustando mucho.[61]

> (I took the remote control from her. I put down on the bedside table the book I'd been holding in my hands, without reading a line. The book was *Pnin* by Nabokov. I never did finish it, although I was really enjoying it.)[62]

Once again, in the absence of any further indication from Marías as to his intention, we are reduced to speculation.

Of all his novels, *TLA* is the one that contains the greatest number of direct references to Nabokov and his works. The reasons are not hard to find. Nabokov was no stranger to England's great university cities, having spent time at Cambridge from 1919 to 1922, where he must have experienced the same feelings of alienation and perplexity that characterize the narrator of *TLA*'s reaction to Oxford. Nor was the campus novel a genre

---

[59] *EHS*, p. 77.
[60] JM, *The Man of Feeling*, trans. by Margaret Jull Costa (London: Harvill, 2003), p. 50.
[61] *CTB*, p. 196.  [62] *A Heart So White*, p. 142.

Nabokov was averse to cultivating: *Pnin* is a prominent example. As if these biographical and artistic parallels were insufficient, Marías added another point of contact with Nabokov by applying for leave from Oxford in the first term of his second year so that he could lecture at Wellesley College, the American University where Nabokov had famously taught. While living there during this second visit, Marías tried to imagine him pacing the room above, grappling with the intransigent *Lolita* ('Los imposibles pasos del exiliado ruso').[63]

The Marías who wrote *TLA* undoubtedly had Nabokov very much on his mind. The novel's anonymous narrator reveals a familiarity with the 'Translator's Foreword' to the version of Lermontov's *A Hero of Our Time* written collaboratively by Vladimir Nabokov and his son Dmitri. The narrator explains the meaning of the English verb 'to eavesdrop', noting that Spanish does not have a direct equivalent by which to translate it. He then describes the embarrassing and pathetic conversation, on which he eavesdrops, between Cromer-Blake and a young man, who seems to be a reluctant lover or a rent-boy. Nabokov maintains that the frequency with which eavesdropping recurs in *A Hero of Our Time* as a narrative device 'ceases to strike the reader as a marvellous vagary of chance and becomes, as it were, the barely noticeable routine of fate'.[64] As if to head off any criticism that his own use of the device is contrived, the narrator of *TLA* translates and quotes these exact words when explaining that eavesdropping is commonplace in the university cities of Oxford and Cambridge: 'En Oxford (y en Cambridge, supongo) *eavesdropping*, como dijo Nabokov que sucedía en la novela de Lermontov mencionada, se convierte en la "apenas perceptible rutina del destino"' ('In Oxford [and Cambridge too, I imagine], eavesdropping becomes exactly what Nabokov describes in the Lermontov novel mentioned above: "the barely noticeable routine of fate"').[65]

The mysterious Russian teacher, Rook (a probable allusion to Nabokov's penchant for chess), is described as having known Nabokov; he demonstrates his familiarity by ostentatiously using Nabokov's name and patronymic when referring to him. Rook unnerves the narrator and his lover Clare Bayes by his presence on the train that returns the illicit lovers to Oxford after an encounter in a Reading hotel. A combination of their own carelessness and bad luck have left them in danger of being caught:

---

[63] *Desde que te vi morir*, p. 19–23.
[64] Mikhail Lermontov, *A Hero of Our Time*, trans. by Vladimir and Dmitri Nabokov (London: Everyman, 1992 [1st edn 1958]), p. 5.
[65] *TLA*, p. 229. *All Souls*, p. 172.

carelessness in that they had lingered in the hotel and left only one train on which they could return, it being their usual custom to travel separately; bad luck in that the train happened to contain Rook.

> Habíamos llegado por tanto juntos a la estación de Oxford y habíamos caminado juntos bajo una luna pulposa y móvil, de cara al viento, hasta separarnos en una esquina aún distante de nuestras respectivas casas.... Luego, mientras por vez primera caminábamos solos y juntos por las calles de Oxford bajo la luna pulposa y móvil y de cara al viento, oímos sus pasos a poca distancia, detrás, resonando al mismo ritmo que los nuestros, o eso creímos—creímos que eran los suyos, y no el eco.[66]

> (Anyway, we'd arrived at Oxford station and walked together beneath a fickle, mellow moon, our faces to the wind, until on a corner still some distance from our respective houses, we went our separate ways...Afterwards, when we walked the streets of Oxford, for the first time together and alone, beneath the fickle, mellow moon, our faces to the wind, we heard his footsteps a little way behind, echoing the rhythm of our steps, or at least we thought they were his and not just the echo of our own.)[67]

The phrase 'pulposa luna', unusual in Spanish, appears in Marías's translation of Nabokov's poem 'Hotel Room'. I quote the final stanza, followed by Marías's version.

> Stirless I stand there at the window,/and in the black bowl of the sky/glows like a golden drop of honey/the mellow moon.

> Inmóvil, me quedo junto a la ventana,/y en la negra vasija del firmamento/ como gota dorada de miel refulge/la pulposa luna.[68]

'Hotel Room' is an enigmatic poem. It records the alienation the poet feels in a room that is inhospitable and not his own—'Not quite a bed, not quite a bench./Wallpaper: a grim yellow'. The final stanza acts as an upturn. Looking out over the night sky, the poet watches the moon: the 'grim yellow' of the room's walls is replaced by the succulent invitingness of 'a golden drop of honey'. Nabokov builds a sequence of alliterations that contribute to the sense of harmony—'Stirless I stand', 'black bowl', 'glows like golden', 'mellow moon'—alliterative effects Marías reproduces with 'refulge/la pulposa luna'.[69] It is as if the sight of the moon allowed the poet to glimpse something better than his immediate surroundings. What the larger significance is of seeing the moon remains unsaid, though the vista it offers suggests an opening out of the poet's mind to wider, more transcendent thoughts. By contrast, in *TLA*, the 'luna pulposa'

[66] *TLA*, pp. 37–8.   [67] *All Souls*, pp. 24–5.
[68] *Desde que te vi morir*, pp. 40–1.   [69] *Desde que te vi morir*, p. 41.

seems to add to the narrator's sense of menace on his wary homeward journey through a deserted city.[70]

All that the narrator knows about Rook, beyond the inscrutability of his private life, is that he is preparing a new translation of *Anna Karenina*, the principal innovation of which will be a change in the heroine's name— Anna Karenin, not Karenina. As the narrator points out, this misuse of Russian naming practices was one of Nabokov's bugbears:

> Su traducción iba a ser—nadie había visto aún una línea, ni siquiera el editor—canónica e incomparable, empezando por la fundamental innovación en el título, pues lo adecuado, según Rook y según Nabokov... era Karenin y no Karenina, ya que Anna no era una bailarina, una cantante ni una actriz, únicas mujeres, por muy rusas que fueran, a las que en un texto inglés o en cualquier otra lengua occidental sería admisible feminizar el apellido.[71]

> (His translation—though no one, not even the publisher, had as yet seen a line of it—was to be both definitive and incomparable, beginning with a fundamental innovation in the title, for according to both Rook and Nabokov... the correct title was *Karenin* not *Karenina*, since Anna was neither ballerina, singer or actress, the only women, however authentically Russian, whose family name it would be admissible to feminise in a text in English or in any other Western language.)[72]

Nabokov dispatches the subject with his customary forthrightness in *Strong Opinions*: '([*Anna Karenin*] should be transliterated without the closing "a"—she was not a ballerina)'.[73]

Yet another occasion on which we find Marías's protagonists reading works by Nabokov is in *Mañana en la batalla piensa en mí* (*MBPM*). There it is Luisa Téllez who buys a copy of *Lolita* when out shopping while Víctor Francés watches her from a distance. But rather than follow up this fleeting allusion—any pursuit of which would again demand large amounts of speculation—I intend to examine 'La novela más melancólica: *Lolita* recontada' to see how Marías retells *Lolita* in his own words. My reasons for doing so are twofold. Firstly, with the exception of Pittarello, no critic has yet demonstrated the degree to which his piece is a condensed translation of the original novel. I examine how Marías summarizes, paraphrases, and translates key passages from the novel to recreate its melancholic atmosphere, uncomfortable frankness, and daring use of language. Secondly, I believe that his short story 'Mientras ellas duermen' must be read as alluding to Nabokov's novel and it is revealing to explore what Marías adds to his artistry by so alluding.

---

[70] The phrase reappears in *CTB*, p. 49.
[71] *TLA*, p. 38.      [72] *All Souls*, pp. 26–7.      [73] *Strong Opinions*, p. 112.

## MARÍAS, AZÚA, AND *LOLITA*

Marías's response to *Lolita* is usefully compared with that of another writer of his generation, Féliz de Azúa, who wrote a prologue to Nabokov's masterpiece in 1982. Before their collaboration on the Nabokov translation project, *Dieciocho Poemas y Dieciocho Problemas* (1979), Marías and Azúa had published, along with Molina Foix, the anthology *Tres cuentos didácticos* (1975) that was intended to show solidarity among the young prose writers of the 'Novísimos' generation. On the basis of these collaborative projects, indicative of shared aesthetic and literary tastes, we might expect the two writers to coincide in their views on Nabokov. Were that not to be the case, it would have made their collaboration more difficult and, to some extent, less understandable. However, on examining Azúa's *Lolita* prologue, we find a divergence of interpretation.[74] In my view, his prologue offers little useful commentary on the novel, and instead pursues an idiosyncratic reading that helps little in deciphering this controversial and unsettling text. Marías, on the other hand, attempts only to recreate its essence through paraphrase and translation. Azúa starts from the premise that Nabokov was interested in how Lolita epitomizes the American teenager who must learn to work her feminine wiles until she has found the man of her dreams; that in a twisted, satirical form, Nabokov depicts Lolita's apprenticeship as the good American housewife, 'su aprendizaje hasta el matrimonio'. This process

> Suele consistir en un ir y venir de poseedor en poseedor, hasta que aprenden la técnica de la explotación, hasta que no les falta por adquirir ni uno solo de los trucos de la posesión y el ahorro. En ese arduo aprendizaje, la cadena de sinvergüenzas, macarras, chorizos y hombres de buena fe es sólo un primer eslabón pedagógico que se olvida por completo una vez alcanzado el primer amor conyugal.[75]

> (Usually consists of going from owner to owner, until they learn the techniques of exploitation, until they lack none of the tricks of acquisition and money saving. During that arduous apprenticeship, the succession of scoundrels, thugs, crooks, and well-meaning men is only a first pedagogical step that is forgotten entirely once the first marital love has been achieved.)

Azúa's tone here is one of heavy sarcasm. Were it not to be, what could we make of his bizarre remarks? The idea that *Lolita* is satirizing the adolescent development of America's female youth is one that its author was

[74] Félix de Azúa, 'Prólogo para "Lolita"', in *Lecturas compulsivas*, pp. 112–15 (p. 115). The author explains that the prologue was written for the pocket edition of *Lolita* published by Grijalbo but that it was never used by the publisher, for reasons he cannot remember.
[75] 'Prólogo para "Lolita"', p. 114.

always anxious to quash. That Lolita learns to prostitute herself is undoubt-edly true, but her move is born of desperation, the only means at her disposal of wresting some control back from her tormentor. The squalid marital home she is sharing with Dick by the end of the novel—'dismal district, all dump and ditch, and wormy vegetable garden, and shack and gray drizzle, and red mud'—is indeed a pale shadow of the destiny to which she might have aspired, but even so, Nabokov's emphasis does not lie there.[76] As Michael Wood puts it, what is pathetic about the married Lolita is that she is no longer the goddess of Humbert's imagination, but rather stands in 'her sheer ruined ordinariness, her old lost ordinariness found again only as a ruin'.[77] Summoned by her plea for money, Humbert watches Lolita survey her past life with him:

> In her washed-out gray eyes, strangely spectacled, our poor romance was for a moment reflected, pondered upon, and dismissed like a dull party, like a rainy picnic to which only the dullest bores had come, like a humdrum exercise, like a bit of mud caking her childhood.[78]

Humbert's perception of her reaction is couched in terms that heighten its pathos for him—how could Lolita think so little of the attention he lavished on her for so long?—whilst the reader might see the pathos resid-ing more on her side: this latest, brief consideration of 'our poor romance' confirms perhaps her long-held belief that life was not fun as a sex-slave at the hands of a paedophile who ought to have been her legal protector. Their association has not been 'our romance', but rather, his.[79] This brings us to my final point, which is that Humbert allows the reader only his version of events. '[Humbert's confession] is about "Lolita", about the obsessive dream of Lolita which captured the actual child and took her away', as Wood puts it.[80] Humbert's monopoly on the truth about his relationship with Lolita is the final act of violence committed against a girl who is only ever seen through his eyes. He is certainly not interested in Lolita as a product of capitalist society and neither is Nabokov.[81]

And yet, Azúa does see the pathos of '*this* Lolita, pale and polluted, and big with another man's child', though he captures its emphasis rather oddly:[82] 'La aventura sexual con H. H. fue sólo un aspecto mecánico, un error de engranajes; la aventura con Kilt [*sic*] fue la verdadera educación

[76] *Lolita*, p. 285.
[77] Michael Wood, *The Magician's Doubts: Nabokov and the Risks of Fiction* (London: Pimlico, 1995), p. 136.
[78] *Lolita*, p. 256.        [79] Wood, pp. 136–7.        [80] Wood, p. 115.
[81] We might also note that Nabokov rejected all implications that *Lolita* was intended as a satirical attack on American capitalism. See *Strong Opinions*, pp. 22–3.
[82] *Lolita*, p. 295.

sentimental. Y, ahora, Lolita, la señora Lola, sin vida ni corazón, puede casarse con Dick' ('Her sexual adventure with H. H. was simply a mechanical aspect, an operational error; her adventure with Kilt [*sic*] was her true sentimental education. And now, Lolita, Mrs Lola, lifeless and heartless, can marry Dick').[83] He sees the novel as recording that most poignant of losses—the loss of youth—but this leaves out of account the voice of Humbert himself, surely *Lolita*'s most compelling aspect.[84] Marías, by contrast, retells the novel privileging the point of view that, as Wood observes, marks its essential core—that of Humbert Humbert, the arch sentimentalist: 'De Vladimir Nabokov recomendaría *Lolita*, que pese a antiguos escándalos y tergiversaciones posteriores, yo veo, más que nada, como la historia de una fidelidad, tan dura como melancólica como lírica' ('Among Vladimir Nabokov's works I would recommend *Lolita* which I see, despite old scandals and subsequent distortions, as, above all, the story of an enduring passion, as hard as it is melancholic as it is lyrical').[85]

## 'LA NOVELA MÁS MELANCÓLICA: (*LOLITA* RECONTADA)'

In its original version, the essay 'El canon Nabokov'—another of the pieces Marías gathered into *Desde que te vi morir*—was a review of a translation by Rafael Ruiz de la Cuesta of *Una belleza rusa*, a collection of Nabokov short stories published in 1992 by Anagrama. The edited and extended version that made its way into the later anthology removes all reference to the article's original purpose. However, the final paragraph of that first version offers considerable insight into what Marías believed to be the challenges of translating Nabokov:

> Una palabra sobre la traducción: traducir a Nabokov, con su inglés original o procedente del ruso—tanto da—, lleno de utilizaciones arriesgadas e insólitas de la lengua, con su amor al detalle que sobresalta y al adjetivo impensado y oblicuo, es una tarea dificilísima: algunos traductores logran no hacer el ridículo, otros fracasan e indignan. Por ello esta versión de *Una belleza rusa* merece destacarse, pues por ello resulta doblemente excepcional.[86]

(A word on the translation: translating Nabokov and his use of English (which can either be described as idiosyncratic or coming from Russian, who cares, the effect is much the same) with its abundant daring and

[83] 'Prólogo para "Lolita"', p. 115.  [84] 'Prólogo para "Lolita"', p. 115.
[85] JM, 'De memoria locuaz leída', in *AVC*, pp. 355–8 (p. 356).
[86] JM, 'El canon Nabokov', in *VF*, pp. 436–8 (p. 438).

unheard of linguistic feints, its love of the detail that jumps off the page and the unexpected, oblique adjective, is an extremely demanding task: some translators manage not to make fools of themselves, others fail and cause indignation. For that reason this version of *A Russian Beauty* deserves to stand out, since its ability to avoid those pitfalls makes it doubly exceptional.)

Marías was speaking from experience here, gained both generally through years of work as a professional translator and more particularly through his own work on Nabokov's poems. However, 'El canon Nabokov' appeared in *El País* in January 1993, five months after 'La novela más melancólica (*Lolita* recontada)' had been published in the Babelia section of the same newspaper. The editors had commissioned 'La novela más melancólica' to form part of a series in which famous writers recreated, in abbreviated form, a novel of their choice. That Marías should have chosen *Lolita* ought not to surprise us. When asked about his favourite fictional characters, he listed Humbert Humbert among them, adding that he counts *Lolita* among the novels that move him the most.[87] How he went about the task of retelling *Lolita* goes a long way to explaining why, in early 1993 more than ever, he was able to pass comment on the challenges posed by translating Nabokov: 'La novela más melancólica' is a palimpsest in which his own retelling is interwoven with translated phrases and sentences from the original novel. In this section I hope to show the veracity of that assertion and the literary merits of the retelling itself.

Strangely perhaps, Marías chose not to retell Humbert's tale in the first person. Rather than write in Humbert's voice—an option which must have tempted him, given his preference for writing in the first person—he adopts the perspective of an omniscient narrator. There are several possible explanations. He may have done so in order to create the necessary distance between his creation and Nabokov's; to avoid producing a pastiche of Humbert's rich diction. His decision could also reflect something central to Humbert's character, which is that, though given to moments of devastating brevity—'(picnic, lightning)'[88]—he often draws his scenes in the kind of excruciating detail that would make a paraphrased account incongruous. Marías may have written from the omniscient viewpoint to mirror his position in relation to his own fiction: that of using another's voice while retaining absolute control over the characterization of the speaker. In his own fiction, that control comes naturally since Marías

---

[87] Interview with *Star* magazine (http://www.javiermarias.es/PAGINASDEENTRE-VISTAS/cuestionario.html end of 1993); María José Obiol, 'El dominio de la sensación', *El País*, 23 July 1989, Domingo, p. 20.

[88] *Lolita*, p. 10. Thus summarizes Humbert the circumstances around his mother's death.

*translation and palimpsest*

decides how the narrator is characterized, how and where information is deployed in the text. When retelling *Lolita* the crucial difference is that Nabokov has already performed that task in the voice of Humbert. To wrest control back from an already written text, Marías takes up a position at one remove from it.

However, this is only half the story. His version mixes the voices of the characters with that of the omniscient narrator, weaving in Humbert's descriptions, Charlotte Haze's trite utterances, Lolita's impish disobedience, while not forgetting Quilty's drunken foray at the Enchanted Hunters Hotel. The result is a text that is as much a translation and a palimpsest as anything else. Let us examine the opening of the second paragraph. As the reader will see, in the translations that follow the Spanish quotations, I have italicized and referenced the phrases from Nabokov's original that he is translating or paraphrasing:

> Lolita, luz de mi vida, fuego de mis entrañas, mi pecado, mi alma, la primera invocación del narrador Humbert Humbert, quien en su oscura infancia europea se enamoró impúdica y frenéticamente de una niña de su edad llamada Annabel, muerta de tifus cuatro años después de su primera y última agonía estival: nos queríamos con amor prematuro, con la violencia que a menudo destruye vidas adultas.[89]

> (*Lolita, light of my life, fire of my loins, my sin, my soul,* the narrator Humbert Humbert's first invocation, he who in his dimly seen European childhood fell *shamelessly, agonizingly* in love with a girl of his own age, Annabel, who, four months after their first and last agonizing summer, died of typhus: we loved each other with a premature love, *with a violence that frequently destroys adult lives.*)

The privileging of one viewpoint begins immediately, though how else could a retelling of *Lolita* start? Marías opens with Humbert's spell-like incantation—'Lolita, light of my life, fire of my loins. My sin, my soul'.[90] What Wood calls 'Humbert's dandyish taste for alliteration' immediately comes to the fore, as does the wistful rhythmic quality of his prose, achieved through the use of two four-syllable clauses, followed by two-syllable clauses separated by commas;[91] both the alliteration and falling rhythm are difficult to retain in Spanish, which lacks the single-syllable equivalents that would allow Marías to reproduce the effect. He importantly describes Humbert's words as an 'invocación', a summoning of Lolita's spirit, because, as Humbert makes clear, by the time the text has reached the reader's hands, both he and his girl-bride must be dead. In other words, Marías adopts the guise of one of his favourite literary

---

[89] *Desde que te vi morir,* p. 131.    [90] *Lolita,* p. 9.
[91] Wood, *The Magician's Doubts,* p. 112.

personae, that of the ghost. Juan Ranz, Víctor Francés, Deza all survey finite and closed time periods, events over which they no longer have any influence but which they commit to memory through the medium of print. These events are characterized by trauma, loss or self-doubt, often brought on by affairs of the heart, which, Pittarello points out, are amongst the riskiest for their identity and destiny.[92] Humbert's task, as Marías is aware, is to make his Lolita immortal, the 'refuge of art... is the only immortality you and I may share, my Lolita'.[93]

Marías translates from Humbert's account so that his words are woven seamlessly into the text, with no speech marks to identify the quotations. As I have shown in relation to Browne, Marías's habit of incorporating phrases pregnant with meaning into Spanish goes right to the heart of his endeavour as a translator and enricher of his mother tongue. Exercising the same degree of control as Humbert does over Lolita, who is glimpsed only partially in the text, Marías must select the particular anecdote and turn of phrase that provide the essentials of Humbert's narrative. Hence we have Humbert's slippery description of his first love for Annabel, 'All at once we were madly, clumsily, shamelessly, agonizingly in love with each other',[94] which is paraphrased as 'impúdica y frenéticamente', Marías's rendering of the final two Humbertian adverbs. The description is slippery because, as Marías points out, Humbert shows no desire to 'despejar la duda de si su amor infantil fue la primera manifestación de algo *inherente a su personalidad* o si su biografía quedó para siempre fijada en aquella inicial imagen de su adoración' ('apparently indifferent to the doubt surrounding whether his childhood romance was the first evidence of an inherent singularity or if his life story was left forever fixed on that initial worshipped image').[95] This mysterious 'algo inherente a su personalidad' is Humbert's phrase, his 'inherent singularity', as he somewhat grandly calls it, in hopes of casting himself as the tragic lover and victim of fate's cruel twists.[96] Marías's description of Humbert's love for Annabel as an 'agonía estival' could not be more apt: 'agonía' because it was destroyed soon after by her premature death; 'agonía' in a sexual sense because it remained unconsummated, as Humbert describes in self-flagellating detail. Marías again translates Humbert's words, 'We loved each with a premature love, marked by a fierceness that so often destroys adult lives':[97] 'con la violencia que a menudo destruye vidas adultas'. Eva García Valle, Deán's lover in *MBPM*, is well aware that it is not just experiences that reach their fruition that leave indelible and deep marks.

[92] Elide Pittarello, 'Rewriting Nabokov: the shortened *Lolita* by Javier Marías', in *Nabokov. Un'eredità letteraria*, ed. by Alide Cagidemetrio and Daniela Rizzi (Milan: Univesità Ca' Foscari di Venezia, 2006), pp. 87–95, *passim*. My own English translation of '*Lolita* recontada' appears in this volume as an appendix to Pittarello's article, pp. 96–109.
[93] *Lolita*, p. 327.    [94] *Lolita*, p. 12.    [95] *Desde que te vi morir*, p. 131.
[96] *Lolita*, p. 14.    [97] *Lolita*, p. 18.

While recounting Eva's attempts to dupe him, Deán remarks that her scheme to keep him by her by faking an abortion was a good one: 'quizá une más la renuncia a lo que pudo ser y era común que su aceptación o su consumación o su desarrollo sin trabas' ('perhaps the renunciation of what might have been and was common to you both unites you more than its acceptance or accomplishment or unfettered development').[98]

Marías continues to use Humbert's first invocation to punctuate the text, repeating the incantation, one phrase at a time. Taken on their own, Humbert's words juxtapose contrasting impulses and express how his sense of self is bound up with sexual desire and a concomitant inability to satisfy that need without harming others—'light of my life, fire of my loins. My sin, my soul'. Nabokov does not repeat the invocation as Marías does, showing that the idea is the latter's innovation. The first two clauses appear at sinisterly apt moments in the retelling.

> [Charlotte Haze] era para Humbert esa cosa lamentable y chata que se llama una mujer atractiva, pero vivía con una niña de doce años, su hija Dolores, Lolita, luz de mi vida.

> ([Charlotte Haze] was to Humbert that *most sorry and dull thing known commonly as a handsome woman*; yet she lived with a twelve-year old girl, her daughter Dolores, Lolita, light of my life.)[99]

> Humbert es un hombre muy apuesto o muy atractivo, lo es para las mujeres y lo es para la niña Lolita, fuego de mis entrañas, con quien juega y tontea amparado en el contacto físico a que obliga todo trato afectuoso con los menores.[100]

> (Humbert is a very handsome and attractive man, women find him so, as do girls, as does the girl-child Lolita, fire of my loins, with whom he plays and fools around under cover of the physical contact inherent in adopting an affectionate manner with children.)

Marías recreates Humbert's cunning. He puts up with Charlotte so he can get to her daughter; he plays with Lolita under cover of innocence to gain sexual gratification. The continued use of these epithets throughout the text, always in their original order, acts as a refrain, the effect of which becomes almost hypnotic: the kind of musical variation Marías has mentioned hoping to achieve in his prose.[101] The continuing spell her memory

---

[98] *MBPM*, p. 428; *Tomorrow in the Battle Think on Me*, p. 297.
[99] The original reads 'that sorry and dull thing: a handsome woman'. *Lolita*, p. 76.
[100] *Desde que te vi morir*, p. 132.
[101] See Catrina Visani interview (http://www.javiermarias.es/PAGINASDEENTRE-VISTAS/entrevistaCaterinaVisani.html): 'hay prosas que, como la música, invitan rápido a seguir el ritmo, o a seguir la melodía, y frecuentemente depende de cada lector escoger el ritmo o no. En este sentido, de una manera vaga, y absolutamente poco científica, en mis libros intento buscar al menos un tipo de prosa rítmica' ('there are some sorts of prose that,

casts over Humbert, reiterated in that form, heightens the melancholy and yearning that punctuate the novel, while not shying away from the monstrous premise. Hence it is that Marías starts the paragraph detailing Lolita's account of her sexual initiation, 'Lolita, fuego de mis entrañas, le relató después sus iniciaciones en el campamento'. Readers familiar with the novel will recall the difficult scenes where Humbert cannot help boasting of his virility—'fire of my loins'—and the painful results for the sexually immature Lolita.

Marías is alive to the horrible ironies in the novel, and not just in the fact of Lolita having become sexually active in the weeks before Humbert anticipated getting his hands on her. Charlotte's letter to him, left in the house while she takes her daughter to Camp Q, begins '*Esto es una confesión: te amo…*':[102] a confession within a confession, Charlotte's gushing prose within Humbert's prison cell account of his crimes. Likewise the passing car 'que no había podido esquivar a la figura lamentable y chata que corría hacia el buzón' to post the letters warning Lolita of Humbert's intentions towards her. The scene has a reprise in *MBPM* when Deán's lover Eva flees the London bus on which they have both been travelling and runs straight into the path of an oncoming taxi, dying instantly.

The letters Mrs Haze was so anxious to post 'las recogió del suelo, las hizo pedazos, se los guardó en el bolsillo, no serían jamás leídas, ni por él siquiera. Y entonces, Lolita, Lolita, Lolita. *Repítelo hasta llenar la página, tipógrafo*' ('Humbert picked them up from the ground, tore them to pieces, and put them in his trouser pocket, never to be read, not by him

---

like music, quickly invite you to follow their rhythm or melody, and often it's up to the reader whether or not to choose the rhythm. With that in mind, in a vague and utterly unscientific way, in my books I at least aim towards rhythmical prose'); Jaime Bello León interview (www.javiermarias.es/main.html): 'pudiéramos decir que hay una tentativa de aproximarse a una de las muchas cosas que la música consigue mejor que ninguna otra forma artística, desde luego no normalmente la literatura. A veces uno está escuchando un concierto y hay un tema, una melodía, que aparece tocada la primera vez sólo por el piano y después, al cabo de un rato, aparece y esta vez son los violines los que la tocan con alguna variación y luego es la orquesta entera, entonces se produce un reconocimiento. Aunque uno ya haya oído eso la primera vez, la segunda, la tercera, puede darse que la repetición sea exacta o no, pero eso es algo que conmueve mucho siempre y cuando la melodía, probablemente sea hermosa. Entonces en mis novelas últimas intento que eso exista, tomando como modelo lo que la música hace' ('we could say that there is an attempt to approach one of the things that music does better than any other artistic form, and that literature of course does not normally do. Sometimes you are listening to a concert and there is a theme, a melody, that at first appears played only by the piano and then, a while later, reappears, this time played with slight variations by the violins, and then by the whole orchestra, at which point you feel a moment of recognition. Even though you might have heard it the first, second, third times, the repetition might be exact or not, but it's something that proves very moving, as long as the melody is lovely. So in my last few novels I've been trying to make that exist, taking my cue from what music does').

[102] *Desde que te vi morir*, p. 133; *Lolita*, p. 71.

even. And then, Lolita, Lolita, Lolita. Repeat till the page is full, printer').[103] The final two sentences here translated actually occur in chapter twenty-six, whereas Humbert's destruction of the letters occurs three chapters earlier. By bringing together the two passages, Marías hints at the fulfilment of Humbert's schemes and the depth of his obsession. In the retelling, it is as if Humbert were anticipating the repeated consummations of his relationship with his girl-bride. When the moment comes to describe their first tryst in the Enchanted Hunters Hotel, Marías again conflates and translates sentences from two distinct chapters: '*A las seis de la mañana despertaron del todo ambos, a las seis de la mañana ya eran amantes. A partir de ahora Humbert debe andar con tiento, debe hablar en un susurro*'.[104] His conflation captures the essence of Humbert's shame, while sparing the reader his boasts about the sexual conquest itself.

From these heights of happiness, the descent to final misery and ruin is slow and painful. Humbert realizes that his only hope of keeping Lolita at his side is by terrorizing and enslaving her. His devastatingly matter-of-fact admission that once she had realized her mother was dead is translated and rendered as 'Al día siguiente Lolita, mi pecado, insistió en llamar a su madre, y Humbert tuvo que hablarle por fin de su muerte. Y entonces, *¿comprenden ustedes?, Lo no tenía absolutamente ningún sitio a donde ir*' ('Next day Lolita, my sin, insisted on calling her mother, and Humbert had finally to admit that she was dead. And then, you see, Lo had absolutely nowhere else to go'). Sparing the reader Humbert's account of her anger followed by her submission, out of fear and desperation, to a sexual reconciliation: 'At the hotel we had separate rooms, but in the middle of the night she came sobbing into mine, and we made it up very gently. You see, she had absolutely nowhere else to go'.[105] Marías traces with great economy their journey across America, a journey that, as he observes in his prologue to the retelling, 'ha inventado una América—la de moteles y carreteras—de la que aún se nutre buena parte de la narrativa americana contemporánea' ('has invented a version of America—that of motels and freeways—on which a good part of contemporary North American fiction still feeds').[106] Faced with the wide range of activities from which he

---

[103] *Desde que te vi morir*, p. 133. Marías has either misremembered the precise details of the retrieval of the letters or, as is more likely, changed the text for artistic effect. The original English has 'a pretty child in a dirty pink frock' hand them back to Humbert: *Lolita*, p. 104. The original instruction to the 'tipógrafo' reads 'Repeat till the page is full, printer': *Lolita*, p. 116.

[104] *Desde que te vi morir*, p. 134. The original English passages read 'but by six she was wide awake, and by six fifteen we were technically lovers': *Lolita*, p. 140; 'I have to tread carefully. I have to speak in a whisper': *Lolita*, p. 142.

[105] *Lolita*, p. 150.     [106] *Desde que te vi morir*, p. 130.

could choose to render their journey—sun-splashed afternoons playing tennis, visits to National Parks, stays in teepees, trysts in the backseat of the car—he instead emphasizes the confines and sordidness of that American motel landscape: 'ruido de camiones y empleados negligentes, habitaciones sin decorar, toallas ajadas y cisternas anémicas'.[107] Such details have direct textual equivalents but do not appear together at any point; the fact that he is not translating directly, but rather offering an impressionistic summary of the journey, shows his desire to reach the underlying melancholy of this itinerant peregrination across America.

Once Lolita has escaped his clutches and disappeared with Quilty, Humbert is left, like Marías's narrators, to survey the ruin of what once was, incapable of changing the past, and left only to contemplate it through the lens of language. The broken, down-trodden Lolita Humbert encounters in her marital home several years afterwards is just such a moment and Marías's selection of telling detail again captures the deep sense of loss that permeates the description:

> *Qué madura, qué desconocida la sombría división entre los pechos pálidos de Lolita, mi alma, cuando se inclinó un momento. Aun así, pese a sus diecisiete años, quiero que te vengas a vivir conmigo, que mueras conmigo, que lo hagas todo conmigo.*[108]

> (How womanish and never seen before was the shadowy division between Lolita's pale breasts, my soul, when she bent down for a moment. Even so, despite her seventeen years, I want you to come to live with me, and die with me, and everything with me.)

The switch into Humbert's voice, from pained observation to his heartfelt plea, is extremely affecting.

In one passage 'La novela más melancólica' betrays how much the text has been suffused by Marías's other reading of Nabokov: 'Con la vida sedentaria, con una percepción más fuerte de lo que se llama "realidad", la capacidad de aterrorizar de Humbert disminuyó pero no su amor ni su deseo (la niña seguía siendo nínfula: chupaba los lápices)' ('With sedentary life, and its greater grounding in so-called "reality", came a diminution of Humbert's capacity to frighten his charge, which was not matched by a fall in either his love or his lust [the girl continued to be a nymphet: she used to suck on pencils]').[109] Marías's reference to 'realidad' has no

---

[107] *Desde que te vi morir*, p. 134.
[108] The original English reads, 'How womanish and somehow never seen that way before was the shadowy division between her pale breasts when she bent down over the man's hand!'; '"I want you to leave your incidental Dick, and this awful hole, and come to live with me, and die with me, and everything with me" (words to that effect).' *Lolita*, pp. 290, 295.
[109] *Desde que te vi morir*, p. 135.

textual equivalent in *Lolita* but must come instead from Nabokov's repeated refusal in interviews to acknowledge that there is any such thing as objective reality: 'there is an average reality, perceived by all of us, but it is not true reality: it is only the reality of general ideas, conventional forms of humdrummery, current editorials'.[110] He reminds his interviewers that the perceived world is little more than a group of interacting subjectivities. Marías's qualification of the term is no doubt a nod towards a shared aesthetic standpoint—that there is nothing so fragile as human perception.

Evidence that his own artistic predilections govern selection of detail from Humbert's account comes in the following excerpt: quoted first is the original Nabokov, followed by Marías's paraphrase.

> Up to the end of 1949, I cherished and adored, and stained with my kisses and merman tears, a pair of old sneakers, a boy's shirt she had worn, some ancient blue jeans I found in the trunk compartment, a crumpled school cap, suchlike wanton treasures.[111]

> Regresó a Beardsley, contrató a un detective inútil, *acarició y besó unos zapatos de goma y unos vaqueros usados por ella, hallados un día en el maletero del coche. Tesoros fútiles.*[112]

> (He returned to Beardsley, hired an imbecilic detective,[113] cherished and kissed a pair of old sneakers and some ancient blue jeans of hers found one day in the trunk compartment of the car. Wanton treasures.)

Marías's interest in the physical objects accumulated during a person's existence, objects that concertina time and become laden with associations has long been a feature of his writing. The sentimental response to physical objects had been a characteristic of Noguer/Noriega/Navarro in *EHS*. He could not face being in the same house as his ex-wife's possessions and planned to have a bonfire of them shortly after her death. Víctor Francés thinks Marta's thoughts as she lies dying in *MBPM*. He imagines her wondering what will become of her possessions if she dies, investing the objects with the life they gain by virtue of their association with a private, idiosyncratic world:

> No tiene sentido que mis faldas permanezcan vivas en esa silla si yo ya no voy a ponérmelas, o mis libros respirando en las estanterías si yo ya no voy a mirarlos, mis pendientes y collares y anillos esperando en su caja el turno que nunca les llegaría.[114]

> (It doesn't make sense that my skirts should remain alive on that chair if I'm not going to put them on again, or that my books should continue to

[110] *Strong Opinions*, p. 118.     [111] *Lolita*, p. 270.
[112] *Desde que te vi morir*, p. 136.     [113] *Lolita*, p. 269.
[114] *MBPM*, p. 46.

breathe on the shelves if I'm not going to look at them any more, my ear-
rings and necklaces and rings waiting in their box for their turn which will
never come)[115]

'La novela más melancólica' ends with reference to yet another such physical object that Humbert hopes will survive into the future to provide
testimony to lives now lost—the text itself. Marías's translation beautifully captures the melancholy wistfulness of Humbert's final words to the
reader:

> *Ninguno de los dos vivirá cuando el lector abra este libro. Pero mientras palpite*
> *la sangre en mi mano que escribe, tú y yo seremos parte de la bendita materia y*
> *aún podré hablarte.* Lolita, luz de mi vida, fuego de mis entrañas, mi pecado,
> mi alma.[116]

(Neither of us will be alive when the reader opens this book. But while the
blood still throbs through my writing hand, you and I will be a part of
blessed matter, and I will still be able to talk to you. Lolita, light of my life,
fire of my loins, my sin, my soul.)

## 'MIENTRAS ELLAS DUERMEN' AS PALIMPSEST

Given that Marías has maintained that one of his reasons for translating
Browne into Spanish was to make available to his readers a set of works
from which he had drawn inspiration, we might well ask whether he
intended his retelling of *Lolita* to fulfil a similar purpose. There can be
little doubt that his short story 'Mientras ellas duermen' draws on and
pays homage to Nabokov's novel, such that it becomes a palimpsest of the
earlier text.

'Mientras ellas duermen' is narrated by its anonymous protagonist, a
married man from Madrid who, during the time covered by the story, is
holidaying in Menorca with his wife Luisa. The two of them become
intrigued by the eccentric behaviour of two fellow holidaymakers, a couple consisting of a middle-aged and overweight man and his beautiful
young 'novia'. While the latter suns every inch of her body with what
seems disproportionate attention to detail, her husband spends his time
filming that same body with obsessive assiduity and regularity:

[115] *Tomorrow in the Battle Think on Me*, p. 28.
[116] *Desde que te vi morir*, p. 137. The original English reads 'Thus neither of us is alive
when the reader opens this book. But while the blood still throbs through my writing
hand, you are still as much part of blessed matter as I am, and I can still talk to you from
here to Alaska': *Lolita*, p. 327.

él no cesaba de dar vueltas a su alrededor para filmarla incansablemente, se empinaba, se retorcía, se tiraba por tierra, boca arriba y boca abajo, le hacía planos generales, planos americanos, primeros planos, travellings y panorámicas, picados y contrapicados, la tomaba de frente, de costado y de espaldas.[117]

(he never ceased circling her, tirelessly filming her: he would stand on tiptoe, bend double, lie on the ground, face up and face down, take pan shots, medium shots, close-ups, tracking shots and panoramic shots, from above and from below, full face, from the side, from behind.)[118]

This morbidly fascinating spectacle proves irresistible for the narrator and his wife who comment on the man's relentless attention to detail. Our narrator is, however, short-sighted and because he refuses to wear either glasses or contact lenses on the beach—a combination of vanity and practicality—must observe the strange pair through the mesh of his straw hat: the ingenious device has much the same effect as his glasses, he claims. When he later meets Alberto Viana, as the voyeur is called, this screening tool gains retrospective connotations of a barrier to the full horror of the spectacle he has been witnessing. Viana seen close up without the aid of this filter turns out to be a more sinister individual than the narrator could have imagined and the scales well and truly fall from his eyes.

The two men meet late one night at the hotel where they are both staying with their partners. While the latter sleep upstairs—hence the title of the story—our narrator, suffering from insomnia, spots Viana sitting in a lounger next to the swimming pool and decides to satisfy his curiosity about this most eccentric of men. They strike up a conversation during which Viana explains that his reason for filming his girlfriend, Inés, so often and so assiduously is that he wants to be sure to have a complete record of her final day of life. The narrator is confused by such behaviour: Inés is still young and, according to her husband, not in ill health. And yet, Viana maintains that in all certainty she will predecease him. It emerges that his 'adoración' for her does not fit within the normal parameters of such feelings and the background to their relationship is similarly unconventional.

It is at this point that the Nabokovian parallels emerge. Earlier in the story, the narrator had described Inés's attractions in the following terms: 'Era la belleza en la que piensan los niños, que es casi siempre (excepto en los ya desviados) una belleza pulcra, sin ninguna arista, en reposo, mansa, privada de gestos, de piel muy blanca y pecho muy grande' ('It's what

[117] JM, 'Mientras ellas duermen', in *MED*, pp. 175–208 (p. 183).
[118] JM, 'While the Women Are Sleeping', in *While the Women Are Sleeping*, pp. 1–30 (p. 7).

children think of a beauty and which is almost always (unless the children are already deviants) an immaculate beauty, unmarked, in repose, docile, gestureless, with very white skin and large breasts').[119] The passing allusion to aberrant sexual desire, placed there as an apparently inconsequential remark, turns out to have been anything but gratuitous. Viana is a Humbertian echo, a lover of nymphets. He met Inés, the daughter of friends, when she was just seven years old and decided there and then that he would make her his own. In order to win his prize, he, like Humbert, went through the same chillingly calculated process of self-education in the ways of a young girl's mind: 'Durante ese año el cuarentón y cultivado Humbert fue al cine doscientas veces, compró muchos refrescos, helados, chicles, pulseras, tebeos. Hasta leyó un libro titulado *Conoce a tu propia hija*' ('In the course of that year, forty-something, cultured Humbert went to the cinema some two hundred times, bought countless sodas, ice creams, sticks of gum, bracelets, comics. He even read a book entitled *Know Your Own Daughter*').[120] Except that Marías captures with great economy Humbert's sense that such childish activities are beneath him: the adjectives 'cuarentón y cultivado' jar with the list of items he must buy to sate Lolita's need for entertainment he regards as no more than trash— 'refrescos, helados, chicles, pulseras, tebeos'. Viana on the other hand took to the task with relish; he even calls it 'la preparación del espíritu' ('preparing myself spiritually'): 'escuchando discos de los que ella oía, aprendiendo juegos, viendo mucha televisión, programas de tarde y todos los anuncios de todos los años, me sé las canciones' ('listening to the same records she listened to, learning games, watching loads of TV, children's programmes and years of ads, I know all the jingles by heart'). He too read comics, moving on to adventure novels, romantic fiction, 'literatura española cuando le tocó estudiarla' ('Spanish literature when she was studying that at school'), in step with the development of the young girl's mind, despite being in his late thirties when he first met her:[121] 'he llevado durante todos estos años una existencia infantil paralela a la mía' ('all these years I've led a parallel existence to my own').[122] He even proved himself more careful and restrained in his preparations than Humbert: while the latter would satisfy his lusts on the 'busconas aniñadas' ('prostitutes who retained a childish something') he encountered in Paris brothels, Viana spent all those years 'evitando mujeres, evitando contagios' ('avoiding other women, avoiding diseases'), a twisted version of the groom who

---

[119] 'Mientras ellas duermen', pp. 181–2; 'While the Women Are Sleeping', p. 5.
[120] *Desde que te vi morir*, p. 135.
[121] 'Mientras ellas duermen', p. 200; 'While the Women Are Sleeping', p. 21.
[122] 'Mientras ellas duermen', p. 201; 'While the Women Are Sleeping', p. 22.

saves his virginity until marriage.[123] And yet, both men had to confront the threat posed by other men and boys of their girl-bride's own age: Viana feared the 'niños que las cortejan, niños absurdos que quieren jugar a mayores desde muy temprano. No se controlan y pueden hacerles daño' ('boys chasing after them, absurd boys who want to play at being adults from early on. They lack self-control and can cause the girls great harm').[124] Whereas Marías writes of Humbert 'hay que vigilar, a los tipos de las estaciones, a los dueños de automóviles lujosos, a los heladeros, a los jovenzuelos tostados junto a piscinas azuladas' ('he must keep an eagle eye on all around him, on garage fellows, owners of luxury cars, ice cream parlor employees, bronzed youths next to blued pools');[125] a good example of Nabokov's 'amor al detalle que sobresalta y al adjetivo impensado y oblicuo'. The original English reads 'garage fellows, hotel pages, vacationists, goons in luxurious cars, maroon morons near blued pools'.[126] 'Maroon' is perhaps as equally unexpected as 'tostados'.

The late-night dialogue between the two men is superbly realized and unsettling not just for the content of the discussion but also because of another, artfully placed detail. While the two men are still discussing Viana's eccentric filming habits and before the conversation has reached the revelations about how he wooed Inés, he dips his silk-socked toe into the water of the swimming pool: 'había mojado el pulgar de su calcetín en el agua, la agitaba de un lado a otro con su pulgar, lentamente' ('He had stretched out his stockinged foot and dipped his big toe into the water, moving it slowly back and forth').[127] At this juncture of the dialogue, the narrator is still wondering whether or not to return to the sleeping Luisa upstairs—'Dudé si despedirme y regresar a la habitación' ('I considered saying goodnight and going up to my room').[128] His lack of tiredness and unwillingness to wake his wife keep him at Viana's side. But the toe dipped in the water begins to act as a synecdoche for the morbid fascination that Viana is exerting over him: he finds himself 'mirando el pie', and follows its movement with his eyes—'había sacado el calcetín del agua y lo había posado de nuevo mojado y oscurecido en la planta, sobre la hierba' ('now he had removed his foot from the water and placed it again—with the tip of the sock wet and dark—on the grass').[129] And sure enough, the damp sock will only get wetter and less comfortable while the narrator will be

---

[123] 'Mientras ellas duermen', pp. 200–1; 'While the Women Are Sleeping', p. 22.
[124] 'Mientras ellas duermen', p. 199; 'While the Women Are Sleeping', p. 21.
[125] *Desde que te vi morir*, pp. 134–5.
[126] *Lolita*, p. 168.
[127] 'Mientras ellas duermen', p. 192; 'While the Women Are Sleeping', p. 16.
[128] 'Mientras ellas duermen', p. 193; 'While the Women Are Sleeping', p. 17.
[129] 'Mientras ellas duermen', p. 193; 'While the Women Are Sleeping', p. 17.

figuratively inundated with information that he did not want to know
but which he cannot quickly forget: 'Viana rió de nuevo y, estirando otra
vez la pierna, ahora metió el pie encalcetinado entero en el agua y volvía a
agitarla lentamente, pesadamente, más pesadamente que antes porque
ahora era el pie entero—el pie gordo y seboso—lo que estaba sumergido'
('Viana laughed again and, stretching his leg out still further, dipped his
whole stockinged foot into the water this time and began to move it
slowly, heavily around, more heavily than before because now his whole
foot—that fat, obese foot—was submerged').[130] Viana eventually removes
his drenched sock and places it over the back of the lounger where he is
lying. The narrator communicates to the reader the disgust he too experienced by engaging four of the five senses in the revolting description.
First, touch:—'Lo sostuvo entre los dedos unos segundos, con asco' ('he
held it, still distastefully, between two fingers'); then sound—'lo dejó col-
gado del respaldo de su tumbona, desde donde empezó a gotear' ('[he]
draped it over the back of his lounger, where it began to drip'); smell—'el
olor de la tela tras pasar por el agua' ('the smell of wet cloth'); and sight—
'A duras penas podía yo apartar la vista de aquello' ('I found it hard to
look away from the former').[131] This detail complements and conveys the
narrator's squirming unease in Viana's presence. The latter, it transpires, is
another of Marías's 'sentimental' male characters, men whose obsessive
and selfish hold over the women they love goes well beyond the boundaries of natural affection. His most obvious precedent is Manur from *EHS*,
who had enslaved his wife Natalia in the hope that she would one day
return his love. When she leaves him for el León de Nápoles, he shoots
himself in the lung, dying slowly and painfully over the following two
weeks.

And yet, Viana is more sinister even than that. Marías has said that
when writing *EHS* he had been toying with the idea that love is 'el sentimiento que exige mayores dosis de imaginación' ('the feeling that
demands the largest doses of imagination'), that it exists as much as an
imagined or anticipated state than in any more tangible form.[132] The danger with such 'hombres sentimentales' ('men of feeling') is that the 'love'
they experience robs them of the ability to empathize with their loved one
to such an extent that the latter becomes no more than a projection of
themselves to be treated as they wish. Hence why Manur is able to live
alongside a woman who despises him in the hope that one day she will
reciprocate his affection. When that hope is gone, it is he who suffers, not

[130] 'Mientras ellas duermen', p. 196; 'While the Women Are Sleeping', p. 18.
[131] 'Mientras ellas duermen', pp. 198–9; 'While the Women Are Sleeping', p. 20.
[132] JM, 'Lo que no se ha cumplido', in *LF*, pp. 79–82 (p. 80).

her. Viana will ensure that Inés dies before he does—and wants, more-over, to have a perfect record of her final day of life—because he can anticipate the time when the image of her that he cherishes in his mind's eye will no longer bear comparison with the reality. He anticipates mur-dering her in the near future because he has noticed her increasing discon-tent with the life they lead: she misses the parental relationship that her decision to accept Viana destroyed, and wants to see what a life after him would be like. But Viana, unlike most human beings—'lo normal es que la gente crea desear lo que le va llegando naturalmente'—and full of Nietzschean will to power, has already decided what form his life will take: he will not countenance Inés dying by any other means than at his hand.

Viana taunts the narrator with the fact that, were the latter to go to the police with the story of Viana's intentions, he is unlikely to be believed. The importance of the story's scenario stares both narrator and reader in the face when they realize that the two men will leave Menorca for their homes, in all likelihood never to meet again. Constantino Bértolo calls the tone of the dénouement 'una desolación no sentimentalista llena de eficacia' ('an unsentimentalized desolation full of effectiveness').[133] The uncomfortable, late-night dialogue between narrator and Viana only comes to an end when Luisa comes out onto the balcony of the hotel room to call her husband back inside. An eerie silence surrounds the room in which Inés must be sleeping—'A la terraza de Inés, cualquiera que fuese, no salió sin embargo nadie' ('On Inés' balcony, though, whichever it was, there was no one')—and, as so often in Marías's fiction, the narra-tor becomes the bearer of a disturbing tale that he can only reproduce in all its horror, unsure of or unwilling to fathom its wider meanings.[134]

---

[133] Constantino Bértolo, 'Realismo de almas', *El País*, 22 April 1990, Libros section, p. 5.
[134] 'Mientras ellas duermen', p. 208; 'While the Women Are Sleeping', p. 30.

# 9

## The Culmination of his Art:
### *Tu rostro mañana*

### *TU ROSTRO MAÑANA*: A NOVEL OF OUR TIMES

#### Introduction

In the preceding chapters I have shown how prolonged contact with
Sterne, Browne, and Nabokov has left discernible traces in Marías's articles, short stories, and novels. The time and effort expended rewriting
their works in his own language or, to use his own phrase, 'speaking in
their voices' were clearly not in vain. His claims to their influence upon
him have a refreshing substance to them that sets him apart from the
herd of writers (particularly in the Hispanic world) who are at pains to
'acknowledge' their 'debts' to Faulkner, Henry James, Joyce, or Proust,
seeking to ally themselves with Anglo- or Francophone masters whose
comparison with their own work usually does them a greater disservice
than they imagine. What is clear in Marías's case is that Sterne gave him
a confidence to allow his narrators to digress at leisure; to slow down or
even temporarily suspend the narrative flow in order to pursue reflections of a personal or philosophical nature. It is likewise clear that
Browne's *Hydriotaphia* has supplied him with a vocabulary to discuss
memory, loss, forgetting, and transience. Rewriting Nabokov's *Lolita*, as
we shall see in the second half of this chapter, showed him what could
be achieved by the use of palimpsest—paraphrasing and hybridizing a
text in search of the precise artistic effect he desired. In this final chapter
I will bring this approach to bear on his longest, richest, and most ambitious novel to date, *TRM* (2002–2007). Fundamental to this examination will be two questions that shall be dealt with in the first and second
halves of this chapter. Thus in the first half, I will be examining how the
novel *TRM* addresses and develops thematic concerns that have been
the author's lasting preoccupations throughout his career. I will give an
initial summary of the novel, trace briefly its links with his previous fiction, and draw out the novel's central themes, seeing how they emerge
both explicitly through the narrative voice—what the narrator indicates

are his reasons for sitting down to describe recent events—and implicitly through what he cannot or will not tell us directly. If this last statement appears cryptic, I trust that its meaning will become clearer in the discussion that follows. I will then link the novel to Marías's journalistic output over the period of *TRM*'s gestation in an effort to see the common ground between the two and to understand why a novel should be a fundamentally richer medium in which to explore those shared concerns. In the second half of the chapter I will be asking how translation and palimpsest are employed in the text as a means of building the complex and nuanced character portraits that are among *TRM*'s greatest strengths.

## A Rich Tapestry: Understanding the Narrator

The novel comprises three parts, each one of which was originally published separately with its own title—*Fiebre y lanza* (hence *FL*, 2002), *Baile y sueño* (hence *BS*, 2004), and *Veneno y sombra y adiós* (hence *VSA*, 2007).[1] Together they make up close to 1600 pages. The tripartite structure and individual publication of each volume were largely dictated by the novel's considerable length since the author was reluctant to keep his readers waiting for the years he knew it would take to complete the whole work before publishing it.[2] But he also had a pressing personal reason for so dividing what he has called his best novel, as he was finally able to admit in interviews after the publication of *VSA*.[3] Two of the novel's principal characters were based on men close to him who were, even when he started, well advanced in years. His father, Julián, and the eminent Hispanist, Lusophonist, and former spy, Sir Peter Russell, whom Marías had met in Oxford in the early 1980s, supplied him respectively with the background for Juan Deza, the narrator's father, and Sir Peter Wheeler, the narrator's friend and confidant. Marías asked permission of both men to use their life experiences for the characters and wanted them to be able to read some if not all of the resulting work, hence his decision to issue *TRM* in three instalments. As it transpired, neither lived long enough to read the completed text, though they did see *BS* published: Julián Marías died on 15 December 2005 at the age of 91; Russell passed away on

---

[1] In the present chapter I shall be using the following abbreviations: (*FL/BS/VSA*, page number).

[2] See, for example, Ángeles García, ' "En el hablar y el callar se descubre la esencia de las personas" ', *El País*, 15 September 2002, p. 34; Paka Díaz, ' "Ni hago relaciones ni adulo a nadie" ', *El Semanal*, 20–26 October 2002, pp. 52–6 (p. 52).

[3] Juan Cruz, 'Javier Marías: Escribir para ver', *El País Semanal*, 23 September 2007, pp. 12–20 (p. 20).

22 June 2006, aged 92.[4] As we have already seen, the betrayal Julián Marías suffered in the final months of the Spanish Civil War shaped his son's early life as much as it did his later fiction. His long-standing interest in the knowability of others is no less apparent in *TRM*, where the thematic development of how well we might know those around us is realized more richly than ever before. It also retells his father's betrayal much as that episode had been told in *NET*, though in a fictional framework that increases its artistic resonances and possibilities.

One of the reasons for saying so is that *TRM* is once again narrated by the son of a betrayed father, one who has taken the wrong very much to heart, just as the real-life Marías has done. Jaime/Jacobo/Jacques/Jack/ Iago Deza—his first name varies depending on with whom he is talking, although Jacques is his preferred form[5]—is that son and our narrator. He writes, as Marías's narrators so often do, from an unspecified present moment about the experiences of the last few years, the period of his separation from his wife Luisa Juárez and their two children, Guillermo and Marina. Precisely how long this period is remains unspecified and is by no means easy to determine, although indications in the text suggest that he first separated from his wife three years before sitting down to write. '[P] or no seguir cerca de mi mujer mientras ella se me alejaba' ('so as not to be near her while she was slowly distancing herself from me')[6] is the beautifully balanced and simple antithesis he uses to explain why he felt the need to leave his native Madrid and flee to London following the failure of his marriage:[7] because its understatement hints at a sense of loss with which Deza finds it hard to cope; because it plays on physical proximity and emotional closeness, suggesting that where they had previously gone hand in hand, the lack of the latter now makes the former unbearable. His flight to Britain is a reprise of a former two-year stay in the country, before his marriage, during which he worked as a Spanish lecturer at the University of Oxford. Deza, it transpires, was in fact the unnamed narrator of Marías's earlier novel *TLA*.[8] Deza initially finds a job working for the BBC, producing programming on Spain. He renews his

---

[4] The tripartite division of the novel irked at least one British reviewer: 'the two volumes published so far have no clear intrinsic reason for their separate existence'. See Stephen Mitchelmore, 'The upraised sword', *Times Literary Supplement*, 14 July 2006, p. 23.

[5] *FL*, pp. 309, 329.

[6] *FL*, p. 31.

[7] *Fever and Spear*, p. 18.

[8] Although doubtless worth exploring further, the links between *TLA* and *TRM* will not be the subject of comment in this chapter, largely for reasons of economy. Other than allowing Marías to situate *TRM*'s action once more in the cultured world of Oxford's ageing dons and their pasts pregnant with espionage, the novels are, in my opinion, largely self-contained.

friendship with Wheeler, whom he met while working at Oxford (much as Marías met Russell).[9] Wheeler invites him to a party at his home on the banks of the River Cherwell so that he can introduce him to Bertram Tupra, the man who will become Deza's boss in a shadowy group that works on the fringes of the British intelligence services. The meeting with Tupra, it transpires, had been a form of job interview staged by Wheeler who believes he has found in Deza a potential protégé. Because Deza has a 'don' ('gift'), an—according to Wheeler—increasingly rare ability, the ability to read people's future possibilities, to be able to predict their behaviour in particular circumstances or under certain pressures. Himself a former spy, Wheeler has seen in Deza a potential recruit, a view Tupra comes to share. So it is that Deza finds himself handsomely paid and living alone in London's Dorset Square with at first only occasional 'interpreting' jobs to undertake in the company of either Tupra or one of their colleagues in the mysterious 'edifico sin nombre' ('building with no name') where the group is based.[10] Interpreting here means not only translating from Spanish to English and vice versa when the subject of their investigations is someone of Hispanic extraction but also predicting the future possibilities of that same subject. Deza's narrative, and the novel *TRM*, thus describe the period of his employment under Tupra until his decision to resign and return to Spain, by which time he has achieved a partial reconciliation with Luisa. And by which time he has done far more than submit strangers to stringent analysis. He has also participated in the savage beating of Rafael de la Garza, a hapless cultural attaché at the Spanish embassy who had been present at Wheeler's initial soirée and who later inadvertently butts in on the carefully planned night out with which Tupra is hoping to flatter two married Italian clients. He has also acceded to a request from his Spanish female colleague Pérez Nuix to lie during an interpretation session so as to favour a business associate of her father's. And most unexpectedly of all, he has physically attacked and warned off

---

[9] In the dedication of *TRM* to Sir Peter Russell, Marías mentions his friend's 'long shadow' (*FL*, p. 9; *BS*, p. 9), one it seems that Russell was casting over the author before they had even met. In the dedicated edition of *El siglo* he gave to Russell in December 1983, he wrote 'Para Peter Russell esta novela que sin duda no tiene tan buenas referencias como yo tengo de él. Con gran simpatía y la amistad segura' ('For Peter Russell, this novel that has not received such good notices as I have received of him. With warmest wishes and in certain friendship'), strongly suggesting that it was a gift offered before they had met in person: suggested by the 'referencias...de él' which are the dedicator's only corroboration of an 'amistad segura'. Russell, who had recently retired as Alfonso XIII Professor of Spanish, was away from Oxford teaching in the United States for a large part of Marías's time there. It is intriguing to note that Russell's reputation preceded him to such an extent that Marías should have wanted to offer him a gift of friendship before they had even met.

[10] *FL*, p. 267; *Fever and Spear*, p. 210.

the man who had taken his place at Luisa's side during their separation, an art forger named Custardoy.

As we can see from this brief synopsis, Marías chose to frame Deza's ability in a context that highlights its origins in early life as well as its paradoxically fallible nature. On the one hand, his ability is just the kind of skill the son of a betrayed father might seek to cultivate, while on the other, that ability has failed him in the one relationship that matters to him most—his marriage—the breakdown of which he clearly did not see coming.[11] Once again, Marías explores the unknowability of those closest to us, the suggestion being that—and Deza's case is particularly emblematic of this—our self-esteem, desire to love and be loved are so much at stake in such relationships that all objectivity is impossible: even if we do see troubling signs or presages of disaster we prefer to pretend they were not there. Deza tries to face up to a troubling relativism under which there is no such thing as an objectively benevolent act. He behaves with the best of intentions towards his estranged wife, lending a sympathetic ear on the phone at the end of her long day, sending home generous sums from the pay packets he receives in his new job, only to find her frosty attitude towards him unthawed. He comes to realize that there is little he can do to change that, until such time as she should consent to look once more upon his actions with the kindness she did before their marriage began to founder. As he repeats throughout the novel, he has come to realize that 'el sentimiento se elige o . . . en él se consiente' ('one chooses a feeling or, . . . agrees to it').[12]

This troubling relativism is further explored in a historical context throughout the novel, epitomized by Tupra's observation that 'hasta lo más descabellado e inverosímil tiene su tiempo para ser creído' ('even the craziest, most unlikely things have their moment to be believed').[13] Hence, Andreu Nin, leader of the POUM (Partido Obrero de Unificación Marxista) during the Spanish Civil War, can one day be a hero of the fight against Fascism, the next an untouchable, portrayed as a Nazi stooge and subjected to prolonged torture before death.[14] Or botulin toxin, the drug once used to assassinate the Nazi leader Reinhard Heydrich[15] can sixty years later be the beauty treatment of choice for the idle rich.[16] However,

---

[11] One reviewer wrote that 'His struggles to come to terms with betrayals both personal and historical—his father's traducement in the Spanish Civil War, his wife's indifference, the nature of his own employment, in which he waits for people to give themselves away—leave Deza brooding'. See Tim Martin, 'Smile, or you might ruin your future', *The Independent on Sunday*, ABC section, 5 June 2006, p. 26.

[12] *BS*, p. 234; *Dance and Dream*, p. 191.

[13] *FL*, p. 89; *Fever and Spear*, p. 66.      [14] *FL*, pp. 89–90, 141–50.

[15] *FL*, pp. 282–4.      [16] *BS*, pp. 195–210.

these historical reflections are not gratuitous forays or displays of erudition. Rather they are carefully chosen examples from the hours of conversation Deza shares with his two mentors—Tupra and Wheeler. Tupra it is who mentions Nin during their first conversation, as if issuing Deza with an early warning that even the most preposterous supposition might one day come true: a warning that, in retrospect, Deza realizes he failed to heed. Heydrich comes up in conversation with Wheeler as the latter recounts the botched operation to kill the Nazi leader and the terrible price paid for his death by the inhabitants of Lidice, the Bohemian village where the fatal ambush took place: in revenge for his murder the Nazis killed all the inhabitants and razed it to the ground. Nor are these forays into twentieth-century history gratuitous because they have their correlative in the small story of Deza's failed marriage. He is 'a self-indulgent hostage to the ups and downs of his own broken marriage', as the Scottish novelist and critic Ali Smith eloquently put it.[17] On the evening that Wheeler's phone call alerts him to the impending meeting with Tupra, he is trying to get through to Luisa and his children for one of his regular catch-ups. An engaged tone is all that greets his repeated attempts and he thinks of the life that his family will be leading without him, one in which he was until all too recently an essential element:

> [U]no queda fijado en la tela de araña del escenario y el ritmo que construyó y que parecían imposibles sin su contribución y sin su existencia, largo prisionero de lo presenciado y llevado a cabo tantas veces, y es incapaz de imaginar que se vayan produciendo cambios.[18]

> ([You] remain caught in the web of settings and rhythms that you established and which sheltered you and seemed impossible without your contribution and without your existence, the long-term prisoner of what was seen and done so many times, and you are incapable of imagining any changes.)[19]

When he finally gets through, his cheerless conversation with Luisa leaves him feeling flatter than before. Marías captures beautifully the casual but unconscious cruelty in her explanation for the line being occupied: 'mi hermana me ha tenido una hora al teléfono haciéndole de psiquiatra, está fatal con su marido y ahora me considera experta. Imagínate' ('my sister has had me on the phone playing psychiatrist, she's going through a really rough patch with her husband and she considers me to be an expert on the subject now. Honestly').[20] That others now see her as a woman who

---

[17] Ali Smith, 'Review of *Your Face Tomorrow 2: Dance and Dream*', *The Sunday Telegraph*, section Seven, 23 July 2006, p. 39.
[18] *FL*, p. 44.    [19] *FL*, p. 58; *Fever and Spear*, p. 28.
[20] *Fever and Spear*, p. 40.

has successfully negotiated a marital breakdown throws cold water over
his continued hopes of reconciliation. Just as the fact that she feels no
embarrassment about sharing the information suggests they are at very
different stages on the path towards resigning themselves to a definitive
split. Their brief conversation over, Deza remembers an evening when he
had asked Luisa what seemed then like a silly question—would their son
(their first-born child) always live with them? To which Luisa had replied
that of course he would, provided nothing bad happened to either of
them. The Deza who can predict the future possibilities of total strangers
evidently did not see coming the differences that have driven him apart
from his wife and he is left only to reflect on a state of affairs he failed to
predict:

> Ahora el niño era todavía niño y no vivía con nosotros sino con ella tan sólo,
> y con nuestra niña nueva a la que también habría tocado vivir siempre así,
> con nosotros. Tenía que habernos pasado algo malo, entonces, o quizá no a
> los dos, sino a mí. O bien a ella.[21]

> (Our son was still only a child and he did not live with us, but with her
> alone, and with our daughter, who should also always have lived like that,
> with us. Something bad must have happened, or perhaps not to both of us,
> but only to me. Or to her.)[22]

His nostalgia for the simple stability of the marital home, tinged with
regret that his children will grow up without their father nearby ('Ahora
el niño era todavía niño'), gives Deza's voice an affecting inflection.

And yet, subsequent revelations might leave us wondering whether
Deza's presentation of his predicament is not in part disingenuous. In the
first section of *VSA*, Deza recalls the night on which he slept with his colleague Pérez Nuix, an event that he is assuming gives him something in
common with their boss, Tupra. The delicate negotiations over who will
sleep where on a rainy night when Pérez Nuix has lingered so long at his
flat that it seemed easier if she stayed until morning, cause Deza to reflect
on his reluctance, as he grows older, gallantly to relinquish his own bed
and offer it to a lady:

> Y claro que me importaba, ya no era aquel joven ni solía dormir más que en
> mi propia cama, y llevaba demasiados años acostumbrado a hacerlo sólo al
> lado de Luisa, ni siquiera al de mi breve y estúpida amante que echó a perder
> mucho de lo que había, o de lo atesorado, aunque Luisa nunca supiera de
> ella a ciencia cierta.[23]

> (And of course I did mind, I no longer was that young man nor was I accus-
> tomed to sleeping anywhere but in my own bed, and I spent too many years

---

[21] *FL*, p. 62.       [22] *Fever and Spear*, p. 43.       [23] *VSA*, p. 142.

getting used to sleeping only beside Luisa, not even by the side of the stupid short-lived lover who ruined much of what I had, or what I treasured, even though Luisa never knew for certain about her existence.)[24]

Was his earlier comment thus disingenuous or are we now to see it as an admission of guilt, the 'algo malo' that happened to Luisa, his suspected but never confirmed infidelity? Or is Deza shying away from painful self-scrutiny when it comes to his marriage because that marriage is simply too precious and the suggestion that he has only himself to blame for its failure too close to the bone? Is Deza the epitome of an impulsive philanderer, one who lusts first and worries about the consequences later? As ever with Marías's fiction, we are not told what to believe, merely invited to speculate.

This ambivalent figure is made more complex still through revelations about the origins of his predictive ability—its deep roots in childhood experience and the way his father encouraged him to interact with the world. Among the reasons for his disquiet as his interpretations of complete strangers become more audacious is that he seems to be abusing a skill cultivated from an early age. According to his son's account, Juan Deza raised his children to keep digging, reasoning, thinking in the discussions and arguments they shared, never to content themselves with superficial solutions, and always to look deeper than they might at first think necessary.[25] It is not difficult to imagine that this formidable paternal figure has cast a long shadow over Jacobo. Nor is it difficult to imagine that he has developed his talent for identifying the future possibilities of those around him in a form of self-defence against the treachery his father suffered. Recalling that betrayal committed by the man identified as Del Real, he asks himself a series of searching questions about the years leading up to it:[26]

---

[24] *Poison, Shadow and Farewell*, p. 105.

[25] *FL*, pp. 343–4, 380; *BS*, p. 370; *VSA*, p. 471.

[26] The men responsible for the malicious allegations against Julián Marías are partially identified in the novel. We are told that Del Real, the principal accuser, had co-authored a book of travel narratives in conjunction with Juan Deza (Julián Marías) and a third person before the Civil War. Deza also states that he has the vague recollection that Del Real 'alcanzó la cátedra en alguna Universidad del norte (La Coruña, Oviedo, Santander, Santiago, no lo sé)' (*FL*, pp. 194–5) ('received a chair in some university in the north (La Coruña, Oviedo, Santander, Santiago, I'm not sure)') (*Fever and Spear*, p. 151). From these details it is not difficult to identify Del Real as Carlos Alonso del Real Ramos (1914–1993), who held the Chair in Ancient and Medieval History and Culture at the University of Santiago de Compostela between 1955 and 1981. The book published in conjunction with Julián is the following: Carlos Alonso del Real Ramos, Julián Marías, and Manuel Granell, *Juventud en el mundo antiguo: (crucero universitario por el Mediterráneo)* (Madrid: Espasa, 1934). Javier Marías facilitated the identification of Julio Martínez Santa Olalla as the 'profesor de aquella misma Facultad...de fanatismo reconocido' (*FL*, p. 194) ('lecturer...from

¿Cómo era posible pasar media vida junto a un compañero, un amigo íntimo—
—media vida de la niñez, de pupitre, de la juventud—, sin percatarse de su
naturaleza, o al menos de su naturaleza *posible*?...¿Cómo puede no verse en el
tiempo largo que quien acabará y acaba perdiéndonos nos va a perder?[27]

(How could he have spent half his life with a colleague, a close friend—half
his childhood, his schooldays, his youth—without having so much as an
inkling of his true nature, or, at least, of his *possible* nature?...How can
someone not see, in the long term, that the person who does end up ruining
us will indeed ruin us?)[28]

Deza recalls the occasion on which he had asked his father about Del
Real, wondering how it could be that his suspicions were never aroused:
' "Pero a lo largo de tantos años de trato" había insistido yo, "¿no habías
tenido nunca el menor indicio, ningún recelo, una advertencia interior,
una punzada, un presentimiento, algo?" ' ( ' "But throughout all those
years of knowing each other," I had said, "had you never had the slightest
indication, the slightest moment of doubt, no inner warning, a pang, a
presentiment, something?" ').[29] By framing Deza's ability in this context,
Marías manages to construct a novel in which his narrator's past and
present, public, private, emotional, and intellectual selves are consum-
mately intertwined. In his brief career as a secret service agent, Deza has
learnt a good deal about the flexibility of his own moral boundaries, about
what he is capable of when under duress or when he believes himself to be
acting for the best. Again, the structure of his account highlights the way
in which he might—perhaps ought to—have seen this coming, since
Tupra ends their first interpretation session by asking:

Déjeme preguntarle: ¿hasta qué punto es usted capaz de dejar los principios
de lado? Quiero decir, ¿hasta qué punto suele usted? Prescindir de eso, de la
teoría, ¿verdad? Todos lo hacemos de vez en cuando, o no podríamos vivir:
por conveniencia, por temor, por necesidad. Por sacrificio, por generosidad.
Por amor, por odio. ¿En qué medida suele usted?[30]

---

that same faculty, a man known for his fanaticism') (*Fever and Spear*, p. 151) who also put
his name to the allegations, by publishing the article entitled 'Un poco de memoria
histórica' in *El País Semanal* on the day he was admitted to the Real Academia Española,
27 April 2008. There he reminds readers of an article published in the main newspaper of
*El País* three Sundays before in which Jacinto Antón reported on recent research that had
brought to light the fervent pro-Nazi sympathies of Julio Martínez Santa Olalla, a prominent archaeologist at Madrid's Universidad Complutense during and after the Civil War.
According to this research, during the Second World War, Santa Olalla endeavoured to
help Nazi colleagues substantiate their claims surrounding the existence of an Aryan racial
type. See *LNVD*, pp. 199–201. See also Jacinto Antón, 'Himmler buscó la raza aria en
España', *El País*, 6 April 2008, pp. 44–5.

[27] *FL*, p. 199.    [28] *Fever and Spear*, p. 155.
[29] *FL*, p. 204; *Fever and Spear*, p. 159.    [30] *FL*, p. 258.

(Allow me to ask you a question: up to what point do you usually do so? That is, disregard it, theory I mean? It's something we all do now and then; we couldn't live otherwise, whether out of convenience, fear or need. Or out of a sense of sacrifice or generosity. Out of love, out of hate. To what extent do you?)[31]

His reply—'Puedo dejarlos bastante de lado, para opinar en una conver-sación. Algo menos, para juzgar. Para juzgar a amigos, mucho más, soy parcial. Para obrar, mucho menos, creo yo' ('I can leave them aside almost entirely if it's just in the interests of conversation, less if I'm called on to make a judgement. Still less if I'm judging friends, because then I'm par-tial. When it comes to taking action, hardly at all')—turns out to be wrong in one important respect:[32] he can and does leave his principles to one side when it comes to taking action. Hence, it is this period that he has sat down to describe: the strong suspicion being that he wishes to lay the immediate past to rest, just as the narrators of all of Marías's novels since *EHS* are evidently trying to do. However, although the accounts given by 'el León de Nápoles' (*EHS*), Juan Ranz (*CTB*), or Víctor Francés (*MBPM*) turn on pressing moral issues, those narrators write them with the detached air of those who believe they have acted for the best, or at least limited the potential damage of their actions. 'El León' has con-ducted an affair with Natalia Manur, one that leads directly to her hus-band's suicide. And yet, Manur's death does not weigh heavily on his conscience since the Belgian banker had held Natalia captive in a forced and loveless marriage for many years. Juan Ranz must confront the fact that his father is a murderer and, though he obviously finds the knowl-edge troubling, the crime is not his and all he can do is put it behind him. Víctor Francés has tried hard to do right by the family of Marta Téllez, the woman who died in his arms as they were about to consummate their extramarital affair. Again, he discovers that his actions have inadvertently led to the death of Marta's husband's lover, a woman who had tried to tie him to her with bonds of guilt by claiming to go through the trauma of an abortion for his benefit. When he discovers her deceit, he tries to throt-tle her, causing her to flee the bus on which they are travelling and run straight into the oncoming traffic, dying instantly. Marta's husband dis-covers soon after that he has lost both of the women in his life in a matter of hours. Had he known that Marta was dead, he might have looked more benevolently on his lover's attempted duplicity. Víctor can only contem-plate the horrific interconnectedness and randomness of a cruel universe,

---

[31] *Fever and Spear*, p. 204.
[32] *FL*, p. 259; *Fever and Spear*, p. 204.

but still knows that he could have done no more than what he did. Deza's situation is altogether different: he knows he has done wrong.

Critics have long remarked on the passivity of Marías's narrators, who are often outwardly successful but emotionally deprived men whose relationship with the world is one of observer to object.[33] Some critics have even gone so far as to suggest that his narrators are voyeurs, submitting women in particular to unflinching and unflattering sexual appraisal.[34] Deza is thus a departure in both of these senses. He is or becomes a man of action, decisively taking matters into his own hands when warning off Custardoy, the art forger who, in his absence, has inveigled his way into Luisa's affections and, he strongly suspects, been beating her. Deza is also a furtive but undoubted voyeur, a trait he displays when spying on the energetic dancer who lives opposite him on the other side of Dorset Square and whose dancing partners often end up sharing his bed.[35] Although Deza claims that 'en principio espiar no es mi estilo' ('spying isn't really my style'), he still keeps binoculars by the window so that he can monitor the dancer's sexual conquests.[36] Confirmation of his disconcertingly puerile interest in women's anatomy comes during the nightclub incident, when he bursts into the ladies' toilets in his frantic search for De la Garza and Flavia Manoia, the errant wife of Tupra's Italian business client. There Deza lingers, enjoying the sight of the startled women hastily pulling up their underwear or giving him what he interprets as appreciative glances.[37] There follows an extended reverie about the perils for a menstruating woman of wearing a short skirt and no knickers.

Among the multiple factors that we must bear in mind when it comes to interpreting Deza's personality is that he appears to have a need for female attention that borders on the pathological. The reader might wonder whether it is just this need that persuaded him to conduct the much-regretted affair that so nearly ends his marriage. And yet, even by his own account, he lacks much real interest in the women he meets, including

---

[33] See, for example, Steenmeijer, 'Javier Marías, columnista: el otro, el mismo', p. 269; Encarnación García de León, 'El narrador en Javier Marías: Metáfora de la mirada de un voyeur literario', *Barcarola: Revista de creación literaria*, 68–9 (2006), 393–412 (pp. 395, 399, 400–2).

[34] Margaret Drabble drew attention to Deza's 'openly sexist [attitudes]' in a review of *VSA*'s English translation. See her 'Spies and Mirrors', *Times Literary Supplement*, 13 November 2009, p. 25.

[35] This aspect of his character was also noted by reviewers. See Sarah Emily Miano, 'The voyeur, the shady businessman and his missus', *The Daily Telegraph*, Arts & Books section, 29 July 2006, p. 9; Tim Martin, 'That shouldn't happen in a disabled loo', *The Independent on Sunday*, ABC section, 23 July 2006, p. 26.

[36] *FL*, p. 55; *BS*, p. 40; *Fever and Spear*, p. 37; *Dance and Dream*, p. 24.

[37] *BS*, p. 137.

those he sleeps with. As he describes the night Pérez Nuix spent at his flat, he rails against the social niceties and inane rituals that surround one-night stands. Above all, what he cannot abide is that once he and his fleeting lover have had sex she often wants to linger, spend the night, prepare breakfast, perhaps see him again a few days later. A long sequence of his grievances pour out in sentences beginning 'Sí, me ha fastidiado…Me ha irritado…Me ha sublevado…Me ha airado…Y me ha reventado…Pero lo que más me ha enfurecido' ('Yes, it's often bothered me…I've found it irritating…It has infuriated me…It has angered me…And it's really riled me…However, what has most enraged me').[38] Some might see in this combination of sexual predation that dwindles into scorn as soon as the sex act is complete misogyny in its purest form.

## The Novel as Moral Enquiry

To return to our point of departure—the suggestion that *TRM* is a novel that deals in pressing moral issues, the slippery boundaries between right and wrong—it stems above all from Deza's decisions to intervene, to act, to use violence to achieve his aims. Those decisions take the novel into ethical territory that Marías has never entered in the same way before.[39] Deza's involvement in an escalating spiral of violence is finally ended by the realization that his interpretation of the circumstances in which an ageing popstar (identified here only as Dick Dearlove) would be capable of murder, have been used to set a deadly honey trap: deadly that is for the young man used as bait, not for Dearlove, who has proved Deza's suppositions to be correct. It had been his contention that Dearlove would only be capable of murder if it were to protect his memory and public reputation. He sees that Dearlove's tastes extend to the illegal end of the sexual spectrum. Hence he suggests that were Dearlove to find himself the victim of—for example—a honey trap baited with a youngster below the age of consent, he would be capable of killing those who had conspired against him in order to avoid going down in history as a deviant.[40] It is only when

---

[38] *VSA*, pp. 58–9; *Poison, Shadow and Farewell*, pp. 39–40.

[39] In her review of the English translation of volume two of the novel, Ali Smith called it 'an intellectual, poetic and moral epic for our time'. See 'Review of *Your Face Tomorrow 2: Dance and Dream*', p. 39.

[40] Some months later when Deza meets Dearlove in person he adds the proviso that the ageing star might actually kill precisely so that he can be remembered for the awful deed, fearful as he is that his music might not be good enough to have secured his immortality in the popular imagination. Deza (and Marías) have fun inventing ludicrous song titles for the hits of this grotesque individual—'Peanuts from Heaven' and 'Bouncing Bowels' the two mentioned (*VSA*, p. 245)—reinforcing the idea that Dearlove is not destined for music's hall of fame.

Deza reads in the British press the account of a young man's death at Dearlove's hand that the penny drops, and he realizes that the webs of supposition and prediction he has been weaving 'llevan consigo no sólo una carga ética, sino también una responsabilidad moral' ('carry with them not only an ethical charge, but also a moral responsibility'), as David Herzberger suggests.[41]

Marías drew attention to this particular aspect of Deza's psychology in a 2010 interview:

> Lo que me interesa a mí es observar que haber sido violento le causa menos pesar de haber causado involuntariamente una muerte. Hay una frase en la novela: "Nunca hay repugnancia hacia uno mismo, eso es lo que nos permite hacer todo, según nos vamos acostumbrando a las ideas que nos surgen". Bueno, lo que uno decide hacer, aunque sea algo que uno reprueba, es más fácil de aceptar y asumir que las cosas que suceden por causa de uno sin que uno lo quiera.... Lo que le pasa a Jacobo Deza no es natural: de hecho, la capacidad de las personas para justificarse por cualquier descuido, negligencia o *careless talk* es extraordinaria. Y la novela hace hincapié en lo contrario: precisamente lo que se hizo por descuido, por negligencia o *careless talk* es lo que menos se puede perdonar Jacobo Deza.[42]

> (What I'm interested in observing is that having used violence troubles him less than having involuntarily caused someone's death. There is a sentence in the novel: 'You never feel disgust towards yourself and, as we come round to the ideas that occur to us, that lack of disgust allows us to do absolutely anything.' Well, what you decide to do, although it may be something you disapprove of, is easier to accept and come to terms with than the things that happen because of you and without your wanting them to.... What happens to Deza is entirely natural: in fact, people's capacity to excuse themselves any kind of oversight, negligence, or *careless talk* is extraordinary. And my novel lays the emphasis on the exact opposite: what came about because of an oversight, negligence, or *careless talk* is precisely what Jacobo Deza can least forgive himself.)

Deza's behaviour runs contrary to what the author perceives as a human tendency to hide behind plausible denial or the defence that one's actions have had unforeseeable consequences. Rather than claim that he could not have predicted how his interpretation of Dearlove would be used, Deza finds the fact that his words have helped to plot a murder unbearable.

[41] David K. Herzberger, 'La autoridad transformadora de la narración en *Tu rostro mañana*', in *Allí donde uno diría que ya no puede haber nada: Tu rostro mañana de Javier Marías*, ed. by Maarten Steenmeijer and Alexis Grohmann, Foro Hispánico, 35 (Amsterdam: Rodopi, 2009), pp. 189–201 (p. 194).

[42] Juan Gabriel Vásquez, 'Los rostros y el tiempo: Entrevista con Javier Marías', *Letras libres*, 105 (2010), 46–54 (p. 49).

The explanation is best found in the dialogue with his father Juan that immediately precedes news of Dearlove's arrest.

*TRM* offers portraits of several contrasting mentors (Wheeler, Juan Deza, even Tupra), among whom the narrator's father stands for a moral rectitude which looms large in his son's outlook. Not only has Deza realized that he put to shameful use the deductive powers his father helped to foster, Dearlove's death means that he will also fail to match the latter's ethical summation of his life, delivered during their final conversation together shortly before Juan Deza's death. His son asks him why he has kept for so many years the handgun he was thankfully never called upon to use during the Civil War. His father's reply is that the experience of wartime remained so vivid in his memory that the possibility of its return could never seem unreal enough for him to divest himself of the gun with comfort.[43] Juan further wonders whether, had his wife and children been in grave danger, he might have been able to wield it in their defence. Although until now his words offer Deza a retrospective justification for the beating he has just delivered to Custardoy, what Juan gives with one hand he unwittingly takes away with the other. What he is most proud of, he claims, is that 'nadie haya muerto nunca por lo que haya dicho o contado' ('no one ever died because of something I said or reported').[44] Having himself been accused by cowardly academic rivals—men who wanted others to do the dirty work of dispatching him because they had not the courage to do it themselves—it is not surprising that he holds those who act only as instigators in the deepest contempt. But his judgement sits heavily on his son's conscience and Deza knows that, however unintentionally, he has come to resemble the loathed creature that lurked on the fringes of his imagination as a child—the informer. The question that continues to burn in his mind is how much that 'unintentionally' in fact absolves him of blame. If he could see Dearlove's future possibilities written in his expression, gestures, and speech patterns, why could he not do the same when it came to assessing the threat posed by Tupra? Juan Deza's pride in never having caused a death through 'careless talk' also helps the reader to see why it was that the narrator gives so prominent a place in his account to the search for information on the fate of Nin: the POUM leader is said to have resisted the best efforts of his inhuman torturers and divulged no information that could have implicated his comrades.

An added reason for suggesting that the novel takes us into territory where morality is to the fore is that Deza's account reads like the confes-

---

[43] *VSA*, pp. 519–20.
[44] *VSA*, p. 521; *Poison, Shadow and Farewell*, p. 402.

sion of a guilty man. It even begins with what Grohmann has rightly
~~described~~ as an admonition:[45] 'No debería uno contar nunca nada, ni dar
datos ni aportar historias' ('One should never tell anyone anything or give
information or pass on stories').[46] That admonition is moreover a reworking of separate but almost identically worded pieces of advice from his
two prominent mentors—Wheeler[47] and his father.[48] Perhaps the most
curious but telling indication of Deza's uneasy conscience is the fact that
he uses the alias Dick Dearlove instead of the ageing popstar's real name,
explaining that he has just picked out a pseudonym from the batches of
files he seen in the cabinets of the nameless building.[49] This is an odd
move if, as seems likely, his intention is that his words should never fall
beneath anyone's gaze but his own. We have to surmise this anyway
because Deza makes it abundantly clear that his wife must never find out
why her relationship with Custardoy ended so abruptly: she would never
forgive Deza for that kind of paternalistic interference in her life. With
that in mind and given that he describes in painstaking detail how he first
threatened Custardoy with a gun then mangled his hand with repeated
blows of a poker, his intention must be for his account never to see the
light of day. Were it to be found it would certainly scupper his recent
marital reconciliation, something he clearly wishes to avoid, having gone
to so much trouble to win Luisa back. Why then should he change the
name of the ageing popstar? The answer can only be that he fears one day
being implicated in Dearlove's death, that his account is a physical sheaf
of papers that he is afraid might be found. Further corroboration of this
impression is offered by the fact that Deza also claims to have witnessed
'un jefe del Pentágono' ('a Pentagon chief') taking cocaine, adding coyly
'aunque esto no puedo contarlo, quiero decir quién ni dónde ni las circunstancias' ('although I can say no more than that, I mean, who or where
or what the circumstances were').[50] From Marías's viewpoint, Dearlove's
alias performs a pleasing dual function. Firstly, Dick Dearlove is the shortened form of Richard Dearlove, head of MI6 between 1999 and 2004,
and a name that might plausibly be found by an employee making a
search of the organization's records: it adds a neat touch of verisimilitude
for those familiar with Britain's intelligence services. Secondly, and more
salaciously, the popstar is described as possessing a voracious sexual appe-
tite, a 'hipersexualidad o pansexualidad o heptasexualidad' ('hypersexuality
or pansexuality or heptasexuality') that does not discriminate between

---

[45] Alexis Grohmann, 'La literatura como paradoja', in *Allí donde uno diría que ya no
puede haber nada*, pp. 161–9 (p. 161).
[46] *FL*, p. 13; *Fever and Spear*, p. 3.      [47] *FL*, p. 473.      [48] *BS*, p. 305.
[49] *FL*, p. 349; *VSA*, p. 245.      [50] *BS*, p. 269; *Dance and Dream*, p. 221.

sexes or age groups.[51] The name Dick Dearlove could hardly be a more appropriate word play for such a committed sexual athlete.[52]

While the importance of the fact that Deza is actually writing his experiences down may not seem great, it is a departure for Marías. His previous narrators had been evidently putting past experience to bed, and using the act of ordering demanded by writing to do so, but there had been little evidence before that they were writing for an implied audience. Of all of Marías's overtly fictional, first-person narrators, 'el León de Nápoles' is unique in addressing an implied readership, when he assures them that he would be incapable of following Hierónimo Manur's example and killing himself after his own split from Natalia: 'Pero no debéis preocuparos, yo sería incapaz de seguir su ejemplo' ('But don't worry, I would be incapable of following his example').[53] Even the fact that Deza is writing for an audience he does not want to discover his manuscript paradoxically implies that, all the same, they remain in the back of his mind. We find evidence of this during the disco scene in *BS*, where Deza reassures the reader that he will explain in a moment a piece of information he has just given: 'Me irritó ya tantísimo con aquellas pequeñas frases...que pese a haber decidido a la postre responderle en inglés turbio *por lo que diré en seguida*...no pude contenerme' ('These small comments of his so enraged me...that despite my determination to respond to him in obscure English—*for a reason I give below*...I could not control myself').[54]

Deza's sense of guilt is thus at least twofold. He fears public exposure as implicated in the Dearlove scandal and he fears the private retribution of his wife for interfering in her love life during their separation. That sense of guilt has further facets the closer we look at Deza's account. He is at pains to explain his behaviour in England, to ask himself how he could have sunk low enough to stand idly by while his compatriot De la Garza was threatened with a sword, half drowned in a toilet, then smashed repeatedly against metal bars, fracturing his ribs. Marías is not interested in flatly condemning Deza, nor does he wish the reader to do so.

---

[51] *VSA*, p. 248; *Poison, Shadow and Farewell*, p. 189.

[52] The matter of Dearlove's name is complicated somewhat by the rude joke he makes of the fact that the shortened form of his first name 'Richard' is 'Dick' when he meets Deza in Edinburgh: 'Llámame Dick—dijo en seguida—. Todo el mundo me llama así, con buen criterio y mejor tino' (*VSA*, pp. 247–8) ('"Oh, please, call me Dick," he said at once. "Everyone does, and with good reason too"') (*Poison, Shadow and Farewell*, p. 189). From this we must conclude one of three things: either Deza has made the incident up to reinforce his characterization; or he is adapting another rude joke based around Dearlove's name that the singer did make; or his first name was indeed Richard.

[53] *EHS*, p. 180; *The Man of Feeling*, p. 132.

[54] *BS*, p. 91 (my italics); *Dance and Dream*, pp. 67–8.

Condemnation and moral superiority are the kind of knee-jerk responses that do not interest a writer like him who has stated and written repeatedly that he wants his novels to explore areas of human behaviour that remain dark to him. He restated this position at least twice while writing *TRM*, once in March 2002 when nearing the culmination of *FL*, and again in May 2005 when *VSA* was taking shape.[55] The earlier instance came in the form of one of his weekly columns in which he was responding to a survey that indicated that 46 per cent of Spaniards never read so much as a newspaper. Apologizing '[por] ponerme algo solemne y quién sabe si un poco pelma' ('for going all solemn on you and who knows if a bit dull'), he delivered a manifesto for the novel, a genre that remains, he argued, the perfect space in which to explore the following questions:

> ¿Qué nos entristece y por qué lo hace? ¿A qué se debe este llanto, esta emoción, esta vergüenza? ¿Y este amor insoportable, o este odio que me corroe? ¿Por qué me siento aquí ridículo y aquí rechazado, y por qué quiero vengarme? Pero es que además están las contradicciones: ¿por qué admiro tanto al que ansío ver destruido? ¿Por qué me faltaría en el mundo aquel a quien busco borrar de su faz, si lo consiguiera? ¿Por qué mis sentimientos y anhelos ni siquiera son puros, y al mismo tiempo amo y detesto? ¿Y por qué yo vivo y se mueren los otros, por qué no me mato, por qué debo estar seguro de que también me moriré algún día, por qué nadie se salva? ¿Y qué sentido tiene que pasemos por aquí algún tiempo y nos desvivamos por lo que pronto no va a importarnos? ¿Por qué lo pasado nos parece algo fútil siempre, hasta lo más doloroso y triste? ¿Por qué recordamos? ¿Por qué lo olvidamos? ¿Por qué lo uno o lo otro, si no elegimos? Y si no depende de nuestra voluntad, ¿qué es entonces lo decisivo? ¿Por qué percibimos y por qué pensamos?[56]

> (What makes us sad and why does it? What's causing this weeping, this emotion, this shame? And this unbearable love, or this hatred that's consuming me? Why do I feel ridiculous and rejected here, and why do I want to get revenge? But besides them, there are the contradictions: why do I admire so much the person I want to see destroyed? Why, if I succeeded, would I miss the presence in the world of the one person I am trying to wipe from its surface? Why are my feelings and desires not even pure, and why do I love and hate at the same time? And why do I live on while others die, why don't I kill myself, why do I have to be sure that one day I will die, why is no one saved? And what sense is there in our spending a while around here and devoting all our energies to something that soon won't matter to us at all? Why does the past always seem pointless, even its most sad and painful episodes? Why do we remember? Why do we forget? Why the one and not

---

[55] For the 2005 example, see Pittarello, *Entrevistos*, p. 28.
[56] JM, 'Ni como bultos ni como idiotas', in *HMC*, pp. 193–5 (pp. 194–5).

the other, if we don't choose? If our will is not involved, what in that case is the decisive factor? Why do we perceive and why do we think?)

Having reeled off this substantial list of questions that he believes the novel to be the best place to explore, he reiterates that the novel can do precisely that and no more: 'Ojo, no es un lapsus, he dicho preguntas y no respuestas. Estas y muchas más' ('Take note, it's not a lapse on my part, I said questions and not answers. These and many more').[57] Instead of seeking to elicit knee-jerk responses, *TRM* is a gradual exploration of the problem of how to behave morally in the modern world. And the longer one looks at that exploration the richer, more complex, intelligent, and rewarding it becomes.[58]

Of interest here is the question of how much Deza can account retrospectively for his actions and see in hindsight the personal vulnerabilities that were affecting his decisions. How much is the act of writing up those experiences providing him with a clarity of thought that he lacked then? On the face of it, he appears now to have a good understanding of the forces that were acting upon him but is that awareness enough to ensure that he will not err in the same direction again? We might well want to ask whether his entire account is not the first meaningful piece of self-scrutiny ever undertaken by a man of, on the one hand, tremendous culture and, on the other, surprising moral blind spots. That at least is the conclusion reached by the anonymous writer of a report on Deza that the narrator himself finds one day while rummaging in the filing cabinets of the 'edificio sin nombre':

> A veces lo veo como a un enigma. Y a veces creo que él también lo es para sí mismo. Y que no se presta atención porque en realidad ha renunciado a ello, a entenderse. Se considera un caso perdido con el que no ha de malgastar reflexiones. Sabe que no se comprende y que no va a hacerlo. Y así, no se dedica a intentarlo. Creo que no encierra peligro. Pero sí que hay que temerlo.[59]

> (Sometimes he seems to me to be a complete enigma. And sometimes I think he's an enigma to himself. Then I go back to the idea that he doesn't know himself very well. And that he doesn't pay much attention to himself because he's given up understanding himself. He considers himself a lost cause upon whom it would be pointless squandering thought. He knows he

---

[57] 'Ni como bultos ni como idiotas', p. 195.
[58] Jordi Gracia agrees with the fundamental point argued here, idiosyncratically describing *TRM* as 'un póquer de problemas sobre la mesa mejor que…crucigrama con las soluciones halladas' ('a poker game of problems on the table rather than…a crossword with the solutions already written in'). Jordi Gracia, 'Javier Marías o pensar por novelas', *Claves de razón práctica*, 177 (2007), 77–8 (p. 78).
[59] *FL*, p. 347.

doesn't understand himself and that he never will. And so he doesn't waste his time trying to do so. I don't think he's dangerous. But he is to be feared.)[60]

For Marías the report brilliantly solves the significant problem of how to gain an outside perspective on the narrator in a novel narrated exclusively in the first person. In *Lolita*, as we have seen, Nabokov used the framing device of Dr John Ray, Jr's idiotic preface.[61] However, for Deza the report becomes an important touchstone and he has recourse to its insights repeatedly throughout his account and his interpretation of it offers a significant indication as to why he has decided to write up his experiences at all.[62]

What the report gives him is an enticing explanation for his detachment. If he has indeed 'renunciado...a entenderse', that would help to explain how he has allowed himself to be sucked into Tupra's shady world. If he considers himself 'un caso perdido con el que no ha de malgastar reflexiones', what else can he expect of himself but unreflective behaviour? And yet, the reader notices that Deza begins to discuss the report in the past tense, making the following remarks as he tries to explain his failure to stop Tupra's assault on De la Garza: 'ni a mí mismo me veía...era cierto lo que apuntaba aquel texto relativo a mi nombre...nunca me había interesado ni preocupado nada' ('I could not even see myself...because the report about me...was quite right: this had never interested or worried me in the least').[63] Has his view changed? Has he decided that he is worth worrying about after all? As I shall discuss shortly and as touched on briefly above, Deza knows from the breakdown of his marriage that a significant part of belief is made up of the will to believe. How much credence can he legitimately place in the report when he knows that it is telling him something he fervently wants to believe? Because it absolves him of the responsibility to confront his current and past selves, is its conclusion not too intoxicating for comfort?

The examination of his troubled conscience continues as he appears to hint at why the account the reader holds has been written down at all:

Lo que ocurrió, en lo que participé anteanoche en este país que para mí volverá a ser "el otro" algún día, se hará cada vez más brumoso, irreal, sobre todo si no se repite ni yo lo cuento ni insisto, llegará entonces a ser recordado como un mal sueño a lo sumo, y tras todos los sueños siempre puede decirse: "Oh no, yo no quise, no era mi intención, no tuve parte y fui ajeno, yo no elegí, qué voy a hacerle, si aparecieron esa asquerosidad o esa violencia

---

[60] *Fever and Spear*, p. 274.    [61] *Lolita*, p. 5.
[62] *FL*, pp. 345–7; *BS*, pp. 59, 188, 357, 360; *VSA*, pp. 353, 500, 564–5, 609.
[63] *BS*, p. 188; *Dance and Dream*, pp. 150–1.

que yo mismo causo, o que no he impedido…". Eso piensa el iluso y eso pensamos todos y quién no lo ha hecho, de vez en cuando.[64]

(What happened the night before last, and in which I participated, in this country which for me will one day revert to being "other", will become increasingly hazy, unreal, especially if it doesn't happen again or if I don't keep thinking about it, then it will come to be remembered as, at most, a bad dream, and after every dream in which some appalling or violent act occurs, caused by me or which I did nothing to prevent, I can always say: "I didn't want it, that wasn't my intention, I took no part, it had nothing to do with me, I didn't choose it, what can I do about it…" That is what the dreamer thinks and what we all think, and who, from time to time, hasn't done the same?)[65]

The extended self-scrutiny involved in writing down his experiences and weaving a web of their intimate interconnectedness is perhaps the best antidote to any tendency for the past to slip beneath the horizon of his memory. On the night she spends with Deza in his apartment, Pérez Nuix suggests that the blindness he experiences in relation to himself is in fact a trait germane to each of the 'intérpretes de vidas': 'Hasta los más dotados y los más entrenados para ahondar en el prójimo y descifrarlo nos volvemos tuertos y tontos cuando nos miramos' ('Even people like us—gifted and highly trained in examining and deciphering our fellow man—become one-eyed idiots when we make ourselves the object of our studies').[66] The only explanation she can offer is that they suffer from a 'falta de perspectiva' when it comes to themselves. Deza's account could equally be interpreted as an effort to gain precisely that perspective.

I have already stated that his account reads like a confession. What is surprising about this confession is the length of time it takes for the narrator to give any indication of what it is he has done wrong.[67] Not until half way through the second volume (approximately 750 pages into the text), when the attack on De la Garza in the nightclub toilets begins, do we get the first real information on the nature of his transgression. Until this point he has peppered the text with coy hints and indications:

Pero la conciencia no tiene presentes las leyes, ni el sentido común le interesa ni atañe, sólo a cada conciencia su sentido propio, y esa línea tan delgada se difumina a menudo según mi experiencia, y ya no separa nada cuando

---

[64] *BS*, pp. 243–4.    [65] *Dance and Dream*, pp. 198–9.
[66] *VSA*, p. 124; *Poison, Shadow and Farewell*, p. 90.
[67] Fernando Valls was among early critics of the novel to suggest that the action could progress with more urgency. See his 'Interpretar y narrar', *Quimera*, 224–5 (2003), pp. 99–101 (p. 101).

desaparece, así que he aprendido a temer cuanto pasa por el pensamiento e incluso lo que el pensamiento aún ignora, porque he visto casi siempre que todo estaba ahí, en algún sitio, antes de llegar a él, o de atravesarlo. He aprendido a temer, por tanto, no sólo lo que se concibe, la idea, sino lo que la antecede o le es previo. Y así yo soy mi propio dolor y mi fiebre.[68]

(But consciousness knows nothing of the law, and common sense neither interests nor concerns it, each consciousness has its own sense, and that very thin line is, in my experience, often blurred and, once it has disappeared, separated nothing, which is why I have learned to fear anything that passes through the mind and even what the mind does not as yet know, because I have noticed that, in almost every case, everything was already there, somewhere, before it even reached or penetrated the mind. I have therefore learned to fear not only what is thought, the idea, but also what precedes it and comes before. For I am myself my own fever and pain.)[69]

Note the use of the perfect tense—'he aprendido'—to express how recently acquired is the knowledge he describes. He indicates early on that his misdemeanour is connected with 'mi época profesional de Londres' (my time working in London) but resists any immediate temptation to elaborate. Specifically, he bemoans the fact that his handlers—Tupra, Mulryan, Rendl, Pérez Nuix—came to expect too much from him, encouraged him to be too daring in his conclusions. This idea makes its first appearance early in his account, where he is trying to describe his ability to discern people's 'faces tomorrow':

algo parecido a [la adivinación] acabó por esperar mi transitorio jefe, o el hombre que me contrató durante un periodo que se hizo largo, más o menos el de mi separación de Luisa, cuando me volví a Inglaterra por no seguir cerca de mi mujer mientras ella se me alejaba. La gente se comporta de manera idiota con notable frecuencia, con su tendencia a creer en la repetición de lo que la complace: si algo bueno se da una vez, entonces debe acontecer de nuevo, o debe propiciarse al menos.[70]

(something rather similar to [divination] was what came to be expected of me by my temporary boss, the man who contracted me to work for him during a period that seemed to go on for a long time, more or less the same period of time as my separation from my wife, Luisa, when I came back to England, so as not to be near her while she was slowly distancing herself from me. People behave idiotically with remarkable frequency, given their tendency to believe in the repetition of what pleases them: if something good happens once, then it should happen again, or at least tend in that direction.)[71]

The ostensible subject of the musing that begins 'La gente se comporta' is the fact that, just because he passed the original test Tupra and Wheeler

[68] *FL*, p. 30.     [69] *Fever and Spear*, p. 17.     [70] *FL*, p. 31.
[71] *Fever and Spear*, p. 18.

set for him, the former expected him to repeat the performance again and again, when all he felt himself doing was pursuing the merest shadow of a hunch. However, Marías has ensured that Deza's musing forms an ambiguous elision, the implications of which even the narrator may not have appreciated. By implication he upbraids Tupra 'con su tendencia a creer en la repetición de lo que l[o] complace', whilst the remark might equally apply to himself. He expects or fervently hopes for the repetition of Luisa's affection for him; that thing that 'la gente' hopes or expects will repeat itself could, because of the flow of Deza's thought, apply equally to Tupra or to his own relationship. Deza does indeed fervently hope that Luisa will one day take him back and spends long, self-lacerating passages imagining what sort of man has come to usurp his place at her side. As we saw in Chapter 7, his description of himself as 'como nieve sobre los hombros' seems to be an expansion of Browne's simile of brushing aside unwanted memories. Is Deza therefore consciously talking about both Tupra *and* himself when he describes this particular human folly? Does he consider himself equally guilty? The elision is sufficiently ambiguous for us not to know the answer, an effect that Marías doubtless created with care, because it throws up the question that is begged by the novel as a whole: is it enough to be able to identify one's own failings to avoid them in the future? Is knowledge the same as moral insight?

At play when Deza felt himself 'perdiendo más escrúpulos cada día' ('each day that passed, I was losing more and more scruples')[72] was a myriad of factors (or what he can now see was a myriad of factors) that were working against him and in favour of Wheeler and Tupra.[73] He goes over them almost obsessively in his account: the fact that he was away from his Madrid home and his life in London seemed like an unreal parenthesis;[74] that he was speaking a language that was not his mother tongue, lending his experiences an air of being at one remove;[75] that he was still reeling from his break-up with Luisa;[76] that, because he never learned the outcome of his deductions, at least until the Dearlove case, there appeared to be no consequences to his actions;[77] that the interpretation sessions simply became routine; that there was a camaraderie among the group. This latter factor is given a sinister twist in *BS* where Deza peppers the narrative with allusions to bullfighting, starting with his observation that 'Varias noches y días mi sensación al respecto fue la de constituir más bien una banda, o una cuadrilla algo taurina' ('On several such nights and days my sense was, rather, of being part of a gang, or of a matador's

---

[72] *FL*, p. 316.    [73] *Fever and Spear*, p. 250.
[74] *BS*, pp. 119, 122–3, 185, 293–4; *VSA*, pp. 117, 329, 450, 502, 672.
[75] *BS*, p. 114.    [76] *FL*, p. 87.    [77] *FL*, pp. 261, 321–2.

*cuadrilla*').[78] These continue with De la Garza's use of bullfighting terminology to illustrate his anticipated sexual conquest of Flavia Manoia—
'Espero que no me lo hayáis jodido ya vosotros, me habéis cortado la
inspiración y la faena al carajo, sois la leche merengada' ('I hope you two
haven't screwed things up for me, you've broken my concentration, you
have, all that hard work down the drain, you arseholes');[79] 'la tenía ya
entregada. Sólo me faltaba cuadrarla y hala: estocada hasta la empuña-
dura, hasta las corvas' ('she was there for the waking man. It was just a
question of manoeuvring her into position and then in I'd go, the *coup de
grâce*, in with sword, up to the gunnels')—and Tupra's movements which
are compared with those of a matador:[80] 'Le cortó la redecilla de un tajo,
habrían bastado una cuchilla, unas tijeras, una navaja suiza para hacer eso,
menos filo del que necesitaba un torero para cortarse la coleta cuando se
retiraba de la plaza' ('He sliced off the hairnet with one blow; a kitchen
knife, scissors, a Swiss army knife would have been sufficient, a far shorter
blade to cut off his pigtail when he retires from the ring').[81] Through these
descriptions Deza consciously links De la Garza's ordeal with that of
Emilio Marés, a young poet who, according to the narrator's father, was
'toreado' to death by nationalist militia during the Civil War, killed as a
bull would have been in the rings of Spain. Or in other words, wounded
first with a lance and then the barbed darts called 'banderillas', made to
pass repeatedly beneath the matador's cape, and eventually killed with a
lunging sword blow to the heart. The associative links drawn between De
la Garza's ordeal and that of Marés continue with Tupra's overcoat brushing the former's abject, defeated figure as they leave the nightclub toilets—'Sólo el faldón del abrigo, en su vuelo como de capote torero, rozó
la cara al salir del caído' ('As he left, only the tail of his overcoat, which
swirled like a matador's cape, brushed the face of the fallen man').[82] The
detail eloquently conveys his humiliation and utter abasement. Any lingering doubts that Deza has deliberately written up his account to highlight this associative chain and concomitant guilt are dispelled by his final
mention of Marés:

> A mí no me costaba nada recuperar el cabreo, de hecho el de fondo no se me
> iba a pasar en mucho tiempo y nunca se me iba a olvidar el mal trago, el
> sentimiento de miserabilidad y abuso que me había infundido, de impoten-
> cia y de chulería y aun de fascismo analógico: me había hecho acordarme de

[78] *BS*, p. 63; *Dance and Dream*, p. 44.
[79] *BS*, p. 204; *Dance and Dream*, p. 164.
[80] *BS*, p. 205; *Dance and Dream*, p. 164.
[81] *BS*, p. 287; *Dance and Dream*, p. 237.
[82] *BS*, p. 350; *Dance and Dream*, p. 290.

la cuadrilla de requetés o de falangistas que había toreado a un hombre en un campo de Ronda, en el remoto octubre o septiembre del 36.[83]

(It was easy enough for me to recover my own anger, I wouldn't get over those deep feelings of rage for a long time and I would never forget the whole awful experience, the feeling of wretchedness and outrage that he had instilled in me, of impotence and menace and even of analogical fascism. If it *was* analogical: it had reminded me of that gang of Carlist militiamen or Falangists who had baited a man in a field outside Ronda, in the remote October or September of 1936.)[84]

However, by no means the least telling factor in prolonging Deza's secret service career was flattery. The deductive challenge set for Deza on the evening of Wheeler's party was one that, as he later points out, even the pitiably drunk De la Garza would have sailed through.[85] Wheeler asks Deza to see what he thinks of Tupra's new girlfriend, Beryl, a woman who during the party, as De la Garza succinctly observes, 'No le hace ni puto caso' ('She doesn't take a blind bit of notice of him').[86] If this is a new relationship, its beginning is far from promising, given the total indifference Beryl displays towards her alleged partner. Deza rightly deduces that theirs is a relationship in its death throes, a deduction which gives Wheeler and, by extension, Tupra the confirmation they need that the narrator is indeed one of those who possess the elusive 'don o maldición' ('ability or curse'). Looked at retrospectively, one might begin to suspect a Machiavellian edge to Wheeler's behaviour in snaring Deza for queen and country; certainly this is how Deza comes to view his mentor's actions: 'había propiciado mi encuentro con Tupra y me había sometido a una pequeña prueba que ahora me parecía inocente e idiota—perfecta para que yo no midiera el riesgo' ('he had made use of my encounter with Tupra and submitted me to a small test that now seemed to me innocent and idiotic—and which in no way prepared me for the possible risks of joining the group').[87] He (Wheeler) follows up this childishly simple first task with a wounding remark on the narrator's marital difficulties. Just as the latter is rounding off his portrait of Beryl and Tupra— a couple who are drifting apart, whose every action is now insufferable to one another—Wheeler asks '¿Fue eso lo que te pasó con Luisa?' ('Was that what happened with you and Luisa?').[88] The reminder of Deza's fallibility proves instrumental later in their conversation when Wheeler suggests that:

Tampoco vas a perder un tiempo que ya das por perdido, el de las convalecencias sentimentales se llena con lo que sea, el contenido es lo de menos, con lo que esté más a mano y más ayude a empujarlo, se tiene poca exigencia,

---

[83] *BS*, pp. 388–9.     [84] *Dance and Dream*, p. 323.     [85] *FL*, pp. 134–5.
[86] *FL*, p. 79; *Fever and Spear*, p. 57.
[87] *VSA*, p. 573; *Poison, Shadow, and Farewell*, p. 443.
[88] *FL*, p. 120; *Fever and Spear*, p. 91.

¿no es cierto? Luego no se recuerdan apenas, esos periodos, ni lo que se hizo
en ellos, como si hubiera estado permitido todo, uno se justifica mucho por
la desorientación y el sufrimiento; es como si no hubieran existido y en su
lugar hubiera un blanco. También un vacío de responsabilidades, "¿Sabe? Yo
no era yo entonces".[89]

(You can't really waste time that you already consider to be wasted, these
periods of sentimental convalescence can be filled up with anything, the
content doesn't really matter, whatever happens by and helps to push them
along will do, one tends, I think I'm right in saying, not to be too choosy.
Afterwards, it's hard even to remember those times or what one did while
they lasted, as if everything had been permissible then, and one can always
cite disorientation and pain as justification; it's as if those times had never
existed and as if, in their place, there was a blank. They're free of responsibilities too, "I wasn't myself at the time, you know.")[90]

Here he is both exposing Deza to the risk of transgressing in the name of
'the cause' and giving him the excuse he can use if anything goes wrong.
When taken alongside Wheeler's later revelations about his own wife's
death, the suspicion of a Machiavellian streak in him is confirmed.
Months later, with Dearlove dead and Deza considering his resignation
from the group, Wheeler reveals that his wife and fellow secret service
operative, Valerie, committed suicide after the Second World War, unable
to cope with her remorse at having, in the cause of undermining enemy
morale, condemned several Austrian friends to the slow death of a concentration camp. In other words, Wheeler knows all too well the potential
pitfalls of a career in which one is encouraged to suspend ethical judgements in pursuit of a greater good. And yet, he has placed his friend and
confidant directly in the line of fire. I shall return to Wheeler's deep and
complex characterization in the second section of this chapter.

Flattered to be asked, still reeling from Luisa's rejection, Wheeler providing him with both his introduction to the service and his conscience-
saving get-out clause should anything go wrong, Deza looks in retrospect
like an easy target. Running alongside the 'sensación de haber aprobado
un examen' ('feeling of having passed an exam')[91] is also the captivating
personality of his new boss, Tupra. Marías renders brilliantly the dynamic
of their first major interpretation session, deciphering the future possibilities of a man who claims to be a Venezuelan army officer with aspirations
to oust Hugo Chávez from power.[92] Tupra wants to know whether the

[89] *FL*, p. 436.    [90] *Fever and Spear*, p. 345.
[91] *FL*, p. 262; *Fever and Spear*, p. 206.
[92] Deza states that it was in fact the third session he was involved in but in the first two
he was present only as an interpreter of the Spanish language and had a peripheral role (*FL*,
pp. 233–4).

man, to whom he ironically gives the alias 'Bonanza', will keep his word and undertake the *coup d'état* he is promising. Once 'Bonanza' has been ruthlessly questioned and brusquely dismissed, Tupra's rapid-fire and implacable questioning of Deza begins: 'Dígame más. Dígame si el venezolano decía la verdad' ('Tell me more. Tell me if the Venezuelan gentleman was telling the truth'); 'Eso ya lo sé, Mr Deza. Le pregunto si alguna de las dos era verdad. En su opinión. Por favor' ('I know that Mr Deza. I'm asking you if either of those two things is true. In your opinion. Please'); 'Explíqueme eso, haga el favor' ('Explain that, will you?'); 'Por qué piensa eso, dígame' ('But, tell me, why do you think that?'); 'Eso no importa. Sí le sigo. Dígame qué detalles' ('That doesn't matter. And I do see what you mean. Tell me, what details?').[93] Even though their conversation took place in English—Deza is translating it from memory into Spanish—he feels justified in using the formal 'usted' form of address, emphasizing the distance Tupra imposes through studied politeness: the superfluous use of 'Mr Deza', repetition of 'por favor', 'haga el favor'. Deza interjects that he would learn later to fear the escalation of that same exaggerated courtesy—'Más adelante comprobé que solía recurrir a esas fórmulas, "tiene la bondad," "se lo ruego," antes de irritarse del todo' ('Later on, I learned that he always resorted to such formulae, "if you would be so kind", "if you wouldn't mind" when he was about to get really annoyed')[94]—because it is the condescending mask Tupra adopts in order to feign respect for his subordinates. Central also to the dynamic is the fact that Deza has been lulled into a false sense of security:[95]

> No hice otra cosa que improvisar, es lo cierto. No tenía nada que perder. Ni que ganar, había sido llamado como traductor y ya había cumplido con mi función. Seguir allí era una deferencia por mi parte, aunque Tupra no me hiciera sentirlo así, si acaso al contrario, era uno de esos raros individuos que piden un préstamo y consiguen que sea quien se lo concede el que se sienta deudor.[96]

> (I merely improvised, that's all. I had nothing to lose. Nor to gain either, I had been summoned to act as a translator and had performed that role. Remaining there was a courtesy on my part, although Tupra did not make me feel this to be the case, rather, perhaps, the opposite, for he was one of those rare individuals who can ask for a loan and manage to make the person giving the loan feel that he is the debtor.)[97]

Nothing more dangerous than offering judgements when the pressure is off and your guard is down. Marías even uses a packet of cigarettes to ratchet up the tension between the two men. No stranger to tobacco or its

[93] *FL*, pp. 246, 247, 251; *Fever and Spear*, pp. 194, 195, 198.        [94] *FL*, p. 247.
[95] *Fever and Spear*, p. 195.        [96] *FL*, p. 248.        [97] *Fever and Spear*, p. 196.

use in art, he was asked in 2003 to come up with a list of his favourite cinema smoking scenes, choosing among his list of ten (five actors, five actresses) no fewer than three starring John Wayne in films directed by John Ford.[98] Of interest to us, however, are not his choices in themselves, rather the fact that he felt able to answer and had evidently noticed how the ritualized aspect of smoking can create tension, supply release, give a scene its rhythm, and convey meaning without words. This simplest of props in *TRM* takes the form of Tupra's packet of 'Rameses II, cigarrillos egipcios de tabaco turco, un poco picantes' ('Rameses II, Egyptian cigarettes made from slightly spicy-tasting Turkish tobacco'), one of which Tupra has extracted but not yet lit.[99] Deza fixates on the tip sitting in Tupra's mouth, imagining it increasingly damp with saliva. The unease this creates in his feverishly working mind leads him to take one out himself and light it: 'ya no pude aguantar y encendí el cigarrillo, no sin embargo el mío, sino un valioso Rameses II que le pedí permiso para coger' ('I could hold out no longer, though, and finally lit a cigarette, not mine, however, but an expensive Rameses II, to which I asked permission to help myself').[100] His nerve fails him soon after when he has delivered the verdict that never in a million years would 'Bonanza' lead a coup against Chávez—'Me había dejado llevar por el atrevimiento, me frené' ('I had got carried away by my boldness, I stopped')[101]—fearful that he has pushed deduction into the realm of fantasy. What seems crucial to his recovering his composure are a few reassuring words from Tupra and, more importantly, the fact that 'Ahora sí encendió su precioso y ensalivado Rameses II, él también' ('Now he too lit his cigarette, his precious, saliva-sodden Rameses II').[102] The release of tension—a post-coital cigarette where coitus is here figuratively replaced by Deza's having reached the right conclusion—enables him to finish off his appraisal of 'Bonanza'.[103]

## Marías the Citizen

I have been arguing that *TRM* has significant ethical resonances and that those are explored with remarkable complexity and richness above all

---

[98] Marías's response to the survey was originally published in *Nickel Odeon*, 30 (2003), 88. His answers can also be found in JM, *Donde todo ha sucedido: Al salir del cine*, ed. by Inés Blanca and Reyes Pinzás (Barcelona: Galaxia Gutenberg, 2005), p. 280.

[99] *FL*, pp. 247–8; *Fever and Spear*, p. 195.

[100] *FL*, p. 249; *Fever and Spear*, p. 196.

[101] *FL*, p. 250; *Fever and Spear*, p. 197.

[102] *Fever and Spear*, pp. 197–8.

[103] The same dynamic plays itself out after Deza's interpretation of Dick Dearlove (*FL*, p. 365). Useful comparisons could be made between the dynamic created by cigarettes in this scene and Juan Ranz's uncomfortable conversation with his father at his wedding, in *CTB*, pp. 103–27.

through the narrative voice. Deza's particular frailties and personality traits mean that the reader is invited to approach the moral issues that the novel explores as challenging ethical dilemmas rather than open and shut cases. His account asks the reader to engage with the difficulty of identifying and choosing 'the good' in a modern world of bewildering moral relativism. This aspect of the novel has not escaped the attention of critics. *TRM* has been called a 'mighty Spanish trilogy about power, surveillance, morality and mortality' possessed of 'contemporary longsightedness and [a] unique ethic-aesthetic agenda';[104] 'a kind of experiment in forensic ethics: a study of the shifting aspect of good and evil over time';[105] 'un relato intelectual de alcance moral' ('an intellectual tale of moral reach').[106] This alongside praise that it 'may very well be the first authentic literary masterpiece of the 21st century';[107] 'no sólo es la mejor novela de Javier Marías sino una de las grandes novelas del siglo XX [*sic*] español' ('not just Javier Marías's best novel but also one of the great novels of the twentieth [*sic*] century in Spain');[108] 'la mejor novela española (y de una de las mejores de cualquier otra literatura) de los últimos cincuenta o sesenta años' ('the best Spanish novel (and one of the best in any other language) of the last fifty or sixty years');[109] 'probably the most powerful and important novel to appear in European literature for some time'.[110] The last of these endorsements from no less a figure than Antony Beevor, a historian no stranger to the conflicts that provide the background to many of the reflections in the novel—the Spanish Civil War and the Second World War.[111]

To reinforce the argument that *TRM* is a novel with wider ethical resonances I wish to show how much the issues it addresses have been the preoccupation of Marías the columnist and public intellectual. I therefore devote the following section of my discussion to examining Marías's journalistic output over the period of the novel's gestation. As will have become clear already in this study, Marías's journalism offers rich pickings for the researcher who wishes to trace his developing preoccupations.

---

[104] Ali Smith, 'Books of the Year', *Times Literary Supplement*, 27 November 2009, p. 15.

[105] James Lasdun, 'Glittering with intent', *The Guardian*, Review section, 21 November 2009, p. 10.

[106] Santos Sanz Villanueva, '*Tu rostro mañana 3: Veneno y sombra y adiós*', *El Mundo*, El Cultural section, 11 October 2007, pagination unknown.

[107] James Lasdun, p. 10.

[108] Jordi Gracia, 'Javier Marías o pensar por novelas', p. 78.

[109] Antonio Iriarte, unpublished text, available at the following URL: http://www.javiermarias.es/main.html (accessed 1 June 2008).

[110] Antony Beevor, 'Christmas Books', *The Guardian*, Review section, 28 November 2009, p. 2.

[111] See also Beevor's review of *VSA*, 'Your Face Tomorrow: Poison, Shadow and Farewell', *The Sunday Telegraph*, section Seven, 8 November 2009, p. 28.

Maarten Steenmeijer has pointed to a change in his persona as evidenced
by his weekly column: from diffident and reserved beginnings, during
which he seldom addressed his readers directly, and only in the formal
'usted' form, he has gained the confidence to adopt a more familiar tone.[112]
He self-consciously assumes the pose of an anachronism in his own
time—'No perteneceré mucho a mi época, pero' ('I may not belong too
readily to my own era but')—a man staggered at the general levels of
rudeness and thoughtlessness with which he and his fellow citizens are
forced to contend.[113] Notes of self-deprecation creep in each Spring when
he writes his obligatory article railing against the Semana Santa processions that paralyse the centre of Madrid, and every other town in Spain,
for the duration of Holy Week: 'Ay Señor—empecemos lo más piadosa-
mente posible—. Ay Señor, Señor. Miren que cada año lo intento, no
escribir sobre la Semana Santa y sus ocho mil procesiones' ('Oh Lord—
let's start as piously as we can—Oh Lord, Lord. Look, I do try every year,
not to write about Holy Week and its eight thousand processions').[114] As
we saw in the last chapter, alongside this irascible pose has run a coherent
and consistent attack on the apparent impunity with which the governments of Britain, Spain, and the United States were able to prosecute the
second Iraq war. The defence of civil liberties in the face of increased pressure from governments eager to protect their citizens from the threat of
global terrorism has been another cornerstone of his position. He believes
that the individual should always seek to guard jealously his or her
freedoms since he or she cannot know when the goalposts of what is and
is not acceptable may be moved.

He has been at pains to draw a clear distinction between his journalistic
and novelistic output. Asked in 2007 what his work as a columnist had
brought to his novels, he replied:

> Tengo que decir que no mucho. Hay una diferencia muy grande entre mis
> columnas periodísticas y mis novelas. Siempre digo que cuando escribo un
> artículo lo hago como ciudadano. Cuando escribo una novela, el ciudadano

[112] Steenmeijer writes: 'Si en un principio el narrador tanteaba su actitud frente a su
público sirviéndose sólo de vez en cuando de fórmulas como "no sé si ustedes recuerdan,"
"no quiero atribular a ustedes" y "eso lo saben ustedes tan bien como yo," luego pasa a
usarlas con gran frecuencia y naturalidad' ('If at first the narrator was feeling his way
towards knowing how to address his audience, using only the occasional formulae like "I
don't know if readers will recall", "I don't wish to trouble you unduly", and "as readers will
know as well as I do", he then goes on to employ them with great frequency and naturalness.'). 'Javier Marías, columnista: el otro, el mismo', pp. 268–9.
[113] JM, 'La prescripción insoportable', in *EOOL*, pp, 137–9 (p. 139). See also 'Harán de
mí un criminal', in *HMC*, pp. 160–2.
[114] JM, 'Inermes', in *DNA*, pp. 39–41 (p. 39). See also 'El encapuchado abuso', in
*EOOL*, pp. 50–2; 'El Christus Corpi', in *EOOL*, pp. 233–6; ' "Botellón" de encapuchados',
in *DNA*, pp. 192–4; 'Presiosa', in *LNVD*, pp. 42–4.

desaparece. En una novela se puede ser salvaje. En un artículo nunca haría afirmaciones como las que hago en mi novela. En un artículo te estás haciendo responsable, y el sentido de la responsabilidad, en la novela desaparece.[115]

(I have to say 'not a great deal'. There is a very considerable difference between my journalistic columns and my novels. I always say that, when I write an article, I write it as a citizen. When I write a novel, the citizen disappears. In a novel you can be brutal. In an article I would never make the kind of statements that I make in my novels. In an article you are making yourself responsible, and that sense of responsibility disappears in the novel.)

The distinction he is drawing appears to be largely one of tone, not necessarily of content, and it would be naïve to assume that the subjects that were of concern to Marías the citizen should not also have influenced Marías the creative writer (to follow his distinction). In fact, many of Deza's stated opinions are those of his creator, the 'préstamos' ('borrowings') of personal characteristics to his creations that have become one of Marías's trademarks. For instance, Deza is a committed and unrepentant smoker, complaining loudly about the war on tobacco being waged by Western health authorities, much as Marías does repeatedly in his weekly column.[116] Both complain bitterly that many of their compatriots lack the most basic courtesy or social grace[117] and Marías in fact admitted that Deza's whipping boy De la Garza was a caricature of a certain kind of loud, obnoxious, and talentless Spaniard whose proliferation alarmed him.[118] There is undoubtedly substance to Jordi Gracia's criticism that some of the pet peeves that irritate Marías the citizen stick out rather obtrusively when put in the mouth of Deza the narrator—the former's dislike of sandals or tourists with backpacks being the most glaring examples.[119] Nevertheless, Deza shares at least part of his creator's disquiet at the ease with which in recent times governments have, in the name of

---

[115] Cruz, Juan, 'Javier Marías: Escribir para ver', *El País Semanal*, 23 September 2007, pp. 12–20, (p. 18).

[116] *FL*, p. 407. See, for example, 'Cuando no es triste la muerte', in *HMC*, pp. 69–72; 'Mentecatómetros', in *EOOL*, pp. 98–100; 'Roben pero no fumen', in *EOOL*, pp. 227–9; 'Las memeces tiránicas', in *EOOL*, pp. 275–7; 'El peligro de engreimiento', in *DNA*, pp. 51–3; 'Sablistas eclesiásticos y sablistas gubernamentales', in *DNA*, pp. 96–8; 'La intromisión que no para', in *DNA*, pp. 144–6.

[117] *FL*, pp. 63–98 *passim*; *BS*, p. 89; *VSA*, p. 504.

[118] Antonio Lozano, 'Javier Marías: El monarca del tiempo' *Man*, 207 (2005). See also his comments in Solanes, '"El grado de ignorancia en España es deprimente"', *Cuadernos hispanoamericanos*, 691 (2008), 87–104 (pp. 94–5).

[119] *BS*, p. 84. Gracia writes: 'Incluso al narrador le llega el contagio del articulista cascarrabias que es a menudo Javier Marías y con ello llega también alguna debilidad extraña a la novela (pero menor: el vituperio de la sandalia o el diagnóstico sobre los niños insaciables, manías de ciudadano que desploman de golpe la altura de la novela)' ('Even the narrator of

protecting society, amended laws on the individual's right to avoid prolonged detention without charge, unauthorized scrutiny of his or her private communications, or being habitually subjected to the gaze of
closed-circuit television cameras.[120] Deza makes the following observations on his impromptu bursting into the female toilets of the nightclub
where De la Garza has disappeared with Flavia Manoia:

> [N]uestros gobernantes aprovechados han metido tanto miedo a la gente
> que ésta se ha vuelto dócil en poco tiempo, sobre todo ante quien esgrime la
> aterradora y dominante palabra que lo justifica todo 'Seguridad. Seguridad':
> hasta los abusos irónicos y las humillaciones que fingen no serlo, no sé: las
> funcionales.[121]

> (The opportunistic people who govern us have made people so afraid that
> we have rapidly grown docile, especially when confronted by someone
> wielding the terrifying, omnipresent word—'Security'—that justifies every-
> thing, even supposedly ironic uses and abuses of it and humiliations that
> pretend not to be humiliations, but, how can I put it, purely functional.)[122]

> [P]ero si la gente se deja hoy registrar por las buenas en cualquier aeropuerto
> u oficina pública, y se descalza y aun se desviste obediente a la orden de un
> aduanero torvo, no es extraño que admita importunaciones e interrupciones
> e impertinentes preguntas hasta en medio de sus ocupaciones íntimas.[123]

> (but given that people now meekly allow themselves to be frisked at any
> airport or public building, and obediently take off their shoes or even get
> undressed at the orders of some grim-faced customs officer, it is little
> wonder that they should accept importunate demands and interruptions
> and impertinent questions even while engaged in the most private of
> occupations.)[124]

This strand of the novel is not only explored through Deza's asides; rather
it forms the basis of lengthy discussions between the narrator and Wheeler
about the ethical implications of state intervention in the lives of not only
its own citizens but also those of other countries. In the final section of

---

the novel experiences contagion from the cantankerous columnist that Javier Marías often
is, and with it a few weaknesses that jar in the novel (but which are minor in nature: the
vituperation aimed at sandals or the diagnostics surrounding insatiable children, pet peeves
of the citizen that cause violent dips in the novel's tone)'). 'Javier Marías o pensar por
novelas', p. 77. For corroboration of the fact that these are indeed among Marías's pet hates,
see 'Engreídos y enrollados', in *LNVD*, pp. 78–80 (p. 79)

[120] See, for example, 'La traición a Henry Adams', in *HMC*, pp. 154–6; 'Cuando una
sociedad está putrefacta', in *HMC*, pp. 254–6; 'Ingenuos hasta la estupidez', in *EOOL*,
pp. 164–6; 'Not forever England', in *EOOL*, pp. 254–6; 'Nuestra pobre vida sin secretos',
in *EOOL*, pp. 278–80; 'Los países irreconocibles', in *DNA*, pp. 33–5; 'La intromisión que
no para', in *DNA*, pp. 144–6; 'Entérenlos', in *DNA*, pp. 165–7.

[121] *BS*, p. 141.     [122] *Dance and Dream*, p. 109.     [123] *BS*, p. 146.

[124] *Dance and Dream*, p. 113.

*FL*, Deza recalls Wheeler's sustained disquisition on the dubious morality and limited effectiveness of the British campaign against 'careless talk' during the Second World War. Symmetry is completed later in the novel when the final section of *VSA* records another of Wheeler's perorations on the pitiless tactics adopted by British intelligence to undermine German morale during that same conflict. It is no accident that Marías should be bringing to the attention of his readers the period of the twentieth century when modern espionage was born. The campaign against careless talk, which had precedents in the Spanish Civil War, as Deza confirms when he finds a book of contemporary posters issuing public warnings against the so-called Fifth Column, is a potent example of the state warning its citizens to look out for the enemy within, guard against the traitor's avid ear. The more recent modern-day example of such practice found its way into Marías's journalism: the encouragement given to US citizens in the wake of the terrorist attacks on 11 September 2001 to report their neighbours' suspicious behaviour to counter-terrorism police. Such a measure he regarded as nothing short of inviting malicious misuse and, given the historical precedents offered by Spain, a sign that the society in question was rotting from within: he entitled his article 'Cuando una sociedad está putrefacta'.

If, as I argue, *TRM* is a novel about the modern world, in what precise relation does it stand to contemporary concerns? In my view, the answer lies in the interrogation of the relationship of the individual to the State, of moral absolutes versus relativism, of personal responsibility versus its abdication. *TRM* is a novel of our times because it encourages the reader to reflect on what the state does in the name of protecting its citizens, whether in peace- or wartime, overtly through legislation or covertly through spying. As Marías's articles so eloquently testify, events since the terrorist attacks on 11 September 2001 and the second Iraq war have shaken what used to be thought of as the solid foundations of Western democratic values. He joined many intellectuals and citizens the world over in looking on with disbelief as the leaders of the United States offered up the principles on which free societies are based, imprisoning foreign nationals with no hope of a trial or right to legal representation, endorsing torture as a legitimate interrogation technique, or making scant effort to build international consensus before invading a sovereign state. Deza's time as a British intelligence agent leaves him reflecting on how he has fallen short of his own moral standards and, perhaps most importantly, those of his upright and honourable father. His is a small story of how a jilted, directionless, and easily flattered man falls into condoning and even using violence against defenceless victims. In Marías's hands, however, that story acquires resonances that echo through Spain's Civil War, the Second World War, to the present day. Ali Smith highlighted the extent to which the novel promotes a sustained examination of our own conduct in a world of complex moral choices:

> What it asks, like any book, is that you get involved. But Marias [*sic*] wants us involved at a depth-charge level of commitment. He wants his readers to make all sorts of interlayered connections: verbal, narrative, historic, humane. Because everything he writes recognises the difficulty of any human negotiation, personal and political, and because he is opposed to what he sees as something akin to a new fascism—a current state of stupidity arising from 'lazy ways of thinking'—Marias demands we admit the profound complexity of any involvement. What does it mean, exactly, to give beggars money in the street? What are the consequences of helping anybody? And say, for instance, you witness someone you actively dislike being beaten to near-death by your supervisor at work, how involved should you get?[125]

Where this becomes problematic, perhaps, is in Marías's oft-stated opposition to moralizing in art. He restated this position in an interview with Ignacio Echevarría shortly after *FL* appeared:

> Creo poder afirmar que en mis novelas no hay sermones, como en tantas otras. Ni tampoco jeremiadas. No me dedico a condenar las acciones o las actitudes de los personajes, por horribles que pudieran resultar, no se trata de eso. Me molesta cada vez más la trampa, la impostura. Lo que más me puede irritar es la complacencia con que el autor de una novela o de una película alardea de su propia posición moral. Me dan ganas de decirle: 'Oye, ya me he dado cuenta de que tienes un alma muy bella, deja de darme la lata y cuéntame algo más interesante'. Es posible, en efecto, que por mi parte sea cada vez más moral la manera de abordar la escritura, pero lo sería en un sentido opuesto a este que señalo.[126]

> (I believe I can claim that there are no sermons in my novels, as there are in so many others. Nor jeremiads. I don't spend time condemning the characters' actions or attitudes, however horrible they may be; it's not about that. I find myself increasingly irritated by traps, imposture. What I find most irritating of all is the self-satisfaction with which a writer or film-director shows off their own moral position. I feel like saying to them: 'Listen, I've got the message that you have a beautiful soul, now get off my case and tell me something more interesting'. It's possible, in fact, that my approach to literature has become more moral, but in the opposite sense from that which I've just been discussing.)

Grudgingly, he concedes that his works may have taken on a more ethical edge but what he gives with one hand he takes away with the other. His

---

[125]    Ali Smith, 'Review of *Your Face Tomorrow 2: Dance and Dream*', p. 39.
[126]    Ignacio Echevarría, 'A medida que uno cumple años se incrementan la confusión y la incertidumbre', *El País*, Babelia section, 26 October 2002, pp. 2–3.

novels may be ethically engaged but never in the sense of congratulating himself or anyone else for their moral rectitude, an activity he would regard as intellectually sterile, perhaps even dishonest. I have shown that *TRM* does precisely the opposite.

## TRANSLATION AND PALIMPSEST IN
### *TU ROSTRO MAÑANA*

Having established what I believe *TRM* to be about, I wish now to discuss how Marías establishes characters and voices in the novel through the use of translation and palimpsest. Of all of his fiction to date, *TRM* could be called his most conversational novel on the basis that long sections of each of its three volumes are taken up with conversations recalled and recreated. Most of those conversations took place in English or, in the case of those between Wheeler and Deza, in a hybrid of English and Spanish. The irony of this fact was not lost on the Marías who had been accused of writing Spanish that sounded like English in his early fiction:

> Me ha divertido en esta novela, a posteriori, pensar que a mí, durante muchos años, con mis primeras novelas sobre todo, se me descalificaba diciéndome que parecían traducidas del inglés. Yo nunca me lo tomé como una descalificación (he traducido, y sé el trabajo que lleva), pero se empleaba como "¡Bah!, este escritor que parece traducido". Al cabo de los años, éste es un libro que parcialmente sería una traducción, porque muchos de los diálogos estarían sucediendo en inglés. Finalmente, ésta sería una novela traducida.[127]

> (It has amused me in this novel, in retrospect, to think that for many years people dismissed my work, my early novels above all, by claiming that they sounded as if they'd been translated from English. I never took it as a dismissal (I've worked as a translator and I know how much work it requires) but the people who said it did so as if to claim 'Huh! this writer sounds like a translation.' All these years later, this book would actually be a partial translation because many of the conversations in it would be happening in English. Finally, this would be a translated novel.)

One early, it might even be said premature critic entitled her article on *FL* '*Tu rostro mañana* de Javier Marías o el arte de la conversación', demonstrating an astonishing prescience over the content of a novel three quarters of which had still to be written.[128] She was nevertheless proved right

[127] Félix Romeo, 'Javier Marías "Me angustia que nada sea olvidable"', *ABC*, Cultura section, 26 October 2002, p. 14.
[128] Geneviève Champeau, '*Tu rostro mañana* de Javier Marías o el arte de la conversación', in *Cuadernos de narrativa: Javier Marías*, pp. 169–88.

and conversations do indeed make up significant sections of each of the three volumes. In *FL*, Deza spars verbally with (separately) Tupra and De la Garza when they meet during Wheeler's soirée and talks at length with his host both that night and the following morning. In *BS*, he recalls his conversation with Pérez Nuix on the night she enlists his help over her father's business affairs. He likewise evokes the occasion on which his father spoke to him about the Civil War atrocities of which the latter had learned both during and after the conflict. He and Luisa maintain a conversation on the subject of botox and menstrual blood that is importantly amusing for both parties and renews Deza's hopes of reconciliation. Each of these last two conversations is interpolated within the narrative of the evening in the nightclub toilets, on which Deza has chance to talk to De la Garza at greater length than at their previous encounter. Later that same evening, he reproaches Tupra for the savage treatment he has just inflicted on his compatriot. By now in *VSA*, to justify himself, Tupra takes the narrator back to his home to show Deza a series of videos featuring celebrities, public figures, or heads of state engaged in grotesque or criminal behaviour, culminating in a video which indicates just what his Italian client Manoia is capable of when it comes to dispatching his enemies: the implication being that De la Garza has got off lightly with a few broken ribs. Throughout this increasingly upsetting session, the two men converse at length on morality, war, and the instrumentalization of fear: according to Tupra, if you can live with and harness fear in the service of your country, you become an inexorable force. Deza also flashes back to complete his account of the night Pérez Nuix spent at his flat a few weeks previously. When Deza is finally able to take some time off from interpreting work, he returns to Madrid where he talks (separately) with Luisa and his now aged father. When his suspicions are aroused about Luisa, he does his best to wheedle information out of her sister, Cristina, to determine the cause of his wife's facial injuries. Once he has identified, stalked, and cornered Custardoy, the two men talk before and during Deza's attack on him. Following Dearlove's arrest, about which Deza reads on the plane journey back to London, he confronts Tupra over the group's involvement, only to meet with his boss's predictable hermeticism. Finally, the narrator becomes the bearer of Wheeler's secrets as the latter unburdens himself of a lifetime's untold experiences: Valerie's death, his intelligence work, and the creation of the group of 'intérpretes de vidas' ('interpreters of lives').

In this section of my discussion I will analyse how Marías characterizes these distinct voices through the use of translation and palimpsest, focusing initially on Wheeler. It is my contention that their characterization is realized predominantly through the content of what they say rather than significant stylistic differentiation between their voices. Some reviewers pointed to the lack of variation between the speech rhythms of different characters as a regrettable aspect of the text and it is true that the voices of Deza himself, Tupra, Pérez Nuix, and Wheeler are not significantly individualized. There are, however, several factors, both internal and external to the novel, that explain this. Firstly, all of these characters share the 'don o maldición' and hence the horror of generalizing or simplifying that shapes Deza's meticulous outlook and prose style. Secondly, their voices are being filtered through Deza's memory and he acknowledges that that process involves artistic licence.[129] Thirdly, Marías is perhaps conscious that one of the novelists he most admires wrote a similarly multi-voiced novel in which little differentiation is made between the speech rhythms of its protagonists. Literary posterity has not looked any less kindly on William Faulkner's *Absalom, Absalom!* (1936) in spite of its undeniably sharing this feature.[130] Other than the content of his speeches, the factors that individualize Wheeler include his world-weariness (his jaded response to Deza early in the novel, 'Qué tontería. Una gran idea') ('An excellent idea, indeed!');[131] his uneasy relationship with past memories that continue to haunt him (crucially the death of his wife);[132] and his long-silenced intelligence work across three continents (Africa, Asia, and Europe).

Wheeler's characterization is realized through his recorded perorations and reflections on a wide range of topics, among them espionage, the Second World War, Shakespeare's representation of kingship, the Day of Judgement, and the Spanish Civil War. (It is not in vain that Marías claimed after publication of *VSA* that 'la novela aspira a hablar de todo' ['the novel aspires to talk about everything'].)[133] As we shall see, however, those extended reflections are not the only means Marías employs. When we first meet him, Wheeler appears to sit at the centre of a benevolent,

---

[129] For example, *FL*, p. 328; *BS*, p. 39.

[130] Marías greatly admires *Absalom, Absalom!*, as we can see from the introduction to his 1997 volume of essays and translated poems in homage to Faulkner. In that pugnacious piece, he discusses why Faulkner's literary reputation should have fallen on hard times in recent years, suggesting that one of the principal causes is the self-interest of mediocre critics and writers who use extraneous and politically correct arguments to disparage the great American novelist. In his view, this drove of mediocrities cannot help but be threatened by novels as great as *Absalom, Absalom!* or *Light in August* because they throw into such sharp relief the inanity and triviality of most works ever published. See *Si yo amaneciera otra vez*, pp. 15–16.

[131] *FL*, p. 140; *Fever and Spear*, p. 108.

[132] *FL*, pp. 471–3.

[133] Justo Barranco, ' "Mi novela aspira a hablar de todo" ', *La Vanguardia*, 25 September 2007, p. 37. See also Antonio Lozano, 'Javier Marías. Hablar o callar, esa es la cuestión', *Qué leer*, October 2007, pp. 62–7 (p. 65).

Shandean world of English eccentrics, one generated through allusion to Sterne's comic masterpiece. By the end of the novel, that impression has given way to a far less cosy and altogether more troubling portrait of a ruthless, determined, but haunted man: a portrait sketched in no small part by allusion to Shakespeare but also the British spy and propagandist Sefton Delmer.

As I indicated in the preceding section of this chapter, Wheeler emerges as a Machiavellian figure, one who knows better than anybody the personal, professional, psychological, and legal dangers to which he is exposing Deza and yet who exposes him to them all the same. In Wheeler's case, a consequence of the novel's long gestation enabled Marías to make his character increasingly nuanced and complex as the novel progressed. The death of Sir Peter Russell brought into the public domain information concerning his secret service career that would otherwise have remained unavailable to the author. Marías is unlikely to have known at the outset all of the facts about Russell's intelligence work that he later included in *VSA*. To begin with, he admitted in 2002 that he had not badgered his distinguished friend for material, in part out of respect for Russell's privacy and also because he was well aware that the Official Secrets Act in any case precludes the divulging of such sensitive information.[134] While Russell may have shared privately with Marías some of his wartime experiences, there is no evidence that such material found its way into the novel since the missions the author attributed to the fictional Wheeler in *VSA* could all be found in the fullest of the obituaries of Russell published in the British press.[135] This information, alongside the fictional account of Valerie's suicide (fictional because Russell never married) provide the framework around which Marías constructed the complete picture of Wheeler that we are given in the final section of *VSA*.

As the novel begins, Marías and Deza seem determined to characterize Wheeler with the help of references to Sterne. Much as Marías had used something of the Shandean world to poke fun at Oxford and its eccentricities in *TLA*, those echoes reappear at Wheeler's soirée, as if situating us once more in those familiar, benevolent surroundings. Lord Rymer, who had presided over the riotous high table at which Deza first met the fascinating Halliwell, reappears, no less dependent on alcohol than

---

[134] Javier Marías and Juan Villoro, 'De espías y otros fantasmas', *Letras libres*, 15 (2002), 44–7 (p. 45); Óscar López, 'Contesto y salto pocas veces para las que podría hacerlo', *Qué leer*, November 2002, pp. 7–9 (p. 8).

[135] I am referring to that written by Bruce Taylor, published in *The Times*, 14 July 2006 p. 80. Although the original obituary was published anonymously, Ian Michael identifies the author in his own obituary of Russell. See Ian Michael, 'Sir Peter Russell (1913–2006)' *Bulletin of Spanish Studies*, 83 (2006), 1133–44 (p. 1137).

before though somewhat becalmed since his intervention in proceedings is limited to an impromptu drinking contest with De la Garza.[136] Another fellow guest is 'la deana viuda' ('the dowager deaness'),[137] the widow of the Dean of York Minster, a woman old enough to be De la Garza's mother but who nevertheless attracts his lustful gazes.[138] Tupra refers to her as 'Mrs Wadman, la Deana viuda' while commenting to Deza that his puerile compatriot is unlikely to find her receptive to his advances.[139] Deza replies that, 'No sabía que la viuda del Deán de York se llamara Mrs Wadman' ('I didn't know the Dean of York's widow was called Mrs Wadman'), only for Tupra to respond ironically, 'Bueno, ese debería ser el nombre, siendo viuda y siendo de York, yo creo' ('Well, that must, I assume, be her name, since she's a widow and the widow of York').[140] The reference to Widow Wadman situates the reader once again in Sterne's world of Shandean eccentrics, where Deza is both strangely at home and able to keep his surroundings at an ironic distance. While De la Garza struggles to make himself understood in English, Deza receives compliments on his command of the language, even trying to bamboozle his compatriot with obscure idiomatic expressions when the latter butts in on his conversations.

This picture of a home away from home is further developed by Deza's forthright comments on Spain itself. It is in this chapter that he makes the first of what become repeated disparaging remarks: on Spaniards' habit of looking through the person they are talking to[141] or congregating vociferously and obnoxiously when abroad.[142] He also despairs of the mediocrity, hypocrisy, and inexplicable success of the political and literary Right in his home country: his political sympathies clearly lie with his Republican father. De la Garza in this sense is lumped with the traditionalist establishment since he has gained his post at the embassy through paternal influence and has a declared soft spot for Spain's fascist writers of the pre-, post-, and interwar period.[143]

With the other guests safely dispatched—or unsafely in the case of those whom De la Garza offers to drive home—Deza and Wheeler are finally able to talk at leisure. Here again, Shandean resonances emerge as the latter begins to wield his walking stick much as Uncle Toby wields his crutch in *TS*.

My good uncle *Toby*, with infinite pleasure, answered it; and full gladly would have ingrafted a sentence of consolation upon the opening it afforded; but having no talents, as I said, that way, and fearing moreover that he might

---

[136] See *TLA*, pp. 51–75.      [137] *FL*, p. 95; *Fever and Spear*, p. 70.
[138] *FL*, p. 80.      [139] *FL*, p. 95.      [140] *FL*, p. 96; *Fever and Spear*, p. 71.
[141] *FL*, p. 67.      [142] *FL*, p. 71.      [143] *FL*, 73–4.

set out with something which might make a bad matter worse, he contented himself with resting his chin placidly upon the cross of his crutch.[144]

Did ever man, brother *Toby*, cried my father, raising himself up upon his elbow, and turning himself round to the opposite side of the bed where my uncle *Toby* was in his old fringed chair, with his chin resting upon his crutch—did ever a poor unfortunate man, brother *Toby*, cried my father, receive so many lashes?[145]

Or this further example in which the crutch takes on a more martial appearance:

Bless your honour! cried *Trim*, advancing three steps as he spoke, does a man think of his christian name when he goes upon the attack?—Or when he stands in the trench, *Trim*? cried my uncle *Toby*, looking firm—Or when he enters a breach? Said *Trim*, pushing in between two chairs—Or forces the lines? cried my uncle, rising up, and pushing his crutch like a pike—Or facing a platoon, cried *Trim*, presenting his stick like a firelock (4.18.??)

Note now the analogues in *FL*:

Había dejado el bastón atravesado sobre su regazo como la carabina o la lanza de un soldado en su descanso[146]

(He had laid his walking-stick across his knees, like the carbine or spear of a soldier at rest)[147]

Había agarrado su bastón con los dos puños por encima, como si fuera definitivamente una lanza, había apoyado en el cenicero el puro poco humeante[148]

(He was holding his walking-stick with his two clenched fists one above the other, as it were definitely a spear, he had placed his still smouldering cigar in the ashtray)[149]

[Wheeler] se reclinó sobre la barandilla y blandió el bastón con la mano izquierda, la punta hacia arriba, como si fuera un látigo más que una lanza, me recordó a un domador de pronto—.[150]

([Wheeler] leaned on the banister and brandished the walking-stick in his left hand, the tip uppermost, as if it were a whip rather than a spear, and suddenly he reminded me of a lion-tamer)[151]

se llevó el bastón al hombro, ahora como el fusil de un soldado en un desfile o de guardia, el mango como la culata, fue un gesto meditativo—.[152]

(he ... raised his walking-stick to his shoulder, like the rifle of a soldier on parade or on guard, with the handle as the rifle butt, it was a meditative gesture)[153]

---

[144] *TS*, 4.2.327.    [145] *TS*, 4.3.328.    [146] *FL*, p. 101.
[147] *Fever and Spear*, p. 75.    [148] *FL*, p. 118.    [149] *Fever and Spear*, p. 89.
[150] *FL*, p. 131.    [151] *Fever and Spear*, p. 100.    [152] *FL*, p. 132.
[153] *Fever and Spear*, p. 102.

All of this play paints a portrait of Wheeler as reliant on his stick as an aid but still dandyish enough to use it as a prop in conversation. But Wheeler is a long way from being the compliment to mankind that Hazlitt so warmly praised. Not only this, his wielding of the walking stick like a lance or soldier's rifle also anticipates revelations about Wheeler the servant of his country, albeit not in the front line of battle, but no less a part of the war effort.

A further Shandean resonance comes after Deza has delivered his tirade about De la Garza, when Wheeler laments that one cannot identify 'hijos de puta' from the first—'parece mentira que no se sepa *ab ovo*' ('it's amazing that people don't realise this *ab ovo*').[154] Recalling Tristram's promise—one that he fulfils in the most literal sense—to follow the tenets of good rhetoric and start his story from the beginning, Wheeler's fleeting remark turns out to be as teasing as it is telling because he is about to invite Deza to join a group of interpreters who seek to know precisely '*ab ovo*' what total strangers are capable of doing: the more nuanced version of whether or not they are an 'hijo de puta' ('son of a bitch').

It is as if Marías wishes to lull the reader into a false sense of security over Wheeler. He is an intriguing mixture of the bullishly youthful and the increasingly jaded, defiantly smoking in spite of his age, seating himself on the stairs rather than the more comfortable sofa nearby while he and Deza talk. These raffish qualities help Deza to imagine the younger Wheeler—'era fácil figurárselo como un galán de los años treinta o quizá cuarenta' ('it was still easy to him, to imagine him as a young heart-throb of the '30s or perhaps '40s')[155]—with the nostalgia for not only his friend's youth but also a bygone age.[156] It is the explosion of such easy nostalgia that will occupy much of Wheeler's characterization in the rest of the novel. Even though Wheeler is a would-be Uncle Toby, fond of playing Lillabullero on the piano,[157] there is a steel to him that belies and undercuts this image.

Clearly it is not only the reader who comes to realize Wheeler's ruthless edge. Although Deza does not state that his attitude towards his one-time mentor changed irrevocably during his brief intelligence career, he does offer the following limp excuses for not attending his funeral: 'Reconozco que me dio pereza, el recuerdo y la pena no tienen por qué hacerse

---

[154] *FL*, p. 105; *Fever and Spear*, p. 79.
[155] *FL*, p. 101; *Fever and Spear*, p. 76.
[156] César Pérez Gracia has also noted the Shandean resonances of this conversation at he foot of the stairs. See his 'Sterne y Marías o el coloquio de los peldaños. En torno a *Tu rostro mañana*', in *Allí donde uno diría que ya no puede haber nada*, pp. 77–85.
[157] *FL*, 457–8.

presentes en las ocasiones sociales. Estaba muy atareado en Madrid. Habría tenido que desempolvar mi birrete y mi toga. Lo dejé estar' ('And the truth is I couldn't be bothered; memory and grief don't always chime with social duty. I was very busy in Madrid. I would have had to dust off my cap and gown. So I just let it go').[158] On the morning after his initial soirée, he and Deza discuss the origins of the group of what Tupra now calls 'intérpretes de personas' ('interpreters of people'),[159] origins that can be traced back to the British campaign against 'careless talk' during the Second World War.[160] According to Wheeler, such was the paranoia that gripped the country over the fear of Nazi sympathizers spying on their countrymen and passing information to the enemy, that British Intelligence sought out those with the talent to see who was trustworthy and who not. But as he clarifies, not only did they need the talent, they also needed the courage to recognize the undesirable traits they had discerned in their subject:

> Por último estaban los muchos que, al igual que hoy sucede, tenían verdadera aversión, más aún, pánico a la arbitrariedad y a la posible injusticia de sus pareceres: los que preferían no pronunciarse nunca, agarrotados por la responsabilidad y por su invencible temor al yerro[161]

> (Then there were the many who, exactly as happens now, had a real aversion, no, more than that, a terror of the arbitrariness and possible unfairness of their own views: the sort who prefer never to declare themselves, hamstrung by the responsibility and by their invincible fear of making a mistake)[162]

Were we seeking an explanation for Wheeler's determination to recruit Deza, we might best find it in this conviction that these rare, chosen individuals have a duty that verges on a moral obligation to use their ability for the greater good. The irony is, of course, that Deza will see during his final conversation with Wheeler that agreement on how best to achieve the greater good was, however, not forthcoming even during a conflict that pitted right against wrong in as clear cut a manner as the Second World War did. He will likewise discover to his cost during his time in Tupra's employ that the boundaries of where the greater good lies have become unsettlingly blurred in recent times: what use should the British government make of videos that incriminate international heads of state if the stable rule they offer is better than any visible alternatives? In fact Marías has stated that *TRM* first began to take shape in his mind as he became aware of the threat of obsolescence that hung over Britain's secret service after the fall of the Iron Curtain:

---

[158] *VSA*, pp. 683–4; *Poison, Shadow and Farewell*, p. 527.     [159] *FL*, p. 469.
[160] *Fever and Spear*, p. 371.     [161] *FL*, p. 467.     [162] *Fever and Spear*, p. 370.

Los servicios secretos británicos pasaron una mala temporada entre la caída del muro de Berlín y los atentados de las torres gemelas. Fueron unos doce años en que no tenían trabajo, y durante los cuales no tuvieron otra manera de sobrevivir que saliendo a la búsqueda de clientes. En la novela lo cuenta uno de los personajes y es algo totalmente cierto, no una invención. Habían perdido a su tradicional enemigo, a los rusos por decirlo de manera simplona, y empezaron a ofrecer sus servicios a grandes compañías, a hacer espionaje industrial. Lo hicieron con el conocimiento de los altos mandos y la manera que encontraron para camuflar esta actividad fue utilizando el argumento de que si estaban sirviendo a las grandes compañías del Reino Unido es que estaban sirviendo a su país.[163]

(The British intelligence services went through a rough patch between the fall of the Berlin Wall and the attacks on the Twin Towers. Those were twelve years in which they had no work, and in the course of which they had no other means of survival than to go out in search of customers. One of the characters in my novel describes the situation and it's something that's absolutely true, by no means invented. They had lost their traditional enemy, the Russians to put it simplistically, and they began to offer their services to big corporations, to carry out industrial espionage. They did so with the full knowledge of their senior commanders, while the pretext they found to camouflage this activity was by using the argument that, if they were helping British companies, they were serving the national interest.)

In the novel itself, Pérez Nuix even alludes to a bona fide article that appeared in *The Independent* 'tan sólo unos días antes del 11 de septiembre [de 2001]' ('only a few days before 11 September [2001]'),[164] reporting the proposal made by Sir Stephen Lander, then head of MI5, to offer his organization's services to private business.[165]

The group's creation was made necessary by the failure of the campaign against 'careless talk', one that can be put down, in Wheeler's view at least, to two interconnected factors. Firstly, far from deterring the British population from sharing their titbits of sensitive information, the campaign gave that exchange an added frisson of transgression. Secondly, it sought to deny a people, who were already suffering the deprivations of rationing and separation from loved ones, the single greatest democratizing social leveller—the ability to interact using language. To illustrate his point that language has always been the tool that most effectively breaks down social

---

[163] José Andrés Rojo, 'Javier Marías, el escritor con brújula', *Turia. Revista Cultural*, 88 (2008–2009), 352–61 (pp. 353–4).

[164] *VSA*, p. 63.

[165] *Poison, Shadow and Farewell*, p. 43. For the article referred to, which did indeed exist, see Steve Boggan, 'MI5 offers to spy for British firms', *The Independent*, 7 September 2001, p. 1.

barriers, Wheeler recalls Act IV Scene I of Shakespeare's *King Henry V*,[166] in which 'el rey se emboza en una capa prestada y se acerca, se mezcla con tres soldados en la víspera de la batalla' ('the kind wraps himself in a borrowed cloak and goes and sits down in the camp with three soldiers').[167] It is here that the increasingly jaded Wheeler emerges, where Marías has carefully constructed his characterization around several key texts that the ageing don refers to or quotes. It is their selection and manipulation that I will now discuss in detail because it epitomizes Marías's technique of creating character through translation and palimpsest.

In Act IV Scene I, Henry wanders among his troops on the eve of the Battle of Agincourt doubting his courage to lead them in the field, racked by guilt at his father's usurpation of the throne, and evoking wistfully the unburdened life that 'private men' enjoy:

> What infinite heart's ease/Must kings neglect that private men enjoy!/And what have kings that privates have not too,/Save ceremony, save general ceremony?[168]

> "¡Qué infinito sosiego de corazón deben los reyes perderse, que los hombres particulares disfrutan! ¿Y qué tienen los reyes que no tengan también los particulares, salvo el ceremonial, salvo la general ceremonia?"[169]

We might note in passing that Marías's translation of this phrase demonstrates his versatile grasp of English since the word 'private' appears in its nominal form in Browne's *Hydriotaphia*: 'Happy are they whom privacy makes innocent; who deal so with men in this world that they are not afraid to meet them in the next'.[170] There, he had rendered it as 'aislamiento': 'Dichosos son aquellos a los que el aislamiento hace inocentes; los que tratan con los hombres en este mundo de manera que no temen encontrárselos en el otro'.[171] Although it is not certain that by 'privacy' Browne means 'withdrawn from the society of others'—hence 'aislamiento'—it is a plausible alternative. When translating Henry's soliloquy, however, Marías translates 'privacy' in the sense of 'not holding public office' that Henry intends, using the Spanish word 'particulares'. According to María Moliner's dictionary of Spanish, 'particular' does indeed mean

---

[166] I should clarify that Wheeler does not name Henry V at this point; he merely describes the Shakespearean scene. It is not until *BS*, p. 158 that we receive confirmation that Deza has subsequently tracked down the play to which his friend and mentor was alluding.
[167] *FL*, p. 416; *Fever and Spear*, p. 329.
[168] William Shakespeare, *King Henry V*, ed. by T. W. Craik (London: Routledge, 1995; repr. London: Arden, 2002), IV. 1. 233–6.
[169] *FL*, pp. 416–17.     [170] *Religio Medici*, pp. 132–3.
[171] *La religión de un médico*, p. 244.

'Persona que no tiene un cargo o una representación oficial' ('Person who does not hold an official post or position').[172]

To return to how this quotation characterizes Wheeler, it reinforces the idea that some individuals are marked out for public duty and that many will, like Henry on the eve of battle, find their conscience racked by the difficult choices that are its unavoidable consequence. His own guilt over the death of his wife, and self-questioning over how ultimately justifiable his actions in the service of his country were, are deferred until the third volume of the novel. The suggestiveness and air of tortured mystery that surround Wheeler make him one of Marías's most captivating characters. We might recall that he too had spoken earlier in *FL* of having a mind too full of memories,[173] much as Henry is all too aware of the murder of Richard II that allowed his father, and now him, to wear the English crown. Henry lists the penances he has put in place to expiate the crime, among which are the re-burial of Richard's body, his own tears for the dead, and alms for five hundred poor. Wheeler summarizes thus:

> Los reyes antiguos eran muy desvergonzados, pero al menos los de Shakespeare no se engañaban del todo: se sabían con las manos manchadas de sangre y no olvidaban a qué debían el poderse ceñir corona, además de a los crímenes y las traiciones y las conspiraciones (yo no sé si fueron demasiado humanos).[174]

> (Kings of old were shameless creatures, but at least Shakespeare's kings did not entirely deceive themselves: they knew their hands were stained with blood and they did not forget how they came to wear the crown, apart from murders and betrayals and plots (perhaps they were too human).)[175]

Both a blessing and a worry to the troubled king is the fact that he can commend his troops to the care of a higher power: a blessing because praying to God holds out the hope that they might win the day in spite of the odds; a worry because, if in God's eyes neither his rule nor his cause in France are just, the weight of thousands more deaths will tip the balance heavily in his disfavour on Judgement Day. This fear is even put into words by one of Henry's unwitting companions round the camp fire, as Wheeler recalls:

> En esa misma escena de Shakespeare, sin ir más lejos, uno de los soldados con los que el rey conversa antes de su soliloquio anuncia que éste se verá en aprietos para rendir cuentas si no es buena causa la de su guerra: "Cuando todas esas piernas y brazos y cabezas segadas en la batalla", dice, "se junten el

---

[172] Listed under 6 in meaning of 'particular'. See María Moliner, *Diccionario del uso del español*, 2 vols (Madrid: Gredos, 1996), I, 650.
[173] *FL*, pp. 126–7.     [174] *FL*, p. 417.     [175] *Fever and Spear*, pp. 310–11.

último día y griten todas 'Morimos en tal lugar' ". Ya lo ves, era creencia, no sólo que hablarían y hasta protestarían los muertos, sino incluso sus cabezas y miembros desperdigados y sueltos, una vez reunidos para presentarse con decoro a juicio.[176]

(In that same scene from Shakespeare, for example, before the king gives his soliloquy, one of the soldiers with whom he speaks says that the king will have a hard time of it should the cause of the war prove to have been a bad one: "When all those legs and arms and heads, chopped off in battle," he says, "shall join together at the latter day, and cry all, 'We died at such a place.'" You see, that was what they believed, not only that the dead would speak and even protest, but that their scattered, separated heads and limbs would protest as well, once reunited to present themselves for judgement with due decorum.)[177]

In Wheeler's view, the gradual erosion of Christian belief and its comforting certainties deprived many of those who fought in the great wars of the twentieth century, himself among them, of a faith in such ultimate justice.[178] We might wonder if Wheeler's nostalgia for the certainties of Christian judgement is not a sublimated desire for punishment of his wrongdoing. The sad truth is that, even though language may be the great social leveller, there is one boundary that it cannot overcome—that between the living and the dead, as Wheeler wistfully observes:

Ahora en cambio miró hacia abajo un segundo, y aún tenía la vista en la hierba o más allá, en la invisible tierra bajo la tierra, cuando añadió tras tan breve pausa: 'Los únicos que no lo [el hablar] comparten, Jacobo, son los vivos con los muertos'.[179]

(He looked down for a second, and still had his eyes fixed on the grass, or perhaps beyond that, on the earth beneath the grass, or beyond that, on the invisible earth beneath the earth, then added after a brief pause: 'The only ones who do not share a common language Jacobo, are the living and the dead.')[180]

Deza's observes his friend's haunted figure, beautifully capturing Wheeler's stare, that appears to search beneath the ground for those who lie uneasy in their graves, as well as into a past too full of troubling memories ever to be far from his mind.

We already know that Wheeler has no faith in such restorative justice: today's victims will not see their murderers punished tomorrow. What was once the comforting reassurance of an ultimate redressing of the balance has found a modern equivalent in the self-interested search for

---

[176] *FL*, p. 422.        [177] *Fever and Spear*, p. 334.        [178] *FL*, pp. 424–5.
[179] *FL*, p. 419.        [180] *Fever and Spear*, p. 332.

compensation indulged by the descendants of those wronged. Wheeler rails against the tendency for governments or groups to seek apologies, or financial gain, for events that took place long in the past.[181] He has a secular cynicism about such claims:

> Cada persona es cada persona y no se prolonga en sus remotos vástagos, ni siquiera en los inmediatos, que a menudo son infieles; y de nada sirven estas transacciones y gestos a quienes fueron damnificados, a quienes se persiguió y torturó, se esclavizó y asesinó de veras en su única y verdadera vida: esos están bien perdidos en la noche de los tiempos y en la de las infamias, que sin duda no será menos larga.[182]

> (A person is a person and does not continue to exist through his remote descendants, not even his immediate ones, who often prove unfaithful; and these transactions and gestures do nothing for those who suffered, for those who really were persecuted and tortured, enslaved and murdered in their one real life: they are lost for ever in the night of time and in the night of infamy, which is doubtless no less long.)[183]

He is denying the belief in metempsychosis that had featured so prominently in *ES*, as we have seen. Wheeler's words act as the mirror image of the Brownean thought, quoted in *ES*, that human lives are lived over again. In the sentence up to the first semicolon we might detect the cadence of Browne's prose, with each clause shortening in syllable length and creating the falling rhythm that is so characteristic of *Hydriotaphia*. Browne's influence could well have supplied Marías with the phrase 'noche de los tiempos', which has an identical equivalent in *Hydriotaphia*: 'the night of time far surpasseth the day—and who knows when was the equinox?' and in Marías's version 'la noche del tiempo con creces supera al día, ¿y quién sabe cuándo fue el equinoccio?'.[184] The phrase reveals Browne's awareness that large parts of human history shall forever remain dark to efforts to illuminate them. Laurence Stapleton reminds us that '[Browne's] words are moving because he ponders the ties binding generations of men to each other, and shows their frailty compared with the eventual contemporaneity of all in the resurrection'.[185] Wheeler's world view finds no place for that Christian certainty and underlying the bitterness of his atheistic

---

[181] For example, *FL*, p. 300. Here we can clearly see another 'préstamo' ('borrowing') from author to character of Marías's views as a columnist for *El País Semanal*: he has attacked the culture of victimhood through which some groups seek political capital from the crimes inflicted on their forefathers.

[182] *FL*, p. 300.

[183] *Fever and Spear*, p. 237.

[184] *Religio Medici, Hydriotaphia*, and *The Garden of Cyrus*, p. 130; *La religión de un médico* p. 239.

[185] Laurence Stapleton, *The Elected Circle: Studies in the Art of Prose* (Princeton: Princeton University Press, 1973), p. 58.

scepticism is the awareness that so many victims have no redress and no opportunity to confront their murderers. His is another of Marías's complex and rich psychological portraits. He is reluctant to discuss his past openly or to elaborate further on Valerie's mysterious death, despite speculating whether the foundation of the espionage group Deza is to join might have saved her life. 'La lástima fue que no surgiera la idea unos pocos meses antes, quién sabe si Val, si mi mujer, si Valerie, no habría muerto en ese caso' ('It's just a shame that the idea didn't come up a few months earlier, who knows, Val, my wife Valerie, might not have died').[186] Until the final volume of *VSA*, his past is a closed book of which only glimpses are to be had.

Shortly after Deza has observed Wheeler's troubled stare, the latter's mind turns to dreams, the one place, according to him, in which the living and dead can communicate. He cites the example of Milton's sonnet to his dead second wife, Catherine Woodcock, the same sonnet Casaldáliga had used to anticipate his role as a bereaved husband in *ES*:

> Y al inclinarse ella para abrazarlo en el sueño, entonces "*I wak'd, she fled, and day brought back my night*", así termina.' ('Desperté, ella se deshizo, y el día devolvió mi noche'.) 'Con los muertos se vuelve a la noche siempre, y a no oír más que su silencio, y a no obtener nunca respuesta. No, no hablan, son los únicos; y son también la mayoría, si contamos a cuantos atravesaron y dejaron atrás el mundo. Aunque todos hablaran sin duda durante su estancia.[187]

> (And as she leaned forwards to embrace him in the dream, "I wak'd, she fled, and day brought back my night", that's how it ends. With the dead you always return to night and to hearing only their silence and to never receiving a reply. No, they never talk, they are the only ones; and they are also the majority, if we count all those who have passed through the world and left it behind. Although they all doubtless talked while they were here.)[188]

Once again, his characterization is brilliantly reinforced through this use of translated passages. Wheeler is an adoptive British man, born just as the Great War was erupting, the product of a rigorous formal education system and years of reticence about painful memories enforced by governmental and social edict. Were we not yet to have fully grasped the implications of this, his act of revealing his own emotional state through reference to Milton makes the point abundantly clear. One not given to conspicuous self-revelation, who would not lightly discuss an episode as

---

[186] *FL*, p. 387; *Fever and Spear*, p. 305.     [187] *FL*, pp. 427–8.

[188] *Fever and Spear*, p. 338. I have corrected what appears to be an exceedingly rare mistake in Jull Costa's English version. Her original reads 'as he leaned forward to embrace her' where the Spanish makes clear that it is the other way round.

personal and painful as the death of his wife, literary allusion is for him more like a strategy of indirectness. In this case Deza picks up the inferences clearly enough, if only because he is an attentive interlocutor, but they keep Wheeler's self-revelation at several crucial removes from himself. He is, moreover, a literary critic by trade and just as he could not resist the temptation to offer wider assessment of Shakespeare's representation of kingship in his comments about *King Henry V*—'(yo no sé si fueron demasiado humanos)'—when describing Milton's sonnet on his dead wife, he is similarly precise:

> Y en ella recupera [Milton] la visión triplemente: la suya, como facultad y sentido; la imagen de su mujer imposible, pues no sólo él, sino nadie puede verla ya en el presente, se ha borrado de la tierra; y sobre todo el rostro y la figura de ella, que en él no son recordados siquiera sino imaginados, nuevos y nunca antes vistos, porque él jamás la había contemplado en vida más que con la mente y el tacto, fueron sus segundas nupcias y estaba ciego al casarse.[189]

> (And in that dimension he recovered his vision threefold: his own, as faculty and sense; the impossible image of his wife, for neither he nor anyone else could still see her in the present, she had been erased from the earth; and, above all, her face and figure, which, in him, were not even remembered but imagined, new and never seen before, because he had never seen her in life other than with his mind and with his touch, she was his second wife and he was already blind when they married.)[190]

Later revelations, but also the ongoing sense of mystery over the fate of Valerie, indicate why Marías should have chosen to return to this favourite poem. Rather than dwell here on the implications of the poem either for himself or others, Wheeler immediately turns the conversation back to the subject of careless talk, as if veering away from so personal a subject before Deza can pursue it any further. As *FL* ends and the two friends pause in their discussion to go in for lunch, Deza asks his mentor how Valerie died, the answer to which Wheeler begs they defer for another time: ' "Eso...," dijo. "Déjame que te lo cuente otro día, si te parece. Si no tienes inconveniente." Parecía estar pidiendo un favor, le costó cada palabra' (' "Ah..." he said. "Do you mind if I tell you another day. If that's all right." He seemed to be asking me a favour, every word was painful').[191]

If much of the reflection engaged in by Deza throughout *TRM* hinges on the question of whether or not the ends justify the means, his final

---

[189] *FL*, p. 427.    [190] *Fever and Spear*, p. 338.
[191] *FL*, p. 472; *Fever and Spear*, p. 374.

Delmer & Sebald

conversation with Wheeler draws that question out in a rich dialogue of startling force and resonance. Once again, Marías constructs Wheeler's voice as a palimpsest of several other texts, this time histories of the Second World War: the autobiography of Sefton Delmer, who was in charge of Britain's covert propaganda broadcasting to Germany from July 1940, and W. G. Sebald's essay on the Allied fire bombing of German cities, *On the Natural History of Destruction*. Some construction of Wheeler's voice through quotation—notably from Delmer—is freely acknowledged in the text, with the character quoting from memory the former spy's published autobiography. However, what I would like to examine is the selection and editing of material from Delmer, a labour that is also one of translation since Marías is rendering the English in Spanish. The borrowing from Sebald takes the form of a more subtle homage and translational hybridization, with the German writer's name nowhere to be found in the text. In his case, of course, Marías is also translating and hybridizing a text that has already been translated from German into English.[192] What he is using both texts to develop above all is an interrogation of the idea that wartime and peacetime are mutually exclusive in the human mind—that each is inconceivable to the other when one holds sway. It is worth noting further that he is not interested in these texts for their particular truth value—the fact that the authors claim to be describing events that actually happened—but rather for the particular examples they offer of warfare taken to its most ethically troubling extremes.

This point was reinforced by a speech entitled 'Para empezar por el principio' he gave in 2008. There he described his aversion to fictional works that attempt to bolster their interest or legitimacy by declaring themselves ' "Basados en hechos reales" ' (' "Based on real events" ').[193] Such an assurance, he suggested, ought to warn the potential reader against the defensiveness of the artists involved. Is what they have produced so lacking in verisimilitude, coherence, or interest on its own terms, so reliant on outrageous coincidence or on cheap emotional tricks ('baraturas'), that the only legitimacy they can still call upon for their work is that it is indeed based on a true story?[194] Marías cites the example of his great-grandfather, Enrique Manera y Cao, the first man in the author's family (to his knowledge) to publish a work of fiction. Manera y Cao was moreover the subject of what he calls 'una de las primeras historias que yo

---

[192] We can assert this with confidence given that Marías does not speak or read German.

[193] JM, 'Para empezar por el principio', in Mario Vargas Llosa, Javier Marías, and Arturo Pérez-Reverte, *Lecciones y maestros: II Cita Internacional de la literatura en español* (Santillana del Mar: Santillana, 2008), pp. 109–33 (p. 111).

[194] 'Para empezar por el principio', pp. 111–12.

escuché como si se tratara de un cuento, es decir, de una ficción' ('one of the first stories that I listened to as if it were a tale, that is, a work of fiction').[195] According to that tale, the Cuban-Spanish Manera y Cao was the victim of a curse uttered by a mulatto beggar on a road near La Habana in response to the former's refusal to give alms. That curse warned him that he and his first-born son would die before their fiftieth birthday, far from home, and without receiving a proper burial. Not only did this triumvirate of indignities befall Manera y Cao when he died at sea at the age of forty-nine on his way back to Spain after the fall of Cuba to the United States in 1898, it also came to pass in the case of his eldest son. He was lost in combat in 1921 at the age of forty-six during Spain's disastrous colonial war in Morocco and his body never recovered. It was at that moment that, in Marías's view, the story of the curse began to be worth telling, not because it was true but because in its picturesque details, improbable coincidences, and uncertain particulars it sounded like fiction:

> Fue allí y entonces cuando pasó a ser parte de una historia, o aún es más, se convirtió en su desencadenante. Y, por mucho que ocurriera en la realidad, fue sólo en aquel momento cuando mereció ser contada, esto es: cuando de pronto pareció ficción. No sólo un relato acabado, sino sin ningún cabo suelto.[196]

> (It was there and then that it became part of a story, or to go even further, that it became the story's trigger. And, irrespective of the fact that it happened in reality, it was only at that moment that the story deserved to be told, that is: when all of a sudden it seemed like a work of fiction. Not just a nicely rounded-off story, but one without a single thread left dangling.)

In other words, what the author himself will have been aiming at when he hybridized Delmer and Sebald for the purposes of Wheeler's speech is a poetic truth, a sense of roundedness and coherence exemplified by this family anecdote and first heard at his grandmother's knee.

The ostensible subject of Wheeler's peroration is the death of Valerie, but in order to explain her demise, he sets the scene of the Allied propaganda war against the Third Reich and the lengths to which British intelligence was prepared to go in its search for victory. Like many passages in *TRM* it makes for uncomfortable reading not because of sensationalist elements or cheap fireworks, but because of the matter-of-fact presentation of actions that, viewed from the comfort of a peaceful Europe, look like the most gratuitous cruelty. Wheeler describes how his young wife became embroiled in the activities of the Political Warfare Executive

---

[195] 'Para empezar por el principio', p. 123.
[196] 'Para empezar por el principio', p. 130.

(PWE), an organization that acted with apparent impunity in waging all-out propaganda war on the German people. Marías is thus weaving the fictional character into a narrative which has documentary evidence to sustain it. Paraphrasing Delmer's autobiography, Wheeler evokes the PWE practice of sending letters to the bereaved relatives of German soldiers who had died of their wounds in hospital, purporting to be from a concerned comrade and informing the family that their son/father/husband had died not from injuries received in battle but from a lethal injection administered by the medical authorities: the ruthless doctors had needed their wounded relative's bed for a soldier with a better chance of returning to the front line.[197] Wheeler continues:

> No es que a Delmer y a su unidad se les escapara que la verdadera crueldad era la suya, extrema, al hacer creer semejante falacia (verosímil, por otra parte) a una desolada viuda, a unos padres ancianos o a unos hijos huérfanos. Pero si eso servía para crear descontento y rencor entre la población, rebajar la moral de los combatientes, desunir a la tropa y propiciar deserciones, estaba por encima de cualquier otra consideración.[198]

> (Delmer and his unit were perfectly aware that they were the ones who were practising real and extreme cruelty by making a grief-stricken widow or someone's aged parents or orphaned children believe such a falsehood (which was, on the other hand, quite believable). However, if this served to feed discontent and rancour among the population, to lower the morale of the combatants, spread disunity among the troops and encourage desertions, that was what mattered.)[199]

The choice of adjectives is sober in spite of the stark picture being painted: the only one that carries a heavy emotional load is 'desolada', the others—'ancianos' and 'huérfanos'—are factual in their content. Delmer and his team operated in full knowledge of the cruelty of their actions—'No es que... se les escapara'—and yet all they could muster by way of justification was the hope—'si eso servía'—of provoking discontent and rancour among the enemy. Looked at with today's eyes, Wheeler tacitly acknowledges, this tactic interferes with our sense that even in the heat of battle some spaces and people should remain inviolate—the relatives of the dead being high on that list.

Wheeler goes on to speculate that there was a degree of embarrassment even at the establishment level over Delmer's conduct of the dirty war against Germany. He reinforces the point by quoting the speech Delmer made to his team of black operatives shortly before the disbanding of

[197] Sefton Delmer, *An Autobiography*, 2 vols (London: Secker & Warburg, 1961–1962), I: *Black Boomerang* (1962), p. 134.
[198] *VSA*, pp. 619–20.          [199] *Poison, Shadow and Farewell*, p. 480.

their unit and once victory had been secured.²⁰⁰ Importantly, however, Wheeler/Marías do not acknowledge Delmer as the source, instead introducing it with 'las instrucciones a sus miembros negros fueron de este tenor, más o menos' ('its black members were given more or less the following instructions'). Equally importantly and as we shall see, he also heavily edits Delmer's words:

'Durante años nos hemos abstenido de hablar de nuestro trabajo con toda persona ajena a nuestra unidad, así que poco se sabe de nosotros y de nuestras técnicas. La gente puede tener sus sospechas, pero no sabe a ciencia cierta. Queremos que sigáis igual, que así se mantenga. Que nada ni nadie os lleve a jactaros de las tareas que hemos llevado a cabo, de los trucos y trampas que hemos tendido al enemigo. Si empezamos a presumir de nuestras ingeniosidades, quién sabe en qué pararía eso. Así que punto en boca'.—'*So mum's the word*', fue lo que dijo aquí Wheeler, y me sonó haber visto la expresión en alguno de los carteles de la *careless talk*—.²⁰¹

("For years we have abstained from talking about our work to anyone not in our unit, and therefore little is known about us or our techniques. People may have their suspicions, but they don't know anything for certain. And to keep it that way, we want you to continue as you have up until now. Don't allow anything or anyone to provoke you into boasting about the work we've done, about the tricks and traps we laid for the enemy. If we start to show off to people about the ingenious things we got up to, who knows where it will end. So mum's the word." And I remembered having seen that last expression on one of the 'careless talk' posters.)²⁰²

The passage in Delmer in fact reads as follows:

"Our security has been excellent up to now," I said. "You have not talked about our work with outsiders and nothing much is known about us or our technique. People may have their suspicions, but they don't know. I want to keep it that way. Don't be misled into boasting about the jobs we have done, the tricks we have played on the enemy.... "If we start boasting of the clever things we did, who knows what the result of that will be. So mum's the word. Propaganda is something one keeps quiet about. Are you *einverstanden?*"²⁰³

With the ellipsis in this second quotation I have obviously indicated the material that Marías elected to omit from his quotation and hybridization of this speech. What the ellipsis cannot indicate is the size of the omission,

²⁰⁰ 'Black operatives' here refers to the name given to covert operations—black operations, the black arts—by British Intelligence.
²⁰¹ *VSA*, pp. 620–1.
²⁰² *Poison, Shadow and Farewell*, pp. 480–1.
²⁰³ *Black Boomerang*, pp. 218–19.

which is in fact of five paragraphs of text comprising thirty-two lines. In these, Delmer explains to his unit that their silence is vital in avoiding a repeat of the rumours and innuendo that circulated in Germany after the Great War in response to Lord Northcliffe's revelations over the propaganda campaign he had been responsible for waging during that conflict. According to Delmer, Lord Northcliffe's hunger for public acclaim played into the hands of those in Germany—Hitler foremost among them—who had sought to explain away their defeat as owing more to the dirty tricks of enemy propagandists than to their inferior military might. By editing out these considerations from Delmer's speech, Marías is able to use it to suggest a degree of official ambivalence or unease over the tactics employed by the PWE. We also note that Marías adds alliteration to the speech, lending it a greater sense of rhetorical flair: 'Don't be misled' becomes 'Que nada ni nadie'; 'the tricks we have played on the enemy' become 'los trucos y trampas que hemos tendido al enemigo'. Nor can he resist reproducing the original English phrase 'So mum's the word', one that in its old-world charm sits in incongruous contrast to the events that that same old world witnessed.

Wheeler substantiates his claims over official unease concerning the PWE by evoking one of the most chilling passages in Delmer's autobiography, where even its author's customary pugnacious self-confidence wavers. We note again Marías's eye for selecting incidents that sit delicately on the cusp of moral acceptability. This pitiless episode in the war on the German civilian population involved hijacking radio transmission signals in order to spread false information through what were regarded as bona fide channels. Wheeler explains that Delmer and his team managed to make misleading broadcasts in perfect German (among the prisoners of war who collaborated with the PWE was a trained radio announcer) telling civilians of the alleged 'safety zones' that had been agreed with the Allies, areas that would remain free from aerial attack and to which many beleaguered families made their way in the mistaken belief that shelter awaited them. Churchill hoped that these columns of desperate refugees would 'impede the strategic communications of the Hun armies'.[204] Delmer was able to see for himself the effects of his handiwork when he travelled to Germany in March 1945. But far from experiencing a rush of pride in the achievements of his team, he looked with pity on the

> miserable, ragged families, trudging wearily along the Autobahn and through debris-cluttered streets of bomb ruins. Behind them they dragged carts,

[204] *Black Boomerang*, p. 200.

hybridization



> buses that had no fuel for their engines, and even hearses. All were loaded with bedding and babies. I did not stop to question any of them whether it was a message on Radio Cologne or Radio Frankfurt that had first started them on their trek. I did not want to know. I feared the answer might be 'yes'.[205]

Marías appears to have hybridized Delmer's account with W. G. Sebald's equally distressing evocation of a group of refugees from the bombed out remains of Hamburg, a passage to which Marías had drawn attention in a 2003 article, shortly after reading *On the Natural History of Destruction* for the first time:[206]

> The exodus of survivors ... had begun on the night of the air raid itself. It started, as Nossack writes, with 'constant movement in all the neighbouring streets ... going no one knew where.' ... Friedrich Reck describes a group of forty to fifty such refugees trying to force their way into a train at a station in Upper Bavaria. As they do so a cardboard suitcase 'falls on the platform, bursts open and spills its contents. Toys, a manicure case, singed underwear. And last of all, the roasted corpse of a child, shrunk like a mummy, which its half-deranged mother has been carrying about with her, the relic of a past that was still intact a few days ago.'[207]

Notice how the incident Sebald quotes has been hybridized with Delmer's account to masterly effect in the speech by Wheeler:

[205] *Black Boomerang*, p. 205.

[206] The relevant passage reads as follows: 'En una cita del extraordinario diario de Reck-Malleczewan, éste cuenta cómo días después, ya en otro sitio, a una refugiada hamburguesa se le abrió la maleta al subir a un tren abarrotado, y cómo de ella salieron primero objetos ya inútiles y privados de sentido, y luego el cadáver achicharrado de un bebé, "encogido como una momia," que la madre llevaba de un lado a otro, "reliquia de un pasado que poco antes estaba intacto"' ('In a quotation from the extraordinary diary of Reck-Malleczewan, the latter describes how, days later and by then elsewhere, the suitcase of a refugeed mother from Hamburg burst open onto the platform as she tried to board a packed train, spilling at first only objects that were by now useless and robbed of their purpose, then the roasted corpse of a child, "shrunk like a mummy" that she had been carrying about with her, "relic of a past that was still intact a few days ago"). See 'Moscas y olor y gritos', in *EOOL*, pp. 44–6 (p. 45).

[207] W. G. Sebald, *On the Natural History of Destruction*, trans. by Anthea Bell (London: Hamish Hamilton, 2003), p. 29. When Marías was asked to contribute to an *El País* article canvassing the opinions of Spanish writers as to what novels, films, television series, or historical works they would recommend on the Second World War, Sebald's essay featured among his choices. He also recommended *Band of Brothers* (HBO, 2001); *The Longest Day* (Dir. Andrew Marton, Bernhard Wicki, Darryl F. Zanuck, Ken Annakin. 20th-Century Fox, 1962); *Night and Fog* (Dir. Alan Resnais, Nouveaux Pictures, 1955); *Tora! Tora! Tora!* (Dir. Richard Fleischer, 20th-Century Fox, 1970); Field Marshall Lord Alanbrooke, *War Diaries 1939–1945*; Antony Beevor, *Berlin: The Downfall 1945*; Winston Churchill, *The Second World War*; Marie Vassiltchikov, *Berlin Diaries, 1940–1945*; Rebecca West, *The Meaning of Treason*. See Winston Manrique, 'Los últimos días de la Segunda Guerra Mundial', *El País*, 25 July 2005, pp. 28, 31.

las gentes huyendo sin saber dónde iban y atravesando sucesivos paisajes de ruinas, arrastrando consigo lo poco que les había quedado o que habían podido meter en sus precarios vehículos que no funcionaban, o marchando a pie por las carreteras y campos con niños muy pequeños a cuestas y las miradas ausentes o aterrorizadas, a veces con niños ya muertos que no se decidían a enterrar en mitad de un sendero, o de los que no se atrevían a desprenderse y que seguían cargando como si fueran efigies, sin el menor sentido... Y decía Sefton Delmer que no se paró a preguntarle a nadie si lo que les había impulsado a lanzarse a los caminos había sido por ventura mensajes de Radio Colonia o de Radio Francfort, cuyas frecuencias él había ocupado. 'No quería saberlo. Temía que la respuesta pudiera ser "sí",' escribió, recuerdo.[208]

(people aimlessly fleeing, trudging through a series of ruined landscapes, dragging with them all that remained of their possessions or that they had been able to pile into their broken-down vehicles, or walking along roads and across fields with very young children on their backs, their eyes empty or terrified, sometimes with dead children whom they didn't dare to abandon, but continued pointlessly to carry as if they were efigies... And Sefton Delmer said that he didn't stop to ask anyone if, by any chance, what had first impelled them to set off along the roads and begin their aimless wanderings had been the messages broadcast on Radio Cologne or Radio Frankfurt, whose frequencies he had taken over. I remember that he wrote: "I didn't want to know. I feared the answer might be 'yes' ".)[209]

He has reworked the detailing here: the specificity of a single incident that in Sebald is so striking—the child's body falling incongruously from the sprung-open suitcase—has been altered such that the homage is recognizable without the original being pillaged. In fact, the specificity has dissolved into an indeterminate number of people bearing their dead because they lack the certainty of return that would allow them to bury them along their routeless journey. What the hybridization achieves is to lend the suffering of many a particularity of detail that heightens its impact on the mind's eye. What we might also note here is the effect created by the alternating use of hypotaxis and parataxis, which is of a bewildering proliferation of suffering that the sentence structure itself struggles to contain.[210]

---

[208] *VSA*, pp. 626–7.        [209] *Poison, Shadow and Farewell*, p. 484.

[210] Further material Marías has gleaned from Delmer includes the PWE tactic of printing and distributing fake 'Wanted' posts of members of the German SS (*VSA*, p. 618; *Black Boomerang*, pp. 126–7); the presence in Delmer's team of a collector of German official documentation and typefaces who was also a prodigious forger (*VSA*, p. 641; *Black Boomerang*, pp. 127–8); the fact that Delmer allowed his beard to grow during the conflict, though Marías does not include the Dorian Gray-like experience he had when shaving it off at the end of the war (*VSA*, p. 635; *Black Boomerang*, pp. 217–18). Interestingly, the account of Wheeler's first meeting with Hewlett Johnson, the Red Dean, is not inspired by

With this homage in mind, we might further detect the tone of Sebald's essay in the remarks Wheeler makes on Arthur 'Bomber' Harris. *On the Natural History of Destruction* is an extended examination of why it was that in the years after the Second World War so few German writers attempted to record or describe the levelling of so many of their cities by Allied bombing raids. Although Sebald recognizes that their reluctance must in large part have been caused by collective guilt over the millions of war dead scattered across Europe, he has no hesitation in characterizing the fire bombing of German cities as an indefensible policy. On Harris, Sebald makes the following observations:

> In fact there is much to suggest that in Harris a man had risen to the head of Bomber Command who, according to Solly Zuckerman, liked destruction for its own sake, and was thus in perfect sympathy with the innermost principle of every war, which is to aim for as wholesale an annihilation of the enemy with his dwellings, his history and his natural environment as can possibly be achieved. Elias Canetti has linked the fascination of power in its purest form to the growing number of its accumulated victims. In line with this idea, Sir Arthur Harris's position was unassailable *because* of his unlimited interest in destruction. His plan for successive devastating strikes, which he followed uncompromisingly to the end, was overwhelmingly simple in its logic, and by comparison any real strategic alternatives such as disabling the fuel supply were bound to look like mere diversionary tactics. The war in the air was war pure and undisguised.[211]

Wheeler allows himself an unguarded and darkly humorous condemnation of Harris, one whose spirit chimes in harmony with Sebald's text:

> Arthur Harris, el Mariscal del Aire, fue el que ordenó cocer a cincuenta mil hamburgueses y a ciento cincuenta mil dresdeneses hacia el final de la Guerra bajo la cínica pretensión de estar atacando objetivos militares, y también arrasó Colonia y Francfort, Düsseldorf y Mannheim, era un hombre implacable con demasiado poder, casi un psicópata al que le valía todo para aplastar al enemigo y ganar.[212]

---

Delmer's autobiography, though Johnson and Delmer did meet during the latter's time in Spain as a war correspondent for the *Daily Express*. His account of their first meeting, rather than a tale of the heroic breaking of the naval blockade on Bilbao, is a more scabrous anecdote concerning Johnson moving into a hotel room that was formerly the site of a brothel. See Sefton Delmer, *An Autobiography*, 2 vols (London: Secker & Warburg, 1961–1962), I: *Trail Sinister* (1961), pp. 317–18. Johnson does mention the breaking of the naval blockade in his autobiography. See Hewlett Johnson, *Searching for light: an autobiography* (London: Michael Joseph, 1968), pp. 144–5. A final possible influence of Delmer on Marías is in the choice of Deza's profession prior to his recruitment into the Secret Service. Before heading the propaganda broadcasting unit, Delmer was working for the BBC. Unlike Deza, who describes his salary as more than ample (*FL*, pp. 261–2), Delmer apparently had to take a considerable pay cut in order to serve his country (*Black Boomerang*, p. 34).

[211] *On the Natural History of Destruction*, pp. 19–20.      [212] *VSA*, p. 615.

(Arthur Harris, the Air Marshal, was the one who ordered the burning of fifty thousand Hamburg citizens and one hundred and fifty thousand Dresden citizens towards the end of the War on the cynical pretence that he was attacking military targets; he also flattened Cologne, Frankfurt, Düsseddorf and Mannheim; he was an implacable man with too much power, almost a psychopath really, willing to use any means at his disposal to crush the enemy and win.)[213]

The pun is on 'hamburgueses' (residents of Hamburg) and 'hamburguesas' (hamburgers), which Harris 'ordenó cocer' ('ordered cooked'), in words that once again expertly characterize him. They do so because their jarring gallows humour offers a snapshot of a time now lost. Only by seeing such days can Wheeler acquire the sense of distance to ironize them in quite this way. Seen from the pusillanimous perspective of today, his words appear oddly distasteful.

Where Wheeler is a nuanced and troubled figure, his modern-day counterpart in the interpreting group, Tupra, offers little room for ambiguity; if only because his true personality is never stable enough for the reader to form a complex opinion which might then be altered by further revelations. Tupra appears simply unknowable. Chameleon-like, he goes by different names—Ure, Dundas, Reresby—depending on which nightclub or city the group are visiting. He carries himself with apparent ease among Italian mafiosi, British high society, Oxford academics, and military figures. He is, in Deza's estimation, a sexual rival against whom no serious opposition could ever be mounted. It can hardly be coincidental in this regard that he drives the same car as James Bond—an Aston Martin. Above all, he is untroubled by the violence he either inflicts or witnesses: he injects what Deza calls the 'veneno' of familiarity with extreme violence in a forensic, cold manner while expressing only amused contempt at his colleague's squeamishness as they watch scenes of unalloyed savagery in the viewing room at his home. And yet, this inscrutable figure is characterized, even if only partially, through the use of translated texts.

There are only two occasions in the novel on which we gain a glimpse of a potential vulnerability in Tupra, moments when the mask of imperviousness briefly slips. The first comes when Deza enters his boss's home, a place so striking in its cosiness and charm that the only meaningful comparison he can call to mind to evoke it adequately is the London townhouse occupied by the Darling family in Disney's *Peter Pan* (1953). The juxtaposition of this warm impression with the barbaric scenes Tupra forces him to endure could scarcely be more stark. All until the end of

---

[213] *Poison, Shadow and Farewell*, p. 476.

that late-night video session, when a woman unknown to Deza but who must be Tupra's passing conquest or long-term partner opens the door of the viewing room and asks when he will be coming to bed. Her lithe silhouette framed in the doorway—chiffon gown, high-heeled slippers—calls to his mind a pin-up girl from the 1950s, an old-school elegance once more evocative of the world of James Bond. But what most strikes Deza is the incongruity of Tupra having someone to come home to, the fixed emotional point that he has felt the lack of so keenly during his time in London: 'Así que a él sí lo esperaba alguien y no vive solo, o al menos no le falta compañía querida algunas noches...Así que tiene un punto flaco, una persona a su lado' ('So there was someone waiting for him, and he doesn't live alone, or at least on some nights he doesn't lack company...So he does have a weak point, someone at his side').[214] Far from resenting the intrusion, Tupra acquiesces uncomplainingly: '—Un poco de trabajo tardío con un colega. En seguida voy, querida' ('Just working late with a colleague. I'll be right with you, my dear').[215] Perhaps because he misses his family so bitterly and feels so at sea without them, Deza has a conservative sense that the home is a foundational space. To him it is the place where, to adapt the quotation from *King Henry IV* that he cites, he can be more himself. He is intrigued to discover that Tupra is, he assumes, not immune to that same need.

This privileged if fleeting glimpse of the private life behind the professional façade acts as prelude to the second moment at which Tupra offers a window onto his inner world. While he and Deza are travelling to Edinburgh by train, the latter reads aloud some of Stevenson's final poems to while away the journey. In them the dying writer evokes with nostalgia the mindscape of his youth and the cold bleakness of his childhood in the Scottish capital. Such memories sit in heavy contrast to the home he has made for himself in the South Sea Islands, to which Stevenson had travelled in hopes of relieving what was assumed to be tuberculosis. Believing that he had 'only the nurse and undertaker to expect', he described himself as being 'not unwilling to visit like a ghost, and be carried like a bale, among scenes that had attracted me in youth and health'. His pessimistic outlook soon gave way to renewed hope and he recovered his health long enough to live six years among the island peoples, of whom he grew deeply fond. As he wrote in his South Seas travelogue:

> Few men who come to the islands leave them; they grow grey where they alighted; the palm shades and trade winds fan them till they die, perhaps

---

[214] *Poison, Shadow and Farewell*, pp. 169–70.
[215] *VSA*, p. 223; *Poison, Shadow and Farewell*, p. 169.

cherishing to the last the fancy of a visit home, which is rarely made, more rarely enjoyed, and yet more rarely repeated.[216]

Against this backdrop, it was only in his mind's eye that he could behold the scenes of Edinburgh years before. Deza wonders aloud whether the Scottish writer's late-flowering nostalgia for childhood and his roots is not a universal human trait, whether in our final hours those are the only memories that matter. (I give the original English first, then the translations as they appear in *VSA*, with, in square brackets, the changes made to the original versions of these poems published in *De vuelta del mar*, Marías's collection of Stevenson's verse:)

> The belching winter wind, the missile rain,/The rare and welcome silence of the snows,/The laggard morn, the haggard day, the night,/The grimy spell of the nocturnal town,/Do you remember?—Ah, could one forget![217]

> El viento vomitante del invierno, la arrojadiza lluvia, el infrecuente [raro] y bienvenido silencio de las nieves, la mañana tardía, el día macilento, la noche, el mugriento sortilegio de la ciudad nocturna, ¿os acordáis?...Ah, si pudiera uno olvidarse[!]'[218]

We note how Marías has endeavoured to maintain what he calls in his translator's note 'un *ritmo equivalente*' (his italics).[219] Hence the alliterative and rhythmic effect of 'winter wind' is transferred to 'viento vomitante', an acceptable alternative translation than the more literal 'eructante' (belching, burping). The same preservation of internal rhyme within a single phrase occurs with the rhyme of 'laggard...haggard' transferred to 'tardía...día'. He has further tidied up his original translation, removing the ambiguity from 'raro', which could mean 'strange', and replacing it with 'infrecuente', bringing it better into line with Stevenson's original where 'rare' undoubtedly means 'uncommon, infrequent'. Looked at through Deza's eyes, the inclusion of the poems is no small task since he must be translating into Spanish poems he read to his boss in their original English, begging the question why he should have taken the trouble. What might seem like a relatively minor episode in their acquaintance has its impact implicitly amplified by the care the narrator takes to recreate it. Marías invited speculation on this episode by drawing attention to its intriguing inconclusiveness in a 2008 interview:

> Tupra es el que mueve los hilos...Y es el rostro que no cambia, el que parece impenetrable. Pero también tiene sus momentos de debilidad. Ocurre

---

[216] Robert Louis Stevenson, *In the South Seas*, ed. by Neil Rennie (London: Penguin, 1998), p. 5.

[217] *De vuelta del mar*, p. 162.

[218] *VSA*, p. 240.        [219] *De vuelta del mar*, p. 10.

cuando vuelve en tren de Edimburgo y Jacobo Deza le va leyendo unos poemas. Entonces le pide más, que siga leyendo. Y se nota que podría tener más debilidades que las que se apuntan.[220]

(Tupra is the man who pulls the strings... And his is the face that does not change, that seems impenetrable. But he too has his moments of weakness. It happens as he returns from Edimburgh by train and Jacobo Deza reads him some poems over the course of the journey. It's then that Tupra asks him for more, asks him to continue reading. We become aware that he might have more weaknesses than those recorded.)

So how do these poems act as a frame within which to see Tupra or what do his reactions to them tell us about him? To take the first of these questions, I would suggest that by implication they frame Tupra within the limits of Stevenson's thought. They hint at a man whose abiding concerns remain domestic and subject to a conservative centredness; one who fights for queen and country out of a fierce protectiveness of what he treasures at home, just as Deza commits grave crimes while sheltering those he holds most dear. In fact, the only line at which Tupra baulks during the extended reading session is one in which Stevenson suggests that he could relinquish his concern for the love of his life, an idea Tupra finds ludicrous:

Cuando la luz de mis ojos expirantes disminuya y ceda, y la voz del amor llegue insignificante a mis oídos que estarán cerrándose, ¿qué sonido vendrá sino el viejo grito del viento de nuestra ciudad inclemente? ¿Qué volverá sino la imagen del vacío de la juventud, llenado [llenada] por el ruido de pasos y aquella voz de descontento y embeleso y desesperanza?[221]

—'Yet when the voice of love shall fall insignificant on my closing ears...'

—Tonterías—me cortó Tupra. '*Nonsense*', fue la palabra en su lengua—. Eso no fue lo mejor que escribió Stevenson. Desde luego no era un gran poeta.

—Volvió a quedarse callado, como para subrayar su veredicto, y después añadió, para mi sorpresa—: Pero léeme más, anda.[222]

And yet, through all this we should remember that his outlook is seen through Deza's eyes. These are Deza's interpretations of a man whom he

---

[220] José Antonio Rojo, 'Javier Marías, el escritor con brújula', *Turia: Revista Cultural*, 88 (2008–2009), 352–61 (p. 358).

[221] *VSA*, p. 240. The original English reads: Yet when the lamp from my expiring eyes/ Shall dwindle and recede, the voice of love/Fall insignificant on my closing ears,/What sound shall come but the old cry of the wind/In our inclement city? what return/But the image of the emptiness of youth,/Filled with the sound of footsteps and that voice/Of discontent and rapture and despair? See *De vuelta del mar*, p. 164. Again Marías has cleared up an infelicity in his earlier version, changing the noun to which the adjective 'llenado' applies from 'youth' to 'emptiness'. The adjustment seems quite correct since it is the emptiness that is filled.

[222] *VSA*, p. 243.

admits he cannot interpret convincingly. We might well ask whether these attempts to 'domesticate' Tupra are designed to attribute purpose and order to a man whose actions are for Deza unsettlingly inscrutable, even amoral. Moreover, there is not a little self-interest in Deza's needing to situate Tupra in a framework that goes some way towards explaining him. As we saw in the first half of this chapter and Marías pointed out, there is a side to Deza that wants to surrender control of others, to immolate himself:

> [Tupra] es el personaje sin rostro, el que lo sabe todo, el que corrompe al narrador y lo envenena.... Lo más sorprendente es que el narrador, cuando ya todo ha pasado y ha vuelto a instalarse en Madrid, y las cosas siguen su curso, sigue pensando en Tupra como en un amigo. El que tiene al demonio como aliado. Porque el demonio sabe manejarse en cualquier situación.[223]

> ([Tupra] is the faceless character, the who knows all, who corrupts and poisons the narrator.... The most surprising thing of all is that, when everything is over and done with and the narrator has gone back to live in Madrid, he continues to think of Tupra as a friend. He who has the devil on his side. Because the devil knows how to carry himself in any situation.)

By the time Deza sits down to write his account, he has repaired his marriage to Luisa to the extent that he and his wife are back in a relationship, albeit that they occupy different living spaces to avoid taking one another for granted. Yet Deza is conscious of the fact that he may in the future need to call on the services of a man like his former boss both because he knows that Custardoy is still in Madrid and because his own dabbling in interpreting human beings has not ended. Much as MI5 was planning to do just before the terrorist attacks in 2001, Deza has gone private: he now works for a friend in business advising on the trustworthiness of potential clients.

To conclude this analysis of *TRM*, the final question I wish to address is what Marías achieves through constructing characters through translated and hybridized texts. In the first instance my analysis has shown how much the author's imagination draws on those texts he has translated for inspiration. I have shown how these character portraits have come together in his mind and been realized on the page. On a wider scale, seeing the degree to which Deza, Wheeler, and even Tupra are inhabited by texts, by the best articulations and formulations of complex human thought, suggests how much their lengthy perorations are a search for meaning itself. I noted above that Deza and Wheeler speak in an alternating hybrid of English and Spanish, a phenomenon on which Steenmeijer comments: 'No son raras las veces que el cambio o trasvase lingüístico se limita a una sola palabra si resulta que no hay un equivalente adecuado o satisfactorio en el propio idioma' ('On plenty of occasions the linguistic change or transfer is limited to a single word if it turns out that there is no adequate or satisfactory equivalent in their own language').[224] What the two men are inadvertently creating is a perfected inter-language where each concept that their minds desire to express finds its best formulation. In the article just quoted, Steenmeijer develops the idea that Deza, Wheeler, and Tupra are 'figuras inacabadas' ('unfinished figures') whose defining characteristic is precisely their instability or unknowability: a suggestion he further supports by reference to the fact that, in the case of the first two at least, they have shifting names (Wheeler having changed his surname as a teenager, Deza having a first name that varies depending on his interlocutor), and are between nationalities (Wheeler a New Zealander by birth and British by adoption, Deza a reluctant Spaniard). Both lack their wives (Wheeler permanently, Deza temporarily) and inhabit two languages (with the concomitant problems of dissociation for Deza in particular). Both feel themselves anachronisms in an increasingly frivolous world.[225] Steenmeijer also notes how much Deza's language becomes inflected or infected through contact with De la Garza, whose liberal use of expletives and recherché sexual slang creeps into the narrator's diction.[226] That argument might be extended even further to include the fact that Deza's Spanish begins to suffer from sporadic English inflections because he uses it so infrequently[227] just as that of his colleague Pérez Nuix does.[228] Deza describes how much of his early assimilation to the group of interpreters was a matter of adopting the linguistic tics that were the common currency of its members. He notes with dismay how the desire to please his handlers quickly turned fleeting impressions into certainties or the vocabulary of trust and mistrust into second nature. Beyond these examples is the vast number of quotations that pepper both Deza's narrative and his conversations: from among others John Ashbery, Cervantes, T. S. Eliot, Lope de Vega, Antonio Machado, Marlowe, Milton,

---

[224] Maarten Steenmeijer, 'Figuras acabadas y figuras inacabadas en *Tu rostro mañana* de Javier Marías', *Siglo XXI, literautra y cultura españolas: revista de la cátedra Miguel Delibes*, 3 (2005), 197–209 (p. 202).

[225] 'Figuras acabadas y figuras inacabadas en *Tu rostro mañana* de Javier Marías', pp. 201–2.

[226] 'Figuras acabadas y figuras inacabadas en *Tu rostro mañana* de Javier Marías', p. 203.

[227] *BS*, pp. 37, 236.     [228] *BS*, pp. 50, 53; *VSA*, pp. 75, 559.

Rilke, and Shakespeare, as well as Irish folk poetry and Bob Dylan.[229]
What Marías may be hinting at by constructing his characters from
such a web of literary quotation is that they are like Borges's Shakespeare—everything and nothing: men who see and interpret the world
in its infinite variety but for whom that interpretative capacity leaves
room only for doubt.[230] It is their task to pick at the remains and try to
salvage what they can:

> al final del tiempo sólo quedan vestigios o cercos y en cada uno se rastrea a
> lo sumo la sombra de una historia incompleta, llena de lagunas, fantasmal,
> jeroglífica, cadavérica o fragmentaria como trozos de lápidas o como ruinas
> de tímpanos con inscripciones quebradas[231]

> (at the end of time there are only vestiges or remnants or rims and in each
> can be traced, at most, the shadow of an incomplete story, full of lacunae, as
> ghostly, hieroglyphic, cadaverous or fragmentary as pieces of tombstones or
> the broken inscriptions on ruined tympana)[232]

Deza's phrase is, not surprisingly, inspired once again by Browne's *Hydriotaphia*: 'Gravestones tell truth scarce forty years; generations pass while
some trees stand, and old families last not three oaks'.[233]

---

[229] To give an idea of the sheer number of quotations in the text, the following article by
Antonio Iriarte, which runs to sixty-three pages, gives a comprehensive set of sources for the
attributed and unattributed citations in the novel. See his '"Cito a menudo para mis adentros": citas y alusiones en *Tu rostro mañana* de Javier Marías', in *Allí donde uno diría que ya no
puede haber nada*, pp. 303–66.
[230] Borges, *Obras completas*, II, pp. 181–2.       [231] *VSA*, pp. 493–4.
[232] *Poison, Shadow and Farewell*, pp. 379–80.       [233] *Religio Medici*, p. 128.

# Conclusion

I introduced this study of Marías's debt to translation by citing two examples of works by Stevenson and Conrad that he translated into Spanish and that have since served him as significant literary touchstones. We saw in Chapter 9 that more than a quarter of a century after his versions of Stevenson's poems had seen print, they remained a crucial reference point on which to draw when characterizing Tupra in *TRM*. To conclude my consideration of Marías's praxis in this area, I wish to highlight a final example from Conrad, summarize what my work has shown, and suggest further lines of enquiry.

The scene in the nightclub toilets in *BS*, during which Tupra menaces De la Garza with a sword, is pivotal in the larger novel of which it forms part. There Deza experiences for the first time the unsettling horror of physical violence. It is there too that he realizes the power it can wield over others, that he begins to make connections between the present and his father's accounts of atrocities perpetrated during the Civil War. In interviews after the novel's publication, Marías was quick to acknowledge that the scene was a homage to the interrupted tale of the 'vizcaíno' ('man from Vizcaya') in chapters 8 and 9 of *Don Quijote*, a deliberate suspension of narrative time.[1] While he also noted that translating Sterne had shown him that 'un minuto puede durar ochenta páginas' ('a minute can last for eighty pages') underlining the way in which the Cervantine inheritance, that could be thought his natural birthright as a Spanish novelist, will always be refracted through the author of *Tristram Shandy*.[2] The gap between Tupra raising his sword and bringing it down on De la Garza's exposed neck is filled with Deza's thoughts on how his compatriot might narrate his death on the Day of Judgement, the depiction of the sword in art (Velázquez and Durer), and the sword's long and bloody history in

---

[1] Ángeles García, '"Quiero dar presencia al tiempo que no percibimos"', *El País*, 3 October 2004, pp. 39–40.
[2] María Luisa Blanco, 'Javier Marías, todas las voces', *El País*, Babelia section, 29 September 2007, pp. 2–3. He makes the same point in 'Los rostros y el tiempo', p. 48.

human warfare.[3] What I wish to show in the following brief analysis is that this pivotal scene owes its inspiration not only to Cervantes but also to Conrad. Repeated allusions to the latter in *TRM* rhyme with one another to create coherence and meaning in a way that ought by now to be familiar from my analyses of the repeated imagery in *NET*—the passengers in the street awaiting their bus—and *TRM*—the repeated allusions to bullfighting. As we saw in Chapter 1, Marías was 're-translating' *The Mirror of the Sea* at the same time that he was writing *BS*.

In the most memorable passages of *The Mirror of the Sea*, Conrad describes with great pathos and beauty the predicament of seamen whose misfortune has been to encounter the sea in one of its more implacable moods. One such passage relates the torment suffered by the crew of a steamer left to drift helplessly in the Southern Ocean after storm waves had ripped off its propeller; the second officer diligently plotting its crazy, rudderless course on his charts as it strayed farther and farther away from the shipping lanes and any hope of rescue.[4] Another recounts the fate of a 'water-logged derelict', a dismasted and slowly sinking ship, whose crew stoically man the pumps day after day, hoping to stay afloat long enough to attract the attention of another vessel, only for their will to break when the prolonged waiting conquers what optimism they had managed to retain:

> But they went on trying to keep the brig afloat as long as possible, and working the pumps constantly on insufficient food, mostly raw, till "yesterday evening," [the captain] continued, monotonously, "just as the sun went down, the men's hearts broke."[5]

This latter anecdote, which forms the centrepiece of the section aptly entitled 'Initiation', ends with Conrad recalling the respect he learned for the sea by witnessing the fear-lined faces of the rescued seamen. They had in their faces the unforgettable and unmistakeable look of those who had for many long days contemplated their own imminent demise. It is these passages of *The Mirror of the Sea* that Marías had in mind when crafting the nightclub scene in *BS*.

We can surmise this from how Deza describes De la Garza's subsequent reaction to Tupra's attack, one during which he had been described as shielding himself 'los dos brazos sobre la nuca inútiles como un paraguas bajo la tempestad marina'.[6] What the narrator realizes when he sees the cultural attaché several months later is that his compatriot has been every

---

[3] *BS*, pp. 271–9.     [4] *The Mirror of the Sea*, pp. 63–6.
[5] *The Mirror of the Sea*, p. 142.     [6] *BS*, p. 281.

bit as affected by the threat of death as Conrad's sailors were. He realizes this merely on the strength of De la Garza's reaction to seeing him:

> Vi a Rafita desencajado, con los puños apretados aún pegados al cuerpo (no como arma sino como escudo), la mirada turbia, la respiración muy agitada, le había entrado una tos intermitente pero incontenible en cada acceso, presa de un pánico que revivía y que quizá llevaba también meses temiendo. Aún le duraría esa nebulosa de perpetuo miedo, se lo fiaba largo. Muy mal lo habría pasado aquella noche, el peligro real de muerte se percibe siempre y en él se cree inmediatamente, aunque al final se quede sólo en susto de muerte.[7]

> (I saw how shaken Rafita was—his clenched fists still held close to his body (not as a weapon, but as a shield), his eyes wild, his breathing agitated— gripped by a panic that he was now reliving and which he had perhaps been dreading for months, he had also developed an intermittent cough, which, when the fit took him, proved uncontrollable. That cloud of perpetual fear would last for some time yet, it wouldn't be quick to clear. He must have suffered greatly that night, because one is always instantly aware when there is any real danger of death, even if, in the end, it turns out to be something that merely frightened one half to death.)[8]

De la Garza has, like another of Conrad's former colleagues, seen the sword of Damocles suspended over his head:

> A man may be better for it, but he will not be the same. Damocles has seen the sword suspended by a hair over his head, and though a good man need not be made less valuable by such knowledge, the feast shall not henceforth have the same flavour.[9]

In this instance, the former colleague in question is a captain whose ill-judgement has allowed his ship to run aground, a man Conrad believes will be marked forever by the experience. Marías appears to have conflated this passage with those quoted above describing rescued seamen since, in *FL*, Deza comments on the 'careless talk' poster that features a lifeboat full of naval personnel watching their vessel sink: 'unos cuantos supervivientes alejándose de él en un bote de remos sin volverle la espalda,

---

[7] *VSA*, p. 298.  [8] *Poison, Shadow and Farewell*, p. 228.
[9] *The Mirror of the Sea*, p. 69. For Marías's Spanish, see *El espejo del mar* (Reino de Redonda), pp. 134–5. We might also note Conrad's use elsewhere of the image of the sword of Damocles applied to imperilled seamen. For example, the following passage from his novella *Typhoon*: 'But the quietude of the air was startlingly tense and unsafe, like a slender hair holding a sword suspended over his [Captain MacWhirr's] head. By this awful pause the storm penetrated the defences of the man and unsealed his lips. He spoke out in the solitude and the pitch darkness of the cabin, as if addressing another being awakened within his breast'. See Joseph Conrad, *Typhoon and Other Tales*, ed. by Cedric Watts, rev. edn (Oxford: Oxford University Press, 2008), p. 62.

la mirada fija en aquel desastre del que se salvaban tan sólo a medias, como todo tripulante y todo náufrago' ('a few survivors are rowing away from the boat, though like any crew member or shipwreck victim, without turning their backs on it, their gaze fixed on the disaster from which they have only half-escaped').[10] Such survivors 'se salvaban tan sólo a medias' because their memory of so close an encounter with death would live with them forever. We also know that Marías had retained and was using as inspiration Conrad's observation on the sword of Damocles because Wheeler employs the very same image. Recalling with incredulity his secret-service mission to escort the Duke and Duchess of Windsor from Madrid to Lisbon, he remembers that he was to act as their executioner should the two right-wing royals show any signs of wishing to join Hitler in Berlin: 'Me cuesta creer, por ejemplo, mi función de custodio, acompañante, escolta y hasta espada de Damocles de los Duques de Windsor en el verano de 1940' ('I find it hard to believe, for example, that I acted as custodian, companion, escort and even sword of Damocles to the Duke and Duchess of Windsor in the summer of 1940').[11] It is telling to note that, even though Marías's retranslation of *The Mirror of the Sea* turned out to be something of a cosmetic exercise, the process still enabled him to engage once more with Conrad's imagery and conceptualization of fear.

Restrictions of space have meant that wider consideration of Marías's debt to Conrad has not been possible. What I have shown, however, is that Marías's engagement with those writers whose works he so painstakingly wrought in his own language has left profound marks on his thinking and literary praxis. Their insights, outlook, and phraseology have found their way into his articles, novels, and short stories in a way that is the very essence of linguistic incorporation and cross-fertilization. As should by now have become abundantly clear, the study of his efforts as a translator is also the study of his broad culture and frame of reference. This study goes a considerable way towards elucidating precisely how deep that culture is and how broad that frame of reference. It is for future critics of his work to take on the task of exploring his engagement with, among others, Conrad, Dinesen, Eliot, and, most importantly, Shakespeare.

In Marías's case, the study of his debt to translation has opened a window onto how his fiction takes shape: the inspiration that forms it and the praxis that helps it develop. Close analysis of his versions of *TS*, *Hydriotaphia*, and 'Lolita recontada' has shown him to be a translator of rare

---

[10] *FL*, p. 400; *Fever and Spear*, p. 313.
[11] *VSA*, pp. 594–5; *Poison, Shadow and Farewell*, p. 460.

assiduity, flair, and sensitivity. And the unchallenged assumption that because his talents as a writer in his own tongue are beyond question, his versions of others' works in English must be similarly irreproachable proves well founded all the same. His experience of the art exemplifies another of Edith Grossman's insights:

> Translation is, in fact, a powerful, pervasive force that broadens and deepens a writer's perception of style, technique, and structure by allowing him or her to enter literary worlds not necessarily found in one national or linguistic tradition. Far beyond essentially pernicious anxieties of influence, writers learn their craft from one another, just as painters and musicians do.[12]

This study has gone a considerable way towards charting the development of Marías's imaginative vocabulary and his continuing dialogue with the literary masters he chose to translate. The influence they have had and will continue to have on his work underpins what is by now his sustained examination of what sort of role writing, and the semblance of order that it generates, can have in helping human beings to lay the past to rest.

What this study has also shown is that rather than an aloof figure with his eye trained more on Anglophone tradition than the Spain of his own time, Marías has demonstrated a sustained commitment to the contemporary world. That the disquisitions of a narrator like Jacobo Deza resonate throughout the war-torn history of the twentieth century and more recent debates over the ethics of covert intervention in the life of the private individual is testimony to the universalizing reach of Marías's fiction, not his disengagement from Spain. In fact, the voguish trend among some of his contemporaries towards Civil War fiction finds far more sophisticated and ethically coherent expression in *TRM*, where the emphasis is on the wrongs committed by both sides in that conflict. Not only that, but there and elsewhere in his fiction he looks for the causes of human wrongdoing in crucial gaps in what we like to think of as our self-knowledge, rather than in the colour of our political allegiances. He is a writer fascinated by the affective and contingent barriers to real self-awareness. The ghostly narrator of 'Cuando fui mortal' is emblematic in this respect in that his memory, now raw with 'the edge of repetitions', constructs a narrative version of his past which resonates with all the factors that determined who he became and of which he yet remained ignorant. Marías's fiction represents a striving towards understanding and remains utterly engaging both for the quality of the writing itself and the depth of the insight that animates it.

---

[12] *Why Translation Matters*, p. 22.

If, as I fervently hope, this book has shown how rich the study of translation can be for students of Spanish literature in the modern period, perhaps we might expect in the future to receive similar insights into the work of Azúa, Benet, Galdós, Martín Gaite, and Unamuno, as well as the host of other important writers in the last two centuries who have combined their own work with the translator's craft. Were it to be the case, it would be a timely reminder that this frequently overlooked and undervalued activity lies at the heart of cultural exchange rather than at its margins.

# Bibliography

Unless otherwise stated, the place of publication of the following works is Madrid (Spain).

## WORKS BY JAVIER MARÍAS

### (i) Novels

*A Heart So White*, trans. by Margaret Jull Costa (London: Harvill, 1995).

*All Souls*, trans. by Margaret Jull Costa (London: Vintage, 2003).

*Corazón tan blanco* (Alfaguara, 1999 [originally 1992]).

*Corazón tan blanco*, ed. by Elide Pittarello (Barcelona: Crítica, 2006).

*Dark Back of Time*, trans. by Esther Allen (London: Chatto & Windus, 2003).

*El hombre sentimental* (Alfaguara, 1999 [originally 1986]).

*El hombre sentimental* (prologue by Elide Pittarello (Espasa Calpe, 1994 [originally 1986]).

*El siglo* (Barcelona: Seix Barral, 1983).

*El siglo* (Alfaguara, 2000).

*Los dominios del lobo* (Alfaguara, 1999 [originally 1971]).

*Los enamoramientos* (Alfaguara, 2011).

*Mañana en la batalla piensa en mí* (Alfaguara, 2000 [originally 1994]).

*Negra espalda del tiempo* (Alfaguara, 1998).

*The Man of Feeling*, trans. by Margaret Jull Costa (London: Harvill, 2003).

*Todas las almas* (Alfaguara, 2000 [originally 1989]).

*Tomorrow in the Battle Think on Me*, trans. by Margaret Jull Costa (London: Harvill, 1996).

*Travesía del horizonte* (Alfaguara, 1999 [originally 1972]).

*Tu rostro mañana 1: Fiebre y lanza* (Alfaguara, 2002).

*Tu rostro mañana 2: Baile y sueño* (Alfaguara, 2004).

*Tu rostro mañana 3: Veneno y sombra y adiós* (Alfaguara, 2007).

*Voyage Along the Horizon*, trans. by Kristina Cordero (San Franciso: Believer Books, 2006).

*Your Face Tomorrow*, trans. by Margaret Jull Costa, 3 vols (London: Chatto & Windus, 2005–2009).

### (ii) Short Stories

'Caído en desgracia', *El País Semanal*, 21 August 2005, pp. 16–21.

*Cuando fui mortal* (Alfaguara, 1996 [originally 1993]).

*Mientras ellas duermen* (Alfaguara, 2000 [originally 1990]).

*When I Was Mortal*, trans. by Margaret Jull Costa (London: Harvill, 1999).

*While the Women Are Sleeping*, trans. by Margaret Jull Costa (London: Chatto & Windus, 2010).

**(iii) Article collections**

*A veces un caballero* (Alfaguara, 2001).

*Demasiada nieve alrededor* (Alfaguara, 2007).

*Donde todo ha sucedido: Al salir del cine*, ed. by Inés Blanca and Reyes Pinzás (Barcelona: Galaxia Gutenberg, 2005).

*El oficio de oír llover* (Alfaguara, 2005).

*Harán de mí un criminal* (Alfaguara, 2003).

*Literatura y fantasma: Edición ampliada* (Alfaguara, 2001).

*Lo que no vengo a decir* (Alfaguara, 2009).

*Mano de sombra* (Alfaguara, 1997).

*Pasiones pasadas* (Alfaguara, 1999 [originally 1991]).

*Salvajes y sentimentales: Letras de fútbol* (Aguilar, 2000).

*Seré amado cuando falte* (Alfaguara, 1999).

*Vida del fantasma: Cinco años más tenue* (Alfaguara, 2001).

*Vidas escritas: Edición ampliada* (Alfaguara, 2000).

*Written lives*, trans. by Margaret Jull Costa (Edinburgh: Canongate, 2006).

**(iv) Uncollected articles**

'An Open Letter About Iraq', *The Threepenny Review*, 93 (2003), p. 35.

'Aviones marineros', *Granta en español*, 1 (2004), pp. 23–30.

'Borges: un fragment apocryphe de Sir Thomas Browne', *Le Promeneur*, 58 (1988), pp. 20–1.

'El padre', *El País*, 16 December 2005, p. 36.

'Esta absurda aventura', *El País*, Babelia section, 23 August 2008, p. 23.

'*Lolita* recontada', trans. by Gareth Wood, in Alide Cagidemetrio and Daniela Rizzi, eds, *Nabokov. Un'eredità letteraria* (Milan: Univesità Ca' Foscari di Venezia, 2006), pp. 96–109.

'Los reconocimientos', *Revista de Occidente*, July/August (1989), pp. 162–3.

'Los tesoros del olvido', *El País*, 20 October 1982, p. 39.

'Para empezar por el principio', in Mario Vargas Llosa et al., eds, *Lecciones y maestros: II Cita Internacional de la literatura en español*, pp. 109–33.

'Un país grotesco', *El País Semanal*, 10 September 2006, p. 110.

**(v) Anthology**

*El hombre que parecía no querer nada*, ed. by Elide Pittarello (Espasa Calpe, 1996).

**(vi) Interviews**

Alameda, Sol, 'Javier Marías: el éxito europeo de un indeciso', *El País Semanal*, 10 November 1996, pp. 58–64.

Anonymous, 'Javier Marías: The Art of Fiction No. 190', *The Paris Review*, 179 (2006), pp. 10–42.

Appendix ('Eight Questions for Javier Marías'), in *Voyage Along the Horizon*, trans. by Kristina Cordero (San Franciso: Believer Books, 2006), pp. 175–82.

Barranco, Justo, '"Mi novela aspira a hablar de todo', *La Vanguardia*, 25 September 2007, p. 37.

Bello León, Jaime, 'Entrevista con Javier Marías', *La Brújula*, 67–8 (1997). www.javiermarias.es/main.html (accessed 4 November 2008).

Blanca, Inés, interview available at the following URL: http://www.javier-marias.es/PAGINASDEENTREVISTAS/javierybenet.html (accessed 2 January 2008).

Blanco, María Luisa, 'Javier Marías, todas las voces', *El País*, Babelia section, 29 September 2007, pp. 2–3.

Castellanos, Luis H., 'La magia de lo que pudo ser: entrevista con Javier Marías', *Quimera*, 87 (1989), pp. 24–31.

Cruz, Juan, 'Javier Marías y Arturo Pérez-Reverte: el agua y el aceite', *La Nación*, ADN Cultura section, 18 August 2007, pp. 12–20.

——, 'Javier Marías: Escribir para ver', *El País Semanal*, 23 September 2007, pp. 12–20.

Díaz, Paka, '"Ni hago relaciones ni adulo a nadie"', *El Semanal*, 20–26 October 2002, pp. 52–6.

Echevarría, Ignacio, 'A medida que uno cumple años se incrementan la confusión y la incertidumbre', *El País*, Babelia section, 26 October 2002, pp. 2–3.

García, Ángeles, '"En el hablar y el callar se descubre la esencia de las personas"', *El País*, 15 September 2002, p. 34.

——, '"Quiero dar presencia al tiempo que no percibimos"', *El País*, 3 October 2004, pp. 39–40.

——, '"Veo un mal futuro para el español"', *El País*, 2 July 2006, p. 54.

Güemes, César, 'Puedo hacer muchas cosas, menos quejarme de cómo me trata la vida', *Jornada*, 18 November 1998. www.javiermarias.es/PAGINASDEEN-TREVISTAS/JornadaNov98.html (accessed 4 November 2008).

Ingendaay, Paul, 'Interview with Javier Marías', *Bomb*, 73 (2000), http://bomb-site.com/issues/73/articles/2345, pp. 150–8 (accessed 2 November 2008).

López, Ángela, '"La Academia no parece lugar muy divertido"', *La clave*, 197 (2005), pp. 78–81.

López, Jaime, interview available at the following URL: http://www.javiermarias.es/PAGINASDEENTREVISTAS/TribunaSept95.html (accessed 23 February 2008).

López, Óscar, 'Contesto y salto pocas veces para las que podría hacerlo', *Qué leer*, November 2002, pp. 7–9.

Lozano, Antonio, 'Javier Marías: El monarca del tiempo' *Man*, 207 (2005). Available at the following URL: http://www.javiermarias.es/main.html (accessed 15 February 2008).

——, 'Javier Marías. Hablar o callar, esa es la cuestión', *Qué leer*, October 2007, pp. 62–7.

Marías, Javier and Braudeau, Michel, 'À propos d'un certain Javier Marías', *La Nouvelle Revue Française*, 584 (2008), pp. 1–20.

—— and Villoro, Juan, 'De espías y otros fantasmas', *Letras libres*, 15 (2002), pp. 44–7.

Pérez-Lanzac, Carmen, 'El último caballero', *Marie Claire* (Spanish edition), January 2005, pp. 90–92.

Perret, Matthew, 'Telling Stories', *The Broadsheet*, 93 (2000), pp. 30–1.

330 *Bibliography*

Pfeiffer, Michael, 'Javier Marías', in *El destino de la literatura: Diez voces* (Barcelona: El Acantilado, 1999), pp. 107–24.
Pino, Hilario, interview available at the following URL: www.javiermarias.es/main.html (accessed 2 January 2008).
Pittarello, Elide, *Entrevistos: Javier Marías* (Barcelona: RqueR, 2005).
Rojo, José Antonio, 'Javier Marías, el escritor con brújula', *Turia: Revista Cultural*, 88 (2008–2009), pp. 352–61.
Romeo, Félix, 'Javier Marías "Me angustia que nada sea olvidable"', *ABC*, Cultura section, 26 October 2002, p. 14.
Solanes, Ana, 'Javier Marías: "El grado de ignorancia en España es deprimente"', *Cuadernos hispanoamericanos*, 691 (2008), pp. 87–104.
Vásquez, Juan Gabriel, 'Los rostros y el tiempo: Entrevista con Javier Marías', *Letras libres*, 105 (2010), 46–54.
——, '"Tengo a veces la sensación de no estar ya vivo"', *Lateral*, 82 (2001), pp. 13–15.
Visani, Caterina, interview available at the following URL: http://www.javiermarias.es/PAGINASDEENTREVISTAS/entrevistaCaterinaVisani.html (accessed 4 July 2008).

### WORKS TRANSLATED BY JAVIER MARÍAS

Ashbery, John, 'Autorretrato en espejo convexo', *Poesía*, 25 (1985–1986), pp. 87–106.
——, *Autorretrato en espejo convexo* (Visor, 1990).
Auden, W. H., 'Dichtung und Wahrheit (Un poema no escrito)', *Poesía*, 29 (1989), pp. 57–83.
——, *Un poema no escrito* (Valencia: Pre-Textos, 1996).
Brodski, Joseph, 'Catástrofes en el aire', *El País*, 25 October 1987, pp. 42–3.
Browne, Sir Thomas, *La religión de un médico y El enterramiento en urnas* (Barcelona: Reino de Redonda, 2002).
——, *Religio Medici. Hydriotaphia* (Alfaguara, 1986).
Burgess, Anthony, 'Encuentro en Valladolid', *El País Semanal*, 26 July 1987, Libros section, pp. 1–12.
Conrad, Joseph, *El espejo del mar: Recuerdos e impresiones*, 7th edn (Hiperión, 2003).
——, *El espejo del mar: Recuerdos e impresiones* (Barcelona: Reino de Redonda, 2005).
Dinesen, Isak, *Ehrengard* (Barcelona: Bruguera, 1984).
——, *Ehrengard* (Barcelona: Reino de Redonda, 2001).
Douglas, Keith, 'Como matar', *Reloj de arena*, 2 (1992), p. 5.
——, 'Oxford', *Reloj de arena*, 4 (1992), p. 5.
Faulkner, William, 'Doce poemas', *Poesía*, 5–6 (1979–1980), pp. 205–21.
Hardy, Thomas, *El brazo marchito y otros relatos* (Alianza, 1974).
——, 'La tumba de la encrucijada', *Revista de Occidente*, 134 (1974), pp. 166–82.
——, *El brazo marchito y otros relatos* (Barcelona: Reino de Redonda, 2003).

Heaney, Seamus, 'Postscript', included in the article 'Un poema' published in his *Seré amado cuando falte*, pp. 117–19.

Holden, Edith, *La felicidad de vivir con la naturaleza: El diario de Edith Holden*, trans. by Javier Marías et al. (Barcelona: Blume, 1979).

Marías, Javier, ed., *Cuentos únicos* (Siruela, 1989).

——, *Cuentos únicos* (Barcelona: Reino de Redonda, 2004).

—— and de Azúa, Félix, *Desde que te vi morir: Vladimir Nabokov, una superstición* (Alfaguara, 1999).

—— and Rodríguez Rivero, Manuel, *Si yo amaneciera otra vez: William Faulkner—Un entusiasmo* (Alfaguara, 1997).

Nabokov, Vladimir, 'Dieciocho poemas', *Poesía*, 4 (1979), pp. 70–84.

Salinger, J. D., 'Dos cuentos inéditos', *Sur Exprés*, 5 (1987), pp. 99–114.

——, 'El corazón de una historia quebrada', *Poesía*, 29 (1987), 101–16.

Sterne, Laurence, *La vida y opiniones del caballero Tristram Shandy. Los sermones de Mr Yorick*, 2nd edn (Alfaguara, 2000).

Stevens, Wallace, 'Notas para una ficción suprema', *Poesía*, 26 (1986), pp. 71–98.

——, *Notas para una ficción suprema* (Valencia: Pre-Textos, 1996).

Stevenson, Robert Louis, *De vuelta del mar*, 2nd edn (Hiperión, 1998).

Updike, John, 'Museos y mujeres', *Revista de Occidente*, 132 (1974), pp. 261–73.

Yeats, W. B., *El crepúsculo celta* (Alfaguara, 1985).

——, *El crepúsculo celta* y *La rosa secreta*, trans. by Javier Marías and Alejandro García Reyes (Barcelona: Reino de Redonda, 2003).

——, 'En las carreras de Galway', in Fernando Savater, *A caballo entre milenios* (Aguilar, 2001).

## OTHER WORKS IN THE REINO DE REDONDA SERIES

Balzac, Honoré de, *El coronel Chabert*, trans. by Mercedes López Ballesteros (Barcelona: Reino de Redonda, 2011).

Baretti, Giuseppe, *Viaje de Londres a Génova a través de Inglaterra, Portugal, España y Francia*, ed. and trans. by Soledad Martínez de Pinillos Ruiz (Barcelona: Reino de Redonda, 2005).

Crompton, Richmal, *Bruma y otros relatos*, trans. by Juan Antonio Molina Foix (Barcelona: Reino de Redonda, 2001).

——, *La morada maligna*, trans. by Panteleimón Zarín (Barcelona: Reino de Redonda, 2001).

De Contreras, Alonso, *Vida de este capitán* (Barcelona: Reino de Redonda, 2008).

Erckmann, Émile and Chatrian, Alexander, *Cuentos de las orillas del Rin*, trans. by Mercedes López-Ballesteros (Barcelona: Reino de Redonda, 2009).

Harris, Benjamin, *Recuerdos de este fusilero*, trans. by Antonio Iriarte (Barcelona: Reino de Redonda, 2008).

Ibargüengoitia, Jorge, *Revolución en el jardín*, ed. by Juan Villoro (Barcelona: Reino de Redonda, 2008).

Lee, Vernon, *Amour Dure*, ed. and trans. by Antonio Iriarte (Barcelona: Reino de Redonda, 2007).

Runciman, Sir Steven, *La caída de Constantinopla 1453*, trans. by Panteleimón Zarín (Barcelona: Reino de Redonda, 2006).

——, *Las vísperas sicilianas: una historia del mundo mediterráneo a finales del siglo XIII*, trans. by Alicia Bleiberg (Barcelona: Reino de Redonda, 2009).

Shiel, M. P., *La mujer de Huguenin*, trans. by Antonio Iriarte (Barcelona: Reino de Redonda, 2000).

——, *La nube púrpura*, trans. by Soledad Silió (Barcelona: Reino de Redonda, 2005).

Southey, Robert, *La expedición de Ursúa, Los crímenes de Aguirre*, trans. by Soledad Martínez de Pinillos (Barcelona: Reino de Redonda, 2010).

## SECONDARY SOURCES

Abbott, J. H., 'El siglo', *Invitación a la lectura*, 8 (1990), p. 3.

Abós, Ángel Luis, *La historia que nos enseñaron (1937–1975)* (Foca, 2003).

Alberca, Manuel, 'Javier Marías en el umbral de su secreto', *Revista de Occidente*, 286 (2005), pp. 137–53.

Alfau, Felipe, *Cuentos españoles de antaño*, trans. by Carmen Martín Gaite (Siruela, 1991).

Andres-Suárez, Irene, ed., *Mestizaje y disolución de géneros en la literatura hispánica contemporánea* (Verbum, 1998).

——, Irene et al., eds, *Cuadernos de narrativa: Javier Marías* (Universidad de Neuchâtel/Arco, 2005).

Antón, Jacinto, 'Himmler buscó la raza aria en España', *El País*, 6 April 2008, pp. 44–5.

Arce, Begoña, 'Los fantasmas de Oxford', *El Periódico*, 18 November 2004, Libros section, p. 4.

Arce, Joaquín et al., eds, *La literatura española del siglo XVIII y sus fuentes extranjeras* (Oviedo: Universidad de Oviedo, 1968).

Archer, Robert et al., eds, *Antes y después del "Quijote"* (Valencia: Biblioteca Valenciana/Association of Hispanists of Great Britain and Northern Ireland, 2005).

Aristóteles, *Ética a Nicómaco*, trans by Julián Marías and María Araújo (Instituto de Estudios Políticos, 1959).

——, *Política*, trans by Julián Marías and María Araújo (Instituto de Estudios Políticos, 1951).

Armada, Alfonso, '¿Para quién escriben? (I)', *ABC*, 8 January 2006, Cultural section, p. 6.

Ashbery, John, 'Books of the Year', *Times Literary Supplement*, 1 December 2006, p. 7.

Auden, W. H., *Collected Poems*, ed. by Edward Mendelson, rev. edn. (London: Faber & Faber, 1991).

Barbour, Reid and Preston, Claire, *Sir Thomas Browne: the World Proposed* (Oxford: Oxford University Press, 2008).

Barnes, Julian, *Something to Declare* (London: Picador, 2002).

Beevor, Antony, 'Christmas Books', *The Guardian*, Review section, 28 November 2009, p. 2.

——, 'Your Face Tomorrow: Poison, Shadow and Farewell', *The Sunday Telegraph*, section Seven, 8 November 2009, p. 28.

Benet, Juan, *Artículos: Volumen 1 (1962–1977)* (Pluma Rota, 1983).

——, *En ciernes* (Taurus, 1976).

——, *La inspiración y el estilo (Con dos textos inéditos de Carmen Martín Gaite)* (Alfaguara, 1999).

——, *La moviola de Eurípides y otros ensayos* (Taurus, 1981).

——, *Páginas impares* (Alfaguara, 1996).

——, *Una biografía literaria* (Cuatro, 2007).

Bértolo, Constantino, 'Realismo de almas', *El País*, 22 April 1990, Libros section, p. 5.

Bioy Casares, Adolfo, *Borges*, ed. by Daniel Martino (Barcelona: Destino, 2006).

Boggan, Steve, 'MI5 Offers to Spy for British Firms', *The Independent*, 7 September 2001, p. 1.

Bonaddio, Federico et al., eds, *Crossing Fields in Modern Spanish Culture* (Oxford: Legenda, 2003).

Borges, Jorge Luis, *Obras completas*, ed. by María Kodama, 15th edn, 4 vols (Barcelona: Emecé, 2004).

——, *Œuvres complètes*, ed. by Jean Pierre Bernès, trans. by Paul Bénichou et al., Bibliothèque de la Pléiade: 400, 2 vols (Paris: Gallimard, 1993).

Boyd, Carolyn, *Historia patria: Politics, History, and National Identity in Spain, 1875–1975* (Princeton: Princeton University Press, 1997).

Bravo, María Elena, 'Ante la novela de la democracia: Reflexiones sobre sus raíces', *Ínsula*, 444–5 (1983), 1, pp. 24–5.

——, 'Literatura de la distensión: el elemento policíaco', *Ínsula*, 472 (1986), 1, pp. 12–13.

Brontë, Charlotte, *Jane Eyre*, trans. by Carmen Martín Gaite (Barcelona: Alba, 1999).

Brontë, Emily, *Cumbres borrascosas*, trans. by Carmen Martín Gaite (Barcelona: Bruguera, 1984).

Browne, Sir Thomas, 'Quinto capítulo de la "Hydriotaphia"', trans. by Jorge Luis Borges and Bioy Casares, *Sur*, 111 (1944), pp. 15–26.

——, *Religio Medici, Hydriotaphia, and The Garden of Cyrus*, ed. by Robin Robbins (Oxford: Clarendon Press, 1972/ 2001).

——, *The Major Works*, ed. by C.A. Patrides (Harmondsworth: Penguin, 1977).

——, *Sobre errores vulgares o Pseudodoxia Epidemica*, trans. by Daniel Waissbein, 2nd edn (Madrid: Siruela, 2005).

Butt, John and Benjamin, Carmen, *A New Reference of Modern Spanish*, 4th edn (London: Arnold, 2004).

Caballero-Castellet, George et al., eds, *Cine-Lit III: Essays on Hispanic Film and Fiction* (Corvallis: Oregon State University Press, 1997).

Cagidemetrio, Alide and Rizzi, Daniela, eds, *Nabokov. Un'eredità letteraria* (Milan: Univesità Ca' Foscari di Venezia, 2006).

Cantalapiedra, Francisco, 'El misterio del móvil de Javier Marías', *El País*, 6 February 2004, p. 51.

Carlyle, Thomas, *La revolución francesa*, trans. by Miguel de Unamuno, 2 vols (Avrial, [n.d.]).

Castellet, José María, ed., *Nueve novísimos poetas españoles* (Barcelona: Barral, 1970).

Cercas, Javier, *Soldados de Salamina*, 30th edn (Barcelona: Tusquets, 2003).

Cervantes Saavedra, Miguel de, *Don Quijote de la Mancha*, ed. by Francisco Rico, 2nd edn, 2 vols (Barcelona: Instituto Cervantes, 1998).

——, Miguel de, *The Ingenious Hidalgo Don Quixote de la Mancha*, trans. by John Rutherford (London: Penguin, 2003).

Champeau, Geneviève, '*Tu rostro mañana* de Javier Marías o el arte de la conversación', in Andres-Suárez et al., eds, *Cuadernos de narrativa: Javier Marías*, pp. 169–88.

Christie, Ruth, '*Corazón tan blanco*: the Evolution of a Success Story', *Modern Languages Review*, 93 (1993), pp. 83–93.

—— et al., *The Scripted Self: Textual Identities in Contemporary Spanish Narrative* (Warminster: Aris & Phillips, 1995).

Coe, Ada M., 'Richardson in Spain', *Hispanic Review*, 3 (1935), pp. 56–63.

Conrad, Joseph, *The Mirror of the Sea* and *A Personal Record* (London: Dent, 1946).

——, *Typhoon and Other Tales*, ed. by Cedric Watts, rev. edn (Oxford: Oxford Uuniversity Press, 2008).

Conte, Rafael, 'Las paellas (republicanas) de "Tito" Jaime', *El País*, 27 November 2003, p. 14.

Crompton Lamburn, Richmal, *The House* (London: [n.p.], [1926]).

Csuday, Csaba, *Al otro lado del espejo: Conversaciones con José María Álvarez* (Murcia: Universidad de Murcia, 1987).

Cuñado, Isabel, *El espectro de la herencia: La narrativa de Javier Marías*, Portada Hispánica, 17 (Amsterdam: Rodopi, 2004).

Curtis, Lewis Perry, ed., *Letters of Laurence Sterne* (Oxford: Clarendon Press, 1935).

Day, Douglas, 'Borges, Faulkner, and *The Wild Palms*', *The Virginia Quarterly*, 56 (1980), pp. 109–18.

de Azúa, Félix, *Lecturas compulsivas: Una invitación* (Barcelona: Anagrama, 2003).

——, Marías, Javier, and Molina Foix, Vicente, *Tres cuentos didácticos* (Barcelona: La Gaya Ciencia, 1975).

de Goncourt, Edmond, *Los hermanos Zemganno*, trans. by Emilia Pardo Bazán (Saenz de Jubera, 1891).

de Lavergne, Gabriel Joseph, *Cartas de amor de la monja portuguesa Mariana Alcoforado* (Barcelona: Círculo de lectores, [2000]).

de Prada, Juan Manuel, *Desgarrados y excéntricos* (Barcelona: Seix Barral, 2001).

de Voogd, Peter et al., eds, *The Reception of Laurence Sterne in Europe*, The Athlone Critical Tradition Series: The Reception of British Authors in Europe, 2 (London: Thoemmes, 2004).

del Real Ramos, Carlos Alonso et al., *Juventud en el mundo antiguo: (crucero universitario por el Mediterráneo)* (Espasa, 1934).

Delbecque, Nicole et al., eds, *Estudios en honor del profesor Josse de Kock* (Leuven: Leuven University Press, 1998).

Delmer, Sefton, *An Autobiography*, 2 vols (London: Secker & Warburg, 1961–1962), I: *Black Boomerang* (1962).

Dickens, Charles, *Aventuras de Pickwick*, trans. by Benito Pérez Galdós, ed. by Arturo Ramoneda, 2 vols (Ediciones Júcar, 1989).

*10 años de* Corazón tan blanco *de Javier Marías* ([n.p.]: Alfaguara, [n.d.]).

Dinesen, Isak, *Ehrengard* (London: Michael Joseph, 1963).

——, *Últimos cuentos* (Madrid: Debate, 1990).

Dobson, Roger, *'Hail, O King!' The Last Days of John Gawsworth* (Oxford: The Friends of Arthur Machen and Tartarus Press, 2005).

Drabble, Margaret, 'Spies and Mirrors', *Times Literary Supplement*, 13 November 2009, p. 25.

Dreymüller, Cecilia, 'Las leyes del mercado: Acerca del fenómeno literario y editorial Javier Marías', in López de Abiada, ed., *Entre el ocio y el negocio*, pp. 83–92.

Durrell, Lawrence, *Spirit of Place: Letters and Essays on Travel*, ed. by Alan G. Thomas (Northampton: Faber & Faber, 1971).

Eça de Queirós, José Maria and Ramalho Ortigão, José Duarte, *El misterio de la carretera de Sintra*, trans. by Carmen Martín Gaite ([Nostromo], [1974]).

Echevarría, Ignacio, *Trayectos: Un recorrido crítico por la reciente narrativa española* (Barcelona: Debate, 2005).

Edemariam, Aida, 'Looking for Luisa', *The Guardian*, 7 May 2005, Review section, pp. 20–3.

Eliot, T. S., *Selected Essays* (London: Faber & Faber, 1953).

Faber, Sebastian, 'Un pensamiento que hace rimas: el afán universalizador en las novelas de Javier Marías', *Revista Hispánica Moderna*, 56 (2003), pp. 195–204.

Faulkner, William, *Novels 1936–1940* (New York: Library of America, 1990).

——, *Las palmeras salvajes*, trans. by Jorge Luis Borges, 3rd edn (Buenos Aires: Editorial Sudamericana, 1949).

——, *The Wild Palms* (London: Chatto & Windus, 1939).

Figes, Eva, *Actitudes patriarcales: las mujeres en la sociedad*, trans. by Carmen Martín Gaite, 2nd edn (Alianza, 1980).

Finch, Jeremiah S., *Sir Thomas Browne: A Doctor's Life of Science & Faith* (New York: Henry Schuman, 1950).

Fish, Stanley, ed., *Seventeenth-Century Prose: Modern Essays in Criticism* (New York: Oxford University Press, 1971).

Fitzgerald, F. Scott, *A este lado del paraíso*, trans. by Juan Benet (Alianza, 2003 [1st edn. 1968]).

Flaubert, Gustave, *Madame Bovary*, trans. by Carmen Martín Gaite (Barcelona: Bruguera, 1982).

Florenchie, Amélie, 'Marías en clave borgeana', in Andres-Suárez, ed., *Cuadernos de narrativa: Javier Marías*, pp. 155–68.

Fornieles, Javier, '*Corazón tan blanco* de Javier Marías: en el corazón de ideología burguesa', *Revista Hispánica Moderna*, 56 (2003), pp. 205–26.

France, Peter, ed., *The Oxford Guide to Literature in English Translation* (Oxford: Oxford University Press, 2000).

Franco, Dolores, *España como preocupación* (Alianza, 1998).

García, A. and Rojo, J. A., 'Javier Marías entra en la Academia', *El País*, 30 June 2006, p. 49.

García, Carlos Javier, *Contrasentidos (Acercamiento a la novela española contemporánea)*, Anexos de Triopelías, 10 (Zaragoza: Universidad de Zaragoza, 2002).

——, 'Imágenes como palabras y *Corazón tan blanco*, de Javier Marías', *Revista Hispánica Moderna*, 54 (2001), pp. 191–202.

García, Mariano, *Diccionario matemático* (New York: Dorman & Co., 1965).

García de León, Encarnación, 'El narrador en Javier Marías: Metáfora de la mirada de un voyeur literario', *Barcarola: Revista de creación literaria*, 68–9 (2006), pp. 393–412.

Gelida, Roser, 'El discurso de la incertidumbre: Cultura visual y la subjetividad posmoderna en la narrativa de Javier Marías' (unpublished doctoral dissertation, University of Colorado, 1999).

Giménez-Frontín, José Luis, *Woodstock Road en julio: Notas y diario* (Iruña-Pamplona: Pamiela, 1996).

Ginzburg, Natalia, *Nuestros ayeres*, trans. by Carmen Martín Gaite (Debate, 1996).

——, *Querido Miguel*, trans. by Carmen Martín Gaite (Barcelona: Lumen, 1989).

Glendinning, Nigel, 'Influencia de la Literatura inglesa en el siglo VXIII [sic]', in Arce, ed., *La literatura española del siglo XVIII y sus fuentes extranjeras*, pp. 47–93.

Glenn, Kathleen M., 'Marías, Javier. *Corazón tan blanco*', *Hispania*, 76 (1993), p. 492.

Goytisolo, Juan, *El furgón de cola* (Barcelona: Seix Barral, 1976).

Gracia, Jordi, 'Javier Marías o pensar por novelas', *Claves de razón práctica*, 177 (2007), pp. 77–8.

Graham, Helen, *The Spanish Civil War: A Very Short Introduction* (Oxford: Oxford University Press, 2005).

——, et al., eds, *Spanish Cultural Studies: An Introduction* (Oxford: Oxford University Press, 1995).

Grohmann, Alexis, *Coming Into One's Own: The Novelistic Development of Javier Marías* (Amsterdam: Rodopi, 2002).

——, 'Javier Marías's *El siglo*: A question of style', *Modern Languages Review*, 97 (2002), pp. 94–107.

——, 'La errabundia de *Negra espalda del tiempo*', in Andres-Suárez, ed., *Cuadernos de narrativa: Javier Marías*, pp. 135–44.

——, 'La nobleza literaria de Javier Marías' *Quimera*, 252 (2005), pp. 61–6.

——, 'La literatura como paradoja', in Steenmeijer and Grohmann, eds, *Allí donde uno diría que ya no puede haber nada*, pp. 161–9.

——, 'Literatura y digresión: la errabundia de *Negra espalda del tiempo*, in *Cuadernos de narrativa*, pp. 135–44.

——, 'Literatura y errabundia', in Archer et al., eds, *Antes y después del* "Quijote", pp. 373–81.

——, '*Los dominios del lobo* by Javier Marías: Hollywood and *Anticasticismo Novísimo*', in Bonaddio, ed., *Crossing Fields in Modern Spanish Culture*, pp. 165–76.

——, 'Madrid and Interconnectedness of the World in Javier Marías's *Mañana en la batalla piensa en mí*', *Donaire*, 16 (2001), pp. 12–20.

——, 'Pérfida Albión: La (escasa) presencia de la narrativa española reciente en el Reino Unido', *Quimera*, 273 (2006), 36–40.

——, and Steenmeijer, Maarten, eds., *El columnismo de escritores españoles (1975–2005)* (Verbum, 2006).

Grossman, Edith, *Why Translation Matters* (New Haven and London: Yale University Press, 2010).

Halliwell, Stephen, *The Aesthetics of Mimesis: Ancient Texts and Modern Problems* (Woodstock [Oxfordshire]: Princeton University Press, 2002).

Hardy, Thomas, *The Short Stories of Thomas Hardy* (London: Macmillan, 1928).

—— et al., *Los tres forasteros y otras narraciones*, trans. by José Donday (Barcelona: Sociedad General Española de Librería, 1929).

Hazard, Paul, *La crisis de la conciencia europea (1680–1715)*, trans. by Julián Marías (Pegaso, 1941).

Heaney, Seamus, *Opened Ground: Poems 1966–1996* (London: Faber & Faber, 1998).

Herr, Richard, *The Eighteenth-Century Revolution in Spain* (Princeton: Princeton University Press, 1958).

Herzberger, David K., 'La autoridad transformadora de la narración en *Tu rostro mañana*', in Steenmeijer and Grohmann, eds, *Allí donde uno diría que ya no puede haber nada: Tu rostro mañana de Javier Marías*, pp. 189–201.

——, 'The Real and the Make-Believe: Hermeneutic Consciousness in Javier Marías's *Negra espalda del tiempo*', *Romance Studies*, 19 (2001), pp. 87–94.

Holloway, Mark, *John Gawsworth and the Island Kingdom of Redonda* (Oxford: The Lost Club and The Redondan Cultural Foundation, 2002).

Howe, Alan B., ed., *Laurence Sterne: The Critical Heritage* (London and New York: Routledge, 1995).

Hughes, Richard, *A Moment of Time* (London: Chatto & Windus, 1926).

Humblé, Philippe, 'A tradução de *Tristram Shandy*', *Ilha do desterro*, 17 (1987), pp. 63–75.

Infantes, Víctor et al., eds, *Historia de la edición y de la lectura en España 1472–1914* (Fundación Germán Sánchez Ruipérez, 2003).

Iravedra Valea, Araceli et al., eds, *Leopoldo Alas. Un clásico contemporáneo, 12–16 Noviembre de 2001*, 2 vols (Oviedo: Universidad de Oviedo, 2002).

Iriarte, Antonio, '"Cito a menudo para mis adentros": Citas y alusiones en *Tu rostro mañana* de Javier Marías', in Steenmeijer and Grohmann, eds, *Allí donde uno diría que ya no puede haber nada*, pp. 303–66.

Izquierdo, Luis, 'Una aproximación a los relatos de Javier Marías', *Ínsula*, 568 (1994), pp. 19–21.

James, Henry, *Washington Square*, ed. by Brian Lee (Harmondsworth: Penguin, 1986).

Jiménez, Juan Francisco, 'La escritura del exceso: Javier Marías y la palabra íntima', *Crítica hispánica*, 27 (2005), pp. 71–83.

Johnson, Hewlett, *Searching For Light: An Autobiography* (London: Michael Joseph, 1968).

Kercher, Dona, 'Children of the European Union, Crossing Gendered Channels: Javier Marías's Novel, *Todas las almas*, and Gracia Querejeta's Film, *El último viaje de Robert Rylands*', in Caballero-Castellet, ed., *Cine-Lit III: Essays on Hispanic Film and Fiction*, pp. 100–12.

Keymer, Thomas, *Sterne, the Moderns, and the Novel* (Oxford: Oxford University Press, 2002).

Keynes, Geoffrey, ed., *The Works of Sir Thomas Browne*, 4 vols (London: Faber & Gwyer, 1929).

——, *The Works of Sir Thomas Browne*, 4 vols (London: Faber & Faber, 1964).

Kociejowski, Marius, 'Intimate Distances', *Poetry Nation Review*, 29 (2002), pp. 10–12.

Kristal, Efraín, *Invisible Work: Borges and Translation* (Nashville: Vanderbilt University Press, 2002).

Labanyi, Jo, 'Literary Experiment and Cultural Cannibalization' in Graham, ed., *Spanish Cultural Studies: An Introduction*, pp. 295–9.

Lamburn, Richmal Crompton, *The House* (London: [n.p.], [1926]).

Lasdun, James, 'Glittering with Intent', *The Guardian*, Review section, 21 November 2009, p. 10.

Leavis, F. R., *The Great Tradition: George Eliot, Henry James, Joseph Conrad* (Harmondsworth: Peregrine, 1962).

Lee, Abigail E., 'Sterne's Legacy to Juan Goytisolo: A Shandyian Reading of *Juan sin tierra*', *Modern Language Review*, 84 (1989), pp. 351–7.

Leibniz, Gottfried Wilhelm, *Discurso de metafísica*, trans. by Julián Marías (Revista de Occidente, 1942).

Lermontov, Mikhail, *A Hero of Our Time*, trans. by Vladimir and Dmitri Nabokov (London: Everyman, 1992).

Levi, Primo, *El sistema periódico*, trans. by Carmen Martín Gaite (Alianza, 1987).

——, *Historias naturales*, trans. by Carmen Martín Gaite (Alianza, 1988).

Lewis, C. S., *Una pena en observación*, trans. by Carmen Martín Gaite (Barcelona: Anagrama, 1994).

——, *Una pena observada* trans. by Carmen Martín Gaite (Trieste, 1988).

Lindop, Grevel et al., eds, *The Works of Thomas de Quincey*, 21 vols (London: Pickering and Chatto, 2000–3).

Logie, Ilse, 'Aspectos performativos en dos novelas de Javier Marías: *Corazón tan blanco* y *Mañana en la batalla piensa en mí*', in Delbecque, ed., *Estudios en honor del profesor Josse de Kock*, pp. 889–97.

——, 'La traducción, emblema de la obra de Javier Marías', in Steenmeijer, ed., *El pensamiento literario de Javier Marías*, pp. 67–76.

López de Abiada, José Manuel et al., eds, *Entre el ocio y el negocio: industria editorial y literatura en la España de los 90* (Verbum, 2001).

Lynch, Enrique, 'El arte de la digresión: *Sobre errores vulgares o Pseudodoxia Epidemica*', *El País*, 8 April 2006, Babelia section, p. 14.

MacDonald, George, *La princesa y los trasgos*, trans. by Carmen Martín Gaite (Siruela, 1995).

McNeillie, Andrew and Clarke, Stuart N., eds., *The Essays of Virginia Woolf*, 6 vols (London: The Hogarth Press, 1986–2011).

Mainer, José Carlos, 'El pensamiento literario en la postmodernidad', *La página*, 20 (1995), pp. 29–34.

——, *Tramas, libros, nombres: Para entender la literatura española, 1944–2000* (Barcelona: Anagrama, 2005).

Mallafrè, Joaquim, 'Sterne in Catalan: Notes on Translation', *The Shandean*, 9 (1997), pp. 109–21.

Manrique, Winston, 'Las mejores novelas en español', *El País*, 26 March 2007, p. 58.

——, 'Los últimos días de la Segunda Guerra Mundial', *El País*, 25 July 2005, pp. 28, 31.

Marías, Julián, *Una vida presente: Memorias*, 3 vols (Alianza, 1988–1989).

Martín, Aurelio, 'El PP de Castilla y León dice que está abierto al homenaje a Juan Benet', *El País*, 17 March 1993, p. 31.

Martin, Tim, 'Smile, or You Might Ruin your Future', *The Independent on Sunday*, ABC section, 5 June 2006, p. 26.

——, 'That Shouldn't Happen in a Disabled Loo', *The Independent on Sunday*, ABC section, 23 July 2006, p. 26.

Martín Gaite, Carmen, *La búsqueda de interlocutor y otras búsquedas* (Nostromo, 1973).

——, Carmen and Ruiz Tarazona, Andrés, eds. and trans, *Ocho siglos de poesía gallega: Antología bilingüe* (Alianza [1972]).

Martín-Maestro, Abraham, 'La novela española en 1982 y 1983', *ALEC*, 9 (1984), pp. 149–74.

——, 'La novela española en 1984', *ALEC*, 10 (1985), pp. 123–41.

Martínez Cachero, José María, 'Diez años de novela española (1976–1985) por sus pasos contados', *Ínsula*, 464–5 (1985), pp. 3–4.

Martinón, Miguel, 'Narración reflexiva: *Corazón tan blanco*, de Javier Marías', *Letras peninsulares*, 9 (1996), pp. 355–69.

Mendoza, Eduardo, 'El extraño caso de Javier Marías', *El País*, 18 November 1998, p. 40.

——, *El misterio de la cripta embrujada*, 6th edn (Barcelona: Seix Barral, 2002).

——, '"Laudatio" de la puntuación', *El País*, 30 June 2006, p. 50.

Miano, Sarah Emily, 'Betrayal of a Blood Brother', *The Observer*, Books section, 8 May 2005, p. 16.

——, 'The Voyeur, the Shady Businessman and his Missus', *The Daily Telegraph*, Arts & Books section, 29 July 2006, p. 9.

Michael, Ian, 'Sir Peter Russell (1913–2006)', *Bulletin of Spanish Studies*, 83 (2006), pp. 1133–44.

Miller, Stephen, 'Graphic-Lexical Dialogue in Marías and Rivas', *Romance Quarterly*, 51 (2004), pp. 97–110.

——, 'The Spanish Novel from Pérez Galdós to Marías: Tradition and Nescience, Rupture, and Europeanization', *South Central Review*, 18 (2001), pp. 45–65.

Milton, John, *Poetical Works*, ed. by Douglas Bush (London: Oxford University Press, 1970).

Mitchelmore, Stephen, 'The Upraised Sword', *Times Literary Supplement*, 14 July 2006, p. 23.

Molero de la Iglesia, Alicia, 'El narrador psicológico de Javier Marías', in Romera Castillo, ed., *El cuento en la década de los noventa*, pp. 257–66.

Molina-Foix, Vicente, *New Cinema in Spain* (London: BFI, 1977).

——, 'Primera página', *El País*, 6 January 1993, p. 28.

Moliner, María, *Diccionario del uso del español*, 2 vols (Gredos, 1996).

Mollejo, Azucena, *El cuento español de 1970 a 2000: Cuatro escritores de Madrid: Francisco Umbral, Rosa Montero, Almudena Grandes y Javier Marías* (Pliegos, 2002).

Molpeceres Arnaiz, Sara, '*Macbeth* de William Shakespeare en *Corazón tan blanco* de Javier Marías', *Estudios Humanísticos. Filología*, 22 (2000), pp. 161–73.

Montero, Rosa, *La loca de la casa* (Alfaguara, 2003).

Muñoz Molina, Antonio, *Pura alegría* (Alfaguara, 1998).

——, *Sefarad: Una novela de novelas* (Alfaguara, 2001).

——, 'Tarantino y la muerte', *El País*, 19 April 1995, p. 36.

——, 'Tarantino, la muerte y la comedia: Una respuesta a Javier Marías', *El País*, 10 May 1995, p. 40.

——, *Ventanas de Manhattan* (Barcelona: Seix Barral, 2004).

Murillo, Enrique, '"La vida es un mal novelista": "The Paris Review" abre las puertas a Javier Marías en el gran círculo literario anglosajón', *El País*, 15 January 2007, p. 48.

Murphy, Kathryn and Todd, Richard, '*A man very well studyed*': New Contexts for *Thomas Browne* (Leiden: Brill, 2008).

Nabokov, Vladimir, 'The Art of Translation', in *Lectures on Russian Literature*, ed. by Fredson Bowers (London: Harvest, 1981), pp. 315–21.

——, *Lectures on Don Quixote*, ed. by Fredson Bowers (Orlando: Harvest, 1983).

——, *Lectures on Russian Literature*, ed. by Fredson Bowers (London: Harvest, 1981).

——, *Lolita* (London: Everyman, 1992).

——, *Novels and Memoirs 1941–1951* (New York: Library of America, 1996).

——, *Novels 1955–1962: Lolita, Pnin, Pale Fire, Lolita: A Screenplay* (New York: Library of America, 1996).

——, 'Problems of Translation: "Onegin" in English', *Partisan Review*, 22 (1955), pp. 496–512.

——, *Strong Opinions* (New York: Vintage, 1990).

Napoleón, *De Córcega a Santa Elena (Escritos y discursos)*, trans. by Dolores Franco (Pegaso, [1941]).

Nathanson, Leonard, '*Urn Burial*: The Ethics of Mortality', in Fish, ed., *Seventeenth-Century Prose*, pp. 440–61.

Navajas, Gonzalo, *La narrativa española en la era global: Imagen, comunicación, ficción* (Barcelona: EUB, 2002).

Navarro, M. T., '*Corazón tan blanco*: El color de la experiencia', *Reseña de Literatura, Arte y Espectáculos*, 229 (1992), p. 21.

Navarro Gil, Sandra, 'La voz del narrador en las novelas de Javier Marías', *Revista de Literatura*, 65 (2003), pp. 199–210.

New, Melvyn, *Tristram Shandy: A Book for Free Spirits* (New York: Twayne, 1994).

O'Leary, Catherine and Ribeiro de Menezes, Alison, *A Companion to Carmen Martín Gaite* (Woodbridge: Tamesis, 2008).

Obiol, María José, 'El dominio de la sensación', *El País*, Domingo section, 23 July 1989, p. 20.

Ortega y Gasset, José, *Obras completas*, 12 vols (Revista de Occidente, 1946–1983).

Oyata, Martín, 'Matices de la extrañeza en la narrativa de Javier Marías', *Renacimiento*, 51–54 (2006), pp. 74–87.

Pardo Bazán, Emilia, *Obras completas*, ed. by Federico Carlos Saínz de Robles et al., 3 vols (Aguilar, 1963–1973).

Parker, Fred, *Scepticism and Literature: An Essay on Pope, Hume, Sterne, and Johnson* (Oxford: Oxford University Press, 2003).

Patrides, C. A., ed., *Approaches to Sir Thomas Browne: The Ann Arbor Tercentenary Lectures and Essays* (London: University of Missouri Press, 1982).

——, ' "The Best Part of Nothing": Sir Thomas Browne and the Strategy of Indirection', in Patrides, ed., *Approaches to Sir Thomas Browne*, pp. 31–48.

Patterson, Christina, 'In Search of Lost Time', *The Independent*, 28 July 2006, Arts & Books Review section, pp. 20–1.

Pegenaute, Luis, 'Las primeras traducciones de Sterne al español y el problema de la censura', *Livius*, 1 (1992), pp. 133–9.

——, 'Sterne Castles in Spain', in de Voogd et al., eds, *The Reception of Laurence Sterne in Europe*, pp. 234–46.

——, 'The Unfortunate Journey of Laurence Sterne Through Spain: The Translations of his Works into Spanish', *The Shandean*, 6 (1994), pp. 24–53.

Pereda, Rosa, *Contra Franco 1968–1978* (Barcelona: Planeta, 2003).

Pérez Galdós, Benito, *Ensayos de crítica literaria*, ed. by Laureano Bonet (Barcelona: Península, 1999).

——, Benito, *Obras inéditas*, ed. by Alberto Ghiraldo, 12 vols (Renacimiento, 1923–1930).

Pérez Gracia, César, 'Sterne y Marías o el coloquio de los peldaños. En torno a *Tu rostro mañana*', in Steenmeijer and Grohmann, eds, *Allí donde uno diría que ya no puede haber nada*, pp. 77–85.

Pérez-Lanzac, Carmen, 'El último caballero', *Marie Claire* (Spanish edition), January 2005, pp. 90–2.

Perrault, Charles, *Bruno Bettelheim presenta los Cuentos de Perrault*, trans. by Carmen Martín Gaite (Barcelona: Crítica, 1980).

Perriam, Chris et al., eds, *A New History of Spanish Writing: 1939 to the 1990s* (Oxford: Oxford University Press, 2000).

Pescador, Félix Romeo, 'Javier Marías por sus propios ojos', *Invitación a la lectura*, 8 (1990), p. 1.

Pessoa, Fernando, *El marinero*, trans. by Carmen Martín Gaite (Alcalá de Henares: Fundación Colegio del Rey, 1990).

———, *Obras completas*, 11 vols (Lisbon: Ática, 1942–1974).

Pittarello, Elide, 'El mundo depende de sus relatores', *Archipiélago*, 18–19 (1994), pp. 225–7.

———, 'Guardar la distancia', in Javier Marías, *El hombre que parecía no querer nada* (ed. by Pittarello), pp. 11–31.

———, 'Haciendo tiempo con las cosas', in Andres-Suárez, ed., *Cuadernos de narrativa: Javier Marías*, pp. 17–48.

———, '*Negra espalda del tiempo*: instrucciones de uso', in Steenmeijer, ed., *El pensamiento literario de Javier Marías*, pp. 125–34.

———, ' "No he querido saber, pero he sabido": Javier Marías y "Corazón tan blanco"', in Javier Marías, *Corazón tan blanco* (ed. by Pittarello) (Crítica, 2006), pp. 5–94.

———, 'Prólogo: Gente en el tren', in Javier Marías, *El hombre sentimental* (Espasa Calpe, 1994), p. 9–21.

———, 'Rewriting Nabokov: The Shortened *Lolita* by Javier Marías', in Cagidemetrio and Rizzi, eds, *Nabokov. Un'eredità letteraria*, pp. 87–95.

Pont, Jaume, ed., *Brujas, demonios y fantasmas en la literatura fantástica hispánica* (Lleida: Universitat de Lleida, 1999).

Pozuelo Yvancos, José María, '*Tu rostro mañana*, de Javier Marías: autoconciencia y sentido', *Revista de Occidente*, 286 (2005), pp. 124–36.

Preston, Claire, *Thomas Browne and the Writing of Early Modern Science* (Cambridge: Cambridge University Press, 2005).

Resina, Joan Ramon, ed., *Disremembering the Dictatorship: The Politics of Memory in the Spanish Transition to Democracy*, Portada Hispánica, 8 (Amsterdam: Rodopi, 2000).

Ricks, Christopher, 'Introductory Essay', in Laurence Sterne, *The Life and Opinions of Tristram Shandy, Gentleman*, ed. by Melvyn New and Joan New, rev. edn (Harmondsworth: Penguin, 2003), pp. xi–xxxii.

Rilke, Rainer Maria, *Cartas francesas a Merline, 1919–1922*, trans. by Carmen Martín Gaite (Alianza, 1987).

Roas, David, 'Perdidos en Redonda: Javier Marías y lo fantástico', in Andres-Suárez, ed., *Cuadernos de narrativa: Javier Marías*, pp. 217–30.

Rodríguez, Andrés, 'El universo Marías', *Dominical*, 12 December 2004. http://www.javiermarias.es/ByS/entrevistas2.html (accessed 11 November 2008).

Rodríguez Fischer, Ana, 'El revés del tiempo', *Archipiélago* 34–35 (1998) pp. 193–4.

———, 'Siempre habrá nunca. El enigma del tiempo en la narrativa de Javier Marías', *Cuadernos hispanoamericanos*, 644 (2004), pp. 61–76.

Rodríguez Rivero, Manuel, 'Sillón de orejas', *El País*, Babelia section, 10 April 2010, p. 16.

Rollins, Hyder Edward, ed., *The Letters of John Keats 1814–1821*, 2 vols (London: Cambridge University Press, 1958).

Romera Castillo, José et al., eds, *El cuento en la década de los noventa* (Visor, 2001).

Romero, César, 'Del azar y sus nombres. Sobre Javier Marías y su última novela', *Generació*, 7 (1995), pp. 99–116.

Ross, Ian Campbell, *Laurence Sterne: A Life* (Oxford: Oxford University Press, 2001).

Ruiz, Julius, *Franco's Justice: Repression in Madrid After the Spanish Civil War* (Oxford: Oxford University Press, 2005).

Ruskin, John et al., *Cuentos de hadas victorianos*, trans. by Carmen Martín Gaite et al. (Siruela, 1993).

Russell, P. E., *Cervantes* (Oxford: Oxford University Press, 1985).

Rutherford, John, '"Esos pobres truchimanes": Leopoldo Alas y la traducción literaria', in Araceli Iravedra Valea et al., eds, *Leopoldo Alas. Un clásico contemporáneo, 12–16 Noviembre de 2001*, 2 vols (Oviedo: Universidad de Oviedo, 2002), I, pp. 289–302.

Salinger, J. D., *The Complete Uncollected Short Stories of J. D. Salinger* ([n.p.]: [n. pub], [n.d.]).

Sanz Villanueva, Santos, '*Tu rostro mañana 3: Veneno y sombra y adiós*', *El Mundo*, El Cultural section, 11 October 2007, page unknown.

Savater, Fernando, *A caballo entre milenios* (Aguilar, 2001).

———, *Amor a R. L. Stevenson* (Santander: Límite, 1998).

———, *La infancia recuperada*, 10th edn (Taurus, 2002 [1st ed. 1976]).

———, 'La soledad solidaria del poeta', *Quimera*, 15 (1982), 5.

———, *Mira por dónde: Autobiografía razonada* (Taurus, 2003).

Sayle, Charles, *The Works of Sir Thomas Browne* (London/Edinburgh, 1904–1907).

Scheler, Max, *De lo eterno en el hombre*, trans. by Julián Marías (Revista de Occidente, [1940]).

Sebald, W. G., *On the Natural History of Destruction*, trans. by Anthea Bell (London: Hamish Hamilton, 2003).

———, *The Rings of Saturn*, trans. by Michael Hulse (London: Harvill, 1998).

Segal, Erich, *Historia de amor*, trans. by Eduardo Gudiño Kieffer (Buenos Aires: Emecé, 1970).

Séneca, Lucio Anno, *Sobre la felicidad*, trans. by Julián Marías (Revista de Occidente, [1943]).

Shakespeare, William, *Julius Caesar*, ed. by David Daniell (London: Arden, 2003).

———, *King Henry IV: Part 1*, ed. David Scott Kastan (London: Arden, 2003).

———, *King Henry IV: Part 2*, ed. by A. R. Humphreys (London: Arden, 2005).

———, *King Henry V*, ed. by T. W. Craik (London: Routledge, 1995; repr. London: Arden, 2002).

Shakespeare, William, *King Richard III*, ed. by Anthony Hammond (London: Arden, 2004).

——, *Macbeth*, ed. by Kenneth Muir (London: Arden, 2005).

——, *Othello*, ed. by E. A. J. Honigmann (London: Arden, 2003).

——, *The Tempest*, ed. by Virginia Mason Vaughan et al. (London: Arden, 2003).

Sherlo, Arthur, ed., *The Yale Edition of the Works of Samuel Johnson*, 18 + vols (New Haven and London: Yale University Press, 1958–).

Silone, Ignazio, *Vino y pan*, trans. by Carmen Martín Gaite (Alianza, [1968]).

Simonsen, Karen-Margrethe, '*Corazón tan blanco*—A Post-Postmodern Novel by Javier Marías', *Revista Hispánica Moderna*, 52 (1999), pp. 193–212.

Smith, Ali, 'Books of the Year', *Times Literary Supplement*, 27 November 2009, p. 15.

——, 'Review of *Your Face Tomorrow 2: Dance and Dream*', *The Sunday Telegraph*, section Seven, 23 July 2006, p. 39.

Sobejano, Gonzalo, *Novela española contemporánea 1940–1995* (Mare Nostrum, 2003).

Sontag, Susan, *Where the Stress Falls* (London: Vintage, 2003).

Spencer, Herbert, *De las leyes en general* ([Tordesillas], [1909]).

——, *Exceso de legislación* ([Tordesillas], [1910]).

——, *La Beneficencia*, trans. by Miguel de Unamuno (La España Moderna, [1893]).

Spires, Robert C., 'De la información a la comunicación a la comunidad en *Mañana en la batalla piensa en mí*', in Steenmeijer, ed., *El pensamiento literario de Javier Marías*, pp. 113–24.

——, 'Information, Communication, and Spanish Fiction of the 1990s', *Romance Quarterly*, 51 (2004), pp. 141–59.

Stapleton, Laurence, *The Elected Circle: Studies in the Art of Prose* (Princeton: Princeton University Press, 1973).

Steenmeijer, Maarten, ed., *El pensamiento literario de Javier Marías*, Foro Hispánico, 20 (Amsterdam: Rodopi, 2001).

——, 'El tabú del franquismo vivido en la narrativa de Mendoza, Marías y Muñoz Molina', in Resina, ed., *Disremembering the Dictatorship*, pp. 139–55.

——, 'Figuras acabadas y figuras inacabadas en *Tu rostro mañana* de Javier Marías', *Siglo XXI, literatura y cultura españolas: Revista de la cátedra Miguel Delibes*, 3 (2005), pp. 197–209.

——, 'Javier Marías, columnista: el otro, el mismo', in Andres-Suárez, ed., *Cuadernos de narrativa: Javier Marías*, pp. 255–73.

—— and Grohmann, Alexis, eds., *Allí donde uno diría que ya no puede haber nada: Tu rostro mañana de Javier Marías*, Foro Hispánico, 35 (Amsterdam: Rodopi, 2009).

Steiner, George, *After Babel: Aspects of Language and Translation*, 3rd edn (Oxford: Oxford University Press, 1998).

Stephens, Cynthia, 'Borges, Sir Thomas Browne and the Theme of Metempsychosis', *Modern Language Studies*, 28 (1992), pp. 268–79.

Sterne, Laurence, *The Beauties of Sterne: Including all his Pathetic Tales, & Most Distinguished Observations on Life* (London: C. Etherington, 1782).

——, *The Life and Opinions of Tristram Shandy, Gentleman*, ed. by James Aiken Work (New York: Odyssey Press, 1960).

——, *The Life and Opinions of Tristram Shandy, Gentleman*, ed. by Graham Petrie (Harmondsworth: Penguin, 1967).

——, *The Life and Opinions of Tristram Shandy, Gentleman*, ed. by Melvyn New and Joan New, 3 vols (Gainesville: University of Florida Presses, 1978–1984).

——, *The Life and Opinions of Tristram Shandy, Gentleman*, ed. by Melvyn New and Joan New, rev. edn (London: Penguin, 2003).

Stevens, Wallace, *Collected Poems* (London: Faber & Faber, 1959).

Stevenson, Robert Louis, *In the South Seas*, ed. by Neil Rennie (London: Penguin, 1998).

——, *Memories and Portraits* (London: Chatto & Windus, 1887).

——, *Poemas*, trans. by Txatro Santos and José María Álvarez (Hiperión, 1994).

Strachey, Lytton, *Books and Characters: French and English* (London: Chatto & Windus, 1922).

Suñén, Luis, 'Escritura y realidad', *Ínsula*, 464–65 (1985), pp. 5–6.

Svevo, Italo, *Corto viaje sentimental*, trans. by Carmen Martín Gaite (Alianza, 2008).

——, *Senectud*, trans. by Carmen Martín Gaite (Barcelona: Bruguera, 1982).

Taylor, Bruce, 'Sir Peter Russell', *The Times*, 14 July 2006, p. 80.

*The Song of Igor's Campaign*, trans. by Vladimir Nabokov (Woodstock: Ardis, 2003).

Traugott, John, *Tristram Shandy's World: Sterne's Philosophical Rhetoric* (Berkeley: University of California Press, 1954).

Turpin, Enrique, 'La sutil omnisciencia del fantasma: "Cuando fui mortal" de Javier Marías', *La nueva literatura hispánica*, 2 (1998), pp. 127–42.

Updike, John, *The Early Stories 1953–1975* (London: Penguin, 2003).

——, *Museos y mujeres*, trans. by Andrés Bosch (Barcelona: Noguer, 1974).

Valls, Fernando, 'El hombre que fue Reresby o el rostro de Tupra', *Quimera*, 252 (2005), pp. 69–70.

——, 'El porqué de una encuesta, de unas preguntas', *Quimera*, 214–15 (2002), pp. 10–28.

——, 'Interpretar y narrar', *Quimera*, 224–5 (2003), pp. 99–101.

——, *La realidad inventada: Análisis crítico de la novela española actual* (Barcelona: Crítica, 2003).

——, '*Lo que dijo el mayordomo*, de Javier Marías, o la disolución de los géneros literarios narrativos', in Andres-Suárez, ed., *Mestizaje y disolución de géneros en la literatura hispánica contemporánea*, pp. 168–73.

——, 'Un estado de crueldad o el opio del tiempo: Los fantasmas de Javier Marías', in Pont, ed., *Brujas, demonios y fantasmas en la literatura fantástica hispánica*, pp. 361–7.

Vargas Llosa, Mario, Javier Marías, and Arturo Pérez-Reverte, *Lecciones y maestros: II Cita Internacional de la literatura en español* (Santillana del Mar: Santillana, 2008).

Venuti, Lawrence, ed., *A Translation Studies Reader*, 2nd edn (London: Routledge, 2004).

——, 'Translation, Community, Utopia', in Venuti, ed., *A Translation Studies Reader*, pp. 482–502.

Vila-Sanjuán, Sergio, *Pasando página: Autores y editores en la España democrática* (Barcelona: Destino, 2003).

Walker, A. R. and Glover, A., eds, *The Collected Works of William Hazlitt*, 13 vols (London: Dent, 1902–1906).

Warren, Austin, 'The Styles of Sir Thomas Browne', in Fish, ed., *Seventeenth-Century Prose*, pp. 413–23.

Wilde, Oscar, *El retrato de Dorian Grey*, trans. by Carmen Martín Gaite (Salvat, [1970]).

Williams, William Carlos, *Viaje hacia el amor y otros poemas*, trans. by Carmen Martín Gaite (Trieste, 1981).

Wilson, Jason, *Jorge Luis Borges* (London: Reaktion, 2006).

Wood, Gareth, 'The Dark Backward and Abysm of Time', *The London Magazine*, June/July 2004, pp. 105–7.

——, '"La nieve que cae": Algunos antecedentes literarios y fílmicos de una imagen en *MBPM* de Javier Marías', in Andres-Suárez, ed., *Cuadernos de narrativa: Javier Marías*, pp. 125–34.

Wood, Michael, *The Magician's Doubts: Nabokov and the Risks of Fiction* (London: Pimlico, 1995).

Woolf, Virginia, *Al faro*, trans. by Carmen Martín Gaite (Barcelona: Edhasa, 1978).

Wynne-Tyson, Jon, *Finding the Words: A Publishing Life* (Norwich: Michael Russell, 2004).

Zola, Émile, *Trabajo*, trans. by Leopoldo Alas, 2 vols (Barcelona: Maucci, 1901).

——, *Trabajo*, trans. by Leopoldo Alas, ed. by Francisco Caudet (Ediciones de la Torre, 1991).

# Index

Abós, Ángel Luis 44–5
Alas, Leopoldo 4, 46
Almodóvar, Pedro 12, 36, 199
Álvarez, José María 29
Aristotle 3, 106–7
Ashbery, John 2, 31, 36, 319
Auden, Wystan Hugh 32, 102
Azúa, Félix de 27, 30, 48, 50, 53,
    241–3, 326

Barnes, Julian 136–7
Beckett, Samuel 57, 70, 109
Beevor, Antony 36, 285
Benet, Juan 123, 128, 145, 170
    on committed literature 46–8, 49
    on cultural renewal in Spanish
        letters 41, 42, 52
    death 129–30
    on Galdós 97
    *Inspiración y el estilo, La* 24, 30, 46–7,
        50, 76, 107–8, 174
    literary beginnings 24
    as reader of Conrad 30–1
    as reader of Faulkner 24, 30,
        141 n. 10
    remembered in *Negra espalda del tiempo*
        123, 130–1
    as translator 25, 326
Benjamin, Walter 55, 62
Bernhard, Thomas 26, 109
Bioy Casares, Adolfo 16, 139,
    144–67, 221
Blixen, Karen, *see* Dinesen, Iask
Bolaño, Roberto 2
Bonaparte, Napoleon 19–20
Borges, Jorge Luis 16, 39–40, 51, 70,
    106, 139–67, 187, 221, 233, 320
    'El escritor argentino y la
        tradición' 51–2
    translation of Browne 146–67
    translation of Faulkner's *The Wild
        Palms* 39–40, 139–44
Boyd, Carolyn 44–6
Brodsky, Joseph 32
Browne, Thomas 98, 109, 127, 170–2,
    187–8, 204, 252, 279
    dedication of *Hydriotaphia* 196–7
    'On Dreams' 31
    *Hydriotaphia or Urn Burial* 31, 168,

180, 182–4, 206–7, 212, 220–4,
    258, 300–1, 303, 320
    *Religio Medici* 31, 188, 220, 221, 303
Burgess, Anthony 32

Cambridge University 72, 102, 232, 237
careless talk 289, 299, 305
Carpintero, Heliodoro 22
Castellet, José María 29, 42
Catholic Church 12–13, 231
Cela y Trulock, Camilo José 44 n. 9,
    169–70, 231
Cervantes Saaavedra, Miguel de 48, 49,
    72, 97–8, 319
    *Don Quijote* 20, 21, 32, 46, 81–2,
        233–4, 321
civil liberties 285, 286, 288–9
Coetzee, John Michael 2, 36
Conrad, Joseph 5, 7–8, 37–8, 41, 54, 98,
    109, 174, 194, 235, 321–4
Crompton Lamburn, Richmal 20, 33, 42,
    68–9
Cuñado, Isabel 11, 14, 185, 199,
    206, 216

Dearlove, Richard 272
Delmer, Sefton 294, 306–13
Dickens, Charles 3, 49, 60–2, 74, 77
Dinesen, Isak 2, 5, 98, 109, 131,
    235, 324
Dobson, Roger 32
Douglas, Keith 34
Doyle, Arthur Conan 129
Drabble, Margaret 2, 268 n. 34
Dylan, Bob 23 n. 18, 320

Echevarría, Ignacio 291
Edinburgh 315–17
Eliot, Thomas Stearns 39, 51, 54, 58, 324
espionage 170, 272, 285, 289–90, 298–9,
    307–14
Ewart, Wilfrid 112, 113, 116, 122–3,
    127, 128, 135

Faulkner, William 2, 24, 27–8, 30, 34,
    41, 55, 258, 235
    *Absalom, Absalom!* 293
    *As I Lay Dying* 180
    *The Wild Palms* 39–40, 139–44

Fitzgerald, Francis Scott 25
Flaubert, Gustave 47, 49, 60, 136–7
Ford, John 284
France, Peter 143
Franco, Dolores 18, 19–20, 45
Franco, Francisco 13, 14, 19, 22, 42, 45, 125, 170, 205, 232
Franco, Jesús 22–3, 24

Ganivet, Ángel 45
García Hortelano, Juan 26
Gawsworth, John 34–5, 104, 116, 117–18, 122–4, 129, 197–8
Gide, André 48
Giménez-Frontín, José Luis 75–6
Goytisolo, Juan 42, 48–9, 77
Goytisolo, Luis 26
Gracia, Jordi 287
Grohmann, Alexis:
   on *El siglo* 169, 173–4, 176–7, 184, 185, 193–4
   on Marías's translations 11–12, 31 n. 48
   on Marías's early fiction 43, 201
   on Marías's style 107–8
   on *Negra espalda del tiempo* and *Tristram Shandy* 99
   on plagiarism of Marías's works 230 n. 15
   on *Tu rostro mañana* 272
Grossman, Edith 10–11, 325
Guillén, Claudio 27, 75 n. 19

Hardy, Thomas 5, 22, 25, 26–7, 30, 41
Hazlitt, William 77, 87, 297
Heaney, Seamus 39
Herralde, Jorge 119–20
Heydrich, Reinhard 262–3
Holden, Edith 28–9
Holy Week 286
Hughes, Richard 219–20
hybridity, linguistic 291, 319

Ingendaay, Paul 201

James, Henry 98, 215, 258
Johnson, Hewlett (the Red Dean of Canterbury) 126, 312–13 n. 210
Johnson, Samuel 110, 168
Joyce, James 77, 109, 169–70, 258
Jull Costa, Margaret 2

Kafka, Franz 109
Keats, John 108–9
Keymer, Thomas 87–8, 92, 113–14, 117, 118–19
Keynes, Geoffrey 147, 158, 164, 165

Kristal, Efraín 139–44, 157–8, 163, 166 n. 107

Labanyi, Jo 46, 48 n. 30
Larra, Mariano José de 48
Leavis, Frank Raymond 77
Logie, Ilse 8, 11

Machado, Antonio 22, 319
Maeztu, Ramiro de 45
Mallafrè, Joaquim 83, 89–90, 94
Manera y Cao, Enrique 306–7
Marías, Fernando 193
Marías, Javier:
   amends his translations 28–9, 31 n. 49, 37–8, 316
   attends the Universidad Complutense 23, 24
   'Ausencia y memoria en la traducción poética' 55–60
   birth 18
   chooses translation commissions 29–30
   as cinephile 22–4, 198, 199, 284, 314
   commissioned to translate *Tristram Shandy* 27
   on committed literature 47
   *Corazón tan blanco* 34, 38, 39, 40, 107, 110, 208 n. 44, 214–15, 237, 284 n. 103
   as critic of his compatriots 12–14, 297
   criticized for Anglophone tastes 12, 50–1, 229–30
   'Cuando fui mortal' 16, 170, 199–220, 325
   *Cuentos únicos* 32, 35, 37, 197, 199–200, 202–3, 219–20
   debt to translation 10, 53–4, 98–9, 109–10
   'Desde una novela no necesariamente castiza' 41–4, 46, 49–50, 53–4
   devotion to Nabokov 227–8, 243
   doing the rounds of the publishing houses 38 n. 75
   *dominios del lobo, Los* 23, 24, 43, 50, 53, 201
   enters Real Academia Española 2, 69
   *hombre sentimental, El* 15, 42, 181, 194, 218, 236–7, 256, 273
   lives in Barcelona 27, 101–2
   *Mañana en la batalla piensa en mí* 23 n. 17, 38, 40, 170, 222, 240, 246–7, 248, 251–2, 267–8
   marketing foreign fiction 26
   meets Juan Benet 24
   *Monarca del tiempo, El* 27, 43, 53–4

on moralizing in art 216, 227, 234–5, 273–5, 290–1
on musical variations in prose 247–8
narrators of novels as voyeurs 268
*Negra espalda del tiempo* 16, 45, 68, 71, 99, 103–38, 194, 219 n. 84, 221–2, 232, 260, 322
as newspaper columnist 285–91
on obsessive selecting of fictional detail 210–11
on Oxford 230
on political affiliations 231
on poor translations 63–4, 66–9
on readers 226
reasons for turning to translation 53–4
recommends translation to others 9–10
repertoire as a busker 23 n. 18
role as public intellectual 12–14, 226, 285–91
schooling at the Colegio Estudio 21–2, 46
*Siglo, El* 31, 42, 63
on smoking 284
split from *El Semanal* magazine 12
on swearing 226
teaches at Oxford University 31–2, 233
teaches Translation Theory 32–3, 166
*Todas las almas* 103, 117–20, 122, 125, 194, 237–40, 260, 294–5
'La traducción como fingimiento y representación' 60–4
on translating Nabokov 243–4
*Travesía del horizonte* 24–5, 43, 53, 201
*Tu rostro mañana* 222–4, 226, 259–60, 285
use of recurrent imagery 134–8, 279–81
verdict on Borges the translator 40, 139, 145
versatility of knowledge of English 300–1
on why he writes 273–5
on working conditions for translators 67–9
Marías, Julián 2 n. 3, 18–19
betrayal 18–19, 125–7, 169
blighted career 19, 169
death 169, 259
as disciple of Ortega y Gasset 45
helps publish son's first story 199 n. 10
imprisonment 18–19
as inspiration for son's fiction 205 n. 32, 259
takes family to United States 20, 232
as translator 19

Marías, Julianín 18, 117, 125, 129, 132
Martín Gaite, Carmen 4–5, 24, 76–7, 326
Melville, Hermann 119–20
Mendoza, Eduardo 12, 36, 43, 229
Mill, John Stuart 4, 232 n. 28
Milton, John 185–6, 189–90, 304–5, 319
Molina-Foix, Juan Antonio 68 n. 86
Molina-Foix, Vicente 27, 53, 129
Muñoz Molina, Antonio 21, 44, 46, 52–3, 230 n. 15, 233–4

Nabokov, Vladimir 1, 27, 34, 41, 57, 70
as interviewee 228–9
as lecturer on *Don Quijote* 20, 31–2, 233–4
*Lolita* 229, 234, 238, 240, 241–57, 258, 276
*Pnin* 236–7
on political affiliations 231
*Speak, Memory* 236
*Strong Opinions* 236, 240, 250–1
studies at Cambridge University 232, 237
on translation 9, 55, 56, 64, 81, 140, 238
Nathanson, Leonard 183–4
New, Melvyn 77–8
Nin, Andreu 262, 271

O'Hara, Frank 27, 55
Old Walsingham 196
Ortega y Gasset, José 18, 55, 62, 80–1
Ovid 133–4
Oxford 31, 32, 75, 103–4, 125, 164, 230, 233, 260–1, 294–5

Pamuk, Orhan 2, 36
Panero, Leopoldo María 50
Pardo Bazán, Emilia 3–4, 21
*Paris Review, The* 2
Parker, Fred 90
Paz, Octavio 55
Pegenaute, Luis 11, 70, 78, 80
pensamiento literario 106–9
Pérez de Ayala, Gustavo 24
Pérez Galdós, Benito 3, 74–5, 97–8, 326
Pérez-Reverte, Arturo 12, 21, 36
Perriam, Chris 49
Pessoa, Fernando 4, 193
Pino, Hilario 34, 105
Pittarello, Elide 43, 111, 112, 200–1, 202
Poe, Edgar Allan 202
Pombo, Álvaro 30
POUM 223, 262–3, 271
Premio Nacional de Traducción 2, 70, 99
Premio Reino de Redonda 36

Preston, Claire 150, 155, 196–7
Propertius 175
Proust, Marcel 49, 98, 258

Querejeta, Elías 103–4
Querejeta, Gracia 103–4
Quincey, Thomas de 108–9, 148

Real Academia Española 2, 69
Real Ramos, Carlos Alonso del
    265–6 n. 26
Red Dean of Canterbury *see* Johnson,
    Hewlett
Redonda, Dukes of (selected) 36
Redonda, Kingdom of 1, 34–6, 123–4, 147
Reich-Ranicki, Marcel 38
Reino de Redonda press 2, 26, 33, 36–7,
    64, 68–9, 144, 146, 200
Richardson, Samuel 74, 87–8
Ross, Ian Campbell 73
Russell, Peter:
    as critic of Cervantes 233 n. 37
    death 259–60, 294
    as inspiration for fictional character
        259, 261
    met JM 261

Salinas, Jaime 25–6
Salinger, Jerome David 32–3
Sánchez Ferlosio, Rafael 44 n. 9, 114
Savater, Fernando 21, 36, 39, 49, 50,
    202–4, 235
Sebald, Winfried Georg 2, 36, 146,
    306–7, 311–13
    *On the Natural History of Destruction*
        306–7, 311–13
    *The Rings of Saturn* 147
Second World War 111, 262–3, 282, 285,
    289, 293–4, 298, 305–14
Segal, Erich 24
*Semanal, El* 12
September 11 2001 289, 299
Shakespeare, William 2, 293, 294, 315,
    320, 324
    *Hamlet* 40, 209
    *Julius Caesar* 109
    *King Henry IV* 23, 315
    *King Henry V* 23, 300–2, 305
    *King Richard III* 40
    *Macbeth* 40, 107, 109–10
    *Othello* 40, 110, 209, 219
    *The Tempest* 110
Shiel, Matthew Phippps 34–5, 116,
    122, 124
Smith, Ali 263, 269 n. 39, 290
Sontag, Susan 110–11, 113, 115

Soria 22, 38
Southworth, Eric 146, 232 n. 28, 233
Spanish Civil War 15, 18–19, 42, 111,
    125–7, 168–9, 171, 232, 260, 262–3
    285, 289
Stapleton, Laurence 303
Steenmeijer, Maarten 3, 14 n. 39, 286, 319
Steiner, George 3, 33–4, 36, 51 n. 40,
    55–9, 97–8
Stephens, Cynthia 165
Sterne, Laurence 1, 41, 49, 235, 258
    attempts to visit Spain 72, 120
    death 102
    desecration of corpse 102
    fêted in fashionable society 85 n. 59
    financial difficulties 120
    hopes for advancement 82
    ill-health 72, 112, 120
    as inheritor of Cervantes 97–8
    as orator 79, 85
    reception of *Tristram Shandy* 72–3,
        91, 120
    reception of works in Spain 73–4, 77
    Shandy Hall 101–2
    *Tristram Shandy* 27, 70–96, 293–7
Stevens, Wallace 5, 32
Stevenson, Robert Louis 5, 6–7, 28–9,
    41, 55, 185, 235, 315–17, 321
Strachey, Lytton 164–5

touchstone 5–6, 167, 196, 321
translation:
    as allusion 9, 146, 168, 170–2, 182–5,
        190–1, 206–7, 221–5, 322–4
    as appropriation 39, 57, 99, 103, 104,
        111, 117, 121, 138, 196, 197–9,
        219–20
    as compensation 152, 316
    as creativity 55–60, 64, 100–1, 325
    dangers of 33–4, 63–4
    debates on naturalization 54–5, 62–3,
        71, 80–1, 85
    as enrichment 5–6, 53, 62, 98–9, 324
    as haunting 101–2
    as hybridization 306–14, 318–20
    as incorporation 8–9, 54, 58, 65–6, 324
    as palimpsest 241–57, 291–320
    as suspension of disbelief 60–2
Translation Theory 15–16, 18, 32, 55,
    60, 62
*Tres cuentos didácticos* 27, 241
Turpin, Enrique 206, 217 n. 78

Umbral, Francisco 50
Universidad Complutense (Madrid) 23,
    32, 166, 265–6 n. 26

Updike, John 25–6, 30
Unamuno y Jugo, Miguel de 4, 45,
    98, 326

Valle-Inclán, Ramón María del 46
Valls, Fernando 9, 44 n. 9, 206
Vásquez, Juan Gabriel 200
Vega, Montse 16
Vega, Lope de 319
Venuti, Lawrence 54, 81
Verne, Jules 21
Vila-Sanjuán, Sergio 22–3

Villena, Luis Antonio de 36, 50
Visani, Caterina 47, 194

Waissbein, Daniel 144, 165–6
Welles, Orson 23
Wellesley (Massachusetts) 20, 232–3
Wet, Hugh Oloff de 116, 122–3
Wood, Michael 242–3, 245
Woolf, Virginia 4, 77, 101
Wynne-Tyson, Jon 34–6, 124

Yeats, William Butler 5, 31, 39, 50